Chapaev and His Comrades

War and the Russian Literary Hero across the Twentieth Century

Cultural Revolutions:
Russia in the Twentieth Century

Editorial Board:
Anthony Anemone (The New School)
Robert Bird (The University of Chicago)
Eliot Borenstein (New York University)
Angela Brintlinger (The Ohio State University)
Karen Evans-Romaine (Ohio University)
Jochen Hellbeck (Rutgers University)
Lilya Kaganovsky (University of Illinois, Urbana-Champaign)
Christina Kiaer (Northwestern University)
Alaina Lemon (University of Michigan)
Simon Morrison (Princeton University)
Eric Naiman (University of California, Berkeley)
Joan Neuberger (University of Texas, Austin)
Ludmila Parts (McGill University)
Ethan Pollock (Brown University)
Cathy Popkin (Columbia University)
Stephanie Sandler (Harvard University)
Boris Wolfson (Amherst College), Series Editor

Chapaev
and His Comrades

War and the Russian Literary Hero across the Twentieth Century

Angela Brintlinger

Boston
2012

Library of Congress Cataloging-in-Publication Data:
a bibliographic record for this title is available from the Library of Congress.

Copyright © 2012 Academic Studies Press
All rights reserved

ISBN - 978-1-61811-822-6
ISBN - 978-1-61811-203-3, Electronic

Cover design by Ivan Grave
On the cover: "Zatishie na perednem krae," 1942, photograph by Max Alpert.

Published by Academic Studies Press in 2012
28 Montfern Avenue
Brighton, MA 02135, USA
press@academicstudiespress.com
www.academicstudiespress.com

Contents

Introduction. War and the Hero in the Russian Twentieth Century 7

Part I
CREATING HEROES FROM CHAOS

Chapter One. Born in the Crucible of War:
Chapaev and His Socialist Realist Comrades 34

Part II
WORLD WAR II AND THE HERO

Chapter Two. The Peasant-Soldier:
Alexander Tvardovsky and a New Chapaev 66

Chapter Three. Eyewitnesses to Heroism:
Emmanuil Kazakevich and Vera Panova 91

Chapter Four. Retreat:
Viktor Nekrasov and the Truth of the Trenches 117

Part III
COLD WAR REPERCUSSIONS

Chapter Five. From World War to Cold War:
Tvardovsky, Solzhenitsyn, Voinovich,
and Heroism in the Post-Stalin Period 146

Chapter Six. Antiheroes in a Post-heroic Age:
Sergei Dovlatov, Vladimir Makanin, and Cold War Malaise 174

Part IV
CHAPAEV AND WAR: RUSSIAN REDUX

Chapter Seven. Revisiting War:
Viktor Astafiev and the Boys of '24 206

Chapter Eight. Revisiting Chapaev:
Viktor Pelevin and Vasily Aksyonov 232

Afterword 257
References 263
Index 278

Acknowledgements

Chapaev and his Comrades has been in progress for a number of years, and so I have accumulated numerous debts in its writing. Many students and colleagues have been a part of this book project — in courses like *War and Russian Literature in the 20th Century* and at seminars and talks — and I thank them for their aid and indulgence. I tried out versions of some of these chapters in Madison, WI and Bryn Mawr, PA, in London and Stockholm, and in Los Angeles, Providence, RI, Urbana, IL, Columbus, OH and New Brunswick, NJ. I also drew on my 2004 *Slavic Review* article "The Hero in the Madhouse: the Post-Soviet Novel Confronts the Soviet Past" in writing chapters 6 and 8 of the book.

Tatiana Smorodinskaya and Andrei Rogatchevsky have commented on some of the ideas and chapters that have been folded into this book, and Yvonne Howell, Catherine O'Neil, and Carol Apollonio became my elected community and their intellectual and emotional support essential to completing the project. Ruth Melville gave the manuscript a careful read, and I appreciate her insights, and Ian Lanzillotti offered critical technical support during the last set of revisions.

I want to thank the staff at Academic Studies Press, especially Sharona Vedol and Kira Nemirovsky, and series editor Boris Wolfson. Publishing academic monographs today is a risky business, and I appreciate ASP's expertise in bringing my book to an interested audience across several continents. What's more, despite the prosaic and even bloody nature of my subject matter, having the shade of A. S. Pushkin hover over the book — if only in the press's acronym — has felt like a blessing.

Finally, I am fortunate to have family members who are smart and critical, and who moved this book in the right direction, particularly my husband Steven and father-in-law Peter Conn. I am grateful for their input and their belief in me and my work. Steve has been my stalwart comrade through thick and thin, though I married him because he is a peacenik. Ironies never cease, and he appreciates that more than most. Living with me — and Chapaev — has sorely tried his patience, and I thank him for sticking with us.

My interest in war and how it affects literature, readers, and the culture around them stems from visits to Soviet museums and war memorials in the 1980s, but grew more urgent after the arrival of my children and the onset of the Iraq War. I did not want my children to grow up in a war-torn world, and although many of the conflicts remain distant from us geographically, the effects of war in the twenty-first century have spread across the oceans and into the lives of us all. I hope that some of the examples in this book of how war plays out in a culture will prove inspirational, while I am certain that other examples will remind readers of how violence, especially state-sponsored violence, manipulates our psyches and damages our souls.

Introduction

War and the Hero in the Russian Twentieth Century

> For every generation—its own war and its own victims, which also means its own myths . . .
>
> В каждом поколении—своя война и свои жертвы, а значит, и свои мифы . . .
>
> -Mikhail Epstein

Not long after the collapse of the Soviet state in 1991, Moscow poet Olga Sedakova commented, "Something has happened to the hero in our century."

Sedakova was concerned primarily with the hero in lyrical poetry, but she inadvertently put her finger on an issue of central importance for Russian fiction as well. Something had indeed happened to the hero in twentieth-century Russian fiction, and that something was war.

The history of Russia in the twentieth century was, more than anything else, a history of war and the variety of its consequences: the effects that war inevitably brings to the structure of the economy; the toll that it takes on daily life and on social and familial bonds; the physical destruction of cities, towns, and farms; the dislocations both physical and emotional of populations; and finally, the ongoing struggles over the memory and meaning of these cataclysmic events. With the possible exception of China, in the twentieth century no other country has experienced these consequences more than Russia and the Soviet Union did. It is worth reviewing the litany of Russia's militarized twentieth century.

Before the fall of the tsarist regime, Russians fought a war in the Far East with the Japanese. Soon afterward, a decade of almost constant war ensued, with the First World War interrupted by the Revolutions, and the Revolutions devolving into a long and bloody Civil War. The 1920s saw the beginning of the ongoing Soviet terror against the country's own citizens. That terror, orchestrated and justified as "class war"—which, among other things, devastated the peasantry and countryside and decimated the officer corps of the Red Army—eased somewhat as the 1930s drew to a close, but only because Russians were consumed with and by World War II. The terror quickly resumed when World War II ended in victory.

Introduction

The second half of the twentieth century was dominated by the Cold War against the West. This took many forms—proxy wars in the third world; a dizzyingly dangerous arms race with the United States; great military parades through Red Square, featuring tanks, phalanxes of marching soldiers, and intercontinental ballistic missiles; and briefly, from the mid-1950s through the late 1960s, the concomitant space race. It all ended with the chaotic collapse of the Soviet state, a consequence, some have argued, both of an arms race the Soviet Union could not afford and the disastrous decade-long Soviet war in Afghanistan (1979–1989). Even after the dissolution of the Soviet Union, war has remained a central fact of Russian life. Russian leaders have picked up where their Soviet predecessors left off, fighting wars in Chechnya in 1994–1996 and 1999–2009, conducting border skirmishes with Georgia in 2008, and dealing with their own ongoing "war on terror."

Virtually an entire century of war and everything that goes with it—ideological propaganda campaigns, drafts and recruitment into the armed forces, economic mobilization, and the repression of urban and rural populations across the country—created a thoroughly militarized society. The century saw actual fighting in the streets and across the geographic spaces of the Russian empire; incursions into other political spaces, including the annexation of the Baltic Republics and Ukraine; the march of Soviet soldiers all the way to Berlin; failed and costly struggles in the mountains of Afghanistan; civil sacrifices, evacuations, and suffering; self-policing, interrogations, and house arrests; and prison camp sentences, exile, and forced emigration.

It is not an exaggeration to say that the experience of war shaped every twentieth-century Russian generation and left no family untouched. Husbands killed in war left widows and orphans; lost children left grieving parents and grandparents; and all this on a scale that is still hard to even fathom. While it is a commonplace to talk about the "lost generation" of European men who did not return from the First World War, in a very real sense every Russian generation in the twentieth century was lost. And through it all, the state attempted—through education, propaganda, and ideologically manipulative art, and through the obverse, military conscription, prison camps, and psychiatric incarceration—to mold loyal citizens who would support the government and perpetuate a new Soviet way of life.

Wars both generate and require heroes. Thus what constituted the "heroic" in Soviet Russia remained more central than it might have in a less war-torn and less thoroughly militarized country. War was the experience of the Russian people, and it became a dominant trope to represent the Soviet experience in literature as well as other areas of cultural life. This book will trace those war experiences, memories, tropes, and metaphors in the literature of the Soviet and post-Soviet period. Across the "short" twentieth century, we look closely at the work of just over a dozen writers: Dmitry Furmanov, Fyodor Gladkov, Alexander Tvardovsky, Emmanuil Kazakevich, Vera Panova, Viktor Nekrasov, Alexander Solzhenitsyn, Vladimir Voinovich, Sergei Dovlatov, Vladimir Makanin, Viktor Astafiev, Viktor Pelevin, and Vasily Aksyonov. We will glance briefly at half a dozen more.

These authors represented official Soviet literature, underground or dissident literature, and even émigré literature; they fell into or out of favor, were exiled or returned to Russia, died at home or abroad. Most importantly, they were all touched by war, and they reacted to the state of war in their literary works.

War and the Health of the Russian State

Across the twentieth century, Russia was virtually always at war—with Germany, the US, Afghanistan; with the aristocracy, the kulak, the class enemy. Philosopher Mikhail Epstein articulates the problem thus:

> What generation have we had that was not military? We have fought against blue uniforms, white epaulettes, brown shirts and black berets, against the leather coats of commissars and the narrow pants of hipsters, against sandals, hats, bowlers and moccasins . . . Against autocracy and serfdom, the serfs and the intelligentsia, the bourgeois and the aristocracy, literature and religion, society and ourselves. In every generation—its own war and its own victims . . .[1]

This paradigm, the militarization of everyday life in wartime and in peacetime, has characterized Russian and Soviet perceptions of themselves and their place in the world across the twentieth century.

---

[1] "Какое поколение у нас было не военным? Сражались с голубыми мундирами, с белыми погонами, с коричневыми рубашками и с черными беретами, с комиссарскими кожаными куртками и стиляжьими узкими брюками, с лаптями, шляпами, котелками и мокасинами . . . С самодержавием и с крепостным правом, с крестьянством и интеллигенцией, с мещанством и аристократией, с литературой и религией, с обществом и с самими собой. В каждом поколении—своя война и свои жертвы . . ." Mikhail Epstein, "Posle karnavala, ili vechnyi Venichka," in Venedikt Erofeev, *Ostav'te moiu dushu v pokoe* (Moscow: Izdatel'stvo XGS, 1995), 3–30, 26.

Introduction

In this 1995 summary of his nation's contacts with war, Epstein inadvertently echoed some of the ideas first articulated by the American critic and philosopher Randolph Bourne (1886–1918) in his now classic unfinished essay "War Is the Health of the State." Bourne wrote the essay exactly at the moment that gave birth to the Soviet Union, and while his own concerns were with the American involvement in World War I, his astute analysis of the relationship between war and the state is a logical place for us to begin. Indeed, reading that essay today, it feels almost prophetic, just as applicable to the First World War as to the Second World War and even the war in Iraq in the 2000s. In Bourne's reckoning, war brings "a sense of sanctity to the State." In wartime, the individual is suddenly obligated to support the state—with his life and livelihood if necessary—and any dissent or opposition becomes unlawful or is targeted as dangerous. Bourne's words can easily be ascribed to the then-nascent Soviet state:

> War is essentially the health of the State. The ideal of the State is that within its territory its power and influence should be universal. As the Church is the medium for the spiritual salvation of man, the State is thought of as the medium for his political salvation. . . . [In war] we are at last on the way to full realization of that collective community in which each individual somehow contains the virtue of the whole.[2]

Replacing the church, the Soviet state reached for universal influence, for becoming the medium for both man's spiritual and his political salvation. By maintaining this sense of urgency, this sense of war—whether against external enemies or internal—Soviet society and ideology developed as if according to Bourne's blueprint: "Old national ideals are taken out, re-adapted to the purpose, and used as universal touchstones, or molds into which thought is poured." War was indeed the health of the state, and maintaining a state of war enabled the state to keep the nation continually mobilized to defend itself and eliminated any challenge or opposition.

The construction of Socialist society itself was presented through the lens of military metaphors: fighting class wars, throwing all forces onto the industrial front, identifying enemies of the people, and so on. The concept of

---

[2] Randolph Bourne, "War Is the Health of the State" (1918), Bourne Mss., Columbia University Libraries, www.bigeye.com/warstate.htm. All quotes below from Bourne from this edition of the essay.

"hero"—valorized in a militarization of daily life—kept the urgency of war alive even in times of relative external peace. During the first half of the Soviet century, actual warfare was central to the Soviet experience, and literary texts mirrored that experience. However, even though the second half of the Soviet century did not produce the same kinds of war heroes, or indeed the same kinds of war, writers were still confronted with those original war heroes and the state's emphasis on presenting heroic models in literature. Thus an official equivalence between protagonist and hero continued during the period of Cold War. But as writers recognized the falseness of that equivalence, they instead began to create antiheroes, individuals struggling with the state and with the society that surrounded them. If in the first part of the century, writers created characters who could stride alongside Chapaev, in the second part they increasingly wrote against Chapaev, that is to say, in reaction to the notion of the war hero as it had emerged.

The trajectory of *Chapaev and his Comrades* will follow the trajectory of the century. From a moment when the central figure of war and literature was Civil War hero Vasily Chapaev, we will trace that figure as he becomes a vital part of Soviet cultural memory, reflected in literary texts and broader social contexts. By the time the Soviet Union collapsed, Chapaev reemerges, reclaimed from Soviet cant for the purposes of post-Soviet camp.

This book does not aim to be a comprehensive history of war fiction in the Soviet Union nor a complete history of the Chapaev story. Indeed, we will not follow the trajectory, explored by many other scholars over the years, of how Soviet literature was created, transformed, and then deformed into dissident movements.[3] Instead I am looking to distill the constants across the short twentieth century, reifying the value of shared cultural experience and memory as it remains and becomes fodder for the post-Soviet era. In so doing, it is important to include programmatic socialist realist "positive heroes," especially as they fit into war and postwar contexts, and the simple soldiers from well-written, beloved narratives about the war experience; satirical treatments of the theme, particularly portraits of civilians struggling against the state, and soldiers caught in the gears of the military complex; and the post-Soviet reintegration of all three strands of literature from the period—"official" literature, underground literature, and émigré literature. In

---

[3] See, for example, Rufus Mathewson, Jr., *The Positive Hero in Russian Literature* (New York: Columbia University Press, 1958) and Geoffrey Hosking, *Beyond Socialist Realism: Soviet Fiction since Ivan Denisovich* (London, New York: Granada, 1980).

the chapters that follow, I have deliberately chosen to analyze all three types of writers and texts, as well as their protagonists—heroes and antiheroes both.

War and the Hero

Epstein reminds us that though ruptures were created between the old Russia and the new Soviet Russia by major events—World War I and the Bolshevik Revolution—there were continuities as well. The hero in Soviet life had ancestors in the nineteenth century, and as in the nineteenth century, many of the hero's struggles unfolded in the context of literary creations.

Soviet visions have frequently evoked the Romantic period with its rhetoric of a lone and lonely hero struggling with a society and a regime that neither understands nor accepts him. This essentially Romantic view of the role of the hero in society shares much with the ideas of English Romantic historian Thomas Carlyle. Carlyle knew little about Russian society and letters when he permitted himself grand generalizations on the state of the nation of Russia in the early 1840s. In his by-now famous judgment of Russia, published in his book *On Heroes, Hero-Worship, and the Heroic in History* (1841), Carlyle wrote:

> The Czar of all the Russias, he is strong with so many bayonets, Cossacks and cannons; and does a great feat in keeping such a tract of Earth politically together; but he cannot yet speak. [There is] Something great in him, but it is a dumb greatness. He has had no voice of genius, to be heard of all men and times. He must learn to speak. He is a great dumb monster hitherto. His cannons and Cossacks will all have rusted into nonentity while that Dante's voice is still audible. The nation that has a Dante is bound together as no dumb Russia can be.[4]

Carlyle's *On Heroes, Hero-Worship, and the Heroic* describes a society striving toward national consciousness and argues that a nation needs a number of things: military strength (bayonets, Cossacks, and cannons), centralized government (the czar of all the Russias), individual heroes, and a voice (a Dante) to create the nation's touchstones from those heroes. "Society," Carlyle believed, "is founded on Hero-Worship" (13), and it needs heroes around which to coalesce. According to this argument, through the ages heroes of

---

[4] Thomas Carlyle, *On Heroes, Hero-Worship, and the Heroic in History* (New York: D. Appleton and Company, 1841), 132.

different kinds have arisen to fit the needs of societies, and Carlyle in his lectures focused on six of those types: the hero as divinity, prophet, poet, priest, man of letters, and king. Each of these heroes can draw society together, chronicling the myths and histories that bind a nation. Carlyle's project of nation building posits an era of peaceful coalition, a Romantic sensibility that fulfills its mission and perpetuates itself through fixing that national consciousness in words. But the early Soviet state found itself building a nation in an era of war, and it found much in the Romantic idea of nation building, which it could adopt.

Nineteenth-century Russians of Carlyle's generation saw their own Dante in Nikolai Karamzin, author of the great *History of the Russian State*, and in Alexander Pushkin, virtuoso of verse, drama, and prose, both voices that perhaps remained unheard or resonated too softly in England at the time for Carlyle to have heard them. Karamzin, Pushkin, and other poets and historians of the imperial era had embarked upon their own project of nation building and identified specific historical and cultural heroes—from Boris Godunov to the holy fool Nikolka-Kolpak, from Catherine the Great to Novgorod mayor's wife Marfa-Posadnitsa—and the texts in which these heroes featured strove to identify what it meant to be Russian, to belong in one way or another to the Russian imperial enterprise. In the Romantic era, literature both reflected and strove to influence society, and its literary heroes represented that connection.

Judith Kornblatt has also reminded us of another, more specifically Russian, nineteenth-century source for the twentieth-century literary hero. In her study of the Cossack hero in Russian literature, she demonstrates that the "historical narrative" of the socialist realist novel was not particularly revolutionary but instead relied heavily on nineteenth-century models. The novel, she writes, "turns toward traditional *Bildungsroman*. Over the course of the novel, the hero matures from rebellious adolescent to sophisticated ideologue. Such emphasis on psychological development [. . .] belies mythical associations; maturation equals acceptance of the authoritative values of the state."[5] Rooted in nineteenth-century traditions, whether of Romantics or Cossacks, the twentieth-century literary hero would be further shaped by the experience of war.

---

5   Judith Kornblatt, *The Cossack Hero in Russian Literature: A Study in Cultural Mythology* (Madison: University of Wisconsin Press, 1992), 170.

Introduction

Carlyle notably excludes one kind of hero from his lectures in *On Heroes, Hero-Worship, and the Heroic in History*: the warrior hero. In Russian we find the term *geroi* (герой) in many studies of literature, used to refer to the protagonist of a work. But mythical and literary heroes have always been born in the crucible of war, as far back as Homer, and real-life heroes are proclaimed as such on the basis of their wartime service. In many cases, the protagonist and the hero are one and the same.

In Russian literature, the protagonist frequently participates in war as a soldier, observes it as a bystander or a journalist, or defines him- or herself in terms of military rank even if s/he is not actually in uniform. This has been true since Peter the Great created parallel civil and military ranks, a habit that Nikolai Gogol pokes fun at in his 1836 story "The Nose" with his hapless civilian hero, "Major" Kovalev. In Mikhail Lermontov's 1841 Romantic novel *A Hero of Our Time*, Pechorin lives a life parallel to that of military officers and engagements, and his ennui and reckless bravado stem in part from the fact that he falls outside of a clear military chain of command. Equally Romantic were Nadezhda Durova's memoirs in the 1830s, which she titled *The Cavalry Maiden* to identify her dual role as a woman with her own place in the service. Other nineteenth-century novelists followed suit, focusing on the relations between civilian heroes and their military counterparts, the most obvious example perhaps being Leo Tolstoy, with his *Sevastopol Sketches* (1855), journalistic writings from a military observer, *The Cossacks* (1863), fiction about a young man who longs to belong to a warlike people, and *War and Peace* (1865–1869), the epic novel of war and society that looms large for any novelist writing about military engagements, social transformations, and the philosophy of history and war, in Russia and indeed across much of the world.

No condition functions as well as war as the crucible for producing heroes—and for creating conformity. It seems that warrior heroes are made in the reaction to enemy attack, the patience of waiting and preparing, the heat of the battle. But heroic behavior in battle—the bayonet attack, the well-thrown grenade, the definitive flight over enemy lines—is only part of the equation. The status of hero must be conferred from the outside, by authors and journalists and of course primarily the state, who raise up the hero, mark him or her, and present him or her to contemporaries and to history as an example of worthy behavior: the patriot defending the nation, the individual protecting the collective. Thus two components are necessary in the making of a warrior hero—the actual heroic behavior and the ceremonial marking of that behavior. Indeed, the actual heroics, the "truth" of battle, can be invented; the myths and ceremonies have cultural power even when they are based on fictionalized heroism.

Seeking the predecessor of the Soviet hero in his ancestor, the Russian revolutionary, Rufus Mathewson in his 1958 *The Positive Hero in Russian Literature* also looked back to the nineteenth century. In Dostoevsky, Tolstoy, Goncharov, and Turgenev, Mathewson found a "gallery of faltering heroes," who "all demonstrate an intensive effort to center the novelists' moral quest in the figure of the protagonist."[6] Other scholars who have investigated the hero in the realist era found him to be struggling with the conformist society around him and with his own superfluity. Ellen Chances has argued that some twentieth-century fiction follows the nineteenth-century model of conformism: "A character is doomed if he/she swims against the tides; good if with them." In this kind of novel, Chances concludes, "The outsider becomes an insider. By this transformation to an active member of the community, he too erases the split between disparate elements and eliminates the problem of superfluity. Such a hero is then, of course, a 'positive hero.'"[7] Here Chances is describing Fyodor Gladkov's novel *Cement*, to which we will turn in the next chapter, but her argument works just as well for many other texts of the twentieth century. This important moment works two ways: either the outsider turns insider, or the outsider refuses to become "positive," to bow to the collective. Both paradigms will interest us in our study.

The socialist realist hero, officially codified in 1934, was formulaic. Adults and schoolchildren alike complained about, resisted, and lampooned him, and sometimes her, for decades. The many dull and lifeless novels featuring politically conscious heroes should by all rights have eliminated writers' and readers' interest in the central protagonist in fiction. But despite the tired formula and the turgid plotlines, the heroes in twentieth-century Russian novels still offered novelists and readers opportunities to explore psychological, cultural, and historical issues.

In the end, the literary hero survived the trial of socialist realism. Paradoxically, both war and the institution of Soviet censorship facilitated that survival. On the one hand, war, especially the Second World War, pumped life into the socialist realist hero, providing a context for officially sanctioned

---

[6] Rufus Mathewson, *The Positive Hero in Russian Literature,* 14.
[7] Ellen Chances, *Conformity's Children: An Approach to the Superfluous Man in Russian Literature* (Columbus: Slavica, 1978), 166–167.

heroic deeds that were exciting to read about. On the other hand, the confines of censorship created an underground literature and a space to create different kinds of heroism. Beyond socialist realism, issues of heroism remained important within the literary discourse. The Russian literary hero—forged in the fire of warfare—has even outlived the Soviet Union itself.

Chapaev and His Comrades begins by examining the roots of the Russian hero in the early years of the twentieth century. One model of Russian heroism was created by Maxim Gorky, whose 1906–1907 novel *Mother* connected the hero to both the peasantry and the proletariat in a context of political action. Thus the Soviet hero descended from the nineteenth-century, hero-driven realist novel, with its ties to the intelligentsia, but his class politics were reoriented to match Soviet ideology. In another, more viable, model, the soldier-hero was forged in the crucible of the Revolution and Civil War and drew strength from the fabled Vasily Chapaev, "ataman of the steppes."[8] From that soldier was codified the socialist realist "positive" hero, who acted on the labor as well as the military fronts and returned to fight in the trenches and on the battlefields of the Second World War.

During the second half of the twentieth century, the peasant-warrior figure and the socialist realist hero continued to thrive, in war-related fiction and in satires of that genre. As mentioned above, we will deliberately examine both. The doctrinally required positive hero did not damage the Russian literary hero in any way, but I will argue even strengthened the paradigm in continual creative efforts by nonconformist writers who formed various "oppositions" to state-mandated literary models.

This study ranges across the century, taking its beginning in the pre-Soviet period and ending in post-Soviet postmodernism. We will stop along the way at the particularly crucial cultural and historical junctions, especially moments of war—Civil War, World War II, Cold War—and their immediate aftermath, when soldiers return from war and try to reintegrate into a changed society, often bringing their own military culture back with them. Throughout the book I will situate close readings of novels and novelists in these shifting cultural contexts, thus illuminating the evolution of the

---

[8] In his *Men without Women: Masculinity and Revolution in Russian Fiction, 1917–1929* (Durham, NC: Duke University Press, 2000), Eliot Borenstein identified a "masculinist myth," which remains quite relevant to many of the heroes we discuss. See also Justus Grant Hartzok, "Children of Chapaev: The Russian Civil War Cult and the Creation of Soviet Identity, 1918–1941" (PhD diss., University of Iowa, 2009).

protagonist's function within the official literary canon as well as in the "opposition," alternative or underground traditions, always keeping in focus the protagonists' relationship to war, war rhetoric, and concepts of heroism.

As this book demonstrates, the protagonists of twentieth-century Russian novels remained a vital part of the evolution of Russian prose into the postmodern period, and their relationship to war and the state, to society and the collective, forms a fascinating parallel to historical and cultural events beyond literature. Writers' and critics' attitudes toward literary heroes and their social position vis-à-vis war and the state have ranged from the serious to the ironic. But the literary hero offered the perfect mechanism, within the socialist realist tradition or in the subversion of it, to explore central cultural and literary problems of the Soviet period.

Whether the fictional hero-protagonist or the hero marked as such in history, the Hero, by definition, must stand out from his fellow man. In wartime only some soldiers are decorated, and always for specific actions and brave deeds, while others remain unnoticed, regardless of their behavior under fire; some are marked as heroes, and their actions define heroism for the rest. The opposite of a soldier-hero, of course, is the traitor, the coward, the soldier who is singled out and punished for insufficient bravery in the heat of battle. The penal battalions of the Second World War were devised precisely to punish those identified as unworthy soldiers, without losing their manpower at the front—and those punishments were used both for actual cowards and traitors and for any individualist or nonconformist who got in the way of the military high command.

Thus the relationship between military discipline and the collective effort and necessarily individual acts of war (whether manifested in sniper fire, reconnaissance work, setting minefields, or any number of other wartime activities) contributes to the tension of the individual and the collective inherent in the definition of heroism, especially under the Socialist/Communist regime of post-revolutionary Russia. However, as Irina Gutkin, among others, has shown, the religious and ideological "mass enthusiasm" whipped up by the Bolsheviks made the Soviet case very particular, transforming the Soviet understanding of how an individual ought to act and harnessing those individuals to the cart of large-scale economic, cultural, and political construction.[9]

---

[9] Irina Gutkin, *The Cultural Origins of the Socialist Realist Aesthetic* (Evanston: Northwestern University Press: 1999), 21.

The individual hero worked for the collective in war and peaceful construction and was marked as heroic to serve as an exemplar for his comrades to emulate. Official literature followed this prescribed model: the war-hero protagonist was to inspire at the war and on the home front and to trigger a cloning process whereby his comrades too strove for heroism and became heroic.

Which is exactly what Bourne was talking about. War—on economic, cultural, and political fronts—helped maintain the health of the state. And literature during the Soviet era explored questions of war as it upheld—or undermined—that state.

War and Narrative: Paradoxes, Contradictions, Tensions
Astounding.
That was the word Abraham Lincoln used to describe war and all its consequences, and that remains the best single-word description of it. War can be effective at destroying things, but it does little positive work. War does not build nations, it does not make the world safe for democracy or for communism, it does not avenge the wrongs of the past, nor does it fulfill any of the other sanctimonious justifications offered by old men as they send young men off to kill and die. Plutarch knew as much when he wrote, "The poor folk go to war, to fight and to die for the delights, riches and superfluities of others."

Because of that, wars require narratives. As historian Drew Faust has written, war itself is a "narrative invention." As she explained, "Only a story of purpose and legitimation can transform random violence into what human convention has designated as war."[10] Recently she has argued further that "we seek the order that narrative promises to impose on the incoherence of conflict."[11] Narrative is the only thing that can give meaning to war.

Tim O'Brien, a Vietnam veteran turned author, explained the complexities of translating violence into narrative in his chapter "How to Tell a True War Story":

> How do you generalize?
> War is hell, but that's not the half of it, because war is also mystery and terror and adventure and courage and discovery and holiness and

---

[10] Drew Gilpin Faust, "Race, Gender, and Confederate Nationalism: William D. Washington's *Burial of Latane*," *Southern Review* 25 (1989): 301.

[11] Drew Gilpin Faust, 2011 Jefferson Lecture in the Humanities, "Telling War Stories: Reflections of a Civil War Historian," www.neh.gov/news/humanities/2011-05/TellingWarStoriesWeb.pdf, 7.

pity and despair and longing and love. War is nasty; war is fun. War is thrilling; war is drudgery. War makes you a man; war makes you dead.

The truths are contradictory. It can be argued, for instance, that war is grotesque. But in truth war is also beauty. For all its horror, you can't help but gape at the awful majesty of combat.... Like a killer forest fire, like cancer under a microscope, any battle or bombing raid or artillery barrage has the aesthetic purity of absolute moral indifference—a powerful, implacable beauty—and a true war story will tell the truth about this, though the truth is ugly.[12]

This book examines the work of twentieth-century Russian writers as they tried to turn violence into narrative, confronting the challenge of making meaning out of what would otherwise have remained meaningless.

That paradox, the need to make meaning out of violence, sits at the heart of the war experience. But it is only one of several that any writer who would take on the challenge of writing about war has to face. Running through this book will be a number of paradoxes, some intrinsic to the experience of war itself, others more specific to the twentieth- century Russian experience of it. Let me describe them briefly here.

The old cliché says that truth is the first casualty of war. It isn't that simple. Truth about war became a central criterion to judge the merits of the literature we will examine, but as we will see, the definition of what constituted the "truth of war" was debated and changed over time. Given the state-driven model of the production of art and the relationship between war journalism and propaganda, who decided how truth was defined depended on the way the political winds happened to be blowing.

Connected to this is the question of who was best positioned to tell the truth about war. We will examine writers who were eyewitnesses and participants, journalists and political officers, victims and the children of victims of the militarized society. Each staked his or her own claim to a particular authenticity and thus to a particular truth. Therefore, part of what interests me in this study is the tension—sometimes the contradiction—between what we might call "testimony," the firsthand accounts of events, and the myths that are created from those accounts later. This is central to the creation of war heroes in the first place.

---

[12] Tim O'Brien, *The Things They Carried* (New York: Broadway Books, 1998), 80.

Introduction

Many of the authors who write about war were at the front in wartime themselves and experienced what Kali Tal has called the "drive to testify," a common if not universal reaction to the trauma of life in wartime, which we can trace through many wars, from the Russian Civil War through the American war in Vietnam through today's wars across the globe.[13] Their act of witnessing, of testifying, made the details of war real. As World War II poet Ilya Selvinsky wrote, the eyewitness can offer the most significant and convincing voice:

> I saw it!
> You don't have to listen to folk tales,
> Or believe newspaper columns,
> But I saw it. With my own eyes.
> Understand? I saw it. Myself.[14]

Selvinsky's powerful staccato language harnesses to poetry a documentary feature, which exemplifies the need of poets and writers to "witness" from the front or the rear, to contribute to the war effort, and to chronicle the war, both inspiring and explaining the war for their own and future generations.[15]

Heroism is premised on acts of sacrifice—for country or for comrades—even though the experience of war is often and for most participants a struggle for self-preservation. These paradoxes have confronted all nations when they go to war. My sense is that Soviet writers highlighted the differences between bravery—mere acts of impulse—and heroism. We can define hero-

---

[13] See Kali Tal, "Speaking the Language of Pain: Vietnam War Literature in the Context of a Literature of Trauma," in *Fourteen Landing Zones: Approaches to Vietnam War Literature*, ed. Philip K. Jason (Iowa City: University of Iowa Press, 1991), 215–250, 229. Blogging and other electronic communication formats (including WikiLeaks) have made today's wars immediately accessible, although sometimes less "narrativized" than in the past.

[14] I. Sel'vinskii, *Sobranie sochinenii v shesti tomakh*, vol. 1 (Moscow: Khudozhestvennaia literatura, 1971), 352.

[15] Anatoly Abramov, in his book *The Lyric and Epic of the Great Patriotic War*, notes that the "poetic aesthetic at the time was documentary in nature." He points out that cycles of poems published tended to sound like chronicles or news dispatches: Sel'vinsky published the cycles "Crimea, 1941–1942," "Caucasus, 1942–1943," "Kuban', 1943"; A. Yashin published "Baltics, 1941–1942," "Volga, 1942–1943," "Black Sea, 1943–1944"; Konstantin Simonov published "Poems of 1943," "Poems of 1942," "Poems of 1941." See A. M. Abramov, *Lirika i epos Velikoi otechestvennoi voiny: problematika, stil', poetika* (Moscow: Sovetskii pisatel', 1972), 45.

ism in the Soviet context as bravery plus consciousness. Many people might rescue a comrade in danger or put their own lives at risk, but the true Soviet hero did so in order to advance the Soviet cause. Both kinds of actions have merit; both are described in fiction. But only one is heroic.

Thus in Soviet fiction we will meet what we'll call the "rhetoric of *podvig*." *Podvig* is Russian for "feat," an act of bravery that accomplishes something necessary and dangerous and that often ends in sacrifice or death. Framing an act in war as a *podvig* gives it the stamp of consciousness, the label that makes it medal-worthy, worthy of retelling, worthy of becoming "truth" rather than a mere fact of life in battle.

Those facts, those details of the experience of war, came to be called the "truth of the trenches." *Byt*—mundane daily life—included the boredom of war, the waiting, as well as the frenzy of sudden activity. Neither of these things is particularly heroic. Instead, they are described in literature using the details of *byt*. The tension between these two ways of describing war is a tension over which better portrayed the truth of war. In some eras *byt* was lauded and rewarded; in others, Soviet officials noticed that it lacked the higher truth necessary for the health of the state.

An even more charged tension for Soviet war literature was between the individual nature of the hero and the insistence on the collective identity of the new Soviet man. No less than any other country, the Soviet Union wanted to produce war heroes to hold up as exemplars to the nation. How to square that with an ideology that devalued individualism as such, indeed posited it as retrograde, became a particularly Soviet paradox that these writers had to sort out. The relationship between an individual, an "I," and his comrades, the "we," is both an ideological and a practical problem. For some writers, highlighting the experience of one person added to the sensation of authentic truth, but that had to be balanced with the value of the individual act for the collective good, for the nation and the state. In the official literature, the "we" would always have to triumph. For those writing against the grain, the situation was more complicated. They might foreground the integrity of the individual, but that meant a rejection of the idea of *podvig* as such, and it also doomed their work to remaining unpublished, at least in the Soviet Union.

War is hell. That quip is usually attributed to American general William Tecumseh Sherman. But as the philosopher Michael Walzer notes, the quip is not a description so much as "a moral argument, an attempt at self-justification."¹⁶ In the end, to write about war, to turn violence into narrative, is necessarily to confront our most difficult moral and ethical questions. No contemporary thinker has wrestled more deeply with the morality of war than Walzer. Borrowing from medieval theologians, Walzer asks us to confront and distinguish between the justice *of* a war (*jus ad bellum*) and the justice of what goes on *in* that war (*jus in bello*). We want it both ways, Walzer notes: victory in war and moral decency on the battlefield (47). That's the paradox.

Judgments about what constitutes *jus ad bellum* and *jus in bello* can be made by states and by individuals. But in the Soviet context, writers were not allowed to question either. The Soviet Union was not alone in insisting that all the wars it fought were just, nor was it unusual in its refusal to acknowledge that even just wars can be fought immorally. As we will see in the latter chapters of this book, the fight over the meaning and memory of war—the Revolution, the Civil War, Stalin's Terror and other Soviet repressions of citizens, and the Second World War in particular—revolves precisely around how writers forced readers to confront the distinction between the two.

The history of twentieth-century Russia and its militarized society made war an inescapable topic for Soviet writers. In trying to confront the tensions and paradoxes I have just outlined—truth versus fact, testimony versus myth, the rhetoric of *podvig* versus the simple rendering of *byt*, the "I" versus the "we," and the justice of war versus justice in war—they struggled to reinvent literary heroes for their time.

Chapaev and His Comrades

These themes seem to me the central dilemmas faced by writers who have tackled the narration of war over the Russian twentieth century, and they have informed the choices I have made about the writers and texts I have gathered here. Putting the experience of war—and its social, cultural, and moral implications—at the center of my considerations means foregrounding some writers and works that would not necessarily be considered part of the canon of twentieth-century Russian writing. Interestingly, in twenty-first-century Russia, with its new political emphasis on nationalism and patriotism and its renewed state-sponsored veneration of the veterans and narratives of the Second World War in particular, some of these forgotten texts have been

---

16   Michael Walzer, *Just and Unjust Wars: A Moral Argument with Historical Illustrations*, 4th ed. (New York: Basic Books, 2006), 32.

reissued. War sells, and such authors as Vera Panova, Boris Vasiliev, and Viktor Nekrasov now fill the shelves of Moscow bookstores along with the New Russian cookbooks and the dozens of detective novels.

The works we look at in this study, some of which have more literary merit than others, are among the most important ones through which to look at how war formed the central experience of Russians across the twentieth century and into the twenty-first. Furthermore, a number of these works were and remain immensely popular, although due to Soviet censorship not all were published at home in a timely fashion. Such works as the officially approved Alexander Tvardovsky's *Vasily Tyorkin* and—on the parodic side, published initially abroad—Vladimir Voinovich's *Life and Adventures of the Soldier Ivan Chonkin* (*Zhizn' i neobychainye prikliucheniia soldata Ivana Chonkina*) resonated with people, and their enduring popularity stems from the fact that they spoke with pathos and with humor about war and militarization to a nation made up of individuals who had experienced those phenomena firsthand.

It is also the case, necessarily, that I have had to leave out many worthy books and authors whose study would surely enhance my argument. Not only was the twentieth century a century of war for Russia, it was also a century of writing about war. The hundreds of fascinating and telling poems, narratives, and memoirs—along with the hundreds of less interesting texts—mean that this book project might have continued forever. I've had to make some hard choices, but I hope they will prove good ones for my readers. In the chapters below, I look at poets and prose writers, soldier-writers and civilians. I consider some "mainstream" writers—including a number whose books became exemplars of socialist realist fiction and several whose stars set after Stalin's death, only to rise again in the post-Soviet period—and some more marginal figures. Included in the latter are underground and émigré writers as well as those who published some work in official venues and left other works unpublished or resorted to *tamizdat*, publication abroad. I have also included several authors whose popularity soared in post-Soviet times. I hope through this selection to provide a sample from each of what I have called the three strands of Russian literature during the Soviet period: official literature, underground or dissident literature, and émigré literature.

The book proceeds chronologically, but it is sometimes not a straightforward chronology. The history of publication and suppression in the Soviet Union meant that books written in one era might not see the light of day until another; conversely, books published at one moment might find themselves banned in the next. And as we will see, while war defined the Russian twentieth century, the Second World War looms so large in the Russian imagination that it returns over and over again as Soviet and now post-Soviet Russians continue to struggle with what that war ultimately meant.

I explored one reaction to the "man of the future" in my first book, *Writing a Usable Past*, where I argued that authors of the 1920s and 1930s sought to portray a "real life" biographical hero in such a way that these heroes from the past would be useful to readers of the day. Instead of a "man of the future," some writers in the 1920s and 30s placed a "man of the past" at the center of their narratives. At the same time, of course, there were plenty of future socialist realist heroes being developed, many based on the biographies of actual individuals.[17] These biographical sources meant that literary (and filmic) heroes in the 1930s were designed to be emulated; heroic behavior became the expectation. However, the code of heroism by which the individual hero must always represent a collective enterprise created tension within the model itself and affected Soviet society in myriad ways.

After the revolution, writers—and readers—were in search of heroes, historical figures to whom they might turn for models and exemplars of a proper way of viewing the world and their own place in it.[18] Finding literary paradigms in the historical record was one way that early Soviet writers lent the sensation of truth to their fiction. Authors also exploited symbolic patterns for the socialist realist novel: the mentor/disciple pattern, the pattern of martyrdom, and paradigms of family and family metaphors.[19] These patterns, like those based in biography, are predicated on the arc of a human life and draw upon archetypical understandings of the relationship of the individual to history, the present, and the world around him. For Soviet literature, that relationship and those mythmaking narratives are foundational. The "state of war" during which the new Soviet culture was founded meant that writers reached out for their universal touchstones in creating literary heroes and rolling out their narratives during times of actual or metaphorical war. As we

---

[17] On Soviet war films and their heroes, see Denise Youngblood, *Russian War Films: On the Cinema Front, 1914–2005* (Lawrence: University Press of Kansas, 2007).

[18] See my *Writing a Usable Past: Russian Literary Culture, 1917–1937* (Evanston: Northwestern University Press, 2000, 2008).

[19] See Katerina Clark, *The Soviet Novel: History as Ritual*, 3rd ed. (Bloomington: Indiana University Press, 2000).

will see throughout this study, those cultural touchstones have remained in place well into the twenty-first century.

The central characters of Gorky's *Mother*, a proletarian mother and son, were one variant of the heroics in the first part of the century. But by the 1920s, another model had captured the imagination of Russian readers and children alike—the Chapaev model. In chapter 1 of the book, I examine Furmanov's 1923 novel *Chapaev* and Gladkov's 1925 novel *Cement*, contrasting the Civil War hero with his civilian counterpart on the factory front. Chapaev won out, and he became the ideal of boys all over the country. One example of this is seen in Yury Libedinsky's 1930 *Birth of a Hero* (*Rozhdenie geroia*), a book that tracks the relationship between the individual and the collective and features an adolescent who dreams of Chapaev-like stature in his imaginative play at the game of "world revolution." We see in Libedinsky that the new Soviet hero would be modeled on the peasant-warrior Chapaev, not on Gorky's mother or her son. The release of the early talkie film *Chapaev* in 1934, as well as its thirtieth anniversary re-release in 1964, meant that for children and adults all over the Soviet Union, the Chapaev model grew and remained ever more prominent.[20]

For the new Soviet state as well, Chapaev's class identification confirmed his centrality. In the second chapter of the book, we explore the quintessential Soviet peasant-intellectual, Alexander Tvardovsky, who left his peasant family behind for a long and successful career as a journalist and poet.[21] As members of the peasant class began to move into more visible roles in society, in some cases this was facilitated through political sponsorship of specific individuals; in others it was the persistence and raw talent of the former peasant that enabled him (or her) to rise to prominence. Tvardovsky was one of those talented new Soviet peasants.

Tvardovsky's most famous work was an epic poem with the genre designation "A Book about a Soldier" ("Kniga pro boitsa"). His Vasily Tyorkin, a soldier-hero of the Second World War, is not particularly well-known outside Russia, but Tyorkin serves as an iconic figure for Russians, representing both continuity and change: a folkloric peasant thriving in the Soviet era, an enduring and inventive image of Russia herself. Couplets from the poem entered Russian cultural memory on a par with quotes from the Civil War's Chapaev. Through Tvardovsky and his creative process, we explore this new

---

[20] For more, see Hartzok, "Children of Chapaev."
[21] Tvardovsky had to turn his back on his family entirely when they were declared to be kulaks and sent into administrative exile.

rank-and-file Chapaev of what Russians called the Great Fatherland War, a "grown-up" Chapaev who no longer needed a political commissar baby-sitter.

In exploring the relationship between myth and testimony, Russian literature about World War II offers an unusually rich body of work. Some of the greatest, and certainly most influential, fiction of the era was written at the front itself. Ilya Ehrenburg, Vasily Grossman, Viktor Nekrasov, Vera Panova, Boris Polevoi, Konstantin Simonov, even Alexander Tvardovsky—all worked for newspapers, and many wrote their works as dispatches from the front lines.[22] In part this is what makes the works so vivid; this is also the reason that detail, a vital component of *byt*—of the "every day"—in literature, took center stage in this fiction.

Chapters 3 and 4 explore the power of the eyewitness and the documentary detail through the works of several of these authors, including Stalin-prizewinning authors Kazakevich, Panova, and Nekrasov. The perception of truth in their depictions of war made their fiction extremely popular in Soviet Russia. Soldiers and their counterparts in the rear, both during and immediately after the war, needed inspiration, but not the false inspiration that sometimes rang from tribunals; they wanted to read about little men and women like themselves, individuals who took heroic steps, and occasionally made errors, in fighting for the common good and the Soviet motherland. Cognizant of the censorship their work would undergo, these writers strove to find the most expressive ways of chronicling the war while still getting their narratives published.

Like Kazakevich and Panova, Nekrasov won a Stalin Prize in 1947 for his World War II novel *In the Trenches of Stalingrad* (*V okopakh Stalingrada*), and like theirs, his award-winning novel was made into a powerful film. Panova and Kazakevich remained orthodox Soviet writers, however, while Nekrasov was forced to emigrate in the 1970s. In his fiction and in his later memoirs,

---

[22] Vasily Grossman, in particular, has been studied by a number of excellent scholars in recent years, and I will not be addressing his works in this book. See Anatolii Bocharov, *Vasily Grossman: Zhizn', tvorchestvo, sud'ba* (Moscow: Sovetskii pisatel', 1990); Frank Ellis, *Vasiliy Grossman: The Genesis and Evolution of a Russian Heretic* (Providence: Berg, 1994); John and Carol Garrard, *The Bones of Berdichev: The Life and Fate of Vasily Grossman* (New York: Free Press, 1996); see also Antony Beevor and Lara Vinogradova, eds. and trans., *A Writer at War: Vasily Grossman with the Red Army, 1941–1945* (New York: Pantheon, 2005). Grossman should be particularly familiar to an English-language audience since essays about him regularly appear in the *New Yorker* and the *New York Review of Books*. See, for example, Keith Gessen, "Under Siege: A Beloved Soviet Writer's Path to Dissent," 6 March 2006, a review of *A Writer at War*.

Nekrasov explored the role of heroism in wartime and in peacetime. Using specific and arresting details—from a well-worn copy of Jack London's novel *Martin Eden* handed about in the trenches, to the legacy of Stalingrad, the mine- and skeleton-strewn earth of Mamaev Kurgan—Nekrasov investigated the meaning of truth, patriotism, and service to country in the Soviet context. The émigré writer never ceased revisiting the trenches of Stalingrad though he was unable to set foot in his homeland again after his forced retreat abroad.

War heroes—and the writers who chronicle them—dominate the Soviet cultural landscape, but in the background the Soviet state under Stalin had been at war with its own population. In chapter 5 we look at three writers who tried to confront Stalinism and the consequences of Soviet militarized life, which included mazes of bureaucracy and the horrors of prison camp. In the wake of the Twentieth Party Congress, Nikita Krushchev singled out Tvardovsky and the literary journal he edited, *Novy Mir* (*New World*), expressly endorsing Tvardovsky's post-war sequel "Tyorkin in the Other World" and personally approving the journal's publication of *One Day in the Life of Ivan Denisovich* (*Odin den' Ivana Denisovicha*), Alexander Solzhenitsyn's tale of another peasant-soldier hero who was incarcerated at the state's behest at war's end. Though World War II had ended and their enemies had been routed, soldier-heroes continued to make their mark in the 1950s and early 1960s, particularly in Tvardovsky's reprisal of Tyorkin and Solzhenitsyn's memorable character Ivan Denisovich. The chapter considers the woes exposed in these two works and their implicit indictment of a state that went to war against its own people, but it concludes with a look at Voinovich and his contribution to the literature of war—both his celebratory song about the new Soviet space program and his parodic novel of World War II, *The Life and Adventures of the Soldier Ivan Chonkin*, not published in the Soviet Union until *perestroika*.

The 1960s heralded a new kind of writing, perhaps signaled by the new journal *Yunost'*, or *Youth*, which began publishing in 1955. A "renewed realism . . . of the 60s and 70s" included such authors as Yury Trifonov, whose novels of ambiguity portrayed young heroes caught in complicated social and political situations.[23] Youth prose writers such as Vasily Aksyonov wrote

---

[23] For more on Trifonov and other new realists, see Hosking, *Beyond Socialist Realism*, x. The "lieutenants' literature" of the 1960s and early 1970s fills in the gap in Second World War fiction.

against a background of the city prose of Trifonov and pushed the envelope on anti-Western propaganda, doing their best to embrace the music, movies, and literature that were flooding the underground.[24] While this era offered certain freedoms in choice of theme, style, and genre, the authors publishing still had to come to terms with official Soviet culture and socialist realism's positive hero. In the midst of the ongoing Cold War, not every author could get his work into print, but young prose writers continued to explore the relationship between the individual and the totalitarian state.

Sergei Dovlatov's pseudoautobiographical central protagonists seem to many to be antiheroes rather than heroes, characters who do not even take the socialist realist model into account and thus cannot qualify as positive heroes. In chapter 6, I chronicle the emergence of this new kind of hero in life—the dissident hero, the misfit, the "dropout," the outsider. Looking at the prose of Vladimir Makanin and Sergei Dovlatov—one a writer who published throughout the period, and the other a man who never managed to publish any fiction before his emigration to the West—we examine the marginal hero and his place in society. About Dovlatov, Nobel-prizewinning poet Joseph Brodsky once said, "The decisive thing is his tone, which every member of a democratic society can recognize: the individual who won't let himself be cast in the role of a victim, who is not obsessed with what makes him different." Makanin's heroes are victims, but in the post-Thaw retrenchments of official Soviet culture, a victim became a kind of hero too.

As the Soviet state imploded in the early 1990s, the veterans of the Second World War who had chronicled their eyewitness experiences as journalists or as soldiers were nearing the ends of their lives. A new surge of memoirs and novels, each more earnest than the last, burst onto the literary scene as these writers tried to rewrite Soviet history and their own earlier works, this time without Soviet censorship. The Second World War and its memorials had played an enormous role in the formation of Soviet self-identity across the second half of the twentieth century, and the negation of Soviet history caused a true crisis for veterans and many other Soviet citizens and heralded the decline of the country and its regime. In 1988, General Secretary Mikhail Gorbachev cancelled all history exams nationwide, stating, "There

---

[24] For a study of this era, see Sergei Zhuk, *Rock and Roll in the Rocket City: The West, Identity, and Ideology in Soviet Dniepropetrovsk, 1960–1985* (Baltimore: Johns Hopkins University Press, 2010).

is no point in testing their knowledge of lies."[25] Official acknowledgement of the lies was unexpected after the years of stagnation and status quo, and Gorbachev's statement pointed toward the end of Soviet history as Russians had known it.

In the 1990s, author Viktor Astafiev revisited his own war experiences in his two-volume novel *The Accursed and the Dead* (*Prokliaty i ubity*) as well as in some of his shorter fiction, and his work featured a new and honest vision of the soldier's war and postwar experiences. The struggles of veteran-writers such as Astafiev to find a place in a post-Soviet world for their memories of betrayal by their own state have run up against the new patriotism and nationalism championed by President (and Prime Minister) Vladimir Putin. Chapter 7 looks at post-Soviet visions of World War II, contrasting them with the more immediate eyewitness narratives we looked at in previous chapters. Astafiev (1924–2001), a member of the generation I am calling the "boys of '24,"[26] tried to write the *War and Peace* for the twentieth century. His novel *The Accursed and the Dead* strove for detachment and impartiality, but his memories of his own war experience may have kept him from realizing those goals.

The final chapter of this study sums up the ways in which Chapaev brought Soviet society into a post-Soviet world. The icons of the Soviet past—including Chapaev, but in the context of the Cold War expanding to other important figures, his "comrades" in the larger Soviet context, such as the first Soviet cosmonaut, Yury Gagarin[27]—were ripe for revisiting. The children born in the 1960s, who dreamed of Soviet heroism and transformed their games from horse riding and swashbuckling in Russia's steppes to manning their own crafts in the vast far reaches of space, did just that as they approached

---

[25] Gorbachev's quote from Joyce Appleby, Lynn Hunt, and Margaret Jacobs, *Telling the Truth about History* (New York: Norton, 1994), 290. Vladimir Putin has returned to Victory Day and the need to honor Soviet World War II veterans even as those veterans are dying out. See for example http://www.time.com/time/world/article/0,8599,1618531,00.html.

[26] Another "boy of '24" whom I'll include only tangentially is Boris Vasiliev, author of the WWII novel *The Dawns Here Are Quiet*, among other works. *Dawns* was published in *Iunost'* in 1969; Yury Liubimov staged a version of it at his famous Taganka Theatre in 1971, and in 1972 Vasiliev's fellow veteran, director Stanislav Rostotsky (1922–2001), released a film version. Vasiliev's novels have been republished recently by Vagrius in Moscow, and *Dawns* even received a Chinese translation in 2005.

[27] Gagarin's thirtieth birthday was celebrated with pomp and circumstance in 1964, the same year the film *Chapaev* was released in a thirtieth anniversary edition.

the end of the twentieth century. Gagarin—the son of a peasant—represented a victory in the space race and a sign of Soviet superiority in the Cold War,[28] but what had that "superiority" come to mean by the 1980s and 1990s?

One such author, Viktor Pelevin (b. 1962), has questioned the meaning of the Soviet state, the Cold War, and totalitarianism throughout his writing career, most notably in his 1991 text *Omon Ra*—a parodic novel about a school for cosmonauts—and in his 1996 novel *Chapaev and Pustota*, which confronts the chaotic contemporary times of the mid-1990s through a historical reliving of the Civil War period. In the densely layered literary and historical references of the postmodern post-Soviet novel, the central literary protagonist continued to thrive, but in opposition now to both Soviet society and the contemporary post-Soviet world, a Dovlatov antihero reborn, perhaps. Pelevin's heroes confronted traditional "accursed questions" inherited from the nineteenth century, but they also struggled with the meaning of individuality as a new post-Socialist, postcollective society began to emerge.

Thus not just the Second World War and Cold War narratives continued to be relevant through the end of the twentieth and into the twenty-first century, but the revolutionary and Civil War hero Chapaev did as well. Tropes and cultural remnants of Chapaev and the Soviet "Chapaev text"—from an aging steamship to the cult of the memorial statue—are revisited in stories like Vasily Aksyonov's "The Ship of the World: *Vasily Chapaev*" ("Korabl' mira: *Vasilii Chapaev*"), but these "comrades" are already of a new type. Aksyonov's 1995 story seems at first glance to be merely a compilation of send-ups and clichés of post-Soviet postmodern culture, but like much postmodern fiction, on closer examination it reveals surprising depth and seriousness and contributes an important chapter to the question of Soviet and post-Soviet ideas about heroes and heroism.

The "end" of the Soviet Union meant that clichés and tropes of the Soviet period resurfaced, to be reconsidered, replayed, remixed. The objects and places named to honor the heroes and victims of the Soviet era—from Chapaev to the pilot Valery Chkalov, from Maxim Gorky to Alexei Maresiev, from the heroes of Stalingrad to the victims of Magadan—form a three-dimensional history lesson across the landscape of the former Soviet empire. But in the new post-Soviet political situation, these reminders of wars—wars both external

---

[28] Some sources say that Gagarin was chosen for the successful first manned flight into space in 1961 in part due to his social origin as the son of a peasant. See for example http://news.bbc.co.uk/2/hi/special_report/1998/03/98/gagarin/71823.stm.

and internal, "hot" and "cold"—have a new meaning as well, even as in some cases they rust (like Aksyonov's fictional ship) and list (like the enormous motherland monument to the battle of Stalingrad on Mamaev Kurgan).[29]

What was the fate of Chapaev and his comrades? What of the peasant-soldier? The near-continual state of war in the Soviet era shaped the literary hero and ideas of heroism in society, and although Soviet power is a thing of the past, much of its production remains in the monuments, books, and films that dot the physical and cultural landscape of Russia and its neighboring countries. Coming to terms with the Soviet legacy and the legacy of the hero may take another century, but I hope this book starts us on the right path.

A final paradox about war, perhaps the most bitter. Randolph Bourne wrote his devastating and angry essay as a response to his teacher and mentor John Dewey. In 1917, Dewey endorsed American president Woodrow Wilson's call for the United States to enter the Great War. Dewey saw the moment as a "plastic juncture" out of which might come a better future, molded by progressive intellectuals. That is always the promise of war, and nowhere more so than in the wars Russians fought in the twentieth century. In every case, the very future of utopia was at stake in the fighting, making every sacrifice, every act of violence, every loss seem small by comparison.

Bourne knew better. He wrote in response to Dewey, "War determines its own end: Victory. And government crushes out automatically all forces that deflect, or threaten to deflect, energy from the path of organization to that end."[30]

This book examines the way Russian writers and the protagonists they created negotiated between Dewey's hopes and Bourne's truth. Individualist or representative of a collective, "comrade" of Chapaev or orphan of the Soviet state? Who was the Russian hero of the twentieth century, and what was his relationship to the society that birthed him, celebrated him, mocked him, and worshipped him? In the pages that follow, we look at a number of texts and heroes in both the serious and satirical modes in an attempt to find that hero and to ascertain where the end of the Soviet era has left him.

---

[29] Richard Galpin, "Russia's Massive Leaning Statue," BBC News, Moscow, 8 May 2009. See http://news.bbc.co.uk/2/hi/europe/8040471.stm. The statue is due to be taken down in the near future to avoid disaster.

[30] Quoted in Casey Nelson Blake, *Beloved Community: The Cultural Criticism of Randolph Bourne, Van Wyck Brooks, Waldo Frank and Lewis Mumford* (Chapel Hill, NC: UNC Press, 1990), 155.

Introduction

* * *

From *Mother*, this book will trace an arc that takes us through the entire twentieth century, describing a century dominated by war and other forms of state-sanctioned violence. Proletarian heroes in their revolutionary struggles give birth to the socialist realist peasant-hero Vasily Chapaev and his political commissar sidekick. After the Civil War, Soviet children are born with Chapaev's swashbuckling sword in their hands. The Second World War replaced the Revolution and Civil War as the experience in which Soviet identity was forged. The literary heroes produced in response to that war were comrades to Chapaev and included among others peasant-soldiers and their commissars. They are to be found in folk poetry, straight heroic narratives, new Soviet myths, and "true war stories." In the Thaw and post-Thaw era, the Russian military hero goes underground, gently parodied and turned inside out by a different kind of military service in the Zone of the Soviet Gulag and in novels and stories that could not be published in the Soviet Union. As the Soviet Union began to unravel, new assessments of war and heroism forced a reconsideration of the older rhetoric of *podvig* and asked uncomfortable questions about the justice of war and justice in war. For many, the twentieth century ended with the collapse of the Soviet Union, and as Russians picked up those pieces, some postmodern writers turned the notion of heroism and of Chapaev into nothing but irony.

War has indeed been the health of the Russian state from the Revolution through the early twenty-first century. And it has been central to the creation of the Russian literary hero as well.

Part I
Creating Heroes from Chaos

Trofimov, Chapaev, 1935

Chapter One

Born in the Crucible of War
Chapaev and His Socialist Realist Comrades

> In life there is always a place for feats.
> В жизни всегда есть место подвигу.
>
> -Boris Polevoi
>
> Heroism means doing the impossible.
> Геройство—это значит совершить невозможное.
>
> -Fyodor Gladkov

When Maxim Gorky published his novel *Mother* in 1906, it became a prototype for future socialist realist novels. Over a quarter of a century later, when in 1934 the method of socialist realist writing was codified, *Mother* was listed as an officially approved exemplar. Sitting at an estate in the Adirondacks,[1] Gorky had written the novel in the wake of devastating events in Russia: the humiliating defeat in the Russo-Japanese War and the convulsions of the 1905 revolution that failed to bring the tsarist state down. This must have seemed to Gorky like a "plastic juncture," to use John Dewey's term, though that assessment turned out to be premature. His novel *Mother* was in its own way a war novel that confronted the working class problems of Russia and heralded the coming Revolutions.

After a brief discussion of *Mother*, we look in this chapter at two of its progeny, two of the most significant novels to emerge in the immediate aftermath of the Revolution and Civil War. Dmitry Furmanov's *Chapaev* appeared in 1923, and Fyodor Gladkov's *Cement* was published two years later.[2] Vasily Chapaev is pictured in the heat of the Civil War, while Gladkov's Gleb Chumalov has returned home to a destroyed and abandoned factory after his time

---

[1] Barry Scherr, "Gorky and God-Building," 189–210, in *William James in Russian Culture*, ed. Joan Delancey Grossman and Ruth Rischin (Lanham, MD: Lexington Books, 2003), 189–190.

[2] Dmitrii Furmanov, *Chapaev* (Moscow: Gosizdatel'stvo khudozhestvennoi literatury, 1961). This text uses volume 1 of Furmanov's *Sobranie sochinenii v chetyrekh tomakh* (Moscow: Goslitizdat, 1960). The first edition of Gladkov's *Cement* was printed in *Krasnaia nov'* (1925) nos. 1–6, but unless otherwise noted, I will be quoting from the English translation of that edition, A. S. Arthur and C. Ashleigh, trans., *Cement* (New York: Frederick Ungar, 1980).

fighting the White Army.³ These characters represent two possible models of heroism, Russian men fighting for the future in the war and afterward on the economic front. Although the post-Civil War reconstruction work Gleb does in *Cement* is also heroic, it is Chapaev's heroism that little boys dream of.

Both novels were enormously popular with contemporary readers.⁴ Though *Chapaev* and *Cement* were written before the codification of socialist realism, they too wound up as official exemplars of the method. Unlike the characters in *Mother,* the heroes in these novels are soldiers, and war figures centrally as a marker of what is heroic about them. Both were based in part on the experiences of their authors and include autobiographical details. Both novels also feature a conflict between the spontaneous hero who emerges from the people and the more conscious party figure.⁵

Between them, Gorky, Furmanov, and Gladkov attempted to reconfigure the Russian literary hero in the revolutionary period, placing him in conflict with the state, with external enemies, and with internal enemies. Chapaev proved to be the most enduring.

Gorky, Mother, and the Birth of the Socialist Realist Hero

Maxim Gorky (1868–1936) was a writer from the "lower depths." In the convulsions and revolutionary ferment of the early twentieth century, as the tsarist empire began to wane, he stepped onto the public stage.

---

3   Robert Busch notes that the focus on the economic front is new in 1925; in Soviet fiction up to this point the civil war had been the predominant theme. See Robert Busch, "Gladkov's *Cement*: the Making of a Classic," *SEEJ* 22.3 (1978): 348–361, esp. 348–349. This article follows the evolution of the novel from its original publication in 1925 in *Krasnaia nov'* until the time of Gladkov's death, as it conformed to the changing norms of Socialist realism. See also Maurice Friedberg, "New Editions of Soviet Belles-Lettres: A Study in Politics and Palimpsests," *American Slavic and East European Review*, 13.1 (Feb. 1954): 77–88 and L. N. Smirnova, "Kak sozdavalsia *Tsement*," in *Tekstologiia proizvedenii sovetskoi literatury: Voprosy tekstologii* 4 (1967): 140–227.
4   On this, see Evgeny Dobrenko, *The Making of the State Reader* (Stanford: Stanford University Press, 1997), 130–131. Also Osip Brik, "Pochemu ponravilsia "Tsement," *Na literaturnom postu*, 2 (1926): 30–32, and Valer'ian Polianskii, "Tsement i ego kritiki," in *Na literaturnom postu* 5–6 (1926): 50–53. Brik reacted negatively to Chumalov, and we will see why below.
5   Historically Furmanov and Gladkov have been linked as two proletarian writers first published by *Krasnaia nov'*. Indeed, when Alexander Voronsky was dismissed from the editorship of *Krasnaia nov'*, purportedly for denying proletarian writers access to the journal, he replied that "he had always been willing to publish proletarian writing of quality, such as that of Furmanov and Gladkov." See A. Kemp-Welch, *Stalin and the Literary Intelligentsia, 1928–1939* (Basingstoke: Macmillan, 1991), 42–44.

A Romantic and a product of the nineteenth century, Gorky believed in the idea of the Great Man, a hero in Carlyle's terms, and the fact that he sought that Great Man among the common people—and moreover through the exigencies of his own biography came to be seen as that Great Man—was only one of the conundrums of his work and life.[6]

The putative father of Soviet literature, Gorky in his 1901 "Song of the Stormy Petrel" (*"Pesnia o burevestnike"*) drew on Romantic tropes of the nineteenth century.[7] In the song, other birds (the gull, the loon) fear the coming storm, but the petrel earns the appositives "demon of the storm" and "prophet of victory" and yearns for rough weather. No fear.

Interpreters then and now saw revolution in that storm at sea, and in the stormy petrel, a harbinger of change. Like Mikhail Lermontov's sailboat—in his 1841 poem "A Lonely White Sail Gleams" ("Beleet parus odinokii")—the petrel actively seeks a storm. But while Lermontov's hero imagines that in that storm he would find peace, Gorky's here seeks "life's battle."[8] Throughout much of Soviet history, Gorky himself was figured as a Romantic hero, a "stormy petrel" who welcomed and heralded the approaching storm,[9] and he

---

[6] Gorky has been the subject of several new biographies in Russia; Pavel Basinskii published a ZhZL biography in 2005, Viktor Peteli published *Zhizn' Maksima Gor'kogo* (Moscow: Tsentrpoligraf, 2007), and Dmitrii Bykov wrote *Byl li Gor'kii*, a fuller version of his Channel 5 documentary film, in 2008 (Moscow: AST, Astrel', 2008). A new English translation of his classic *Childhood* (translated Graham Hettlinger, Chicago: Ivan Dee, 2010) may get him more attention in the United States in the next decade as well.

[7] The "Song of the Stormy Petrel" is sung by a siskin in the story "Spring Melodies," a short tale about birds in springtime. The censorship forbade the tale itself, but "Song of the Stormy Petrel" was allowed for publication in the April 1901 issue of *Zhizn'*. Maxim Gorky, *Sobranie sochinenii v tridtsati tomakh*, vol. 5 (Moscow: Khudozhestvennaia literatura, 1950), 322–327: "Song" on 326–327; notes and commentary 482–486.

[8] Lenin adopted the last line of the "Song," ending his own article "Before the Storm" with the words "Let the storm come more fiercely!" See Gorky, volume 5: 485, citing V. I. Lenin, *Sochineniia*, 4th ed., vol. 11, 117.

[9] In a 1999 documentary novel about Gorky, Arkady Vaksberg uses the metaphor of the "stormy petrel" for Gorky himself. See *Gibel' burevestnika: Maksim Gor'kii, poslednie dvadtsat' let* (Moscow: Terra-Sport, 1999). Vaksberg believes that his documentary novel replaces mythical approaches to the man that were an inherent part of all previous biographies of Gorky, but he uses the revolutionary romantic image of the *burevestnik* anyway, underscoring the ways in which Gorky's myths and life are mutually inextricable. On the reassessment of the "Gorky Myth," see Andrew Barratt and Edith W. Clowes, "Gor'ky, Glasnost' and Perestroika: The Death of a Cultural Superhero?," *Soviet Studies* 43, 6 (1991): 1123–1142.

worked hard to fashion and be true to that image. As Vladislav Khodasevich recalled in his 1936 memoir essay about Gorky, by the 1920s Gorky felt that any potential course of action must be subsumed to his image. Sometimes he told Khodasevich that he had an urge to act in unexpected ways, but he chose not to. "It's impossible. I would damage my biography," he would say.[10] His effective management of his image enabled Soviet commentators to praise Gorky as a prophet of revolution, though Gorky well understood the horrors and dangers of warfare.

In the phenomenon of the First World War—like his American counterpart Randolph Bourne—Gorky saw a loss of culture, a decline in humanity that foretold a future of violence against which he felt compelled to struggle. In January of 1917, Gorky shared with French writer Romain Rolland an idea that would bring back a "voice of Dante" to speak to Russians of all ages:

> We adults, who are fated to abandon this world in due time—we will leave our children a pathetic inheritance, we are bequeathing them a very sad life. This absurd war is stunning proof of our moral weakness, of the decline of culture. Let's remind our children that people were not always as weak and wicked as—alas!—we are now; let's remind them that all nations had—and have now—great people and noble hearts! It is essential that we do this precisely in our days of victorious cruelty and brutality.[11]

According to Gorky, a true hero complete with a heroic voice was precisely what Russia needed in the twentieth century. Gorky proposed the *Lives of Remarkable People* (*Zhizn' zamechatel'nykh liudei*), a series of biographies that were to present "great people and noble hearts" to readers, grounding them in a romantic worldview that would enable them to become citizens of the world and of their own nation and that would counter the brutalities

---

[10] "Нельзя. Биографию испортишь" (372). Khodasevich was in fairly close contact with Gorky from 1918 through 1925, what he would call "personal, not business or literary" relations (354). See Khodasevich, "Gor'kii," *Koleblemyi trenozhnik* (Moscow: Sovetskii pisatel', 1991), 353–374.

[11] A. M. Gorky, "Letter to Romain Rolland," in *Sobranie sochinenii v tridtsati tomakh*, vol. 29 (Moscow, 1955), 374–375. Gorky's relations with Rolland, and the latter's disappointment in 1935 when he visited Moscow and discovered that Gorky had become part of the "privileged class," are fascinating, though not relevant to the present discussion. See *Voprosy literatury* 3 (1989): 239–240.

of world war, militarization, famine, and suffering. The *Lives* series finally got off the ground in 1933, publishing seventeen volumes in its first year, including a biography of Italian poet Dante Alighieri. It continues publishing to this day.[12]

In his fiction and in his life, Gorky consciously set out to create a new kind of protagonist for the society from which he himself had emerged, one who could function as a hero for the proletariat. He does this twice over in his classic novel *Mother*.[13] The events of *Mother* transpire during a time of social unrest, although Gorky does not mention any actual war in the narrative. Nonetheless, the situation he chronicles is one of class war and underground revolutionary activity, as representatives of the workers struggled with the authorities and the factory owners to promote their desires for access to learning and power.

In this revolutionary novel, we can trace the origins of the Soviet war hero. After the Revolution, literature drew on the activist-heroes who peopled novels such as Gorky's, and the towns and factories of Soviet life served as the stage for the conflicts of a militarized society, between retrograde elements such as Christians, tsarists, and individualists and the newly collectivist state. Novels such as Gorky's *Mother (Mat')* and Fyodor Gladkov's *Cement* (*Tsement*, 1925) presented the creation of the new protagonist as a part of the revolutionary project—related to, in some cases presaging, and stemming from actual war. The relationship between the creation of this social hero and the Romantic roots of the Russian literary hero (and often his creator) can be seen clearly in Maxim Gorky himself.

---

[12] In 2010 a new volume was published on exiled writer Sergei Dovlatov—an interesting addition to the pantheon of twentieth-century "Remarkable Lives." In 1931 Gorky headed up a different series: "History of the Civil War." With this work he hoped to keep the heroic efforts of the Red Army soldiers alive for their descendents; the participants in the Civil War themselves were to research and write the books "with maximal simplicity, clarity and truthfulness." See "To the Participants of the Civil War," *Sobranie sochinenii v tridtsati tomakh*, vol. 26, 116–119, quote on 117. For details about the plan, see Gorky's letter to Stalin of November 27, 1929, translated in *Maksim Gorky: Selected Letters*, ed. Andrew Barratt and Barry P. Scherr (Oxford: Clarendon Press, 1977), 319–320. Two volumes of what were to be books for peasants "to be read like a novel" were published in 1937 and 1942. For more on the Civil War series, see Hartzok, *Children of Chapaev*, 2009, chapter 4.

[13] First published in English in an American edition of 1907, the novel was revised, shortened, and made more concise in its Russian publication. See Scherr, *Maxim Gorky*, 43–45.

1. Born in the Crucible of War: Chapaev and His Socialist Realist Comrades

When Gorky chose the title for *Mother*, he had a number of things in mind. The novel features a proletarian protagonist named Pavel Vlasov, who gets arrested in the first part of the novel and by the end is sent into exile in Siberia. Pavel's mother, initially a conservative and timid woman who focuses inward on her personal family, is transformed over the course of the narrative to become a true "mother" to the movement. Her Christian devotion to the church and God is also transformed into a belief in something larger—a struggle for change on this earth to benefit all. By naming the novel after his secondary character, the mother Nilovna (called, moreover, by her patronymic rather than her given name), Gorky offers a generative model for future revolutionary action. As Barry Scherr has written, these two characters, the son and the mother, are "revolutionary archetypes," representing their respective generations: the generation of the son—revolutionary—and that of the parents destined to join their offspring.[14] "Mother" with a capital *M* defines Gorky's attitude toward revolution: not only can the older generation be reformed, but they can "give birth" to more and more youth willing to work and fight for changes in society.

What Scherr identifies as the "myth of the revolutionary spirit" is contagious, and it penetrates generational boundaries in unexpected ways, counteracting the biological assumption that a mother gives birth to a son. Here instead, the son Pavel reverses genealogy and passes his legacy on to his mother, who inherits his comrades and the movement he loves. A mother is a generative figure, and Gorky uses the metaphor of the family to indicate that though beyond her reproductive years, Nilovna can continue to have children and to bring more and more of them into the larger revolutionary "family." Thus Gorky harnesses the instincts of the mother to a larger cause and demonstrates how she can exchange her loyalty to a "personal" family for loyalty to the larger social family.

What's more, Gorky's "mother" is presented as a kind of metamother. In the novel, we hear one of Pavel's comrades say to her, "You, mother, are capable of a great deal. You have a great capacity for motherliness!"[15] This is her main characteristic. Not a woman, really, or even an individualized person; we never find out her first name, for example, but continue to think of her as the other characters do, with the class-based habit of calling people by their

---

14 Scherr, *Maxim Gorky*, 44.
15 Maksim Gor'kii, *Mat'* (Leningrad: Khudozhestvennaia literatura, 1986); Maxim Gorky, *Mother* (Secaucus, NJ: Citadel, 1972), 97.

patronymic. Nilovna is rather motherhood personified and indeed amplified beyond her personal status. As we follow Nilovna's speeches throughout the novel, we see that family is paramount for her, and instead of losing a son when Pavel is arrested, she gains an entire generation of sons and daughters, a fact demonstrated by her frequent use of child metaphors.[16]

As she comes to realize what her son's comrades are up to, she feels concern for them as an adult observing children who do not understand the significance of their actions:

> The mother felt that she knew the life of the workingmen better than these people and saw more clearly than they the enormity of the task they assumed. She could look upon them with the somewhat melancholy indulgence of a grown-up person toward children who play man and wife without understanding the drama of the relationship. (Gorky, *Mother*, 244)

Later in the novel, she begins to feel the ties of family for Pavel's comrades, though she has trouble at first with the vocabulary to express herself. When Rybin—a broad-shouldered, black-bearded peasant who has been converted to Pavel's cause—is arrested, Nilovna at first describes this neighbor as a stranger to her, "chuzhoi," but this doesn't feel right. She then brings him into her family with a simile: "I respect him like a brother—an elder brother" (*"uvazhaiu kak rodnogo brata—starshego,"* 305), but that is not quite right either. Ultimately, she comes to embrace her role as mother to all, as the narrator tells us, "Her heart beat tenderly with 'My dears, my children, my own'" (*"Deti! Rodnye moi!"* 341).

Gorky's mother begins her road to consciousness spontaneously, as the "disciple" in the "mentor/disciple" pattern should. She feels that "deep inside her, words were being born, words of a great, all-embracing love." (188) Somewhat later, she comes to understand the importance of words: "Perhaps in our day a word is worth more than a person." (312) Gradually, she moves from pure emoting to articulating the truth (as we are told, the "word is born" in her [*rozhdaetsia slovo*]). By the end of the novel, she speaks, and her words are worth heeding: "You are in truth comrades all, kinsmen all, for you are all children of one mother, of truth. Truth has brought you forth; and by its power you live!" (393)

---

[16] On Gorky's use of the term "comrade," see Borenstein, *Men without Women*, 286, n. 46.

In Gorky's transformative narrative, a spontaneously good woman must become conscious (and know the truth) and must spread that consciousness (and thus speak the truth). This process is facilitated by exposure to the best influences, such as those of Pavel Vlasov and his revolutionary circle. Truth itself, as is obvious in the Russian, is feminine, *Pravda*—an archetypal mother of the comrades Nilovna addresses. As she endures the beating she receives at the end of the novel—the ambiguous scene that leaves the reader uncertain whether she perishes or merely succumbs to unconsciousness, to rise anew another day—we see her kinship with the people. Though she is beaten and down, "her eyes did not fade and they saw many other eyes—those [eyes] burned with the brave, piercing fire so familiar to her—the fire that was dear to her heart" (*"rodnym ee serdtsu ognem,"* 401).

Although the Vlasovs (mother and son) and their comrades are fighting the state, they are in the process creating their own symbols and touchstones of national spirit: the red banner held up by the revolutionaries, the notion of Truth as a rallying point in the struggle with the tsarist regime, the "fiery eyes" that hold kinship within them.

Mother is built on three symbolic paradigms: the "family" spirit the comrades find in Nilovna after she has ascended to revolutionary mother status; Pavel's teaching his mother to understand and view the world in a wider, more communal sense; and the martyred son who will go into exile and perhaps return one day.[17] But Gorky's doubled characters in *Mother* set up yet another pattern for Soviet fiction: Nilovna is the true protagonist of the novel, and by picking up the banner dropped by her son, she symbolically takes on his embattled position vis-à-vis the state.

This militarization of life through revolutionary struggle—with its secret cells, its comradely spirit, its ideological leaders, its foot soldiers, and, most importantly, its enemies—transformed the literary protagonist into a military hero. Nilovna, the Mother, became a touchstone in the new proto-Soviet nationalism, a sign that members of the older, conservative generation were capable of change and of unity with the younger generation. In the novel we see Pavel Vlasov recruit and train his own mother to his cause. The mother brings new qualities to the concept of heroics, with her maternal instincts, her gentle nature, and her ability to become firm once she too believes.

---

17   See Clark, *The Soviet Novel: History as Ritual*.

Gorky planned to write a sequel to this novel, entitled *Son*, in which Pavel Vlasov would have returned from exile to continue his work. The fact that he did not do so leaves Nilovna in a powerful position: the legatee of revolutionary dreams, the meek woman celebrated in the title of the novel, grown larger than life. Eponymous women in Russian literature before her included Leo Tolstoy's *Anna Karenina*, the tragic adulterous noblewoman; Nadezhda Durova's autobiographical *Cavalry Maiden (Kavalerist – devitsa)*, again a noblewoman, cross-dressing to find her place in a male military world; or Anton Chekhov's "The Darling" ("Dushechka", 1898), who took on the characteristics of all the men around her but had no essence of her own. Nilovna is grounded, thoughtful—puzzling out relationships and new vocabulary and attitudes when they are not immediately clear to her—and most importantly a member of the lower peasant/proletarian classes, the classes who would inherit Russia after the Revolution. She is a new woman.

Nilovna occupies the niche of Mother of the Revolution and Mother of Socialist Realism with a quiet fortitude. However, she did not rise to the stature of a hero in Carlyle's sense, nor did she prove a lasting Soviet heroine. Perhaps because she was a woman and a mother, or perhaps because the crucial war context was missing in her creation and development, Nilovna remained a part of the pre-Soviet past. She did not capture the imagination of Russian writers seeking to found new generations of heroes. That role belonged to Chapaev.

From Life to Myth: Furmanov Creates Chapaev

This book takes its title from both the hero Chapaev and the "Chapaev text" of Soviet literature because Chapaev looms so large in the Soviet imagination. In the years since the novel was published in 1923, Chapaev's name and image have been evoked in virtually every war narrative that has followed, and many other narratives besides, especially fiction about children and their development. To reiterate, playing Chapaev and Reds versus Whites became the Soviet child's version of cops and robbers or cowboys and Indians.[18]

---

[18] In his *Folklore for Stalin*, Frank Miller describes the many pseudo–folk songs and folk poems that emerged as part of the "Chapaev text." These celebrations of key moments in Chapaev's history were prototypes for the popular series of anecdotes that satirized the heroic Chapaev. See Frank Miller, *Folklore for Stalin: Russian Folklore and Pseudofolklore of the Stalin Era* (Armonk, NY: M.E. Sharpe, 1990), and Seth Graham, *Resonant Dissonance: The Russian Joke in Cultural Context* (Evanston: Northwestern University Press, 2009). See also Hartzok, *Children of Chapaev*, 2009.

For the novel, Furmanov drew much of his ideological underpinning from the polemics of the 1860s and categories used by his predecessors Dostoevsky, Chernyshevsky, and Ivan Turgenev: Furmanov characterized Chapaev as a person who "love[d] strong, decisive, firm words. And he loved decisive, firm and intelligent actions even more!"[19] Words and deeds—these conflicting dichotomous categories tortured nineteenth-century literary heroes from Turgenev's Rudin and Bazarov to Dostoevsky's Raskolnikov. Furmanov harnessed them together in his novel in order to try and pull the peasantry into a conscious future.

Furmanov himself was thinking about issues of heroism in war in 1919, as he fought side-by-side with the real Chapaev in the Civil War. In an essay from that year, "Conscious Heroes," Furmanov explained the difference between a mere "brave person" (*khrabrets*) and a hero: "The heroism of communists inevitably emerges *from their deep conviction of the righteousness of their cause*. They are firm and manly, passionate and decisive. They are staunch and calm, for they have *consciously entered into the struggle*."[20] Spontaneity and elemental energy are hallmarks of bravery. Passionate, decisive, manly action bolstered by awareness of the cause and conscious struggle—this is how Furmanov defines heroism, and these are the characteristics of the new Soviet hero. As we discussed in the last chapter, Soviet heroism—both in war and in peacetime—equals bravery plus consciousness.

Dmitri Furmanov was born in 1891, the third child of a displaced peasant, and he personally saw the 1905 worker strikes in Ivanovo-Voznesensk at an impressionable age. Indeed, he was witness to the very type of strikes and demonstrations described in Gorky's novel *Mother*. The young Furmanov became fascinated with ideas of anarchy and dreamed of joining in the action of overthrowing bureaucrats and administrators. The admiration the novelist would express for Chapaev, whom he called a "horse of the steppes," came in part from that adolescent experience of watching adults rebel against the controls that impeded their freedom.

As a young man, Furmanov imagined himself becoming a writer and chronicled his hopes in his diary. "Before me," he wrote, "I can see my future literary life—not as formidable and turbulent as those of Belinsky, Pisarev and Dobrolyubov, but nonetheless a wonderfully fruitful one." Furmanov's early

---

[19] Furmanov, *Chapaev*, 156 [emphasis mine].
[20] Dmitrii Furmanov, *Nezabyvaemye dni*, in the series *Biblioteka molodogo rabochego* (Leningrad: Lenizdat, 1983), 205–06.

thoughts on the role of writers and critics and the meaning of art were very much related to the "word and deed" debates of Turgenev and Chernyshevsky: against "art for art's sake." Furmanov believed that art must have a purpose, a goal, and for him that goal was engendered by what he called "holy acts."

As the First World War broke out, Furmanov tried to figure out whether war could create a new society, whether this war was a just war. Speaking out at a prowar rally at Moscow State University, Furmanov compared the current war to the War of 1812. "Is war ruinous or beneficial?" he asked. "One cannot answer this question with certainty, without knowing what kind of war we're speaking about; everything depends on circumstances, time, and place. The War of 1812 was salutary for the Russian people. But what about this war? Will it be good for the people?"[21] Soon after this outburst, Furmanov had the opportunity to find the answer himself: he joined the war effort, first as a medical orderly, and by 1915 as a war correspondent. He joined the Bolsheviks but continued to write about his experiences of war: "Grey Heroes," "Medical Assistants," "The Death of a Pilot." These war sketches, most of which remained unpublished, served as raw material and practice for the future novelist of the Civil War.

Furmanov returned to Ivanovo-Voznesensk in 1917 to do propaganda work among the textile workers and the new local Soviet of Workers' and Soldiers' Deputies. By August of 1917 Furmanov had become one of the main leaders of the Ivanovo Soviet, and on October 25 it was his phone call to *Izvestiia* in Moscow that brought the news of the Bolsheviks taking power to Ivanovo. On that day, Furmanov was appointed chairman of the Provisional Revolutionary Headquarters of Ivanovo-Voznesensk. His status as a provincial political leader continued to rise throughout 1918, and in February of 1919 he became the political commissar of Chapaev's forces.

Furmanov based the novel *Chapaev* on the few months he served as commissar with the Twenty-fifth Division, between March and August of 1919, after which he was transferred to the Turkestan front. "There were many talented, brave, charming commanders in the civil war era. Chapaev was lucky," wrote Yury Libedinsky, "that Furmanov was assigned to him."[22]

---

[21] Aleksandr Isbakh, *Furmanov*, in series *Zhizn' zamechatel'nykh liudei* (Moscow: Molodaia gvardiia, 1968), 42.

[22] Yury Libedinsky, "Bol'shevik, voin, pisatel'," *Furmanov v vospominaniiakh sovremennikov*, ed. A. Isbakh and D. Zonov (Moscow: Sovetskii pisatel', 1959), 172–192; quote on 185.

A regional critic from Ivanovo-Voznesensk called *Chapaev* Furmanov's "hymn in honor of the Bolshevik textile workers of Ivanovo" and maintained that this novel was also a "hymn to the Party."[23] In fact, of course, Furmanov was lucky to have been assigned to the historical Chapaev. In the end they made each other's reputation.

In writing *Chapaev*, Furmanov participated in what LEF (Left Front of Art) critics called "a literature of fact." Furmanov's Chapaev is believable as a character precisely because he is drawn from life. But the novel becomes more credible in addition because of its "conscious" character, Bolshevik political commissar Fyodor Klychkov, who was drawn from Furmanov's autobiography. Thus in a sense Furmanov assigned the "bravery" to Chapaev and the "consciousness" to Klychkov, creating a story of heroism from his own Civil War experiences and through this staging of historical events contributing to the growth of Soviet concepts of *podvig*. In Chapaev, Furmanov created the new Soviet hero.

Chapaev and the Historical Roots of the New Soviet Hero

Familiar though Chapaev remains, let us take a moment to review the plot of the original novel. The action takes place on the Eastern Front, over the course of six months during the Civil War. Our hero Chapaev is a peasant serving now in the Red Army as the commander of the Stenka Razin Division. He is already an exemplary leader of men—disciplining them when necessary, instructing them to treat civilians with respect, strategizing against the Whites. His actions as a military leader would merely make him brave. What makes him heroic over the course of the novel is his evolution, his ideological growth under the tutelage of the division's political commissar Fyodor Klychkov. During the course of the Civil War, Chapaev is transformed from a peasant-soldier who fights into a Soviet soldier who fights for the right reasons. He is a brave peasant who gains consciousness to become a true military hero. This, at one level, is the most important action in the book. And at the end of the novel, the hero dies, shot while crossing a river.

It is a simple story, and part of its appeal lies in the fact that this new Soviet hero drew on models from the Russian past which would have resonated with readers at the time. As Randolph Bourne explained, in times of war "old

---

[23] Pavel V. Kupriianovsky, *Gor'kii. Furmanov. Serafimovich. A. Tolstoi* (Ivanovo: Ivanovo knizhnoe izdatel'stvo: 1960). Quotes on 109 and 169.

national ideals" are readapted by the state into "universal touchstones." The powerful image of Chapaev has its roots in and represents a continuity with nineteenth-century literary heroes in the realist tradition.

Judith Kornblatt has argued that the figure of Chapaev, as presented by novelist Dmitry Furmanov (and then later by filmmakers Sergei and Georgy Vasiliev), was perceived by readers and viewers as a Cossack because the creators of his myth accessed the cultural code of the Cossack in creating his character. "The harnessing of Chapaev . . . may be the main theme of the entire novel," says Kornblatt. She adds, "For Furmanov and his readers, 'Cossack' had become firmly equivalent to 'mythic hero.'"[24] Thus Furmanov in fixing Vasily Chapaev on paper transformed the historical figure, utilizing literary ideas of the Cossack hero drawn from authors like Pushkin and Gogol, Mordovtsev and Kukolnik, and of course Leo Tolstoy.

Another reason for this may have been the prominence of the Cossack figure as an embodiment of the "Russian spirit" in iconography from the First World War. The actual Cossack Kozma Kryuchkov who fought in that war was, as Stephen Norris notes, the first soldier to be awarded a St. George's Cross. Kryuchkov had the qualities of a Russian folk hero, of a *bogatyr*; among other feats, he was said to have defeated eleven German soldiers single-handedly. Those alleged actions in wartime earned him more than just a medal. This Cossack became immortal, with his image reproduced in numerous prints, songs, books, even in film.[25] As a Cossack war hero immortalized in celluloid, Kryuchkov's fate prefigured that of Furmanov's Chapaev.

Furmanov reached for another nineteenth-century source as well in creating the character of Chapaev—the "superman" or extraordinary man of nineteenth-century Russian fiction. Chernyshevsky's Rakhmetov in *What Is to Be Done?* (1862) and Dostoevsky's Raskolnikov in *Crime and Punishment* (1866) were two passionate and physical beings who chose to submit to discipline—asceticism in Rakhmetov's case and intellectual rigor in Raskolnikov's. Dostoevsky "breaks" Raskolnikov, having him recant and regret his intellectual pride, but his strength of character and will remain in the reader's

---

[24] Kornblatt, *Cossack Hero*, 166–168.
[25] Stephen M. Norris, *A War of Images: Russian Popular Prints, Wartime Culture, and National Identity, 1812–1945* (DeKalb, IL: Northern Illinois University Press, 2006). See also Karen Petrone, "Family, Masculinity, and Heroism in Russian War Posters of the First World War," in *Borderlines*, ed. Billie Melman, 95–120 (New York: Routledge, 1998).

mind despite his transformation in the novel's epilogue into a repentant sinner and potential lamb of God. In the Russian tradition, hagiography led to biography. *Chapaev* brought that tradition into the twentieth century for the Soviet state.

Thus Furmanov also participated in the wider literary phenomenon in the 1920s of combining biography and autobiography as sources for fiction. We know that readers of the time were interested in biography, in the *Bildungsroman*. They sought models for their own lives in contemporary heroes as well as in historical biographical fiction. Again according to Dobrenko, readers wanted "thick books, so they can describe a person's life from the cradle to the grave." In the words of one librarian:

> Thick novels about everyday life attract the reader more than anything else. He doesn't want the hero to be in a hurry, or to say just a few quick phrases here and there. He wants a realistic novel, realistically written, one that solves the problems of life that concern him.

Some readers liked *Chapaev* for just this reason. "A good book. I like it because it's big," responded a contemporary.[26]

From Cossack War Hero to Soviet Military Hero

It is important not to forget that though all the topoi of the Cossack myth are present in Furmanov's novel, the historical Chapaev was no Cossack. Born in 1887, Vasily Chapaev was a real peasant from the Chuvash region. He fought as a soldier and then as a noncommissioned officer in the tsarist army during World War I and outdid Kryuchkov by receiving the Cross of St. George three times.

Late in 1917 Chapaev was elected to head an infantry regiment. But leaving his tsarist war record behind, Chapaev joined the Reds and received his own division. Fighting the armies of General Kolchak, Chapaev led his brigades on the "most crucial part of the front."[27] On September 5, 1919, the forces he led were ambushed by the White Army, and Chapaev drowned in the Ural River as he tried to escape. Famed pedagogy expert Anton Makarenko, glorying in Furmanov's portrayal, proclaimed:

---

[26] Quotes from Dobrenko, 130–31.
[27] See A. Makarenko, "*Chapaev* D. Furmanova," *Literaturnyi kritik* 10–11 (1934): 102–19; 106.

> Even in these deficiencies we see Chapaev's steady, admirable strength, his deep and clear humanity, his indefatigable, courageous passion for victory, his wide, open personality. Chapaev gave more than his sword for victory. He gave all of himself . . . not for the beauty of the feat (*podvig*), not for glory, not for moral perfection. He gave everything for the victory of the revolution, for the practical but grandiose goal of the party. (118)

Podvig was not an aesthetic or moral goal. Chapaev, in Makarenko's view, was not in the war effort for himself or for individual glory. He did it all, and was sacrificed, for the party, for the good of the collective.

The much-decorated hero of the tsarist army was transformed into a symbol of peasant know-how and revolutionary courage and martyred in the waters of Siberia. Furmanov took the rudiments of the historical biography and turned Chapaev into a model for the peasant revolutionary, the Soviet military hero. As such, his character is overtly built on his historical predecessors, leaders of peasant revolts such as the Cossacks Emelian Pugachev and Stenka Razin. In the novel, Klychkov, "consciousness" personified, strives to lead Chapaev from his inherent "spontaneous" state into that of the socialist realist positive hero. The mentor/disciple pattern is clearly visible here as Chapaev "grows" and matures over the course of the novel.

This mentoring is all the education Chapaev gets; the tragedy of the novel, in the view of Makarenko and others, is not simply that Chapaev died at the end but that he perished before having a chance at a formal education, still only dreaming of studying "algebra" (109). He learned from life, and from war, melding his natural talents with the lessons of his political commissar and his experiences in battle to help create a new Soviet culture.

In *Chapaev* Klychkov serves as the voice of the author, offering cultural analysis in the expository sections of the novel. Before he meets his future commander, Klychkov imagines him as "the fairytale figure of Chapaev, ataman of the steppes." As we read the section of the novel before the two protagonists meet, we essentially see how those old national ideals are transformed into new universal touchstones under the pressures of war. Klychkov muses:

> He is truly a popular hero . . . a hero from the camp of outlaws—Emelka Pugachev, Stenka Razin, Ermak Timofeevich . . . Those men did their deeds in their own time, and this one has been given a different time—

> so he has another kind of deed . . . it's clear that daring and mettle are Chapaev's main character traits. He is more of a true *hero* than a fighter, more a fiery adventure-lover than a conscious revolutionary. Clearly in him the elements of restlessness and thirst for new impressions are primary and unusually strong. But what an original personality against the background of the peasant insurgency, what an original, striking, colorful figure! (33)

Thus Chapaev is portrayed as a peasant in the Cossack leader model. This quote clearly demonstrates the link, for Furmanov, between the Romantic hero from the people and the Soviet military figure.

Klychkov is able to master Chapaev's "Cossack-like" skills—horsemanship and bravery in battle—much more easily than Chapaev masters Klychkov's political clarity.[28] Furmanov wanted to make Chapaev's path to true Soviet heroism a difficult one, to avoid creating a "superman." In the early stages of work on his novel, Furmanov wrote, "Should I present Chapai with all his faults, his sins, with his human entrails [showing], or, as is usually done, present a fantastic figure, that is to say a striking but in some ways castrated man?"[29] He added, "I am tending toward the former [strategy]." The innovation in Furmanov's novel—sometimes forgotten now, given the legacy of the Chapaev cult—was to make his revolutionary peasant-hero *human*.

There was, however, a conflict in Furmanov's concept of the hero. While he still celebrates the elemental in Chapaev, he explicitly connects restraint with being cultured and considers that to be the goal for revolutionary peasants and workers. When Klychkov notices that Chapaev stands out among the other peasant-soldiers, it is precisely because "he already seemed to have a bit of culture; he did not look as primitive, did not hold himself as others did: *as if a horse of the steppe was holding his own bridle in check*" (61, emphasis mine). This bridle, this emblem of culture and control, represents the "rein" of consciousness over the elemental.

---

[28] Furmanov, *Chapaev* (Moscow: Gosizdatel'stvo khudozhestvennoi literatury, 1961), 33. See Kornblatt: "The message is obvious, although heroic spontaneity is all fine and good, the Soviet ideal requires order. [. . .] The new 'Cossack' was not unbounded but rather carefully confined by Soviet strictures" (Kornblatt, *The Cossack Hero*, 168).

[29] Furmanov, *Sobranie sochinenii v chetyrekh tomakh,* vol. 4 (Moscow: Goslitizdat, 1961), 285, cited in M.N. Sotskova, *Dmitrii Furmanov* (Moscow: Prosveshchenie, 1969), 44.

The political commissar Klychkov gives a running commentary in the novel that explains the process of transformation as he watches it unfold. Although he almost idolizes Chapaev for his iconic and mythical behavior, he struggles with the definition of "hero." Consciousness is the prerogative of the workers, not accessible to the "spontaneous" peasant character, but that cannot take away from Chapaev's heroic traits. "Chapaev is a hero," he says. "He personifies everything irrepressible, *elemental*, furious and protesting that has built up among the peasantry over a long period of time" (68–69, emphasis mine).

After some months, Klychkov recognizes that Chapaev has made progress ("he was already drawn to much that was reasonable and right *consciously* and not only *instinctively*" [298, emphasis mine]). These two qualities, the instinctive or spontaneous and the rational or conscious, again evoke Dostoevsky's Raskolnikov, with the polarity of positive/negative reversed. For Dostoevsky, it was the instinctively Russian (and orthodox) feelings of Raskolnikov that had to take the fore in order for him to reenter society; the nineteenth-century city, with its intellectual depravity, had corrupted the innocent young man and drawn him into intellectual errors. Dostoevsky's tortured intellectual convinces himself to commit a crime; his overly conscious man still does good *instinctively* but rejects that good through much of the novel with his rational, ideological mind. In the postrevolutionary context, consciousness and reason have become good, and instinct must be reined in.

Thus, while Chapaev's instinctual talents and impulses are not labeled as bad per se, the instinctual Chapaev must learn consciousness and rationality in order to become a proper Soviet hero. In examining the rhetorical strategies of *Chapaev*, Ronald Vroon has argued that "the tale of Chapaev may be read . . . as a kind of allegory on the role of rhetoric in an ideological context." He writes, "For Furmanov, the word had to be harnessed, like Chapaev himself, in order to ensure ideological purity and, more importantly, the stability of the new political order."[30]

Chapaev was warmly received and became almost instantly beloved. Furmanov's contemporary Libedinsky celebrated the author as the "first in

---

[30] Ronald Vroon, "Dmitry Furmanov's *Chapaev* and the Aesthetics of the Russian Avant-Garde," in *Laboratory of Dreams: The Russian Avant-Garde and Cultural Experiment*, ed. John E. Bowlt and Olga Matich (Stanford: Stanford University Press, 1996), 219–236, 236.

our literature to show the heroic persona of Soviet man in his full glory." He adds, "He offered a model for a realistic portrayal of important civic events, he showed the newly born beauty of our society as it was reorganizing itself along revolutionary lines and rushing toward communism."[31] That "rush" was portrayed in the novel as well. At one point as he muses on Chapaev's development, commissar Klychkov reminds the reader of just how volatile the situation of war can be. "But the elements," Klychkov warns, "the devil knows where they may go! We've had incidents [. . .] where there was just such a splendid commander, like Chapaev, and then suddenly he went and bumped off his commissar! . . . Or you look and he's gone off to the whites with his '*elemental*' division . . . The workers, they're another thing entirely; they *will never leave, not under any circumstances*, that is, if they have *consciously* joined the struggle" (68).

Worrying that he himself might be "bumped off," Klychkov personalizes the much larger threat the Civil War posed for the Soviet state. War is indeed a "plastic juncture" with results that are seldom predictable. In unleashing the "elemental," the state had to control it. Heroism, as embodied in Chapaev, was the way the state could discipline what might otherwise be chaotic violence and turn it to its own purposes: beating back the Whites and offering a heroic model for the future.

When Maxim Gorky, the arbiter of official Soviet literary taste, wrote to Furmanov about his work, he offered measured praise. Furmanov's writing was "interesting and deeply instructive," but Gorky was not fully confident in Furmanov's creative abilities. In his letter to Furmanov, Gorky asserted, "You narrate like a witness, but do not portray like an artist."[32]

A witness, not an artist. Here was a fundamental problem for anyone who would turn the experience of war into fiction. To write without having been a witness would have been hollow, but to turn the testimony of witness into the material of art undoubtedly required some betrayal of that experience of witnessing. For the early years of Soviet literature—when readers burned for the "literature of fact," for the "sensation of life," for characters based in the revolutionary events through which they themselves had lived—the witness was enough. Furmanov immortalized his own "path to Bolshevism" in his memoirs of that name, but he incarnated his adolescent

---

[31] Libedinsky, "Bol'shevik, voin," 183.
[32] Isbakh, *Furmanov*, 254.

anarchist spirit perhaps equally convincingly in the peasant leader Vasily Chapaev and then "harnessed" that spirit to his autobiographical political commissar. His characters and their Civil War struggles became iconic for the rest of the century.

War on the Domestic Front in Gladkov's *Cement*

Not long after the publication of *Chapaev*, Fyodor Gladkov penned his classic factory and production novel *Cement*. As mentioned earlier, the two novels have much in common, and Gladkov must certainly have noticed Furmanov's success with Chapaev as he was writing. We might see these two novels loosely as a paired set, providing for readers an account of heroism in the Civil War and then in the immediate aftermath of the war. Chapaev perished in a glorious cause, fully aware of that cause, in some ways the "easier" ending. In contrast, Gladkov grappled with the concept of postwar demobilization: Gleb Chumalov must rebuild his life after the destruction of war and in so doing make good on the promise that the war had made way for a better future. Chumalov embraces a slogan that originated in an 1895 story by Maxim Gorky: "In life there is always a place for feats."[33] This oft-repeated quote is the origin of the rhetoric of *podvig*, of great feats, that played a vital role in Soviet literature and in everyday life. Gladkov's hero must apply the rhetoric of *podvig* to the quotidian task of restarting a factory.

Cement is the first Soviet attempt at an important subset of war literature: novels that explore the lives of soldiers returning to a society they neither participated in building nor really understand after their months or years away from it. The shift in landscape between the two novels is dramatic: while Vasily Chapaev rode the steppe on his dashing mount ("*na likhom kone*"), the

---

[33] A version of this phrase—a favorite with such Socialist realist novelists as Boris Polevoi, the author of *A Story of a Real Man* (*Povest' o nastoiashchem cheloveke*, 1946, film version 1949)—was uttered by the heroine of Gor'kii's 1895 story "The Old Woman Izergil," who uses it in describing a former Polish lover who had fought in the Greek War of Independence, against the Turks, merely because "he loved feats." The story reads, "Why should he care about the Greeks, if he is a Pole? Here's why: he loved feats. And when a person loves feats, he can always do them, and he finds opportunities. In life, you know, there is always room for feats. And people who don't find them for themselves,—they are simply lazy cowards, or they don't understand life, because if they did understand life, everyone would want to leave his mark on it. And then life would not consume people without a trace . . ."

hero of *Cement* drags himself back from his Civil War duties to a world that no longer resembles his pre-war home. Nor does he find there the comradeship and sense of purpose of his wartime life, a common enough problem for soldiers returning from the adrenaline-soaked experience of war to the mundane business of civilian life.

In *Cement*, Gleb's struggles do not end when he arrives home from the war. Instead, he begins to fight on a new front: fighting the disarray of postwar life, the bourgeois-ification of his factory town, the bureaucratic obstacles to reconstruction, and the private and personal instincts of his former mates. In this sense, *Cement* stands as the first important attempt to portray Soviet society as constantly at war; it militarizes daily life in a way that would come to characterize the entire Soviet period.

The task presented in Gladkov's novel is a monumental one. Gleb must relaunch a factory after its destruction by the White Army, resurrect it from its ruined state (characterized as *razrukha*), and set it humming. The task is made more arduous because of continuing destructive action by partisan fighters, because of squabbles within the local Communist Party ranks and the disruptive purge of that party, because of a reluctance to help from all state organs above the factory workers and—perhaps most significantly—because of the absurdity of producing cement for a country where no one is building anything. More than anything, this task is a symbolic one: the city had a history of production, and to enter into a new era the factory needed to access its past. New ideas and new thoughts would be poured into the cement molds of old.

The novel is set somewhere in the southern Russian periphery, paralleling the site of Chapaev's regiment, which ranged across the vast steppes. The periphery, as Clark has noted, is the perfect space for novels focused on the ordinary characters who make up the Soviet people. She writes:

> Socialist realist novels are generally set in the periphery. This is not just because it provides a pared-down microcosm for representing processes that take place in the greater arena of society at large, but also because the periphery is the space of the masses.[34]

---

[34] Katerina Clark, "Socialist Realism and the Sacralizing of Space" in *The Landscape of Stalinism: The Art and Ideology of Soviet Space*, ed. Evgeny Dobrenko and Eric Naiman (Seattle: University of Washington Press, 2003), 3–18; 14.

Having himself been exiled to the periphery in 1906, in the 1920s Gladkov found himself with just the right personal experience to write construction novels of and for the masses. The factory town of *Cement* appears to be modelled on Novorossiysk, the main Russian port on the Black Sea, where Gladkov lived for a time. Peripheral though it may be, this formerly bustling port is populated with thousands of workers, as well as a number of intellectuals and former members of the aristocracy. We are told that the factory once sold much of its cement abroad, but in the post–Civil War era, that market has become inaccessible.

Gladkov's construction novels were heralded in the early 1930s—in the midst of active discussions of the advent of a "socialist" realism—as constituting a specifically "proletarian realism."[35] And while he would not have denied the "realism" ascribed to him, Gladkov saw his own work as belonging to the movement of revolutionary romanticism started by Maxim Gorky.

Gladkov's style includes the expansive use of metaphors and other prose embellishments.[36] In discussing his own methods, Gladkov stressed that authors should never be afraid of *romanticizing* the hero, of highlighting the positive traits of the main character of a work. He aimed for what he called *zhivuchost'*—a "living quality"—in his characters, but that living quality included a "heroism" that he believed to be characteristic of the Soviet man (in his own words, "our man").

> The significance of the protagonist of a fictional work, his "living quality" [*zhivuchest'*] for our history is defined by his typicality for his epoch, that is to say the power of the synthesis of the more characteristic qualities of that social environment which a given protagonist represents.[37]

In constructing his new Soviet novel, Gladkov took up a central metaphor straight out of Turgenev. From his bloody days in the Civil War, Gleb

---

[35] A. Kemp-Welch, *Stalin and the Literary Intelligentsia*, 142. Gladkov was at the forefront of the Sovietization of Russian literature, one of seven named to the commission on union membership as the Union of Soviet Writers was being formed (Kemp-Welch, *Stalin and the Literary Intelligentsia*, 171).

[36] As Robert Busch has commented, referring to the nineteenth-century Romantic writer Alexander Bestuzhev-Marlinsky, Gladkov tended "toward the Marlinskian principle of never putting simply what could be said with a flourish." Busch, "Making of a Classic," 357.

[37] Fedor Gladkov, "Moia rabota nad 'Tsementom' (V poriadke samokritiki)," in Gladkov, *Sobranie sochinenii v vos'mi tomakh*, vol. 2 (Moscow: Gosizdatkhudlit, 1958), 421.

Chumalov returns to the home he identifies as his "nest"—and finds that nest empty.[38] This symbol of nineteenth-century family happiness—the nest—is a recurring metaphor throughout the novel, now a neutral concept, now tragic, now negative. Turgenev's cherished but often problematic "nest of the gentry" has received new life in a new stratum of society as Gladkov reinvents the old chronotope for new purposes in a new age.[39]

The settlement to which Gleb returns has the traditional but telling name of "Cozy Colony" ("*Uyutnaya koloniya*").[40] This image of the cozy home would have been welcome to the warrior returning from the peripatetic life of army camps and battles, but in the postwar era there is nothing cozy about this place. The conventional home Gleb left has been transformed and is empty both physically and psychologically. As the omniscient narrator describes it:

> Now he was back in the home he had once left to go out into the empty night. [...] Now the nest was empty, and his wife Dasha, who had clung to him so desperately at the time of their parting, had not welcomed him as a wife should. (*Cement*, 6)

No welcoming expressions of love, no sexual reunion, indeed, no nuclear family to greet the returning war hero. Instead, Gleb finds an empty and sterile Soviet hearth. Dasha Chumalova has taken their child Nyura to the communal children's home to be raised by the state rather than her parents, and she herself has joined the Zhenotdel, the women's department, and prefers to live in a dormitory. Much to Gleb's disappointment after his three-year absence, she cannot stay and celebrate his homecoming but instead rushes off on a business trip for her new Soviet work.

The Chumalovs are not the only ones whose "nest" has been destroyed by the revolution, the ensuing chaos, and the new world order of post–Civil War life. Gleb's neighbors Motya and Savchuk have suffered as well. Motya mourns her losses, lamenting, "I had children—little boys—and was a decent happy

---

[38] Unless otherwise specified, I am quoting from A. S. Arthur and C. Ashleigh, trans., *Cement* (New York: Frederick Ungar, 1980), 6.

[39] On homes and "nests" throughout Russian literature, see Joost van Baak, *The House in Russian Literature: A Mythopoetic Exploration* (Amsterdam, New York: Rodopi, 2009).

[40] Arthur and Ashleigh translate it as "Pleasant Colony" (*Cement*, 1), but *uyut* has the essential connotation of home and health.

mother. Where are they now, Gleb? Why am I no longer a mother? I want a nest; like a hen, I want chicks. But they have perished . . .." (*Cement*, 10). *Her* once cozy home is transformed into a raucous site of screeching and fighting, and the love she and her family shared has turned into animosity between the parents.

Remembering the past in conversation with her husband, Motya continues, "We had a rich nest, Savchuk . . . And our children were dear little starlings . . . Let's weave a new nest, Savchuk [. . .] I shall go along the highway to find other people's orphaned little chicks."[41] Like Gorky's Nilovna, Motya is willing to take on any children she can find to reconstitute her "family." Thus one solution—offered rhetorically but never fulfilled—for this bereft mother hen was a socialist vision of family on a larger, societal scale. But unlike Nilovna, Motya is stuck in her old way of thinking and has not undergone revolutionary training; even if she could gather together orphaned chicks, the result would be another nuclear family or a private version of the state children's home, not a larger socialist family.

The family fire has been extinguished, and the hearth in Gleb's home has gone cold. In a chapter by that name ("The Cold Hearth"), Gleb finds his room to be "strange, uninhabitable and stifling." In former years his wife had met him when he returned home at night. "In those days it was cozy and cheerful in the room." Warm and inviting and filled with flowers that "signalled welcome to him [from the windowsill] like little flames," his home had been full of life and the laughter of his wife and daughter; the floor shone like a mirror, the bed was soft and white, and the table laden with fine-smelling platters of food. The samovar—the central image of prosperous prerevolutionary peasant life, which played such an important role in the stories of Chekhov,[42] among others—was at a boil, and the tea set clattered merrily.

Now, in contrast, these memories of the past are painful, and Gleb feels nauseated thinking of "this abandoned and mildewed home. Where the mice have fouled there can be no rest. Where the cozy fire has died the stinking

---

[41] *Tsement, Krasnaia nov'* [no. 1], I, ii. 74. The literal meaning and ornithological metaphors disappear in Arthur and Ashleigh's translation: "We had a decent home, Savchuk, and our children were such dear little things. Your blood and my blood. Let's make a new home, Savchuk. I can't bear it; I can't, Savchuk. I shall go along the highway to find homeless children" (*Cement*, 11).

[42] I have in mind here especially "The Peasants" (1897), in which the samovar is confiscated for lack of tax payment, leaving the peasant home empty and bereft.

vermin now swarm" (*Cement*, 26–27). All remnants of his former life have vanished, and what remains is a cold and dirty hearth in an empty, abandoned home.

The concept of the nest is larger than the individual home; for Gleb the family should be a microcosm of a larger social entity, the workers' collective. And here it is, the empty home echoes the empty factory, which rather than being a nest of activity is described as a "gigantic tomb, a place of desolation and destruction. . . . Like a dead planet, the factory slept in these idle days" (*Cement*, 13, 14). Evoking cosmic scale, Gladkov emphasizes the barrenness of the empty factory, but with his verb "slept," he offers hope that someone—some hero or collection of heroes fighting on the economic front—can awaken this enterprise from its slumber and set it going again.

Finding both of his homes ruined, Gleb throws himself into the work of reviving the factory, even while he tries to understand the changed circumstances of his personal home front.[43] He realizes that he no longer has the rights of "a master" over his wife, Dasha, and cannot simply keep her with him, though he tries, saying, "Without you there is no warm comfortable home, and my bed will be cold and grow soiled" (*Cement*, 290). She leaves him anyway to go live with her friend and comrade Polina Mekhova.

The neglect of their small family leads to the death of their little daughter in her communal home. Gleb is devastated, but not so self-focused as to forget to make the analogy between his own personal situation and the situation at the cement factory:

> Now everything was suddenly bare, oppressive and strange; this dwelling, the garden path, the little garden itself, and this wall which separated him from Dasha and which surrounded him like the wall of a prison. What was the good of the empty, musty room now? [. . .] Dasha was no longer there, and he was alone. Nurka had died. No Dasha. No Nurka. He was alone. A damnable life! It was like the crusher: it broke everything, destiny, habits, love. (*Cement*, 293)

---

43 In the 1958 version of the novel, Polya Mekhova teases Gleb that his trouble with Dasha must have come from trying to assert his conjugal rights. When he blushes in response, she says, "Oh you, men, men! . . . The *domostroevshchina* is still strong in you! . . . You still lack the manliness to respect a woman . . ." (*Tsement* 1958: 128). In the last chapter of this revised version, Dasha finds that "there was still too much of the old husband in him—an excessive desire for tenderness, and a torturous jealousy, and a persistent desire to nail her to the home nest" (*Tsement* 1958: 260).

In the post–Civil War era, Gleb comes to realize, he must tackle the question of home and personal happiness in the same way that he is tirelessly putting the factory into order. In a moment of optimism, he says to Motya, "We'll build a new nest, Motya . . . What's the big deal? The old nest must have been worthless . . ." (*Cement*, 293). Taking the good—the idea of the nest—from the traditional ideal, Gleb wants to reinvent it and make it better for the future.

In *Cement*, as in Turgenev, the nest does not always have positive connotations. The exploiting Communist Shramm, in particular, is described as living in a "cozy little nest of his own" (*shrammovo gnezdishko*), filled "with fine upholstered furniture, fur rugs and carpets" (*Cement*, 234, 233), where he and his comrades nightly betray the ideals of the revolution, leaving food, drink, and cigarettes to be cleaned up later by the chambermaids at the House of Soviets. Old forms had to die, but one of the main conflicts in the second half of *Cement* centers around the fact that in the post–Civil War period, instead of the promised new life, fragments of the old are returning.

As Comrade Zhidky explains to a Georgian soldier who has been monitoring Shramm's disgraceful behavior:

> We're going to be subjected to a dreadful trial, worse than civil war, ruin, famine and blockade. We're in the presence of a hidden foe who is not going to shoot us, but will spread before us all the charms and temptations of capitalist business [. . .] The *obyvatel'* is crawling out of the womb.[44] He's beginning to get fat and re-incarnates himself in various forms. He is already weaving his nest in our ranks as well, and barricading himself firmly with revolutionary rhetoric and all kinds of red attributes of Bolshevik valour.[45]

The enemy within. Although the armed conflicts had waned, the thrust of the novel reminded readers of the need to remain on guard, to treat everyday life as a continuing battle—outside and even within the party.

If the warmth of the Turgenev-era nest is gone, and the Chekhovian samovar remains extinguished, new forms and metaphors are needed in a

---

[44] Arthur and Ashleigh translate, "The petty trader is crawling out of his hole."
[45] *Cement*, 237. Arthur and Ashleigh translate, "For instance, he's trying to install himself in our own ranks, behind a solid barricade of revolutionary phrases, with all the attributes of Bolshevik valour."

1. Born in the Crucible of War: Chapaev and His Socialist Realist Comrades

new world. Dasha herself says as much in the last conversation she and Gleb have in the book:

> It's not our fault, Gleb. The old life has perished and will not return. We must build up a new life. The time will come when we shall build ourselves new homes. Love will always be love, Gleb, but it requires a new form. Everything will come through and attain new forms, and then we shall know how to forge new links. (*Cement*, 308)

The war in *Cement* comes with casualties for Gleb and Dasha: their original domestic life, their nest of friends and associations, and most tragically their little daughter. Dasha has mourned the death of her daughter personally, but on a societal scale she recognizes that there must be individual sacrifices as the new society comes together.

As a representative of the new Soviet woman, Dasha does not even seem to resent Motya, a holdover from the past. In the first version of the novel, bird metaphors for the women characters abound: Motya is a "brood hen . . . waddling along like a fat duck." When Motya becomes pregnant again in an attempt to fill her family nest, she says to Dasha, "I'm going to have one every year now, if you want to know. I'm going to be a woman, while you're just a barren magpie." Such a metaphor—with Dasha merely making noise while Motya gets down to the business of reproduction—belies the omniscient narrator's empathy for women such as Dasha, who are setting out on a new and uncomfortable path. Motya revels in her traditional life and choices ("looking at [Gleb] sideways—like a hen. In her eyes—full of maternity and inward joy—tears sparked and quivered"), but she is hardly an ideal model for the Communist future.[46] The metaphors of rebirth near the end of *Cement* are not limited to the maternal housewife Motya. In the last celebratory scene of the novel, Gleb is lionized as a hero of labor. He sees the cement factory on the eve of its return to life: "There it was, the factory—a *bogatyr* and a beauty! Not long ago it had been a corpse—a rubbish pile, a ruin, a rat's nest." And now the factory has been reborn—no

---

[46] *Cement*, 292, 293. Her desires eerily foreshadow the kind of pronatalist policies that would be put in place in the Soviet Union and in Nazi Germany, leading to heroine-mothers and the production of sons for the fatherland(s). See Hoffmann, *Stalinist Values: The Cultural Norms of Soviet Modernity, 1917–1941* (Ithaca: Cornell University Press, 2003), 97–105.

longer a rat's nest; Gleb portrays it as a folk hero, a real beauty capable of production. Gleb also gazes at the enormous crowd—twenty thousand people, with more still arriving—and sees them as "a living mountain: stones incarnated in flesh."[47]

But rebirth is not the only paradigm being accessed in this triumphant finale of *Cement*. Gladkov makes another comparison explicit with the banner flying below the railings of the balcony: "We Have Conquered on the Civil War Front. We Shall Conquer Also On The Economic Front". "On the labor front, the same self-denying hero as he was on the field of battle . . ." That is how Gleb is introduced. Wanting to share the glory, Gleb reminds his listeners, "If I am a hero, then you are all heroes! [. . .] We are building up socialism, Comrades, and our proletarian culture. On to victory, Comrades!"[48] The language here is the language of war: battlefields, fronts, victory. Wartime and postwar society are merging. Through Gleb, Gladkov demonstrated that war could be productive and not simply destructive.

* * *

Cement was welcomed by contemporary readers, who—living through the postwar chaos—must have found much that resonated with their own lives.[49] Like Gleb, they too yearned for some hope that out of the rubble a new and better life might emerge. And like Gleb, they had to muster enormous amounts of energy in order to set about building that new life. This, after all, is always the promise of war and its aftermath—the need to build anew.

Certainly when it came out, *Cement* impressed perhaps the most important reader of all. Gorky wrote that *Cement* was "the first novel since the revolution to firmly seize and clearly illuminate the most important theme of the times—labor."[50] As a former member of the Bolshevik underground,

---

[47] *Cement*, 303. Arthur and Ashleigh's version reads, "Stones resuscitated into flesh." Edward Vavra, in his afterword to the English translation of *Cement*, makes an excellent case for interpreting Gleb as a Christ-like figure. He also makes a convincing argument for seeing Gleb and Dasha as two parts of one whole, with Gleb the "spontaneous" and Dasha the "conscious" hero. See *Cement*, 322.

[48] *Cement*, 302, 310, 311.

[49] They were precisely seeking those echoes. Some readers did not find them and reacted to *Cement* negatively: "There's no biography, and since there isn't, there's no understanding it either" (Dobrenko, *Making of the State Reader*, 130).

[50] Gor'kii, *Sobranie sochinenii*, vol. 29, 438–439.

1. Born in the Crucible of War: Chapaev and His Socialist Realist Comrades

Gladkov was able to portray his Communist figures convincingly, and his own experience as a volunteer in the Red Army surely helped him to chronicle that homecoming moment when a warrior from the battlefront must rethink his relationship to the world around him, beginning new battles on the home and economic fronts. The war hero becomes a hero of labor; this portrayal, in Gorky's view, answered the "social order" (*sotsial'nyi zakaz*) of the 1920s.

Critic Osip Brik was not as enthusiastic, but he did give Gladkov credit for understanding what Soviet literature needed—"simultaneously two diametrically opposed things: 'heroism and *byt*.'" Nonetheless, he insisted that Gladkov's efforts did not produce the desired combination:

> If you read *Cement* quickly, it seems like the synthesis has been found, that Gladkov has managed to resolve the problem supposedly standing before Soviet literature. [. . .] In *Cement* there is everything that is recommended in the best cookbooks, but the feast is not edible, because the ingredients are not cooked; they are only pulverized into a literary paté.[51]

Readers paid no attention. In the 1920s *Cement* enjoyed an enormous popularity, perhaps because its problems were real-world problems. The novel offered a view into the myriad post–Civil War struggles returning soldiers faced. How to build a new society on the ruins of the old? A new literature for the proletariat, when many of the models had been written by authors of a nobility no longer welcome in Soviet Russia? New universal touchstones out of old national ideals that had once united a totally different stratum of Russians?

The author of *Cement* was trying to work these problems out in literary form. Readers surely didn't care that Gladkov's portrayals of heroics and *byt* did not belong in one novel, had not been properly cooked. For many Russians in the new Soviet Union in the years after the First World War, the Revolution, and the Civil War, trying to fashion any sort of future at all required not only enormous amounts of energy but also that leap of imagination that could bring *byt* and heroics together.

---

[51] O. M. Brik, "Pochemu ponravilsia 'Tsement'?," *Na literaturnom postu*, 2 (1926): 30–32; reprinted in *Epigony khudozhestva, Literatura fakta: pervyi sbornik materialov rabotnikov Lefa*, ed. N. F. Chuzhak (Moscow: Federatsiia, 1929), 84–88. Quote on 87.

But readers could not sustain that state indefinitely. Vasily Chapaev and Gleb Chumalov both stood as popular war heroes in the 1920s, but only one survived much beyond that. Gleb never found his way into the hearts of Russians the way Chapaev did. In the end, a cement factory did not produce the enduring hero that the Civil War had. That war, at least, ended in victory, one that Chapaev helped achieve. The bright better future promised in *Cement* stayed always in the future, and readers grew weary of reading about it.

Chapaev for Children

Among the first children to play at Chapaev was Boris Shorokhov.

He and his friends do so in Yury Libedinsky's 1930 novel *Birth of a Hero*. With other children in the schoolyard and home alone, dreaming on his bed, Boris plays his favorite imaginative game, world revolution: "And he himself, Boris Shorokhov, he is the head of all the revolutionary forces, he is like Trotsky in the Civil War, and all the soldiers of the Red Army know and love him, as Chapaev, Blyukher and Budyonny were known and loved by their divisions."[52]

The novel is fascinating for a number of reasons, including its exploration of different generations—Communists, Komsomol members, and Young Pioneers—and the way it tracks the relationships between ideology and sex, the individual and the collective, the state and the empire. By turning Boris into a pint-sized Chapaev, however, Libedinsky's novel tried to meld Furmanov's hero with Gladkov's tasks and delegate them to an adolescent. In this story, Libedinsky tried to demonstrate that in the process of tearing down the old Russian society and replacing it with a new Soviet society, new heroes could be born, a whole new blameless generation of them. And in case readers missed the point, those heroes would worship Chapaev.

Libedinsky's Boris Shorokhov is the son of two Old Bolsheviks, and he is the ideal Young Pioneer. Perceptive, thoughtful, and energetic, Borya shows remarkable initiative as well as concern for his fellow Soviet children. With Chapaev as his hero, indeed as more of a father figure than his own disappointing father, Boris throws himself into his duties at Young Pioneer camp. In the meantime, the elder Shorokhov, a Communist functionary in

---

[52] Iurii Libedinskii, *Rozhdenie geroia* (Leningrad: Gosudarstvennoe izdatel'stvo khudozhestvennoi literatury, 1931), 117.

charge of party discipline and maintaining moral clarity for Communists at the center—in Moscow—and the periphery—in far-off Turkestan—embarks upon an affair with the young sister of his deceased wife, losing his own moral compass and neglecting his duties and his children in the process.

The novel, set in 1924, deals in part with the messy sexual relationships and social flux of the post–Civil War era. Confused by their own assessments of stable "bourgeois" marriages as compared to the violence, alcohol abuse, and partner-swapping that seems to go on among their parents, these children who are themselves on the cusp of sexual awakening reject their parents in favor of another ideal entirely: a child-centered commune. A nursery, as it were, where new Soviet heroes can grow up free from the contamination of the old order.

It is worth pausing over this mise-en-scène. With his twelve-year-old protagonist, who is surrounded by a gaggle of orphaned, lost children whose parents are absent literally or figuratively, Libedinsky reminds us of the profound dislocation the period from 1914–1921 had wreaked upon Russian families and on Russian children in particular. A world inhabited by children in this way strikes us now as a literary conceit; for Libedinsky's generation it was a kind of reality. The unprecedented historical upheavals of this period had by 1922 left an estimated seven million abandoned and orphaned children, homeless and without supervision or support.[53] A quarter of a century later, novelist William Golding would use a world of children to explore a dystopian nightmare born of the Cold War in his 1954 novel *Lord of the Flies*. In the wake of the Russian Civil War, Libedinsky used it to build a better future. Caught in the midst of social problems that negatively affect his own life and the lives of his comrades, Boris rejects his childish dreams of revolutionary action in favor of a bold plan to create children's villages—a space he hopes adult problems will not be able to penetrate. These Communist children's villages present an ideal, contrasted in the novel to the organized Pioneer Camp and to the leaderless hordes of orphans (*besprizorniki*) who are the anarchic version of a true collective.

Those bands of orphans with their anarchistic tendency are presented as a negative alternative to the moral center of the novel, Boris Shorokhov,

---

[53] See Alan Ball, *And Now My Soul Is Hardened: Abandoned Children in Soviet Russia, 1918–1930* (Berkeley: University of California Press, 1996), 1. Ball describes the many reasons for the separation of families on 11–13 and elsewhere.

the Chapaev of the next generation. The hero of Libedinsky's novel is born along with the Soviet country itself, and his struggles to find the right path are exemplary. The peasant military hero (uneducated and illiterate, with the *spontaneity* characteristic of an adolescent) is the perfect ideal for a twelve-year-old psyche, whose love of clarity and simplicity will mark the development of the Soviet novel for decades to come. The children who sought to establish their own Soviet "home" in Libedinsky's *Birth of a Hero* were the ones who went off to war against the Nazis, treasuring their affinity to Chapaev and priding themselves on being his comrades.

Part II
World War II and the Hero

Vasily Tyorkin

Chapter Two
The Peasant-Soldier:
Alexander Tvardovsky and a New Chapaev

> Not once did the soldiers or officers
> Add a word about Duty or Faith,
> About Fatherland, Conscience or Honor.
> To their usual answer: "Yessir!"
>
> Но ни разу про Долг и про Веру,
> Про Отечество, Совесть и Честь
> Ни солдаты и ни офицеры
> Не добавили к этому "Есть!"
>
> -Boris Slutsky

Gladkov's *Cement* took its place on what would become a long shelf of "production" novels, created according to the method of socialist realism during the Soviet interwar period. To say that most of them are dreary, forgettable, and deserve their fate now as artifacts rather than as literature is not to say very much.

However, those endless production novels had attempted two things that do interest us here. First, they tried to make the very process of building a new Soviet society, and becoming new Soviet citizens, synonymous with the experience of war—filled with enemies to be defeated, "fronts" to fight on, heroic deeds to be done, and victories to be celebrated. *Podvig* in the service of class warfare and postwar reconstruction. In this sense, these novels surely tried to foster the health of the Soviet state. Second, the novels offered Soviet readers heroes—heroes who engaged in extraordinary feats, fully conscious of their role in advancing the Soviet cause.[1]

---

[1] One of the quintessential heroes of this type is Pavel Korchagin, hero of Nikolai Ostrovsky's 1936 novel *How the Steel Was Tempered* (*Kak zakalialas' stal'*). Even today Russian women continue to complain about having to choose between Pavka Korchagin and Grishka Melikhov when they think about their male counterparts. (Melikhov is the hero of Mikhail Sholokhov's 1940 *Quiet Flows the Don* [*Tikhii Don*].) As Vladimir Kataev has written, the only interesting character in Russian literature was Ostap Bender, leaving women readers crying out, "Rhett Butler, where are you?" V. B. Kataev, *Igra v oskolki: Sud'by russkoi klassiki v epokhu postmodernizma* (Moscow: Izd. Moskovskogo Universiteta, 2002), 80–81.

2. The Peasant-Soldier: Alexander Tvardovsky and a New Chapaev

Those heroes never really stuck. Violence against ordinary people continued throughout the period: purges and collectivization and prison camps. We can see this violence as part of the militarization of civilian life, but it did not prove conducive to the creation of resonant literary heroes. New heroes would have to wait for actual war in order to be "successful" as literary characters. As Randolph Bourne noted, the government might make all sorts of impositions on citizens during times of peace, but only times of war bring on the sense of the "sanctity of the State" and its concomitant feelings of collective will and mobilization for the patriotic good.

But Soviet writers did not have long to wait. Less than twenty years after the conclusion of the Civil War, Russians would find themselves again mobilized to fight. The Second World War stands as the pivotal event of the Russian twentieth century, and its meaning continues to be fought over even into the twenty-first. Consequently, the way Russian writers tried to make meaning out of the events of that war will concern much of the rest of this book.

In this chapter, I focus on the work of Alexander Tvardovsky and his monumental wartime poem *Vasily Tyorkin: A Book about a Soldier*—truly a worthy comrade to Chapaev.

In 1929, Osip Brik had called for a marriage between heroics and the everyday in Soviet literature, between *podvig* and *byt*. The former urges citizens to sacrifice themselves in feats of glory and features the capitalized concepts of Fatherland, Duty, and Honor, of Death and Life on Earth, while the latter grounds those concepts in the particularities of lived experience. Ideally, each should inform the other, though as Brik pointed out, such a marriage was far from easy to negotiate. Great feats, narrated using what we are calling the rhetoric of *podvig*, would never transcend entirely the sense of the collective central to Soviet identity, while everyday life, *byt*, would in the Soviet context be lived framed by a sense of higher calling and obligation. War provided the conditions necessary for that marriage, and what made it possible was duty, described with what we can call the "rhetoric of *est'*." The Russian word *est'*, after all, can be translated as "is" or "exists," "being" or "existence"; "there is," "there are." It is also what Russian soldiers reply when called to attention or given an order: "Yessir!" "Aye, aye, sir!" Boris Slutsky's four-stanza poem, the third stanza of which is quoted in the epigraph to this chapter, ends thus:

> With a terse awareness of duty,
> Silently thinking of the Fatherland,
> They lived well, happily, and long
> Or they instantly died in battle.[2]

In Soviet war literature, *byt* is not a rhetorical strategy; it is the details of the trenches, what some call the blood and mud of wartime existence. But informed by the rhetoric of *est'*, framed by the need to answer the call of the Fatherland, to perform one's duty, the "being" of *byt* is raised to the level of *est'*. With this silence, this "terse awareness", the soldier accepted his fate.

Alexander Tvardovsky was an eyewitness to war. As we explore below, he used his powers of observation and description to bring to life a new hero, a new Chapaev for the Second World War, who cheerfully and without complaint dealt with all the horrors of battle, all the complications of reconnaissance, all the pain of wounds and near-death. *Vasily Tyorkin* was a portrait of the war experience, and in it Tvardovsky used both rhetorical strategies which we've been examining to great effect. He used details of wartime *byt* to encourage and celebrate *podvig* while maintaining a straightforward attitude of the soldier's duty to answer "yessir" when the order came. And for the generation who fought the Second World War, Tyorkin was an enormously successful wartime hero.

Tvardovsky approached the war and its trials from an utterly pragmatic point of view. For example, in the chapter of *Vasily Tyorkin* entitled "About War," the narrator says, "Well, why even discuss it,— / It's all totally clear. / We have to beat the Germans, brother, / No deferment here."[3] No moral ambiguity, no introspection, no chatter, no self-examination, no doubts.

The Poetry of Heroics and the Heroics of Poetry

Less than two months after the war with Germany began, the *Literary Gazette* published an editorial on "the place of the writer in the Fatherland War." It read in part:

> Writers are provided with plenty of material by the thousands of occurrences of individual and collective heroism shown by the Red Army and Navy. A writer should use his skill to create generalizations from these facts so as to reveal artistically in every example of heroism

---

[2] Boris Slutsky, *Bez popravok*... (Moscow: Vremia, 2006), 135.
[3] Tvardovskii, *Vasilii Tyorkin: Kniga pro boitsa* (Moscow: Nauka, 1976), 36–37.

the national character of the Soviet people, the nobility of their ideas, which inculcate a scorn of death and hatred of the enemy.[4]

As this editorial demonstrates neatly, modern war generates propaganda, most of which is designed to inflame feelings of nationalism and a hatred of the enemy that reduces him to something less than human. During the war, using three hundred workers in three daily shifts, the Soviet news agency TASS produced 1,400 different war posters, many of which did precisely that.[5]

Ilya Ehrenburg and Konstantin Simonov, among others, famously treated the theme of hatred of the enemy with powerful propaganda pieces. Ehrenburg's newspaper essay "Kill!" (published in the Red Army newspaper, *Krasnaia zvezda*, on July 24, 1942), for example, begins with details from German letters, marked by real names: Lt. Otto von Schirach, Mathias Dimlich, Helmut Zimlich, Otto Essman, and Lt. Helmut Weigand. The letters demonstrate a disdain for Russians (calling them "animals," "beasts," "types"), and Ehrenburg responds to what he characterizes as the Germans' philosophizing—"Are these really people?"—with a clear answer: "We know everything. We remember everything. We have understood: the Germans are not human. [. . .] We will not speak. We will not be outraged. We will kill." Throughout the article, his rhetoric builds through repetition and escalation: "If you haven't killed at least one German today, your day was wasted." This statement is followed by seven more "if" statements. The repetitive syntax continues, "Do not count days. Do not count versts. Count only one thing: the Germans you have killed," culminating in a call for bloodbath:

> "Kill the Germans!" the old mother requests it. "Kill the Germans!" the child begs it of you. "Kill the Germans!" cries the earth of your homeland. Don't blunder. Don't miss. Kill.[6]

Simonov's poem "Kill Him," also written in July 1942, makes similar exhortations in the hypothetical "if," contrasting the Soviet soldier to the

---

[4] "Mesto literatora v Otechestvennoi voine," *Literaturnaia gazeta* (20 August, 1941): 1.
[5] On TASS during wartime see, for example, Robert Bird, "The Functions of Poetry: TASS Windows and the Soviet Media System in Wartime," in *Windows on the War: Soviet TASS Posters at Home and Abroad, 1941–1945*, ed. Peter Kort Zegers and Douglas Druick (New Haven and London: Art Institute of Chicago and Yale University Press, 2011), 92–103.
[6] *Krasnaia zvezda* No. 173 (5236) (24 July 1942).

German: "If your brother killed a German— / Then he's the soldier, not you, / So kill a German so that he / Not you will lie on the earth, / So that groans will sound, mourning the dead, / Not in your house, but in his. / That's what he wanted, he's at fault, / Let his house burn, not yours, / And let his wife, not yours / Become a widow . . ."[7] This heightened language of hatred finds its place in military newspapers and sometimes with soldiers at the front who spent the war carrying Simonov clippings in their pockets, but "scorn of death," which sounds great in an editorial meeting, was much rarer in the actual trenches.

Effective as this type of propaganda may be in mobilizing citizens to fight, it did not constitute a poetry of heroics. After all, it is actually quite difficult for human beings to sustain anger and hatred indefinitely. The language from the *Literary Gazette* is telling: the description of the "nobility" of Soviet ideas is supposed to breed more than just hatred. Yet the everyday facts from which this rhetoric is to emerge, the "material," the individual acts, were part of the fabric of life in wartime and were equally likely to result in a different set of reactions and literary responses.

Some writers followed this prescribed pattern to highlight *podvig*; others did not. Readers of Soviet fiction, even during wartime, responded better to humor and the everyday (with just a sprinkling of heightened rhetoric) than they did to calls for hatred. Thus in the aftermath of war, it was Vasily Tyorkin who survived.

A New Chapaev: Tvardovsky and his Tyorkin

The biography of the poet, journalist, and editor Alexander Tvardovsky (1910–1971) could have turned out differently, more like a typical tragic peasant story of the early Soviet years. His Smolensk family was made up of hardworking, successful peasants, and he, perhaps, was fortunate to have left home before they were reclassified as "kulaks," arrested and resettled in the far reaches of Soviet Siberia. Tvardovsky himself went on to a successful career, but that shadow followed him throughout his life.

As a young man, Tvardovsky studied at the Smolensk Pedagogical Institute in the hopes of a literary career and began to publish poems as early as 1925 in Smolensk newspapers. Tvardovsky's choice of a career path among

---

[7] Simonov, *Sobranie sochinenii v dvenadtsati tomakh*, vol. 1 (Moscow), 105–107. See Katharine Hodgson, *Written with the Bayonet: Soviet Russian Poetry of World War Two* (Liverpool: Liverpool University Press, 1996), 71–72.

intellectuals and party functionaries in the city resonated in sad and permanent ways when Tvardovsky's family was swept up in the anti-kulak campaign. According to his brother Ivan, the family was subjected to artificially high "individual taxes" beginning in the spring of 1930, and by March 19 of that year they had been sent into administrative exile.

In retrospect, Tvardovsky's choice to strike out on his own path took on an entirely different meaning; his life in the city now represented a rejection of home and family and, certainly in Ivan's eyes, a betrayal of his parents and his heritage. The natural desires of a young man—to make something of himself, to study and join the new society as a contributing member—in essence made an orphan out of Tvardovsky. From that point on, Tvardovsky was on his own, every step accompanied by a label. On every form Tvardovsky ever filled out—and in the Soviet Union there were always plenty of forms—in answer to the question "social origin of parents," Tvardovsky wrote, "Father—kulak, sent into administrative exile from the Western region."[8]

Best known in the West for his role in the 1950s and 1960s as editor of the liberal literary journal *Novyi Mir* (*New World*), the journal that published Solzhenitsyn and Sinyavsky, Panova and Pasternak, Tvardovsky also functioned in the Soviet context as an example of the peasant who became cultured, a peasant who turned away from agricultural work and instead redirected his energy toward a role in the new Soviet society.[9] In that sense, Tvardovsky was a real Chapaev: a character who harnessed the spontaneous energy of the hardworking peasant to a revolutionary, indeed Bolshevik, vehicle. Somehow overcoming the label "son of a kulak," Tvardovsky became

---

[8] See Regina Romanova, *Aleksandr Tvardovskii: trudy i dni* (Moscow: Volodei, 2006), 71, 77.

[9] Tvardovskii had two stints as editor of *Novyi Mir*: 1950–1954 and 1958–1970. For a negative portrayal of the editorial board of *Novyi Mir* in the 1960s, see Alexander Solzhenitsyn's fictional memoir *The Oak and the Calf: Sketches of Literary Life in the Soviet Union*, trans. by Harry Willets (New York: Harper and Row, 1975). In defense of Tvardovskii, Vladimir Lakshin, one of the assistant editors of *Novyi Mir* during the years when *NM* was printing Solzhenitsyn's work, published the essay "Solzhenitsyn, Tvardovskii i *Novyi Mir*," in *The Twentieth Century: A Socio-political Digest and Literary Magazine*, vol. 2 (London: TCD Publications Ltd., 1977). The essay was also published in French and in English. I quote from the English translation by Michael Glenny (Cambridge, MA: MIT Press, 1980). In a warm and touching memorial essay, Viktor Nekrasov recalled that Tvardovsky sighed over this very fact: "Alas, abroad I'm hardly known as a poet, but mostly as the editor of some progressive journal." See "Aleksandr Tvardovskii," in Viktor Nekrasov, *Kak ia stal sheval'e: Rasskazy. Portrety. Ocherki. Povesti* (Ekaterinburg: U-Faktoriia, 2005), 83.

a Soviet hero himself, and he created one of the most beloved literary heroes of the Soviet twentieth century, the soldier Vasily Tyorkin.

With roots in the countryside around Smolensk, Tvardovsky naturally portrayed the peasantry in his early work.[10] And although he continued to keep the collectivized peasants in mind, Tvardovsky turned from "village" to military themes in the late 1930s, expressing a certain satisfaction with this transition through his emphasis of the kinship between peasants and military personnel: "These were those very same Soviet people, living under the conditions of army and frontline life."[11] This connection with the masses, whether in the village or in uniform, reified Tvardovsky's origins as a "man of the people." Forced to turn his back on his own peasant family, Tvardovsky discovered a role for himself as a literate Chapaev, portraying the people he knew in his poetry, and these sometimes amusing and often perceptive psychological portraits populated his pages and charmed his readers.[12] This kind of heroism, drawn in part from Civil War literature and in part from the traditions of Russian folklore, gave new life to socialist realism in the context of the war.

In the best of literary circumstances, war gives birth to memorable characters, either living military heroes or their fictionalized counterparts. Just as Chapaev remained vivid in the Russian imagination long after the Civil War

---

[10] Tvardovskii described the fate of the peasantry under Stalin in his 1936 poem "The Country of Muravia." While the political moral here is orthodox, leading the peasant Nikita Morgunok to embrace collectivization, "Muravia" is not just a propaganda poem. Rather, it has been seen as a "modern counterpart of [Nikolai] Nekrasov's great epic of peasant life, *Who Lives Happily in Russia*?" Gleb Struve, *Russian Literature under Lenin and Stalin* (Norman: University of Oklahoma Press, 1971), 311. Only much later would Tvardovskii write about his own family's arrest and exile.

[11] Aleksandr Tvardovskii, "Kak byl napisan 'Vasilii Tyorkin,'" in *Vasilii Tyorkin: Kniga pro boitsa* (Moscow: Nauka, 1976), 240. Note that when studying at the Smolensk Pedagogical Institute, Tvardovskii worked with a literature professor (Vasilii F. Chistiakov) on his *Slovar' komedii 'Gore ot uma'* (1939), having received "the assignment to write out . . . every instance of the usage of the preposition 'k' ('to') on separate cards." (See V. Lakshin, *Vtoraia vstrecha* (Moscow: Sovetskii pisatel', 1984), 129, quoted in Romanova, *Trudy i dni*, 89.) It was Chistiakov who recommended that Tvardovskii apply to the Moscow Institute of History, Philosophy, and Literature. This intimate familiarity with the most quoted and quotable work of verse drama of the nineteenth century surely taught Tvardovskii to sketch verbal portraits with confident strokes.

[12] In reference to Evgenii Shvarts, Caryl Emerson has written about how the "fairy-tale format provided optimism without the ambitious bombast of the production novel." *Cambridge Introduction to Russian Literature* (Cambridge: Cambridge University Press, 2008), 208. Tvardovskii, too, by focusing his attention on a "simple" hero from village life, gives his Tyorkin an energy that doesn't need propping up with political dogma.

had faded, so too the character of Vasily Tyorkin entered the pantheon of Russian war heroes during the Second World War and lived on as a folk hero in the minds of the postwar Russian populace.

Called by many commentators an "ideal socialist realist hero," Tyorkin was actually somewhat more complicated. For Soviet readers, especially those in the military, Tyorkin played the role of a brother and friend, an "official" hero who was likeable and believable and—perhaps most importantly—who cheered them up wherever they encountered him. Ordinary soldiers read *Tyorkin* in frontline newspapers and recited sections of the poem to each other at their campfires and in the trenches.[13] We can find evidence of these reactions in the memoirs of countless soldiers, but among the most valuable sources is Alexander Solzhenitsyn, whose relationship with Tvardovsky by the time he wrote his memoir *The Oak and the Calf* had soured considerably. Even so, Solzhenitsyn wrote the following about *Vasily Tyorkin*:

> Tvardovsky had succeeded in writing something timeless, courageous and unsullied, helped by a rare sense of proportion, all his own. . . . Though he was not free to tell the whole truth about the war, Tvardovsky nevertheless always stopped just one millimeter short of falsehood. . . . The result was a miracle. I am not speaking only for myself; I had excellent opportunities to observe its effects on soldiers in my battery during the war. . . . Of the many things offered them, they obviously had a special preference for *War and Peace* and *Vasily Tyorkin*.[14]

What's more, as V. M. Akimov has explained, Vasily Tyorkin "made it through all the trials of war without high-sounding slogans or a single mention of the name of Stalin."[15] Wartime poet Boris Slutsky read *Tyorkin* with satisfaction, commenting, "This was true poetry."[16]

---

[13] War participant G. E. Shelud'ko wrote, "Almost every soldier, while resting, marching, fighting, would recite the words of the poem by heart." Qtd. in A.L. Grishunin, "Vasilii Tyorkin A. Tvardovskogo," 463.

[14] Aleksandr I. Solzhenitsyn, *The Oak and the Calf*, 14–15.

[15] V. M. Akimov, *Ot Bloka do Solzhenitsyna: Sud'by russkoi literatury XX veka (posle 1917 goda)* (St. Petersburg: St. Petersburg State Academy of Culture, 1994), 82. Mark Lipovetsky sees Tyorkin as a Stalinist appropriation of what he calls the "trickster trope." See his *Charms of the Cynical Reason: The Trickster's Transformation in Soviet and Post-Soviet Culture* (Boston: Academic Studies Press, 2011), 199; also 40.

[16] Quoted in L. Lazarev, "Vo imia pravdy i dobra: o poezii Borisa Slutskogo," in Slutsky, *Bez popravok . . .* , 46.

Nationalism, patriotism, and hatred are the primary tools the state uses to mobilize a population for war. In Tvardovsky's Vasily Tyorkin, readers found those national characteristics and that patriotism personified and humanized—a soldier-hero who was an authentic everyday guy. He was "our lad," as Tvardovsky wrote in his notebooks. Unlike Chapaev, Vasily Tyorkin worked alone; he was an individual, with his own ideas and ways of doing things, and he didn't seem to have a commissar looking over his shoulder. In that sense, Tyorkin augmented the Civil War model of the heroic soldier as first seen in Furmanov's pair of characters yoked to one another in the spontaneity/consciousness mode. Chapaev represented energy and inventiveness, the instinctual ability to see the best way to lead his men in battle and to discipline them when quartered among civilians, and Furmanov's political commissar, Klychkov, was constantly at his side, correcting and directing him toward the truth of the party. The 1934 film version of Chapaev added humor—and the charms of some of the first vivid talking heroes from the big screen—to that image. Less than a decade later, in the character of Tyorkin, Tvardovsky retains the inventive, instinctual, cheerful peasant, but allows him to work for his country on his own terms, without the interference of the party or a commissar. He is a new Chapaev, both humorous and serious, but also fully grown-up and politically mature.

Critics have commented on the absence of a "recognizably Soviet context" in *Vasily Tyorkin*, where the vocabulary and comparisons frequently draw on "ordinary peace-time existence, even when describing specifically military actions." A poem about a Soviet warrior . . . without war terminology and without Soviet political propaganda. In Katherine Hodgson's words, "Tyorkin is a figure with whom readers could identify, an instantly recognizable type who inspired trust and affection" (196, 170).

There was a reason for this. Tvardovsky saw war fiction as a vital part of national consciousness:

> Life, reality, is not fully real until it is reflected in the mirror of art, only then does it receive its reality, so to speak, and obtain stability, become established, gain meaning for the long term. Without *War and Peace*, what would the year 1812 have been for the consciousness of many generations of Russian people?[17]

---

[17] Tvardovsky, quoted in Igor' Sukhikh, *Knigi XX veka: russkii kanon* (Moscow: Nezavisimaia gazeta, 2001), 13.

This relationship between life and art suggests a social function of literature, a need for narrative in order to understand events as they occur and when we look back at them. We can recall Drew Faust's argument about war as a "narrative invention," transforming violence through a story of purpose. That story is what we tell ourselves about war in order to justify and legitimate actions that otherwise seem barbaric.[18] The literary folk hero Tyorkin fulfilled this task for the author and his audience from the early '40s through the mid-'60s.[19]

War as Muse: The Birth of Tyorkin

Vasily Tyorkin: A Book about a Soldier was written and published during the early years of the Second World War, but the figure of Vasily grew out of an earlier group project. Thus the authorial initiative, in true Soviet fashion, was at first a "collective" one. While working at the newspaper *In Defense of the Homeland* (*Na strazhe rodiny*) during the Finnish war in 1939, Tvardovsky and some colleagues created a kind of comic strip hero named Vasya Tyorkin.[20] This early "collective" version of Tyorkin—specifically called by the nickname Vasya rather than the full name Vasily—was truly unique and unusual ("*neobyknovennyi*") and was identified by his authors in their characteristic quatrains as a hero from the start:

> Vasya Tyorkin? Who is that?
> Let us say quite clearly:
> Very much a man who is
> Unique—absolutely.

---

[18] Faust, "Race, Gender, and Confederate Nationalism," 301.
[19] In 1975 Vladimir Lakshin wrote of the "thrilling years of 1956 to 1961, when the Stalinist 'cult of personality' was denounced, when the whole cleansing process implied by that vague phrase began." In contrast, he characterizes the post-Khrushchev period as "a difficult time" for the Soviet intelligentsia. See Lakshin, "Solzhenitsyn, Tvardovskii i *Novyi Mir*," 85.
[20] These comic strips were modeled on traditional folk *lubki* and on ROSTA posters from the early 1920s. During World War II Tyorkin again became a "collective" hero when artist Veniamin Briskin teamed up with Samuil Marshak to create the poster "How Vasya Tyorkin 'Camouflaged' the Fascists." Other authors and filmmakers used the character as well. For the poster image and discussion of Tyorkin see Bird, "The Functions of Poetry," 99–101.

Despite a surname such as this,
Plain and unassuming,
Untold fame—a hero he—
Ever will be looming.

You might ask us straightaway,
A reasonable query:
Why it is that he is called
Vasya—not Vasily!

'Cause he is so dear to all,
'Cause all kinds of people
Get on famously with him,
'Cause they love that Vasya.

A bogatyr', his shoulders wide,
The lad's well put together.
By nature he's a cheery soul,
A man with guts and know-how.

In battle or wherever he is—
One thing is for certain:
First things first, he eats his fill,
Vasya knows his habit.

But he doesn't spare an ounce
Of his strength so fabled
And the enemy he stabs
Like wheat sheaves with a pitchfork.

Nonetheless, fierce as may be
Our fellow Vasya Tyorkin,—
Without a joke, without a pun
He can't survive a moment . . .[21]

---

[21] "Vasia Tyorkin na fronte," *Frontovaia biblioteka gazety "Na strazhe Rodiny"* (Leningrad: Iskusstvo, 1940).

2. The Peasant-Soldier: Alexander Tvardovsky and a New Chapaev

This hero Vasya Tyorkin has the characteristics of a folk *bogatyr*—strong, broad-shouldered, quick with his bayonet—but also the endearing peasant qualities of cheerfulness, lightheartedness, and a good appetite. In his love of joking, songs, and puns, Vasya Tyorkin did not differ all that much from the original Vasily Chapaev, of whom Furmanov wrote: "To him, songs were like bread and water; Chapaev was always gloomy without singing. [When he felt] depressed, he couldn't live a whole day [without it]."[22]

His name, the chummy Vasya, shows him to be not just a lover of jokes but the butt of jokes as well. The stories in which he was featured—the first written by Tvardovsky, later ones by others of the collective authors—were always illustrated, and Tvardovsky commented later that "they give an impression of naiveté, featuring Vasya's extremely improbable 'feats,' and their humor is of questionable quality" ("Kak byl napisan," 238). Soon after the project began, the collective went their own journalistic ways, and the Red Army poet A. Shcherbakov took over as the main author of "Tyorkin."

While the stories were popular, the inventors of Tyorkin themselves believed them to be hack work: "We did not consider this to be literature," recalled Tvardovsky ("Kak byl napisan," 239). Nonetheless, the "improbable 'feats'" in wartime made this hero a Soviet hero.

Tvardovsky must have seen this potential in him because by 1940 he had decided to write a new version of Tyorkin, one who would be more than just a character from the funny pages:

> "Tyorkin," according to the idea I then had, should combine approachability and flexibility of form—inherited directly from the newspaper "Tyorkin"—with a certain seriousness and even lyricism of content. In thinking about "Tyorkin" as a complete work, a poem, I now tried to pinpoint, to seize that "necessary plot moment" . . . without which I could not begin.
>
> The problem with the "old Tyorkin," I now realize, was that it came out of a very old tradition, when any poetic word addressed to the masses was deliberately simplified and lowered to the specific cultural and political level of the reader. ("Kak byl napisan," 240)

---

[22] Quoted in Sarra Shtut, *Kakov ty, Chelovek?: geroicheskoe v sovetskoi literature* (Moscow: Sovetskii pisatel', 1964), 147.

In his essay "How 'Vasily Tyorkin' Was Written (An Answer to Readers)," Tvardovsky goes on to discuss how his attitude toward this "folk poetry" changed; instead of seeing it as work done with the left hand, as hack work, he came to believe in its inherent worth as a creation for a new kind of reader—the mass audience of the Soviet generation:

> Now [readers] were the children of those revolutionary warriors for whom D. Bedny and V. Mayakovsky had written their songs, *chastushki* [song rhymes] and satirical couplets; they were literate, politically sophisticated, culturally aware people who had grown up under Soviet power. ("Kak byl napisan," 240)

In a word, the children of Chapaev, ready to move into the adult world as his full-fledged comrades.

The search for heroic exemplars from Russian military history to inspire the Soviet people received sanction from above. In his November 7, 1941, speech, Joseph Stalin himself invoked Russian military heroes in trying to encourage the populace: "May you be inspired in this war by the courageous figures of our great ancestors: Alexander Nevsky, Dmitry Donskoy, Kuzma Minin and Dmitry Pozharsky, Aleksei Suvorov and Mikhail Kutuzov!"[23] Konstantin Simonov wrote poems in 1938 and 1939 on the twelfth-century Russian hero Alexander Nevsky and the eighteenth-century general Suvorov. But though he mentioned Suvorov in *Vasily Tyorkin*, Tvardovsky chose to focus on a smaller hero, a simple man to whom the front-line soldier could relate.[24]

---

[23] Qtd. in Nina Tumarkin, *The Living and the Dead: The Rise and Fall of the Cult of World War II in Russia* (New York: Basic Books, 1994), 63. Suvorov was the equivalent of "hero" and "warrior" for Soviet and pre-Soviet discourse. In Mayakovsky's satirical play *The Bedbug*, for example, Ivan Prisypkin claims to have fought the Revolution and Civil War "for the good life . . . Maybe I can raise the standards of the whole proletariat by looking after my own comforts!" In response, a true "proletarian" scoffs at him: "There's a warrior for you! A real Suvorov!" (Mayakovsky, *The Bedbug and Selected Poetry*, ed. Patricia Blake, trans. Max Hayward and George Reavey [Bloomington: Indiana University Press, 1975], 259).

[24] Some scholars have called him an "antihero," though I don't agree. See Tumarkin, who calls Tyorkin the "most widely beloved of wartime personages" but depicts him as "a comic figure and an antihero, simple, mundane, organically bonded to the Russian land" (80). Sheila Fitzpatrick, too, describes Tyorkin as "an anti-hero who possesses all the foraging and survival skills needed by Homo sovieticus [with] the same good-

2. The Peasant-Soldier: Alexander Tvardovsky and a New Chapaev

Until June 22, 1941, the day that war broke out with the Germans, Tvardovsky had found himself frustrated. As he later described it, formal issues kept getting in his way, and because there was no real "need" for his character (no "social order," in the phrasing of socialist realism), he was having trouble with his writing. While Tvardovsky contrasted his "peacetime mood" with his more urgent need to write in time of war, his writer's block stemmed from a set of real problems. First, while official statements had encouraged the reintegration of folklore into Soviet culture since Gorky's 1934 speech at the First Congress of Soviet Writers, Tvardovsky was hesitant to start a long *poèma* in the style of nineteenth-century poet Nikolai Nekrasov or other truly folk literary productions. Second, though he loved his folk hero, that very human quality meant that the character did not seem serious enough to star in a long narrative poem. Likewise, the trochaic tetrameter he had chosen had no precedent in "big" poems and thus also seemed too trivial. Finally, and perhaps worst of all, he couldn't settle on a plot.

With war declared, Tvardovsky's poem gained a purpose, and his muse returned. As he recalled some years later:

> When I decided to break with all my internal feelings of responsibility toward the conventions of form and turn my back on any potential evaluations from literary critics, then I felt free and easy.[25]

Tvardovsky would answer to soldiers and workers in wartime factories, not to sterile critics and literary traditions. He wrote Tyorkin for them, and surely one of the most remarkable things about the poem was that it was written and read while the war raged—in real time, as it were.

---

humored contempt for authority as Jaroslav Hasek's *Good Soldier Schweik*" (Sheila Fitzpatrick, "Everyday Stalinism: Ordinary Life in Extraordinary Times," excerpted in David L. Hoffmann, *Stalinism: The Essential Readings* [Malden, MA: Blackwell, 2003], 169). In contrast, Alexandra Smith identifies the poem as "one of the most typical pieces of Socialist realist writing, portraying a positive super-hero and conveying the sense of moral victory for the Socialist notion of 'collective man'" (Alexandra Smith, "Tvardovskii," in Neil Cornwell, ed., *Reference Guide to Russian Literature* [Chicago, London: Fitzroy Dearborn Publishers, 1998], 853).

[25] Tvardovskii, "Kak byl napisan," 259. Tvardovskii might have benefitted from the advice Anton Chekhov is reported to have given actresses: "Don't think about the reviews, think only about what you are trying to accomplish on stage."

Tvardovsky's timing was perfect, and his poem ideal for its moment. Knowing that it would be published in chapters or even smaller sections in army newspapers, and that his readers in between marches and battles might have only a short time to glance at individual excerpts, Tvardovsky designed the work deliberately so that each part was self-sufficient. A soldier could pick the poem up at any point, even if the previous installation had not reached him. Tvardovsky reminisced about imagining the book published between paperback covers, so the soldier could roll it up and stash it in his boot, hat, or inside his greatcoat, opening it for a few moments at any page when he had a chance. The rhythms of war created the form of the poem.

The result was a series of semi-disconnected chapters, each of which focuses on an important aspect of army life, interspersed with a number of meta-literary chapters from the author. Certain refrains appear, including one that emphasizes the importance of soldiers' work. Numerous chapters repeat the same lines: "A battle rages, right and holy. / A mortal battle not for glory, / But for life on this earth" (from "The Crossing," 34); "A terrible battle rages, bloody, / A mortal battle not for glory, / But for life on this earth" (from "About the Medal," 52); "On the left—the front, on the right—the front, / And in the snowy February gloom, / A terrible battle rages, bloody, / A mortal battle not for glory, / But for life on this earth" (from "The Duel," 84). Terrible, holy, bloody. These adjectives both depict and elevate the war experience, and Tvardovsky's refrain of "for life on this earth" (a refrain highlighted by virtually all critics and commentators on the poem) participated in the rhetoric of *podvig* and placed the military engagement in epic time.[26]

Shining with the aura of a holy truth, the "mortal battle" transformed the simple acts of the knowing trickster Vasily Tyorkin into a mandate for the inevitable successes of a messianic people on a quest to defeat the enemy, expressed through that same rhetoric of *podvig*. The sacred nature of the Red Army's task during the patriotic Great Fatherland War was also highlighted in such works as the "battle hymn" of the war, Vasily Lebedev-Kumach's re-appropriated "Holy War," published in *Izvestia* on June 24, 1941, and set to music the following day—which struck some then and now as ironic, given the officially atheist state that was adopting it. "Holy War" almost teems with capital-letter concepts:

---

[26] Compare with Boris Slutskii's poems, which avoided the rhetoric of *podvig* in favor of simplicity.

Rise up, vast land, / Rise up for a fight to the death! / With the dark forces of fascism, / With the accursed horde. / Let noble fervor / Swell like a wave,— / A people's war is raging, / A holy war![27]

Fight to the Death. Dark Forces of Fascism. Accursed Horde. Noble Fervor. People's War. Holy War. These words screamed out in capital letters that the war was indeed a repeat of the original Fatherland War of 1812, a sacred task to save Russia, taken up now by the new atheist state.

In his poem, Tvardovsky accessed that "heightening" impulse but combined it with the simple language and matter-of-fact cheerfulness of his hero to lower the tone of the sacred call and make his poem more believable and, in the end, more lasting. The rhetoric of *podvig* plus the application of *byt* proved a more appealing formula for readers.

As the writers' collective had mentioned in their early poems, Tyorkin is a common name. In fact, many soldiers wrote to Tvardovsky, convinced that the Tyorkin about whom he wrote, or another prototype for the hero, served with them in their battalion. Tyorkin was rooted in the everyday specifics of the lives of ordinary soldiers. Tvardovsky himself acknowledged the truth of his readers' reactions while denying their claims:

> No, Vasily Tyorkin, as he appears in the book, is a completely invented persona, the fruit of the imagination, a creation of fantasy. And although he does have features which I observed in many living people, it is impossible to call a single one of those people Tyorkin's prototype. ("Kak byl napisan," 230)

These readers' reactions testify to the success of his characterization. Both specific and collective, Tyorkin seemed psychologically "real" to his readers and, we can hope, thus fulfilled his creator's goal of cheering on his soldier-audience in their daily fight with the enemy. While refining the character of Tyorkin, Tvardovsky worked out what he felt the audience, and the theme, needed:

> The (external) "coloring" of frontline life was available to all. Cold, hoarfrost, shell explosions, bunkers, ice-covered army tents—A and

---

[27] For more on Lebedev-Kumach and this song, see Hodgson, *Written with the Bayonet*, 57.

B are writing about this as well. But they don't have the thing which I don't have yet either, or which I'm just hinting at—a person in the individual sense, "our lad,"—not abstracted (on the plane of the "epoch," the country, and so on), but alive, dear, and difficult. ("Kak byl napisan," 246–247)

"Our lad" brings the poem down to earth, to a concrete, prosaic earth where he meets with jokes and laughter and with danger and disappointments. This is the rhetoric of *podvig* combined with the rhetoric of *est'*.[28]

Tvardovsky was well aware that a literary hero in wartime would inherently beg comparison with the famed Civil War hero Vasily Chapaev. In the text of the poem at one point, a Chapaev-like lieutenant ("a cheerful fellow, a dancer, a Cossack" who has a "boyish mustache") rushes to lead the lads into battle: "There he is at the far hut / He raises his hand to his mustache: / "Bravo! Forward, boys!" / He shouted as dashingly, / As if he were Chapaev himself." But the cavalry officer, who leads the troops into battle, himself falls rather quickly. "The commander is wounded!" the soldiers cry. "Forward, boys!" he answers. "I'm not wounded. I am killed. . . ."

In his place, Vasily Tyorkin steps up, and the platoon follows him instead, all forty of them as one. When the general tries to sort out who was the hero at the end of the day, the rest of the platoon explains, "He can't appear himself / He's badly wounded. . . . And then of all the surnames, / All the names of today, / "Tyorkin," they shouted, "Vasily!" / It was, of course, he" (*Vasily Tyorkin*, 147–51).

Although Tyorkin, unlike Chapaev, was not based on the biography of a real soldier, Tvardovsky saw that he was the hero for this particular war. The "Cossack," the "dapper lieutenant" of the Civil War, was not the man of the hour anymore; the peasant-soldier Tyorkin was. Tvardovsky worked on building him a "biography" to underpin his characterization. His notebooks detail how he conceived of this task:

---

[28] As Grishunin notes, "The general direction of the great war is never forgotten in the details of *byt*, the events of the day" ("*Vasily Tyorkin*," 422). This forms a contrast with both Boris Slutskii and Viktor Nekrasov. Nekrasov in particular avoids the "general direction," allowing the reader to focus on the details instead. See chapter 4 below.

> There needs to be more of the hero's early biography. It must come through in his every gesture, action, story. But I must not simply give it outright. It's enough to think it through and imagine it for myself. ("Kak byl napisan," 247)

The other missing part in the Tyorkin tale is the "sidekick," in buddy-film terms, or the personification of political consciousness, to use the terms of socialist realist fiction. Chapaev went through the war with his commissar, Klychkov, showing him the way; and even in the later series of Chapaev jokes (which left out the political commissar entirely), Chapaev had his faithful adjutant, Petya, at his side. Tyorkin too needed a partner.

Tvardovsky recognized this as an issue of literary construction: "Another problem is that such 'amusing,' 'primitive' heroes are usually paired for contrast with a real, lyrical, 'elevated' hero. [I need] more digressions, more of myself in the poem" ("Kak byl napisan," 247). In other words, Tvardovsky decided that the author figure could serve as the missing partner. He supplied that partner in "digressions," which included a number of "From the Author" chapters, and through them Tvardovsky came to serve as his hero Tyorkin's mate.

Furmanov used the character of the political commissar Klychkov as an autobiographical stand-in, and his perspective informs the narrative of *Chapaev*. But Tvardovsky does the same thing without politicizing or indeed incarnating his stand-in. As one critic describes it:

> In the *Book about a Warrior* besides the protagonist, Tyorkin, there is a second hero. This hero is the author-poet himself. He "made friends," became kin to Tyorkin, and travels everywhere with him ("Tyorkin— goes on. The author—after him").[29]

"The author," he explains, "is an intermediary between the hero and the reader, leading a free conversation with readers, whose presence is also felt."[30] The presence of this authorial character, especially in a work written in rhyme,

---

[29] Grishunin, "*Vasilii Tyorkin* A. Tvardovskogo," 434.
[30] The critic compares the "author" character in *Vasilii Tyorkin* to the autobiographical "narrators" of Romantic works such as Pushkin's *Eugene Onegin*, Lermontov's *Hero of our Time*, suggesting that Tvardovskii added authentic data from his own biography to make his invented character Tyorkin seem more real. Grishunin, "*Vasilii Tyorkin* A. Tvardovskogo," 435.

allowed readers to accept the folk poetry aspect of *Vasily Tyorkin* while also feeling that it was grounded in the reality of the 1940s.

Even émigré Russian author Ivan Bunin was enthusiastic about Vasily Tyorkin,[31] in part perhaps for the same reason Soviet readers loved him and the poem. Vasily may be one of "our lads," but the author is a "known" quantity, and the two together give the sensation of authentic truth, of literature that reflects reality and remains contiguous with life and war. *Tyorkin* combines the rhetoric of *podvig* with the rhetoric of *est'* in a thoroughly convincing way, using details of everyday life, of *byt*, to ground the narrative.

Death and the Warrior

Even before creating the hero, and before the onset of war with Germany, Tvardovsky identified the plot elements he imagined including in his epic poem:

> I [even] imagined my hero's path at certain moments of the poem. Crossing the border, being wounded, hospitalization, catching up to his unit that had already gone far ahead. Participation in decisive battles, some kind of meeting with a girl . . .[32]

Narratives about war frequently include these plot elements—crossing borders (especially rivers), participating in battles, being wounded and treated in the hospital, even a fleeting love interest. War narratives, in that sense, mirror the events of war, and the four outcomes in fiction are the same as in war itself: injury, captivity, survival, or death.

Over the course of the Second World War, the Soviet army is estimated to have lost somewhere between eight and ten million soldiers.[33] Some of the

---

[31] Bunin praised especially Tvardovskii's "unusual popular soldier's language." Letter to Teleshov, 10 September 1947, quoted in O. N. Mikhailov, "Put' Bunina-khudozhnika," *Literaturnoe nasledstvo*, vol. 84, part 1, *Ivan Bunin* (Moscow: Nauka, 1973), 53.

[32] 20.IV.1940. Tvardovskii, "S Karel'skogo peresheika (Iz frontovoi tetradi)," in *Vasilii Tyorkin*, 284.

[33] See http://users.erols.com/mwhite28/ww2stats.htm. This site and the related http://users.erols.com/mwhite28/warstat1.htm, part of the *Historical Atlas of the Twentieth Century* put together by Matthew White, try to take published estimates and create an "average," neither too exaggerated nor dismissing the large casualty numbers out of hand. In his book *Bloodlands*, Timothy Snyder includes Soviet

worst losses occurred early in the war, but the death toll continued through to the very last days.

Death looms large in wartime, and it is a common ending to the "narrative invention" of war, to borrow again from Drew Faust. Survivors, among them many of our authors and many thousands of veterans, struggled during and after the war to figure out their own relationship, both to that "narrative invention" in which many had participated personally and to those who remained on the battleground, drowned in river crossings, perished in POW and other camps, et cetera. As Kali Tal has argued, "To be a survivor is to be bound to the dead. . . ." (229). The survivors strove, each in his or her own way, to understand that bond and to create meaning from violence and death.

When they used art to create that meaning, it had a variety of purposes: to lighten the load of the overwhelmed and overburdened soldier, to commemorate and memorialize the trauma experienced by the land and people, to fix physical and psychological experiences on the page and try to make sense of them, for themselves and for their readers. In the Soviet case, this became for many poets and writers a lifelong task, especially as changing political circumstances over the second half of the twentieth century in Russia altered the picture of "purpose and legitimation" for World War II.[34]

Let us notice, however, that in his initial list of possible plot nodes for his poem about Tyorkin, Tvardovsky did not mention death. He faced a certain genre problem: on the one hand, death was omnipresent in war, but on the

---

prisoners of war and besieged citizens (over four million) in the death count, as well as partisan casualties in Belarus and Poland (half a million dead) (Timothy Snyder, *Bloodlands: Europe Between Hitler and Stalin* [New York: Basic Books, 2010], 380).

[34] The rhetoric of *podvig* continued when Soviet rhetoric and the Soviet Union itself were only a historical memory. See for example Aleksandr Boiko, "Geroi strany, kotoroi net," *Sovetskaia Rossiia* (16 February 1995), who reiterates the numbers, nationalities, and names of "heroes of the Soviet Union" in the face of "New Russians" who do not seem to value the sacrifice of his generation and the "victory which we have, alas, ingloriously squandered." He highlights the "boys of '23"—the first born in the Union of Soviet Socialist Republics (founded at the end of December 1922)—who were eighteen when the war began. Ninety-seven percent of this generation, according to Boiko's count, lost their lives in World War II. We will look at the "boys of '24" in chapter 7.

other hand, he was writing an amusing, cheerful poem to keep the warriors' spirits high.

Throughout the poem, rumors fly from time to time of the hero's demise, and from the very start the author hints that a potential outcome for his hero is death. In the introductory section, one of several entitled "From the Author," the narrator presents his book as being incomplete, mere fragments of the saga of this hero:

> What else? That's about it. / In a word, a book about a warrior. / Without beginning and without end. / Why without beginning? / Because there's no time / To start it from the first. / Why with no end? / I just pity the hero. (Tvardovskii, *Vasilii Tyorkin*, 7)

Inherent in the subtitle, "A Book about a Soldier" (*kniga pro boitsa*), is its rhyme, "without an ending" (*bez kontsa*). Here Tvardovsky is deliberately violating genre conventions; after all, a book about a hero should be *biographical*, should describe the natural life arc from birth to death. In wartime, though, there's no time for the details of early life, and the ending is almost inevitably tragic.[35] As we have mentioned, millions of Soviet soldiers saw their lives end before the war did; Tyorkin was in danger as well. As the poem's narrator states a few chapters on:

> By the way, we should just add / Our hero's hale and hearty for now, / But of course he's not charmed, / Against any damned shrapnel, / Any damned bullet, / That might happen, / As it were, to fly blindly, / If he's exposed,—that's the end, brother. (88)

This attitude toward death (in calling names—"damned shrapnel," "damned bullet" ["*oskolok-durak*," "*duratskaia pulia*"]) is marked by a certain bravado but is a far cry from "scorn of death." Later the narrator draws a parallel be-

---

[35] Iu. Burtin has noted that the poem had to be plotless, because a plot would have "inevitably transformed Tyorkin's fate into some kind of individual biography, and thus destroyed the book as a work of 'universal' front content." See Iu. Burtin, "Nestareiushchaia pravda," 136–153 in *"Zhivaia pamiat' pokolenii." Velikaia Otechestvennaia voina v sovetskoi literature. Sbornik statei* (Moscow: Khudozhestvennaia literatura, 1965), 150–151. Tvardovskii's narrator says the same thing: "During war there's no plot" ([Tvardovskii, *Vasilii Tyorkin*, 87]).

tween Tyorkin and the war, acknowledging that Tyorkin is not "real": "Tyorkin's not subject to death, / Until the war is at an end...." (174).

Though as a character Tyorkin became a beloved companion to soldiers at the front as well as in the rear, Tvardovsky regularly comments on his folkloric nature, calling him a "Russian miracle-man" (276) and a *bogatyr* and implying that his very function is tied to war; even Tyorkin himself states, "When I die, the war will end too."[36]

In the poem, as one critic has commented, death in wartime "is shown as an ordinary and even quite likely [event]": "If they kill you, your dead body, / Will lie with others in a row, / They'll cover you / With your worn greatcoat,—sleep, soldier."[37] This attitude toward death is not presented in any kind of elevated, heroic tones, but as merely the result of the facts on the ground; in the end only two of every three soldiers returned from the war at all. Tvardovsky also emphasizes the randomness of death in battle. For example, in the chapter about crossing the river ("Crossing," or *pereprava*, which rhymes with glory [*slava*], but as the poet points out, the two are not synonymous): "Some will be remembered, some will get glory, / And some will [slip into] the dark water,— / Without a sign, without a trace." (26)[38]

In the chapter "Death and the Warrior," the poet presents Tyorkin's struggle with death almost as a seduction, both physical and intellectual. The soldier lies on the battlefield ("not picked up" ["*nepodobrannyi*"]), quite literally on his deathbed. As Death (feminine, of course) leans over him, she offers her friendship/sexual partnership, saying, "Well, soldier, come with me. / I'm your [girl]friend now...." Tyorkin resists ("Tyorkin shuddered, freezing / On his snowy bed") and claims to belong to the living. In a cruel rhyme, Death addresses the warrior as a folk hero, evoking the epithet "good hero" (*dóbryi mólodets*) only to assure him that he is a "goner": "Death, laughing, leaned down further: / 'Enough, enough, young hero, / After all, I know, I can see: / You're alive, but not long for this world.'"[39]

---

[36] In the poem, a wounded soldier is reported as having heard the following lines, with their convincing internal rhyme: "Tyorkin said at that moment: / When I die, the war will end" ("Молвил Тёркин в ту минуту: / 'Мне—конец, войне конец'" [Tvardovskii, *Vasilii Tyorkin*, 174]).
[37] Quoted in A. L. Grishunin, "*Vasily Tyorkin* A. Tvardovskogo," 428–429.
[38] The issue of memorialization deserves a much longer discussion and has received interesting treatments by writers and scholars alike.
[39] Quotes above and below from this chapter in Tvardovskii, *Vasilii Tyorkin*, 151–59.

In the poem's introduction, Tvardovsky had used the rhyme "hero / without an ending" (*molodtsá / bez kontsá*). Here he reiterates, using the voice of Death: the narrative may remain without an ending, out of pity for the doomed soldier, but Death speaks openly: this hero is not long for this world (*molodets / ne zhiléts*). The argument continues, with Death assuring the warrior that he has nothing to live for; even if he survives this night, what awaits him is more of the same: "cold, fear, exhaustion, dirt . . ." not to mention "misery." And she argues that even if he survives the war, as he plans ("I'll fulfill my task, / Finish with the Germans, and head for home"), his return will be pointless. The war has destroyed the Russian land, and if he comes home an invalid, he'll be too weary and damaged to rebuild. Becoming numb, losing blood, Tyorkin is almost ready to give up and give in, "under one condition": he wants to come back on victory day. When Death refuses, he holds firm, following orders, as it were, never to surrender: "Then off with you, Cross-Eyes, / I'm a soldier who's still alive / I'll cry and howl with pain, / Perish without a trace in the field, / But to you I will never / Surrender willingly."

Tvardovsky uses these scenes with Death to enhance the folkloric quality of his character even while filling the narrative with wartime specifics, with *byt*. A burial detail comes out to collect Tyorkin's body and finds that he's alive, but Death does not lose hope that Tyorkin will die on the way back to the medical battalion. Eventually, she has to relent with a sigh, and the chapter ends with her defeat: "Those living ones, they're so / Very friendly among themselves. / That's why I have to manage / To come to terms with the ones who're alone." The power of the collective is reiterated: refusing to give in to Death's seductive arguments, Tyorkin maintains his connection with his fellow soldiers, who literally and symbolically share their warmth with him, placing their own mittens on his nearly frozen hands. Us and them, *svoí* and *chuzhíe*. Death remains "other," the enemy, and the soldiers' solidarity saves their comrade. The war is not yet over, and the hero will rise again.

In the hospital, Tyorkin maintains his trademark calm, jolly attitude, calling himself a "big fan of living." The moral that emerges from this narrative of Death's defeat is clear; brotherhood and unity are the mantra and the protection of the Soviet soldier: "If a third time an evil bullet / Pecks me to death, / Then at least I want to meet, / My final hour / Among you, brothers" (161).

In the end Tvardovsky is unable to kill off his hero. At first he was certain to perish; then he survives two serious injuries (and is once left for dead),[40] but as the war continues, the narrator expresses his hopes for an optimistic ending: "Leaving the ranks now? / Excuse me—Tyorkin lives! / Hale and hearty, more cheerful than before. / Dying? Just the opposite. / I'm now full of hope: / He'll outlive even me" (175).

Instead of chronicling Tyorkin's death, the "duel" in the chapter "Death and the Warrior" is more of a rhetorical struggle, or a struggle between potential seduction by a female and the brotherly bonds of Red Army men. In the end, instead of a corpse, the "brothers" discover that "the warrior is alive"!

In the *Odyssey*, Death is called "the great leveler":

Not even the gods
can defend a man, not even one they love, that day
when fate takes hold and lays him out at last.[41]

In the epic worldview of Homer, Death was all-powerful, but in Tvardovsky's world, the Warrior can rise from his deathbed—especially when surrounded by his comrades. Unity, cohesion, the collective are stronger than death; and the "duel" is not one-on-one, but Death against the entire Red Army.

Tvardovsky wrote for the soldiers in the field, every one of whom lived with the presence of death and with the knowledge, articulated or not, that they too might not return home. The character of Tyorkin was an honest representation of their potential fates, but he also gave them hope that they might survive. Throughout the war, for Tvardovsky and his readers, the hero served two purposes. First, Tyorkin lowered the expectations of what a true *bogatyr* was: "The *bogatyr* is not a fairytale hero— / A carefree giant, / But rather in his field uniform, / A man of simple stuff, / Who feels fear in battle . . ." (292). The hero can be afraid, but in his simplicity he gets the job done. "Yessir."

Secondly, Tyorkin was a companion and encompassed within himself all aspects of war: pain and fear, laughter and rest, wounds, even near-death

---

[40] Tvardovskii recalled that he planned to end his work after Tyorkin's stay in the hospital: "Tyorkin fought, was wounded, and returns to his regiment," and that would be the end. "But my readers' letters taught me that I could not do this" (Tvardovskii, "Kak byl napisan," 264). Thus more and more chapters continued to appear.
[41] Homer, *The Odyssey*, trans. Robert Fagles (New York: Penguin Books, 1996), 115.

experiences, and, of course, *podvig*: "From Moscow to Stalingrad / You are invariably by my side— / My pain, my delight, / My rest and my feat" (224). For Tvardovsky, whose hero was embraced by thousands of soldiers, a "fade-to-black" ending turned out to be the most appropriate of all: "From whence he came, there too he vanished."[42] The folk hero Tyorkin did not perish after all but instead returned to the people,[43] a new Chapaev for a new war.

---

[42] Tvardovskii, "Kak byl napisan," 278. Vykhodtsev argues that Tyorkin in the poem came to represent the "people's immortality," and as such—according to the logic of the fairy tale or bylina—could not be allowed to die (Vykhodtsev, "A.T. Tvardovskii i narodnaia khudozhestvennaia kul'tura [Vasilii Tyorkin]," in *Tvorchestvo A.T. Tvardovskogo: issledovaniia i materialy*, ed. Vykhodtsev and N.A. Groznovaia [Leningrad: Nauka, 1989], 26).

[43] In conjunction with the "continuation" of the tale of Tyorkin after the war, see Tvardovskii's discussions of popular works about his hero (Tvardovskii, "Kak byl napisan," 268–283), as well as chapter 5 below about his "Tyorkin in the Other World."

Chapter Three
Eyewitnesses to Heroism: Emmanuil Kazakevich and Vera Panova

> Here everyone is a hero, just living here is already heroism.
> Здесь все герои, жить здесь уже героизм.
> —Emmanuil Kazakevich

> Though it's odd, you're never more alive than when you're almost dead.
> —Tim O'Brien

War gave new life to Soviet literature and breathed fresh air into socialist realism. During the four years of war, more than 150 major novellas and novels about the war were published in Russian.[1] War literature thrived both during the war and afterward. In effect, the Second World War generated the material for which Soviet writers had been searching.

The best war writing often comes from those who witness the events. They come in two kinds: the observer—often a journalist—and the participant, a soldier or someone who otherwise contributes to the war effort. This is true not only of Soviet fiction: think of Leo Tolstoy, but also Ernest Hemingway and Tim O'Brien. The main writers of the Soviet war experience also fall into these two categories: Alexander Tvardovsky, Ilya Ehrenburg, Konstantin Simonov, and Vasily Grossman were journalists working in and among Soviet battalions for such newspapers as the Red Army's *Krasnaya Zvezda*, *Izvestiya*, or *Pravda*, while writers and poets like Boris Slutsky, Viktor Nekrasov, and Bulat Okudzhava served themselves, as soldiers, reconnaissance men, sappers, etc.[2] We have looked closely at Tvardovsky in the previous chapter. In this chapter we will consider Vera Panova, a

---

[1] P. M. Toper, *Radi zhizni na zemle: Literatura i voina. Traditsii. Resheniia. Geroi*, 3rd ed. (Moscow: Sovetskii pisatel', 1985), 372.

[2] For more on writers in wartime see Anna Krylova, "'Healers of Wounded Souls': The Crisis of Private Life in Soviet Literature, 1944–1946," *Journal of Modern History* 73.1 (2001): 307–331, esp. 313–314 and 330. See also her *Neither Erased Nor Remembered: Soviet "Women Combatants" and Cultural Strategies of Forgetting in Soviet Russia, 1940s–1980s* (New York: Berghahn Books, 2010).

journalist-turned-participant who travelled the rails with a hospital train, and Emmanuil Kazakevich, a poet-turned-reconnaisance man who wrote fiction immediately following the war. Both of these writers memorized the faces, events, and experiences of those around them to reproduce at war's end in narratives that evoked the struggles and individual suffering of World War II.[3]

Participants who become writers fulfill a double function: they both contribute to the war effort and chronicle the war. They witness, and they create meaning out of their experiences and observations for their own and future generations. Gorky had chided Furmanov for writing like a witness rather than an artist, but as we saw in chapter 1, the witness function was essential for creating the feeling of authenticity that Soviet readers sought.[4]

In the Soviet Union, journalists worked in the service of the state. But for participants, there was a double obligation: they may have worked for the state, but they also had personal stock in being truthful to what they saw and did, to their own experiences in war and to those of their comrades. There were thus two levels of truth, the official and the personal. These authors needed to figure out a way to tell their own truths within the strictures of socialist realism and official doctrine. *Literaturnaya gazeta*'s August 1941 editorial on "the place of the writer in the Fatherland War," quoted in a previous chapter, was only one of many official Soviet calls for service to the country. These participants answered that call and their internal call to testify. In their fiction, writers presented actual conflicts and ethical crises in the context of everyday life, and they strove to do so within an ideological framework.

As we saw in the last chapter, Tvardovsky's immensely popular *Vasily Tyorkin* was written and read during the war. In this chapter, we look at Kazakevich's *The Star* (*Zvezda*) and Panova's *The Train Companions* (*Sputniki*), both written in the wake of the war and published in 1946. These works draw their power from the negotiation of the ambiguous wartime boundaries between journalism and fiction, between facts and myths, between the real and the true. Firmly grounded in the *byt* of wartime experience, both narra-

---

[3] Grossman's war writings have been collected and translated into English by Antony Beevor and Luba Vinogradova. See *A Writer at War: Vasily Grossman with the Red Army, 1941–1945* (New York: Pantheon, 2005).

[4] Tolstoy wrote both as a witness and as an artist; compare his work on Sevastopol to *War and Peace*.

tives choose to highlight the collective over the individual, the "we" working together to get the job done on the front and in the rear over the individual hero completing heroic feats.

Witnesses to War

Kazakevich and Panova make an interesting pair. Both came to their fiction about war from journalism. Both won Stalin Prizes for their efforts, and both achieved their success from what we might think of as the margins of Soviet society.

Kazakevich was a Jew—one of the few Soviet writers to emerge from Birobidzhan, the capital of Stalin's Jewish Autonomous Oblast in the Far East near the Chinese border; and Panova was a woman writing about perhaps the world's most quintessentially male activity. Both were witnesses to heroism and cowardice, to triumph and pain and death, and both chronicled those scenes for their fellow Soviet citizens.

Emmanuil Kazakevich (1913–1962) had a peripatetic career. He worked variously as a cultural official, kolkhoz director, journalist, and theater director. He relocated to Moscow in 1938 and during World War II served as a reconnaissance man. Wanting to see action at the front and to store up impressions as literary material, Kazakevich wrote to a fellow soldier, "This is not the pose of a daring person or the naked words of a braggart. This is a question of my burning desire and, if you want, of my future literary life. That's why I'm heading out. . . ."[5] Immediately at war's end he produced the novella *The Star* based on his experiences,[6] and only a few years later, in 1949, *The Star* was adapted as a film for the first time, and directed by Alexander Ivanov.

For decades *The Star* was an integral part of the Russian school curriculum, in great part because it demonstrated the proper attitude toward the homeland and featured the components of love, comradeship, and patriotism in just the right doses, perfect for forming young minds. These components enabled Kazakevich's story to be read by several generations as an inspira-

---

[5] *Voennyi put' E.G. Kazakevicha*, 436, quoted in N. Eidinova, "Negasnushchii svet Zvezdy (O povesti Em. Kazakevicha)," in *Slova, prishedshie iz boia*, ed. A. G. Kogan (Moscow: Kniga, 1980), 37.

[6] I will be quoting from E. Kazakevich, *Zvezda: povest'*, in *Velikaia otechestvennaia*, ed. V. Kozhevnikov, K. Simonov, and A. Surkov (Moscow: Khudozhestvennaia literatura, 1966), 7–80.

tional text about the Great Fatherland War, in which boys from different ethnic backgrounds come together to fight the hated foe.

The story was not too idealized, though: according to one critic, *The Star* "avoids heroic embellishments,"[7] instead offering an engrossing depiction of complex and imperfect relations between soldiers who make mistakes, have some successes, and perish in the end. This ending, in which the entire group dies, leaving the lone female character to mourn, offers a "human element" but also reiterates the trope of the sacrificial warrior from Furmanov's *Chapaev*. The military feat, as appropriate in the rhetoric of *podvig*, is accomplished.

Vera Panova (1905–1973), a dramatist and novelist who was born in Central Russia, worked off and on as a radio and newspaper journalist and as a copy editor before and during the war, and it was in her role as a journalist that she ended up in the war zone. Initially her assignment had her investigating a military hospital train to produce a propaganda piece about it. As she did this, she met and interviewed dozens of military personnel and got to know their stories. In the end, she finished her piece on the hospital train too late in the war to have it contribute to the war effort. But she also transformed the characters she met and the experiences she had on the train into fiction for her novel *The Train Companions*.

Kazakevich and Panova remained successful mainstream writers until their deaths in 1962 and 1973, respectively. Forgotten as the Soviet era waned, Kazakevich lost his foothold in the school curriculum, and his works languished after the breakup of the Soviet Union. Panova remained a middlebrow Soviet writer, winning popularity with many readers because of the empathy she expressed for the everyday lives of her characters, and only in the last versions of her memoirs, published for the one hundredth anniversary of her birth, did her personal struggles with the Soviet regime come out in full.[8] Both novellas have recently been reissued and are again enjoying popularity in post–Soviet Russia.

---

[7] See Wolfgang Kasack, *Dictionary of Russian Literature since 1917*, translated by Maria Carlson and Jane T. Hedges (New York: Columbia University Press, 1988), 164.

[8] See Adele Barker, "V. F. Panova," in *Dictionary of Russian Women Writers*, ed. Marina Ledkovsky, Charlotte Rosenthal, and Mary Zirin (Westport, CT: Greenwood Press, 1994), 483–485. Panova's memoirs, *O moei zhizni, knigakh i chitateliakh*, were first published in the journal *Neva* 4 (1973). See also Xenia Gasiorowska, *Women in Soviet Fiction, 1917–1964* (Madison: University of Wisconsin Press, 1968). The young Sergei Dovlatov, who will feature in chapter 6 below, worked for a time as Panova's secretary.

In *The Star*'s martyred hero Travkin, we can see the continuing evolution of the Chapaev template in war fiction. Kazakevich's Travkin, like Tvardovsky's Tyorkin, is smarter and more selfless than the original, but like Chapaev he is doomed to perish behind enemy lines with no hope of personal happiness. Panova's novel is an ensemble piece, with many featured characters, but her central protagonist is the party boss Danilov, a facilitator who keeps her train moving, and in so doing follows the path of Furmanov's Klychkov. Danilov shares characteristics with Chapaev and Tyorkin, including his roots in a simple peasant family, but his role in wartime as a party worker and bureaucrat creates a parallel with Klychkov. These central protagonists do not feature as heroes per se for the novellas; they are more important as a part of the whole, as leaders within the collective. In these narratives, for Panova and Kazakevich, the war effort was about the "we."

Kazakevich and *The Star*

Kazakevich was one of Tvardovsky's closest friends after the war.[9] Writing Kazakevich's obituary in 1962, Tvardovsky noted:

> The appearance of his novella [*The Star*] marked the arrival in Soviet Russian literature of a great, completely original and striking talent and—more than that—a new step in assimilating the material of World War II.
>
> This novella has become one of the best works of Soviet literature. Its qualities—unusually polished prose, the symmetry of its parts and completeness of the whole, the musical rhyming of the beginning with the ending, along with the deep lyricism and dramatic nature of the plot, the unforgettable vividness of the heroes and their human charm—keep it from losing its power to impact readers, even years later....
>
> I would find it difficult to identify a work by any of today's young prose writers, who are writing at the most auspicious time imaginable for literature, which would come anywhere near the depth of plot and perfection of form of Kazakevich's *The Star*.[10]

---

9   Note that Kazakevich also wrote a biographical book about Lenin, *The Blue Notebook*, about which Nikolai Pogodin, Soviet playwright and himself a winner of the Lenin prize, wrote, "A talented pen has given us a true literary work in which Lenin's mighty heart lives, burns and beats." Kazakevich was a two-time Stalin prizewinner, in 1948 for *Star* and in 1950 for *Spring on the Oder*.

10 Quoted in Margarita Aliger, "Tropinka vo rzhi," *Vospominaniia ob Aleksandre Tvardovskom: sbornik*, 2nd ed. (Moscow: Sovetskii pisatel', 1982), 403.

Obituaries lend themselves to exaggerated encomiums, but if we take Tvardovsky at his word, we get some sense of the significance this book had for the postwar Soviet generation.

As Tvardovsky also commented in the obituary, this novella of reconnaissance units during the war came directly out of Kazakevich's personal experience, and its stylistic perfection in prose seems all the more remarkable considering Kazakevich's pre-war background—as a poet who wrote in Yiddish. But Kazakevich went to war to become a writer, and his experiences there changed him profoundly. As he stated upon the conclusion of the war, "It seems to me that I have experienced everything: suffering, and deprivation, and horror at the sight of depravity, and exultation at the sight of nobility—everything war contains within it."[11]

Kazakevich wrote a number of narratives set in wartime, including *The Star*, *Two in the Steppe* (1948), *Spring on the Oder* (1949), and *The Heart of a Friend* (1953), but *The Star* was by far the most popular and successful, earning him wide acclaim and more than fifty editions in many languages, as well as the Stalin Prize, as already mentioned. According to his friend and colleague Margarita Aliger, later works were criticized for too much "humane pathos," and despite the Thaw, his essay from the late 1950s on Lenin and Stalin—entitled "Genius and Villainy," after Pushkin's formulation—remained unpublishable, even in Tvardovsky's *Novyi Mir*, until the *glasnost* period in the late 1980s.[12]

In *The Star*, a short narrative filled with descriptive language and intense emotions, Kazakevich draws on commonplace Soviet war themes as well as conventional boyhood stories of adventure and exploration. For example, the youngest of Kazakevich's characters, Golub, trembles with ecstasy as he somehow merges his hatred of Germans (who had hung his father) and his recollections of "romantic stories of trappers, Indians, and daring travelers" (*Zvezda*, 54). Dashes across meadows and slow, even marches along ridges—these are the movements of the reconnaissance team; and when they go behind enemy lines, readers hold their breath, hoping against hope for a successful mission.

Hatred and ecstasy, fear and daring—the intense energy of life behind enemy lines is harnessed to the mission before the soldiers, the doctrinally

---

[11] Quoted in L. A. Gladkovskaia, "Emmanuil Kazakevich," 5–24 in Emmanuil Kazakevich, *Sobranie sochinenii*, vol. 1 of 3 (Moscow: Khudozhestvennaia literatura, 1985), 7.

[12] Margarita Aliger, "Zhguchoe stremlenie byt' tvortsom," *Znamia* 11 (1988), 223–25.

required successful mission, which involved a feat and sacrifice. Kazakevich participates in the rhetoric of *podvig* and demonstrates in *The Star* the strength of the tiny reconnaissance unit against an enormous elite Nazi tank division. His novella highlights the protagonist, Lieutenant Travkin, only to show that the individual merges with the "we" in the service of a greater cause. Part of what makes the narrative so exciting is the visual quality of the prose, a quality that served to turn *The Star* into a successful film in the immediate postwar era with Ivanov's 1949 effort, as well as in the recent past, with Alexander Lebedev's remake in 2002.

Volodya Travkin as Heroic Leader

Let us take a closer look at several of the characters from Kazakevich's novella, beginning with the central hero. Travkin strikes the reader as the perfect Soviet officer. The narrator introduces him as "a modest, serious, loyal man who always walks in death's line of sight, closer to death than anyone. . . ." (16). The head of the reconnaissance unit, Travkin surprises some of his men with his selflessness, his dedication to his duties, indeed, what the narrator at one point calls a "fanaticism in fulfilling his duty": "Not to think of his own advantage, but only about his cause—that's how Travkin had been raised . . . [and he was] ready to give up his life for it" (37–38).

This cause—rendered more generally as *delo*—is in wartime very clear, much clearer than it was for Turgenev's and Dostoevsky's characters in imperial Russia, who had struggled with the dichotomy of word versus deed, *slovo* and *delo*. Representative of the New Soviet Man, Travkin and his kind were quick to recognize the nature of the deed, and they moved to act with a sure-footedness that would have been the envy of their nineteenth-century predecessors.[13]

Travkin's leadership style mimics that of Chapaev—always out in front, despite what the manual says about protecting the head of the unit. *The Star* centers around Travkin's unit of military scouts, who penetrate behind enemy lines to discover a huge SS offensive in the making. This discovery and the imperative to stop the offensive provide the primary plot of the novella.

---

[13] Turgenev planted his character Rudin (in the 1859 novel of that name) on the barricades of Paris in 1848, feeling that he needed to make him act after all his speechifying in the Russian country "nest." Where better to act than in a war zone, even if that war was taking place on foreign soil?

A secondary plotline concerns Katya, the radio operator, who falls in love with Travkin. In wartime, Russian soldiers were not to be distracted by women or thoughts of love, and Travkin is no exception, but Kazakevich uses Katya to characterize the leader further, from a woman's point of view:

> In her mind's eye she could see the almost child-like face of the lieutenant. Perhaps she saw in it her own reflection, something like the pain hidden deep in her heart, the persistent pain of a girl from a small town who has encountered life's weight in its most cruel manifestation, at war. (28)

The lieutenant brings out both the maternal and the child in her and without knowing it transforms the young woman into a better Soviet citizen. In Travkin, Katya sees someone so good, so pure, that she too becomes pure, despite having previously defined herself as an "experienced sinner"—not the appropriate heroine to match Travkin. With her new interest in being helpful, she now spends hours in his abode, trying to make his home "homier" and hoping that he will notice her.

Through contact with Lieutenant Travkin, Katya is transformed from fallen woman to Soviet mother-patriot. At one point in the narrative, frustrated that Travkin is deliberately ignoring her devotion to him, she thinks that she may go back to her previous ways with another, less lofty man. The narrator explains, "In Barashkin everything was ordinary, simple and clear, and that seemed to her now just what a person needed to be happy." But soon Katya realizes that "this 'ordinariness' was already foreign and disgusting to her" (43).

The ordinary is sex—taboo in Soviet literature—while the extraordinary is incorporeal, higher than mere sex and the body; indeed, it is exemplified by *podvig*, by feats, and personified in Travkin. As one Soviet critic has written, Katya's unrequited love for the lieutenant showed the "cleansing spiritual strength of Travkin, a fine man and warrior."[14] The warrior-hero does more than defend his country; in Kazakevich's novella, he restores the virginity of Russia's women as well, making them fit to bear further sons for the motherland.

As we have discussed, successful war prose has two characteristics: these stories are filled with detail, to make them seem real, and they somehow

---

[14] Gladkovskaia, "Emmanuil Kazakevich," 10.

transcend the details to make them true. That was certainly what socialist realist doctrine demanded: the "truthful, historically concrete representation of reality" plus "ideological transformation and education." Travkin does not change over the course of this novella, but the other characters who encounter him do. Not just Katya, but some of the soldiers in his unit as well are changed for the better, brought into the collective and made aware of their duty to their country through their contact with this quiet, understated, brave, and conscious hero.

All for One: Unity and Conformity in *The Star*

The Star was based on the author's own experience on reconnaissance duty during the war. In order to make meaning out of that experience, Kazakevich invented Travkin and his men. His narrator also generalizes, however, describing the work of the reconnaissance man in eternal terms. As he prepares for his mission:

> The scout no longer belongs to himself, to his superiors, to his memories. [...] He renounces all human establishments, puts himself outside the law, relying only on himself. He gives his *starshina* all his documents, letters, photographs, awards and medals, to the party head—his party or Komsomol card. Thus he renounces his past and his future, keeping it all only in his heart. Like a forest bird, he has no name [...] in the depths of his brain holding dear only one thought: his *mission*. Thus began the ancient game, in which the only two actors were man and death.[15]

Like Tvardovsky, Kazakevich figures the struggle of the warrior as a confrontation between Man and Death, here presented as a classic duel. Even though the reconnaissance group in this story consists of seven people, they are a unit—a collective that acts as one, led by the intrepid Lieutenant Vladimir Travkin:

> Again and again Travkin looked into his comrades' faces. These were no longer subordinates, but comrades; the life of each depended on all the rest, and he, the commander, felt them not as other people, different

---

[15] Kazakevich, *Zvezda*, 46. Here, as in Tvardovskii's chapter "Duel" (*Poedinok*) the duel pits the Russian against the enemy: "Как на древнем поле боя, / Грудь на грудь, что щит на щит— / Вместо тысяч бьются двое, / Словно схватка все решит" (Tvardovskii, *Vasilii Tyorkin*, 81).

from him, but as parts of his own body. [...] Travkin was satisfied with himself—with himself, multiplied by seven.[16]

"Himself multiplied by seven"—a perfect description of the way individuality could be melded into the larger collective.

Travkin's group is trapped behind enemy lines, and one by one the soldiers are wounded until they all perish. But to turn this sacrifice into a victorious feat, Kazakevich highlights the dueling hand of Death, which deals a blow against the Germans:

> All these Germans—gobbling up food, bellowing, befouling the surrounding forests, all these Hilles, Mullenkamps, Gargasses, all these careerists and punishers, hangsmen and murderers—walk along the forest paths straight to their destruction, and death lowers onto all fifteen thousand of these heads her punishing hand.[17]

The punishers are punished; the division of fifteen thousand crack German SS troops are no match for the hand of Death, nor indeed for the seven-as-one Soviet unit.

In *The Star* Travkin's death, somehow, does not matter. Like Vasily Tyorkin, who faded into the masses of soldiers at war's end, and like Chapaev whose body is lost forever to the river, Travkin's fate is never mentioned, but instead must be intuited through the sad and fruitless waiting of the "hero's fiancée," the radio operator Katya. The star has "set and been extinguished."[18] Travkin does not return from the mission.

Like many Soviet war novels, this one ends with success: the mission is completed, and though the heroes may have perished, their victory lives on. This sacrifice is part of the trajectory of heroism, and it neatly avoids having to deal with the problem of what happens to heroes when they must return home to civilian life.

Kazakevich's narrative celebrates that collective spirit, that ability of a unit to join together, re-forming when one member is lost, and most importantly never questioning the leader. In that sense, Travkin's unit is a microcosm of the Soviet state itself, endlessly willing to follow its leader and endlessly able

---

[16] Kazakevich, *Zvezda*, 55.
[17] Ibid., 75.
[18] Ibid., 80.

to be replenished. Life on Earth (as the base camp is known in the novella's radio lingo) goes on, and though Travkin's unit vanishes, by the end of the narrative a new group of scouts takes its place and heads through Poland in the direction of Berlin and victory.[19]

Socialist realism wanted to have it both ways: to make the prose believable, authors should fill it with concrete details, but to make it inspiring, characters and actions needed to transform the reader, to raise him or her to the level of extraordinariness, of *podvig*. Kazakevich too tries to have it both ways, including details but also aiming at the universal, the transcendent. In presenting the struggle of the "fine warrior" as a duel, Kazakevich alters Tvardovsky's scene of the lonely warrior versus Death; Travkin is the leader of a band of scouts, pitted against a German tank division.

Kazakevich brings the narrative to a melodramatic conclusion as Katya realizes that Travkin is not responding to her repeated radio calls. Having informed his commanders of the secret concentration of the Fifth SS "Viking" Tank Division, the reconnaissance lieutenant perishes along with all of his men. "The circles around Travkin widened in waves along the surface of the earth: to Berlin itself and to Moscow itself" (78). His work has its effect, although he must sacrifice himself and all his men to attain it. Here too, requirements of socialist realist fiction affect the narrative; the hero is represented both by an individual, Travkin, and by the collective. And while death triumphs over Travkin, his heroic deed saves many.[20]

In a memoir, Kazakevich admitted that he was not particularly fond of the characters of *The Star*, in comparison to the fondness he held for some of his later characters. Nonetheless, Kazakevich believed in the concept of the positive hero. As he wrote:

> He exists—you will be able to see him. This is a complicated man, intelligent, thinking, active, suffering as all men should whenever he sees failures, defects, when he encounters pockets of old-fashioned

---

[19] For another recent interpretation of *The Star*, see Frank Ellis, *The Damned and the Dead: The Eastern Front through the Eyes of Soviet and Russian Novelists* (Lawrence: University of Kansas Press, 2011), 36–39.

[20] On this, see L. N. Luzianina, "Dukhovnyi smysl kontsepta 'zvezda' v odnoimennoi povesti E. Kazakevicha," in *Dukhovnost' kak antropologicheskaia universaliia v sovremennom literaturovedenii* (Kirov: Izdatel'stvo Viatskogo gosudarstvennogo gumanitarnogo universiteta, 2009), 96–99.

thinking but not giving up, ready to fight for communism; a lucid, fine, although perfectly ordinary man.[21]

This emphasis on the ordinary belies the wartime propaganda that existed alongside such heroes as Vasily Tyorkin and Volodya Travkin. Travkin is the "ideal hero, who 'teaches the art of victory.'"

As characters and soldiers, Travkin and Tyorkin—cheerful and willing to die without forethought, brave enough to lead the way into battle, across rivers, into woods teeming with enemy forces—must find their way between the capital-*H* Hero embodied in the eighteenth-century general Alexander Suvorov, whose heroic image Stalin evoked in his famous November 7, 1941, speech but surely would not have welcomed in the theatre of battle, and the bravado-filled peasant-hero Vasily Chapaev, while simultaneously showing themselves to be both indispensable and utterly replaceable. In the words of a poet of the time:

> We fight splendidly,
> Slash frightfully,
> Grandsons of Suvorov,
> Children of Chapaev.[22]

Descendents and comrades, indispensable and replaceable. These ironies of the socialist realist canon, and its positive heroes, complicated the idea of the military hero in wartime as well as in war fiction.

A Woman's War: Vera Panova's *The Train Companions*

But it was not only men who faced contradictions real and fictional during the Second World War. Women too were central to the war effort and found themselves in roles previously reserved for men. The films made in the early years of the war depicted the many women mobilized as nurses, soldiers, and journalists as well as those who became partisans.[23]

---

[21] Qtd. in A. Kudriashova, "Kakoi ty, chelovek," *Voprosy literatury* 7 (1965): 203.
[22] Quoted in Shtut, *Kakoi ty, Chelovek?*, 157.
[23] Denise Youngblood, "*Ivan's Childhood* and *Come and See*: Post-Stalinist Cinema and the Myth of World War II," in *World War II, Film and History*, ed. John Whiteclay Chambers II and David Culbert (New York and Oxford: Oxford University Press, 1996), 85–96, 86. In the 1980s journalist Svetlana Aleksievich explores this very question: what does a "female war" look like, as compared to the "male war" of statistics, sacrifice, and *podvig*? See Aleksievich, *U voiny ne zhenskoe litso* (Moscow: Vremia, 2007). See also Krylova, *Soviet Women in Combat*.

Kazakevich confronted this situation and presented one solution to it in the character of Katya and her unrequited crush on Travkin. Katya plays a real role in the war effort, in uniform and engaged directly in the work of reconnaissance and battle. But Kazakevich insists on her femininity, on her yearning for Travkin's love, and on her maternal impulses. Her redemption is not through the higher consciousness of the Soviet collective but through her return to the old-fashioned conventions of female behavior.

War, it turns out, can be a "plastic juncture" for women too, opening up new opportunities for danger, fulfillment, and heroism. In order to keep them from taking too much advantage of that moment, Soviet women in uniform were presented as martial and feminine at the same time.

Among the many women who experienced the war, Vera Panova stands as one of the few who published significantly about it. In her novella *The Train Companions* (*Sputniki*, sometimes translated as *The Train*), Panova portrayed political and medical workers on a hospital train equipped to treat and evacuate war-injured soldiers and civilians.

Though the novel was and remains popular, Panova's work has had a mixed reception from critics over the years. Some of the critique may stem from the fact that the novella won a Stalin Prize in 1947. Catriona Kelly, for example, lumps Panova and her fiction in with writers of socialist realist "kitsch," the term she uses to describe popular literature of the 1940s. Kelly surmises that

> these texts seemed an irritating and even disgusting irrelevance to some readers who had an idea of the realities of the Terror. But for many others they probably functioned as an uplifting or consoling vision of a Socialist utopia just round the corner, or as a wish-fulfilling fantasy of a normal, decent life without stress or hardship, a vital counterbalance to the exigencies of actuality.[24]

---

[24] Catriona Kelly, *A History of Russian Women's Writing, 1880–1992* (Oxford: Clarendon Press, 1994), 252–253. See also Edward J. Brown, *Russian Literature since the Revolution* (London: Collier-Macmillan, 1969), 243 and Ruth Kreutzer, who complains that Panova never wrote a fictional work about her husband Boris Vakhtin, who was arrested and ultimately executed during the mid-1930s (Kreutzer, "Vera Panova," in *Russian Women Writers*, ed. Christine Tomei [New York: Garland Publishing, 1999] 1019). Panova did write about the horrors of Vakhtin's arrest, imprisonment on Solovki, and second sentence in her memoirs, first published in 1989. See Vera Panova, *Moe i tol'ko moe: o moei zhizni, knigakh, i chitateliakh* (St. Petersburg: Izdatel'stvo zhurnala *Zvezda*, 2005), 144–178.

Given that Panova herself was a victim of the Terror, this characterization seems overly dismissive both of her biography and of what she was trying to do with her fiction. Other complaints seem to grow out of the uneasiness a woman writing about war caused for male readers and critics. But the 1940s and '50s in particular were a complex time period in the world of Soviet literature and publishing, and it is possible to take a different approach with more sympathy for the kinds of literature Panova was producing, especially considering Panova's negotiation of her own personal and political biography at the time.

Even before becoming a participant in the war effort, Panova lived the tension between the feminine and the martial. In the purges of 1935 and 1937, her beloved second husband, Boris Vakhtin, had been arrested and exiled to a Siberian prison camp.[25] When Panova was fired from her job at a newspaper because she had now become the wife of an "enemy of the people," she faced real economic problems. As the war loomed, Panova found herself the sole provider for four dependents: two young sons, an older daughter, and her mother.

Panova also exemplifies the complications for Soviet citizens caused by the Soviet war effort following on the heels of the Stalinist purges. Fearing arrest by agents of her own government as an "enemy of the people" herself, she was living near Leningrad in an area that was quickly occupied by the Nazi army near the beginning of the war. She survived the bombing of the area and was nearly conscripted by the Nazis into a work camp. In the midst of all this, the writer managed to make a career and write honest books and plays—no inconsiderable feat.

Indeed, she gets credit from scholar Beth Holmgren as more than just another Stalin-prize-winning novelist for her "key role in precipitating the intermittent thaw in Soviet literature, advocating and demonstrating a greater emphasis on sincerity and emotional expression in [her] work." Holmgren

---

[25] In her memoirs, Panova describes not knowing her husband's fate. "Later I was told that in 1937 all political prisoners were judged a second time and the formula of the sentence I had been given meant, essentially, execution; the camps were being purged to make room for new victims. I don't know whether this was true, but in 1958, when my Buvochka was fully rehabilitated, the paper read 'rehabilitated posthumously.' I don't know if he died from an illness, or in the torture chamber, like [the former Party worker and our acquaintance] Yakov Fal'kner, or whether he really was shot at that time" (Panova, *Moe i tol'ko moe*, 178).

praises Panova's domestication of space and characters in the war narrative *The Train Companions*, arguing that

> the main setting of a hospital train already indicates the move from "masculine" battlefield to a site of human repair and recuperation. The occupants of this gleaming state-of-the-art facility labor to make it a self-sufficient "home," taking on livestock and attaching dust ruffles to the lamps.

This effort, Holmgren argues, launched the process of "writing the female body politic," that is to say, chronicling the contributions women made to postwar Soviet society and clearing a space for women in what has otherwise always been a male sphere.[26] Among other things, women in Panova's fiction—even in *The Train Companions*, with its wartime setting—read books, go to the beauty salon and the movies, and negotiate the boundaries between personal and public life, including everything from fantasies of love and motherhood to efficient workplace behavior.

Wartime Work in Perpetual Motion

In December of 1944, Vera Panova left her Perm newspaper (called, coincidentally, *The Star*) and began her life on a military hospital train, where she was charged with the task of writing about the train for a Sanitary Bureau brochure. The experience of train travel in wartime sharpened the experience of war itself. Both aspects of war—waiting around endlessly and being thrown into frenetic activity—are present in this experience and traumatize the passenger just as they do the soldier in the trenches: the long, unnerving waiting and preparing for action and the sudden, overwhelming, and all-consuming activity of dealing with wounded and dying soldiers and civilians. On the one hand, a journey, living and travelling in the train along railroad tracks that had been laid many decades before. On the other hand, the opposite of a journey. As Panova recalled some years later:

> Here the route can change at any moment, and no one knows how many months and years your trip will last (about days it's not worth

---

[26] Beth Holmgren, "Writing the Female Body Politic (1945–1985)," in *A History of Women's Writing in Russia*, ed. Adele Marie Barker and Jehanne M. Gheith (Cambridge: Cambridge University Press, 2002), 226, 231. See also Krylova, "Soviet Women Writers and the Search for Self," in the same volume, 243–263, esp. 245–246.

> speaking); both the trip and time disappear like the soil beneath your feet.
>
> It's exhausting to rattle around thus in time and space. [...]
>
> The people with whom fate united me lived that way for more than four years: military-hospital train number 312 was formed in July 1941 and dispersed in October 1945. People who were always travelling; at the same time always fixed in one place; not belonging to themselves; losing any sense of time,—such people had to exert an immense amount of effort in order not to lose their equilibrium. They were aided by work.[27]

Panova describes the situation as a kind of work therapy; in the midst of war, blood, and personal tragedy, the work kept her companions sane.

As Panova relates the conditions in this particular hospital train (and metonymically in wartime itself) she focuses almost entirely on the collective. In fact, her fictional train functions as an ideal work collective, and none of the characters on it assume the role of heroic individual. The very cleanliness of the train was for her a metaphor:

> Such cleanliness was perfectly matched to the general spirit of train life: a spirit of decorousness. I did not hear shouting, arguing, rowdy conversations. Everyone was busy with work, filled with dignity. They interacted respectfully. My friends, how wonderful it was, noble and healing. If people would only want it, things could essentially be this way in any place of work. . . . ("Otkuda vzialas'," 336)

Sent as a journalist on assignment, Panova felt compelled to start a novel:

> I'll write down the stories I hear, I'll write it in their words—the story of the female orderly, the story of the doctor, the soldier, the nurse—and the voices of living people, their intonations, will ring out. The book will be read everywhere, and not just at the Main Sanitary Bureau." ("Otkuda vzialas'," 341)

---

[27] Vera Panova, "Otkuda vzialas' kniga *Sputniki*," in *Sputniki* (Leningrad: Sovetskii pisatel', 1967), 337, 338.

3. Eyewitnesses to Heroism: Emmanuil Kazakevich and Vera Panova

The novel would resemble an ensemble play, highlighting a number of the people whom she had interviewed. Panova's individual initiative did not go over well with the train's party organizer, but she persisted, stealing hours late at night to record her wartime experiences in something other than strict journalistic prose. Although Panova spent the war working for radio and newspapers as a journalist, her experience with the military hospital train gave her the start she needed in literature, a start almost stereotypically female, as she carved out time from her personal life to devote to her writing.

Panova continued writing the novel during 1945, mixing the voices, events, and people from Train #312 with other people and events as she created her characters. In great part the structure of the novel emerged from the research itself. As she describes it, Panova sat in a compartment in the pharmacy car and interviewed the staff of the hospital train one by one:

> My work day began at eight thirty.
>
> People came one at a time, and each told about himself, about the train, the war, his own losses and hopes.
>
> The captain sent them. Although unschooled in the subtleties of our profession, he chose the order of visits with a remarkable instinct, organizing them so that sparks flew from the combination of various tales, characters, and features, illuminating from new points of view the story that was building in my imagination. [...]
>
> They all needed a listener. They had already told each other everything long ago, but here was a fresh person, silent, attentive. I didn't interrupt, didn't counter: "And here's what happened to me," only listened. And they could talk an hour, two hours, as much as they liked.
>
> They laughed recalling funny events and cried remembering their dead. Fiancées spoke of their betrothed, husbands about their wives. Some sang me their favorite songs and romances. The Sanitary Bureau needed my pen, but these people needed my ears.[28]

Having over the course of several months travelled with the train twice to pick up the wounded and return them to the rear, she came to believe that literature was her métier: "I will be a writer because I cannot not become

---

[28] Panova, "Otkuda vzialias' kniga *Sputniki*," 339.

one; I cannot not tell the story of these people's feats. I will tell it as I see and understand it. This will be my own contribution to literature and life."[29] Her novel mirrored the "official" work she was doing, the brochure that entered the Museum of Medical Defense in Moscow—along with two of the wagons from Hospital Train #312—when the war was over.

In her fictional train, Panova describes stops and starts, social interactions, constant repairs, and enterprising moneymaking ventures undertaken by some. The train becomes a microcosm of Soviet society, up to and including village life. Part of the train is given over to piglets, which the cook feeds with table scraps, and at one point they even obtain a few dozen chickens in order to have fresh eggs (*Sputniki*, 141–142). Panova's gentle, intelligent Dr. Belov describes the train as a rolling substitute for the homes everyone had left: "The train became overgrown with *byt*, it became a residence, a home, a household" (*Sputniki*, 189). Those details of everyday life, of *byt*, transform the space of the train—devoted to its military mission—into a real place, to which readers could relate regardless of whether they spent the war at the front or in the rear. The *byt* celebrated in Panova's novel humanized the rhetoric of *est'*, the duty-bound, practical attitude of many during the Second World War.

The narrative effectively presents the bifurcated life of military personnel: waiting and preparing and even just killing time, followed by "loading time." Panova describes the difference on the level of personal energy, sounds, and even smells:

> And then noisily, with babble and groans and the knocking of crutches, the War would enter into the wagon-wards, where each wrinkle had been lovingly ironed out of the sheets. Suddenly tobacco smoke began to curl toward the ceilings in dozens of streams. The blankets got bunched up, the pillows were off-kilter. The scents of disinfectants were driven away by the smell of pus, sweat, and heavy male breath. . . .
> A trip with patients was beginning. (*Sputniki*, 142, 143)

This was the rhythm of the train: empty cars in one direction and cars filled with filthy, broken, damaged soldiers in the other direction. *Porózhny reis, gruzhyony reis.* A rhyming rhythm in iambic tetrameter. According to

---

[29] Panova, *Moe i tol'ko moe*, 275.

Panova, it is that motion and the metronome-like alternation of sounds and smells that make up life, particularly the bifurcated life lived in wartime: disinfectant battling with infections, tidy supplies upset by the disorder of the patient-passengers. Her train presents a perfect example of Joseph Brodsky's observation that the details and the tragedy go side-by-side in Soviet war prose.[30]

Individuals within the Collective: Companions on the Train

Panova avoids the rhetoric of *podvig* altogether—despite her statement that she was recording "these people's feats"—and resists any attempt to turn ordinary wartime tragedy into the stuff of heroics. For example, when Dr. Belov receives news that his wife and daughter have perished in the blockade of Leningrad, he can barely function. "He was afraid that he would forever forget how to minister to the sick, to think, to read. The world had receded from him, lost its sounds, its smells, its tangibility" (*Sputniki*, 195). This approach, an understated portrayal of suffering that remains outside the narrative, marks Panova's specific "antiheroism."

Of one eighteen-year-old soldier, Panova writes, "What feats he had achieved, he couldn't really say. He ran, he shot. He crawled, he shot. He sat, he shot. He had a vague understanding of tactics. He had understood his primary function well and he fulfilled it well, so his stories and medals attested" (*Sputniki*, 159). The simplicity of war on an individual level is reduced to this: the boy shooting whenever he could, the wife and daughter perishing in a bomb attack while the doctor, helpless and out of touch, continues to send packages and wait for letters. What other writers might have portrayed as glorious here has no particular glory. Panova neither moralizes nor wallows in the suffering of her characters; she merely relates their fates and gives them voice.

One of the women central to the story is Lena Ogorodnikova, an orphan who has made her own Soviet happiness. Lena works cheerfully through the entire war in honor of her husband, Dania. Her own clarity about her

---

[30] Joseph Brodsky has commented that "in terms of intensity of sentiment, in terms of horrendousness of detail, in terms of hopelessness of the individual's predicament in the course of that war, Russian war prose . . . stands to win hands down [. . .], stay[ing] palpably close to the immediacy of individual tragedy" ("Literature and War: A Symposium. The Soviet Union," *Times Literary Supplement* 17 May, 1985: 543–544). Poetry, Brodsky argues, does a "far more universal job" of chronicling tragedy.

family life, replacing the absent parents with the beloved husband, makes her whole and enables her to tend to patients, to clean and care for them and for the train. Only at the end of the novella is Lena's happiness snatched away from her: it turns out that Dania has found another. "The love that had given her strength, beauty, and happiness now weighed upon her shoulders like a heavy cross" (*Sputniki*, 290). Panova's narrator pities Ogorodnikova, but her fate mirrors a common outcome for a soldier's wife: the end of her marriage through infidelity. The personal "garden" she tended—as her name suggests—has been violated, but her service throughout the war to the unknown patients makes her a valued member of the collective, a loyal "train companion."

A second woman character, the surgical nurse Iuliia Dmitrievna, represents a clear contrast, tied as she is to duty and *byt*. Fully engrossed in her work, Iuliia Dmitrievna dreams of love only in the abstract. Her matter-of-fact attitude keeps the patients moving along, and there is no room for the personal. When near the end of the novella she thinks perhaps marriage awaits her with Dr. Suprugov (whose name, related to the word "spouse," belies his status as a confirmed bachelor), she is mistaken. Instead Panova gives her a child, the thirteen-year-old Vaska, who becomes her apprentice (*Sputniki*, 259–261). Here too the hospital train mirrors the outside world, with its orphaned children set adrift and seeking homes, and lonely women settling for any kind of familial arrangement they can find.

In her real wartime experiences, Panova thought of her political commissar as the "soul" of the train, and in the novel, she embodies him in the character of Danilov. Flashbacks to Danilov's childhood show that he might have featured as a war hero; he inherited a love of hard work from his father, a devout blacksmith, and learned to care for himself from his mother, who always said, teaching him to sew on buttons or wash his clothes, "It will come in handy when you're a soldier" (*Sputniki*, 206). As if to make the point of what a conventional soldier looks like, Danilov and the entire train staff go off to the movies while the train is stopped, and there they see a newsreel and a feature, both about the war:

> The hero was a young man, as good-looking as on a poster, and his girl was the same. They accomplished feats (*sovershali podvigi*) and then the girl was caught by the Fascists and died while being tortured by the butchers. Everyone understood that the fascists on the screen were not

real, but it was all so timely and imminent—the feats, the hatred for the fascists, the good girl giving her life for her country—that they all became agitated while watching the film.[31]

In the official narrative of war, there is no place for love, and in Panova's story too Danilov recalls his own first love (Faina, who will shortly die in their hospital train, unrecognized by him until after her death), but he demonstratively has put love out of his mind. Instead he married coldly, because it was the right thing to do, and loved only the son his wife produced.

He, the father, was creating the life in which his child would live freely and well. In order for the sons to live their lives along a light and smooth road, they, the fathers, were prepared to pave that road with their own bodies. That's how it was. (*Sputniki*, 226)

Danilov does not perish at the end of the novella, as so many Soviet heroes do, perhaps because he is the political officer, what before 1942 would have been called a commissar. His desire to "pave the road with his body" mirrors the idea of *podvig* in the Soviet war discourse, of sacrifice for future generations. But his role in Panova's novella as political officer rather than military hero means that he will survive.

Moving back and forth between military and civilian life, Panova creates with her train companions a model for life in the postwar era. Her hospital train features a work collective that actually functions, and her characters are no less important to the war than Kazakevich's scouts, but they don't have to perish in the end. Just as women in wartime had to negotiate the martial and the feminine, these characters domesticated the space of the train and found ways to execute their military duties while continuing to experience human emotions and human problems. This is what awaited the survivors of World War II: disabled bodies, broken families, personal betrayal, and the need to rebuild once again.

Demobilized soldiers and their civilian counterparts immediately after the war needed inspiration, but not the false inspiration that had rung out in official propaganda and in the poetry of hatred. They wanted to read about little men and women like themselves, individuals who tried to take heroic

---

[31] Panova, *Sputniki*, 203. The frequency with which watching war films forms part of the plot of war novels is fascinating and worth further exploration.

steps, and occasionally made errors, in the daily struggles of fighting for the common good and the Soviet motherland. Both Kazakevich and Panova gave them those individuals in the midst of their *byt*. But in their work, they emphasized the importance of the collective in achieving the feats of victory and the satisfaction of duty, the *podvig* and the *est'*, during World War II. Cognizant of the censorship their work would undergo, these writers strove to find the most expressive ways of chronicling the war while still getting their narratives published, of taking their personal experiences and the actions they witnessed and turning them into literature that mattered and that would reach their readers.

* * *

American writer Tim O'Brien, in trying to define what a "true war story" is, explains:

> You can tell a true war story by the questions you ask. Somebody tells a story, let's say, and afterward you ask, "Is it true?" and if the answer matters, you've got your answer.
> For example, we've all heard this one. Four guys go down a trail. A grenade sails out. One guy jumps on it and takes the blast and saves his three buddies.
> Is it true?
> The answer matters.

O'Brien's story comes straight out of Vietnam, but it certainly rings in the Soviet experience—the individual selflessly sacrificing himself for the sake of the group. Chapaev perished, and the Red Army was victorious. Tyorkin neared death repeatedly, and the Nazis were vanquished in part because of peasant-soldiers like him who kept at their wartime tasks despite the grim conditions and carnage around them. But O'Brien goes on to discuss the risks of such storytelling:

> You'd feel cheated if it never happened. Without the grounding reality, it's just a trite bit of puffery, pure Hollywood, untrue in the way all such stories are untrue. Yet even if it did happen—and maybe it did, anything's possible—even then you know it can't be true, because a true war story does not depend upon that kind of truth. Absolute

occurrence is irrelevant. A thing may happen and be a total lie; another thing may not happen and be truer than the truth. For example: Four guys go down a trail. A grenade sails out. One guy jumps on it and takes the blast, but it's a killer grenade and everybody dies anyway. Before they die, though, one of the dead guys says, "The fuck you do *that* for?" and the jumper says, "Story of my life, man," and the other guy starts to smile but he's dead. That's a true story that never happened. (*Things They Carried*, 83–84)

True stories. Myths. Readers can sometimes tell the difference. Tim O'Brien suggests that irony is at the core of a true story; heroism is less likely to be true, even if we want it to be.

Thinking about O'Brien and his war stories from Vietnam provides a useful way of thinking about the ideologically driven, detail-oriented stories of Soviet World War II heroism. After all, if soldiers, eyewitnesses, and journalists turned the details of real experiences into larger works of fiction, then we ought to remember that the traffic can go both ways. Fictional expectations can structure the way "reality" was perceived and reported.

One such case, the famous story of the twenty-eight Panfilov heroes who perished in a fight with fifty-four German tanks on November 16, 1941, was proven to be utterly fabricated. The investigation is detailed in a secret document dating to 1948. Hints of the results surfaced in 1966, but they were quickly suppressed, and the story finally began to emerge during perestroika, with the full 1948 document published in *Novyi Mir* in 1997.[32] This story—the mythic tale of the heroes, the ways in which the Soviet state and society embraced their heroic feats, and the narrative of how the tale was constructed, how it was discovered, covered up, and rediscovered—can teach us much about war journalism, patriotism, state control, and the relationship between truth and myth, and it is worth relating the story here.

In November of 1941—a time of particularly bad tidings for the Soviet Red Army—a regiment of the Panfilov Division faced an overwhelming attack from German tanks. A correspondent of the Red Army newspaper *Krasnaya Zvezda*, Koroteev, published a small article on November 27 about the battle, taking his information from a commissar of the division who had

---

[32] See N. Petrov and O. Edel'man, "Novoe o sovetskikh geroiakh," *Novyi mir* 6 (1997): 140–151.

himself not participated in the battle, but who wanted the correspondent to know about the "extremely difficult situation at the front."[33]

These are the facts. But what happened from there was pure invention. The editor of *Krasnaya Zvezda* was Major General Ortenberg—the same editor who serialized Vasily Grossman's *The Immortal People* from July 14 to August 12, 1942[34]—and he argued in 1948 that

> the question of Soviet warriors' steadfastness was particularly important at that time. The slogan "Death or Victory," especially in struggles with enemy tanks, was a decisive one. The feats (*podvigi*) of the Panfilov [soldiers] were a model of precisely that kind of steadfastness. I proposed to Krivitsky that he write a lead article about the heroism of the Panfilov [soldiers], and we published it in the newspaper on November 28, 1941.[35]

Thus eight months before Stalin's famous "Not One Step Backward" speech of July 28, 1942, newspaper editors and correspondents were already working to create a culture of *podvig*, a culture of self-sacrificing heroism, through manipulating stories of the front. Ortenburg and others like him saw this as their patriotic duty, their contribution to the war effort; instead of shooting the enemy or mining fields at the front, they used their literary positions to help fight the war against the Germans.

This "invention," as Lieutenant General N. Afanasiev, the head military procurator of the USSR Military Forces, styled the myth of the twenty-eight Panfilov soldiers in his May 10, 1948, report, succeeded in great part for the same reason that the fictional texts we looked at above succeeded: the details made the story. If the story was entirely made up (and it was, by numerous sources in a kind of collective process on its way to becoming a foundational myth of Soviet heroism), why twenty-eight soldiers? Does the answer matter?

It turns out that when asked how many people are usually in a regiment, the original war correspondent replied, "Thirty to forty, but the unit was not at full strength." Thus the number chosen was thirty, but the original story—from the commissar—included two soldiers who surrendered, hands up, to

---

[33] From the evidence by Koroteev, in "Novoe o sovetskikh geroiakh," 147.
[34] See Grossman, *A Writer at War*, 114.
[35] From the evidence by Ortenburg, in "Novoe o sovetskikh geroiakh," 148.

the Germans. Thus 30 - 2 = 28. Then Ortenberg nixed the two traitors, arguing that one was plenty,[36] but he didn't nix the math. 40 - 10 = 30 - 2 = 28. But really twenty-nine.

Another key detail of Krivitsky's second newspaper story was the words of political instructor Klochkov: "Russia is great, and there's nowhere to retreat—Moscow is behind us," a phrase that could under no circumstances have been legitimately "reported speech" (after all, the *Panfilovtsy* died). Krivitsky testified, "I made it up myself."[37] This slogan (great in the telling, unlikely in the trenches) was repeated again and again in story, song, and film in staging the Panfilov tale. But Krivitsky willingly gave evidence to say that "as far as the sensations and actions of the 28 heroes—that was my literary invention."[38] In his article, Krivitsky named names and reported details, and that too contributed to the "real" quality of the reportage:

> Let the army and the country finally know their proud names. In the trench were: Klochkov Vasily Georgievich, Dobrobabin Ivan Evstafevich, Shepetkov Ivan Alekseevich, Kriuchkov Abram Ivanovich, Mitin Gavriil Stepanovich. . . .[39]

And so on.[40]

Soldiers with brave retorts and real names and patronymics. Details and dialogue. These elements helped create a myth that lived on through perestroika and was finally uncovered for the broad public in the late 1990s. Was it a true story, according to O'Brien's criteria? For certain segments of the population, those myths continue to be as dear as ever, their need to believe in the "truth" of Stalin-era Russia and the success of the ideological condi-

---

[36] "Ortenburg said that it's impossible to write about two traitors, and, apparently having conferred with someone, decided to write about only one traitor in the lead article" (From the evidence by Koroteev, "Novoe o sovetskikh geroiakh," 147).
[37] From the evidence by Krivitsky, "Novoe o sovetskikh geroiakh," 147.
[38] Ibid., 147–148.
[39] Ibid., 144–145.
[40] It became awkward when one of those honored posthumously with the title "Hero of the Soviet Union" returned from German captivity . . . but in true Soviet style that offending physical body—a physical body that contradicted a dearly held myth—was quickly swept off to the camps until the mid-'50s. He was later refused rehabilitation and the rights to his title when he emerged from prison, and was even accused in 1990 (now truly posthumously) of trying to horn in on "others' fame" ["*Chuzhaia slava*"] in calling himself (a Red Army soldier who had actually worn a German uniform, after all) a *Panfilovets*. Ibid., 150.

tioning they underwent during that time superseding their own instincts as readers.[41] Indeed, Lebedev's 2002 film remake of *The Star* reifies just this myth of the brave, self-sacrificing Red Army man, exemplifying what Mark Lipovetsky has called "the Soviet myth of war [as] adopted by the post-Soviet rhetoric of national identity."[42] It seems that new generations are buying the Soviet ideological myth of the sacrificial warrior. But for O'Brien, the moral that is required of all Soviet narratives would definitely ring false. As we investigate issues of "truth" and "invention," truth and myth, their genesis and their role in the Soviet understanding of World War II, it is worth keeping O'Brien's categories and the *Panfilovtsy* themselves in mind. The "realism" portion of socialist realism required details, and wartime is full of details, ready to be noticed and narrativized by writers and journalists. Twenty-eight men sacrificing themselves felt real, but perhaps not as real as Panova's piglets on a train.

---

[41] Nina Wieda writes about this as "secular kenosis" and sees the sacrifice of Russian/Soviet military men as mirroring the Christian paradigm of sacrifice. See her unpublished paper "Secular Kenosis in Boris Vasil'ev's *And Dawns Are Quiet Here*," ASEEES 2010, Los Angeles, CA.

[42] Mark Lipovetsky, "War as the Family Value: Failing Fathers and Monstrous Sons in *My Stepbrother Frankenstein*," in *Cinepaternity: Fathers and Sons in Soviet and Post-Soviet Film*, ed. Helena Goscilo and Yana Hashamova (Bloomington: Indiana University Press, 2010), 114–137, 133. Lebedev's remake tells us much more about the Putin era and its love of militaristic patriotism than about World War II.

Chapter Four
Retreat: Viktor Nekrasov and the Truth of the Trenches

> Out of his *Trenches*, as out from under Gogol's "Overcoat," all our honest war prose emerged.
>
> Из его "Окопов", как из "Шинели" Гоголя, вышла вся наша честная военная проза.
>
> -Alexander Parnas[1]
>
> They do it all calmly, with breaks for smoking and joke telling.
>
> И все это спокойно, с перекурами, шуточками.
>
> -Nekrasov, *In the Trenches of Stalingrad*

"The order to retreat comes as a complete surprise."

Thus begins Viktor Nekrasov's 1946 novel *In the Trenches of Stalingrad* (*V okopakh Stalingrada*).[2] That opening line signalled that *In the Trenches of Stalingrad* would not follow the usual formula of Soviet war novels. It starts in the middle of the action, and with the most shameful aspect of war: retreat, in this case a retreat that occurred in 1942 during the bitterly fought Battle of Stalingrad.

For our purposes, Nekrasov's novel stands as a pivot between the formulaics of socialist realism and a different way of writing about the experience of war. It introduces a new tone, leaning toward the irony of *Vasily Tyorkin* and away from the over-earnestness that characterized the official method and that we saw in the heightened metaphors of Kazakevich's *The Star*. Like Panova's *The Train Companions*, it revels in the minutiae of daily life, drawing a contrast with the didacticism imposed by commissars and party ap-

---

[1] Alexander Parnas, *Tot samyi Nekrasov*, excerpted in *Kreshchatik* 27 (Autumn 2005).

[2] According to Nekrasov, the retreat was the portion of the novel about which he was hassled most. On the internal review at *Znamia* someone wrote the words: "The first pages of the story are not particularly interesting," this despite the fact that they were the first written passage in any genre to discuss the retreat. In the end, the editor, Vishnevsky, left this scene intact. See "Kommentarii tretii," in Viktor Nekrasov, *Na voine i posle* (Ekaterinburg: U-faktoriia, 2005), 520.

paratchiks. But with Nekrasov, the reader is in the very trenches, living and experiencing the war along with Soviet soldiers.

In the Trenches of Stalingrad challenges easy notions about the difference between honesty and truth and about the connection between the presentation of facts and the larger meaning of those facts. In these ways, Nekrasov's novel helped create a narrative space about World War II that would later be occupied by writers like Viktor Astafiev, who, in the words of one of Nekrasov's contemporaries, "came out of his *Trenches*."

No wonder Soviet officials didn't quite know what to do with it.

The Strange Career of Nekrasov's *In the Trenches of Stalingrad*

Nekrasov's novel seemed to answer directly the November 1945 call issued to the Central Committee of the Communist Party by F. I. Panferov, senior editor of the journal *October*:

> If a writer were to write of the Fatherland War and dismiss the retreat of the Red Army [to Stalingrad], beginning only with the victorious counterattack, he could not exhibit all the heroism of our country. We do not need a saccharine, comforting literature. We are a nation of great and beautiful truths and are accustomed to looking everything straight in the eye. . . .[3]

Alexander Tvardovsky agreed when he wrote his reader's report of Nekrasov's *Stalingrad* for the original journal publication in November 1946:

> The first obvious merit of this book is that, deprived of external plot and story enticements, it forces one to read it in one sitting. The palpable authenticity of this testimony about the difficult and majestic days of struggle on the eve of the "great turning point," the simplicity and intelligibility of the narrative, the extremely valuable details of trench life and so on—all these qualities herald unquestionable success with readers. About its essential content the following can be said. This is a truthful story about a great victory that arose from thousands of small, imperceptible gains in battle experience and from the moral and political superiority of our warriors long before the victory resounded

---

[3] Qtd. in Elena Zubkova, *Russia after the War: Hopes, Illusions and Disappointments, 1945–1957*, trans. and ed. Hugh Ragsdale (Armonk, NY: M.E. Sharpe, 1988), 95.

across the entire world. This story is also valuable from a literary point of view, original and artistically convincing . . .[4]

It is worth pausing over that review to notice what Tvardovsky has highlighted. "Authentic." "Simple." "Truthful." It would be hard to deny those things. Nekrasov had been there at Stalingrad—he had seen it himself.

Yet those same qualities that Tvardovsky admired seemed to the Writers' Union and official critics to be dangerous, particularly the issue of "truthfulness." Later attacks on Nekrasov accused him of such crimes as "[reveling in] the truth of the trenches," "deheroicization," "slandering," "abstract humanism," and "Remarquism."[5] His work clearly did not follow the official method. As Nekrasov was to recall, in the novel "there wasn't a word about the Party, and only three lines about Stalin."[6] Indeed, Nekrasov claims that at the time he wrote his novel, he did not even know what socialist realism was.[7]

To make matters worse, Nekrasov's own biography cast suspicion on him. Born in 1911, Nekrasov spent several years as a child in Paris with his mother, a doctor. When the family returned to the Soviet Union, Nekrasov grew up in and around Kiev. Of his childhood, Nekrasov recalled "preferring Tarzan's adventures to the Russian classics." This literary preference, ordinary for a boy if not exemplary for a future member of the Soviet intelligentsia, indicates an adventuresome spirit which would serve the young man well when he found himself in the army. But with a mother like that and foreign

---

[4] Internal review, 8 November 1946, published in *Voprosy literatury* 10 (1988): 216.
[5] L. I. Lazarev, "Nekrasov, Viktor Platonovich," in *Russkie pisateli 20 veka. Biograficheskii slovar'*, ed. P.A. Nikolaev (Moscow: Randevu-AM, 2000), 493. For more on Remarquism, see Georgii Markov, *Literaturnaia gazeta* 23 December 1962, 1–2, and 26 December, 1962, 1–3, and Iurii Idashkin, "A esli podumat'," *Oktiabr'* 9 (1962): 212–213. See also Ellis, *Vasiliy Grossman: The Genesis and Evolution of a Russian Heretic*, 36–37, his "The Problem of Remarquism in Soviet Russian War Prose," *Scottish Slavonic Review* 11 (1988): 91–108, and Rosalind J. Marsh, *Soviet Fiction since Stalin: Science, Politics, Literature* (Totowa, NJ: Barnes and Noble Books, 1986), 197–198. Ellis identifies Remarquism as one of his five categories for exploring war literature in his *The Damned and the Dead: The Eastern Front through the Eyes of Soviet and Russian Novelists*.
[6] Nekrasov, *V okopakh Stalingrada* (St. Petersburg: Azbuka-Klassika, 2005), 441.
[7] "V okopakh Stalingrada," radio speech, 12 October 1985. "This man now knows perfectly well what Socialist realism is. Perhaps that's the very reason he left his native Kiev. Just as Aksyonov, Voinovich, Vladimov, Gladilin, Maksimov, Brodsky, Dovlatov—I may have missed someone—left their Moscow or Leningrad. And now they write whatever they like and there is no censorship hanging over them . . ." Published in Nekrasov, *Na voine i posle*, 516.

tastes to boot, Nekrasov made an unlikely orthodox Soviet patriot. An easy decision, then, when Alexander Fadeev, head of the Writers' Union at the time, crossed the novel off that year's Stalin Prize list before passing the list to Stalin for final approval.

Stalin put the novel back on the list. In his address to the Soviet people at the end of the war, Stalin had given the people, not the party, credit for winning the war: "The address contained not a word of the party and its role in the organization of victory. Stalin simply excluded this intermediary link between himself and the people."[8] *Znamia* editor Vsevolod Vishnevsky told Nekrasov that "Stalin himself personally gave the author this most prestigious literary prize."

In awarding the prize, Stalin circumvented the party and bureaucratic apparatus, celebrating Nekrasov, whose novel had also left the party out of the victory, perhaps precisely rewarding the author-veteran for his "in the trenches" emphasis on the people. Historians have called Stalin's move an "inexplicable caprice" that saved Nekrasov's work from the denunciation planned for it by the Writers' Union. An ironic episode of de-Stalinization by Stalin himself.

It is hardly worth speculating about why Stalin decided to do what he did. It may be that Nekrasov was simply the right man in the right place at the right time and it was convenient to forget his family connections.

> Here he was—a junior officer, a battle participant, Russian, twice wounded, with an imposing physical appearance that matched the 1940s aesthetic, a Party member (he joined during the heat of the Stalingrad battle on Mamaev Kurgan)—in the euphoria of victory all of this facilitated the novella's publication.[9]

It may very well have been part of Stalin's specific plan to decimate the literary hierarchy and start again with young authors. Nekrasov certainly

---

[8] Georgii Baklanov, "Vozvrashchenie," *V okopakh Stalingrada* (Moscow: Khudozhestvennaia literatura, 1990), 29.

[9] Lazarev, "Nekrasov," 492–93. After the war, Nekrasov himself was not particularly patient, especially when it came to bureaucracy and protocol. Wanting to continue his education at the construction institute, Nekrasov brought several pastels he had made of the bombing of the "Red October" factory during the siege of Stalingrad to the examination committee, hoping to impress them. When they suggested that he gain some experience by working as a draftsman for a while, he relates, "I didn't bother to wait. I got drunk and became a journalist." See "Stalingrad, October 1942," in Viktor Nekrasov, *Na voine i posle*, 535.

remained puzzled by the prize and later imagined what might have gone on in Stalin's head: "They are all rogues. All! Every one. With that drunk Fadeev at the head of the whole bunch. . . . Things are bad with the writers, bad. I arrested all the good ones, and the new ones are not keeping up. . . ."[10] One way or the other, the prize helped rocket the novel to great success. *In the Trenches* saw more than 130 reprintings between 1947 and 1974.

At which point the novel was unceremoniously banned, and its author, expelled from the Communist Party, emigrated to France. His biography, and his outspoken nature, became too uncomfortable for the Soviet government and the Communist Party. Only when the Communist regime was coming to an end could he be praised again in Russia. And when a new edition of *In the Trenches of Stalingrad* came out in 1990, Grigorii Baklanov lamented in the introduction the generations who had missed out on the novel. "All those years it was as though the novel did not exist, but it did exist and it remains the pride of our literature."[11] Nekrasov could not share in this renewed pride; the author had passed away in Paris in 1987.

During World War II, Nekrasov was a sapper, part of a crew working with land mines at the Battle of Stalingrad. His novel about the battle was published by Vishnevsky in his journal *Znamia* in 1946 under the title *Stalingrad*.[12] An unsparing portrayal of the horrors of war and the complicated relationships among soldiers during wartime, the narrative was based on the author's own experiences of war, the experiences of an eyewitness and a participant. But Nekrasov transformed those experiences, brought them to life for his readers. His incredible eye for detail and use of the "in the trenches" point of view changed the genre of war fiction for Russian literature.

There was something different in *In the Trenches*, something that Nekrasov's contemporary readers felt instinctively. Readers frequently praise the

---

[10] See V. A. Potresov, "Vozvrashchenie Nekrasova," in Viktor Nekrasov, *Zapiski zevaki* (Moscow: Zakharov, 2003), 17–18 and Nekrasov, *Saperlipopet. Esli b da kaby, da vo rtu rosli griby* (London: Overseas Publications, 1983).

[11] Baklanov, "Vozvrashchenie," 6. The Posev edition includes a note from the publisher about the original novella, which had become a "bibliographic rarity" due to being blacklisted in the Soviet Union. See Viktor Nekrasov, *Stalingrad* (Posev: Frankfurt-am-Main, 1981), 6.

[12] As Nekrasov liked to point out in later years, Vishnevsky "was a living classic, one of the most influential leaders of the Writers' Union, a person experienced in all things, who knows what is what, what is possible and what is forbidden" (Nekrasov, *Stalingrad*, 1981, qtd. 441).

book as one of the most "truthful" narratives about the experience of World War II. Among others, Lev Kopelev regarded *In the Trenches of Stalingrad* as his first and favorite book about the war, a book that told the "truth about the war that we cannot and do not want to forget, the bitter taste of which is still alive in us today."[13]

Intonation was the key to most readers' reactions. Fellow exile Efim Etkind described Nekrasov's intonation as "living, natural, like breathing." Told mostly from the point of view of its main character, Lieutenant Kerzhentsev, *In the Trenches of Stalingrad* avoids all loftiness, all pomp and pathos, relying instead on straight talk, frank descriptions, small details. In their 1946 novellas, both Panova and Kazakevich—also eyewitnesses to war—summed up, made larger judgments about the meaning of the events they experienced, even in Kazakevich's case resorted to dramatic allegory, but Nekrasov refrained from any generalizations. In memoirs addressed to Nekrasov, Etkind recalled:

> In an era of loud voices, journalistic eloquence and noisily shouted slogans you began to speak slightly ironically and with a deliberate masculine roughness from which tenderness peeked out. [. . .] You wrote about what is often called a soldier's heroism as if it were the daily behavior of regular guys. Your gentle mocking restraint conquered everyone—then, in 1946, with your *Stalingrad* you inaugurated a new era in literature: the sound of the truth that is born on the edge of life. [. . . T]he truth of masculine solidarity, of daily life in the trenches, and of soldiers' friendship was heard in the intonations of your book.[14]

The fact that Nekrasov drew from his own experiences certainly contributed to a sense of authenticity in the novel and to the "truthfulness" that readers found when they read it. The book neither hid nor apologized.[15]

---

[13] Lev Kopelev, "Pervoe znakomstvo," in "Iz knigi druzei—Viktoru Nekrasovu. Vospominaniia o pisatele," in *Vremia i my* 98, ed. Efim Etkind (New York, Jerusalem, Paris: *Vremia i my*, 1987), 224.

[14] Efim G. Etkind, "Intonatsiia," in "Iz knigi druzei," 214–215. Other critics grouped a number of books together as a "new wave of literature about war," including Grossman's Stalingrad sketches, Kazakevich's *Star*, Panova's *The Train Companions*, and Tvardovsky's *Vasily Tyorkin*. See I. Vinogradov, "Chelovek i voina," in Viktor Nekrasov and Iurii Bondarev, *V okopakh Stalingrada* and *Poslednie zalpy* (Moscow: Izvestiia, 1968), 470–95; 470.

[15] Eisenstein referred to the novella as the "diary of an officer." The style was frequently called "diary-like": "with short phrases, present tense, the author telling only about what he sees, with no literary 'fanciness.'" See Potresov, "Vozvrashchenie Nekrasova," 15.

4. Retreat: Viktor Nekrasov and the Truth of the Trenches

Investing War with Meaning

The plot of *In the Trenches of Stalingrad* does not follow a conventional arc but rather reads like a set of adventures as the protagonist Lieutenant Yury Kerzhentsev moves from one battalion to another across the front near Stalingrad. Important individual events include retreats, a taste of civilian life, attacks, waiting periods, and even disagreements about tactics that lead to a court-martial. Throughout it all, Kerzhentsev tries to find a balance between following orders and doing what makes sense.

Kerzhentsev acts as the first-person narrator; the events of the novel are filtered through his consciousness. In the service, Kerzhentsev is an engineer, though like his creator, Nekrasov, he had studied to be an architect in his native Kiev. Over the course of the novel, Kerzhentsev and his fellow soldiers retreat in a sloppy line toward Stalingrad, spend some amount of time in that peaceful city, watch its partial evacuation, and dig in to defend it. The novel ends with a discussion of Adolf Hitler's Stalingrad speech and the soldiers' musings on why the battle turned out as it did, with the Germans smashed and in retreat and the Russians battered but victorious.[16]

As the narrative begins, Kerzhentsev heads to Stalingrad after a disorganized retreat from a failed defensive position near Voronezh. He hopes to meet up with his battalion there. In Stalingrad, he and his buddy Igor Svidersky experience civilian life: taking tea, walking through the city, visiting the public library. Soon, though, the Germans attack, and Kerzhentsev is assigned to a group that occupies the tractor factory, preparing to blow it up if necessary. These days in the factory illustrate the experience of waiting in wartime, and a certain routine, calm, and even boredom set in.

That routine is interrupted as Kerzhentsev is moved to active positions near the Volga River, where he constructs his entrenchments and works with a small battalion, taking over when the commander is killed. He and his group storm the Mamaev Kurgan hill, but he is relieved of his command when a new man is appointed. Their position is a dangerous one, as they are surrounded, and eventually they are able to escape with serious losses. Other battles ensue. When the head of the division, Captain Abrosimov, insists that they launch a direct attack, Kerzhentsev goes into battle with his fellow soldiers. Half their battalion is lost, including Kerzhentsev's comrade Nikolai Karnaukhov, and in the aftermath Abrosimov is court-martialed and sent to a penal battalion.

---

[16] Nekrasov had planned a third part, but the book was rushed into publication without it. He added part III in 1971. Only the originally published two parts are under discussion in this chapter.

Hoping to maintain a semblance of real life, Kerzhentsev and his comrades try to mark his birthday on November 19, but those celebrations keep being put off by urgent military actions, until finally the lieutenant is wounded and ends up in a medical battalion. The novel ends with him returning to Stalingrad to discover that Igor, from whom he had become separated, is still alive, but before they can be reunited, another attack begins.

The novel is more than the sum of its events. As Vladimir Zubkov has written:

> The author of *In the Trenches of Stalingrad* addressed [. . .] the problems which would in future constantly feed war prose: the traces of prewar life in the consciousness of the frontline soldier, the internal freedom and conscience of the fighting man in the face of the commander who has been deprived of moral reins by the authorities, the indissoluble nature of the individual person and its trace in the general victory.[17]

It was this inner truth, this portrayal of the fighting man as an individual with a past and a part to play in the future, with feelings and desires and reactions to things that were happening around him, that made his novel popular among contemporaries, particularly those who had fought themselves. Nekrasov dismissed praise and accolades that he had written the "best novel about the war." In conversation with Lev Kopelev, for example, Nekrasov insisted:

> "I know, I know, I've heard that before. Were you at the front? . . . Then how the hell, comrade Major, can you say that mine was the 'best novel about the war'? You must know that it only contains part of the truth."
> "Maybe only part, but not a word of nonsense . . ."
> "Perhaps. . . . But partial truth is also nonsense."[18]

This is more than just semantic games, trying to parse the difference between truth, partial truth, and nonsense. This exchange between Nekrasov and Kopelev takes us directly back to the fundamental problems of how to turn war into narrative, which we discussed in the introduction to this book.

Call it a problem of altitude. Wars must be given meaning in order that they can be justified. To create that meaning requires a writer to see the total-

---

[17] See "Ozhidanie? Proshchanie? Segodnia i zavtra khudozhestvennoi prozy o Velikoi otechestvennoi voine," *Ural* 5 (2010).
[18] Kopelev, "Pervoe znakomstvo," 221.

ity of the conflict, the grand purpose, to see it, as it were, from high above. For soldiers on the ground, it is virtually impossible to see that totality and thus to construct larger meaning from their own very limited experience. Nekrasov understood this full well: "In war," Nekrasov's hero tells the reader, "you never know anything except what's going on under your very nose" (*V okopakh Stalingrada*, 16).

That dilemma has been true for all writers trying to narrate all wars, starting with Homer. Nekrasov, however, stands as one of the first Soviet writers to confront it and the first to tell the story of war from underneath his nose. His book is as powerful as it is because he does not try to see the war from the heights, from an altitude that would give the events greater meaning. Instead, he stays in the trenches, and he demonstrates that meaning happens precisely in the trenches, in daily conversations and relationships between individuals.

Duty and Daily Life

The "truth of the trenches," as Nekrasov created it, represents a shift from the truth we saw in Tvardovsky's *Vasily Tyorkin*. *Tyorkin* was part of the visual as well as verbal vocabulary of the war, helping with his cheerful smile and energetic approach to battle to further the propaganda efforts of wartime writers and artists. Through posters and images, as well as in the newspaper publications of Tvardovsky's chapters, Tyorkin and other epic characters put poetry and pictures to work for the state.[19]

But that wartime balance, in which the details of *byt* in *Tyorkin* were augmented by heroism, by the rhetoric of *podvig*, changed after the war. As a witness and participant, Nekrasov was writing for a different audience, no longer for the warrior who needed to keep his spirit up, but for veterans and civilians like himself who were processing the events and effects of the devastating four-year war. In Nekrasov's prose, the rhetoric of *podvig* was replaced by the rhetoric of *est'*, describing how soldiers did their duty in the mud and blood of wartime whether they wanted to or not.[20]

---

[19] For more on this, see Bird, "The Functions of Poetry."
[20] Ellis calls this "heroic pragmatism." Zubkova comments that "soldiers' letters and diaries often represent the experience of the front not in the usual halo of heroism but simply as an ordinary, stressful kind of life, the most terrible part of which was death. As people gradually grew accustomed to this new life, it was not the new but the old prewar life that seemed strange and unimaginable" (Zubkova, *Russia after the War*, 15).

His focus on the quotidian, the everyday, made that duty feel like a real process, a set of decisions and compromises that matched the actual soldier's experience; and with the ironic tone of his first-person narration, Nekrasov reflected many soldiers' ambiguous feelings about what they had done. Irony gave them back their individual right to have an opinion about their own actions, those of their comrades, and those of their commanders. Irony allowed them to feel like human beings, not just automatons performing feats.

The defensive nature of most of the military action in the novel means that Kerzhentsev and his fellow soldiers spend more time smoking, chatting, digging, and planning than they do attacking or actually fighting. Indeed, as the narrator complains:

> The most terrible thing about war is not the shells, not the bombs, one can get used to all that; the most terrible thing is the inactivity, the uncertainty, the lack of an immediate goal. (*V okopakh Stalingrada*, 60)

The novel offers evidence of this observation about wartime, that most of it is spent without purpose or direction. We can compare this feeling with the *porozhny reis* described by Vera Panova, which we explored in the previous chapter; after all, her "empty trips" in the hospital train were also a break, a time of inactivity. But perhaps because the empty trips rhymed with trips full of activity, *gruzhyony reis*, and because during those times the train was in motion back toward the front, for Panova's characters those empty trips did have a purpose and direction. For Nekrasov's Kerzhentsev, especially at the beginning of the Stalingrad campaign, the waiting and not knowing seems more terrible than death.

The pace of the story allows Nekrasov to share with us the musing and philosophizing that goes on during these interminable periods of "uncertainty" and provides us with plenty of details of everyday life in the trenches and even in the city. Nekrasov's language is also the language of *byt*, of everyday life, with informal vocabulary and diction to match the informal interactions between soldiers. With the action being described in the present tense, the reader experiences the frustration, fear, boredom, and panic along with the characters. In his fiction, Nekrasov narrates the war from the inside, offering the reader the feeling of being at the front, experiencing the same priorities and emotions that soldiers experienced.

4. Retreat: Viktor Nekrasov and the Truth of the Trenches

As a narrator and main character, Kerzhentsev is highly observant, with many of his characterizations arresting in their degree of perception. Sudden, unexplained changes in military strategy abound, and in the narration they can seem as random and disconnected for the reader as for the characters. Indeed, it is telling that the novel opens with the "order to retreat." In chapter 2, the narrative catches up with this surprise order:

> Life was flowing calmly and evenly. Even "Pravda" had begun to reach us from Moscow. There were no losses.
> And suddenly like snow on our heads—an order. . . .
> You never know anything in war except what is happening under your very nose.
> When the Germans aren't shooting at you—it seems to you that over all the world peace and silence reign; when they begin to bomb—you are immediately certain that the whole front from the Baltic to the Black Sea has begun to move. (*V okopakh Stalingrada*, 16)

Such musings are paired in the novel with small events, events that move the reader in and of themselves and also stand for something more. For example, when a few shells do reach the soldiers during this first retreat:

> A shard wounds the orange cat who has been living with her kittens in our basement. The first-aid officer binds her wound. She meows, looks at all of us with fearful eyes, and climbs into the box with her kittens. They squeak, crawl on top of each other, and butt at the bandage with their little faces, but they cannot find her nipples. (*V okopakh Stalingrada*, 18)

The little family of cats serves as an understated metaphor for the mutual dependency of soldiers at the front.

This theme of mutual dependency, the need for other human beings to share experiences and to help motivate action in wartime, is brought out more overtly through the introduction of an officer named Maksimov, who impresses Kerzhentsev early in the novel. When he asks the soldiers whether or not they are married and receives a negative reply, Maksimov responds, "Too bad. I'm not married either, and now I regret it. A wife is essential. As necessary as air. Especially now. . . ." (*V okopakh Stalingrada*, 14). During the retreat, the unit is surrounded by German troops, and most of them perish, including Maksimov.

Vasily Grossman wrote a journalistic account of the same retreat:

> Those were hard and dreadful days. . . . The armies were retreating. Men's faces were gloomy. Dust covered their clothes and weapons, dust fell on the barrels of guns, on the canvas covering the boxes full of headquarters documents, on the black shiny covers of staff typewriters, and on the suitcases, sacks and rifles piled chaotically on the carts. The dry, grey dust got into people's nostrils and throats. It made one's lips dry and cracked.
>
> That was a terrible dust, the dust of retreat. It ate up the men's faith, it extinguished the warmth of people's hearts, it stood in a murky cloud in front of the eyes of gun crews. (*A Writer at War*, 130–131)

Grossman's dust evokes the hopelessness of this period of the war. He creates useful and highly descriptive generalizations. But Nekrasov does the same thing, without the summing up, with his cats and his lonely officers who wish they had married in time.

Explicit comparisons of the soldier's life and civilian life emerge in chapter 3, which is filled with recollections. By the "shimmering light of the rockets," Kerzhentsev falls into reminiscences of his street, the chestnut trees of Kiev, and the large soft sofa in his childhood home.

> After dinner grandmother always rested [on that couch]. I would cover her with an old overcoat, which served only this purpose, and give her a book of memoirs or *Anna Karenina*. Then I would look for her glasses. They would turn out to be in the buffet, in the spoon drawer. By the time I found them, grandmother would already be sleeping. And the old cat Fracas with his singed whiskers would squint from under the flaking collar [of the coat]. . . . My God, how long ago that was! . . . Or perhaps it never happened, but it only seems like it did. . . . (*V okopakh Stalingrada*, 19)

The young soldier recalls his mother, his "dear, beloved Kiev," his group of six inseparable friends. Ten months have passed since his last postcard from his mother, the same ten months since Kiev fell to the Germans. While he is performing his duties, mining the territory the army has left, Kerzhentsev gives himself over to these recollections, even mentally walking along the peacetime streets of his town, one at a time, remembering landmarks and events connected with them. He muses on what has happened to his friends from the institute:

> Chizhik perished near Kiev, at Goloseev. [. . .] both of his legs were torn off. I don't know anything concrete about the rest. I think Vergun was captured. Rudensky was not mobilized—he's near-sighted—and I think he was evacuated. He saw me off at the station when I left. I heard from someone, I don't remember who, that Anatoly became a communications officer. And Lyusya? . . . Perhaps she was evacuated? Doubtful. . . . She has an old, sick mother. (*V okopakh Stalingrada*, 22–23)

Now, in wartime, Kerzhentsev has to form a new collective from the soldiers with whom he lives and fights. He even finds a new Lyusya in Stalingrad, though when the opportunity arises he refuses to kiss her, remaining loyal to his old friend instead. Thus, what Catherine Merridale has called "the spirit that emerged at Stalingrad" is in the novel precisely a military brotherhood, a collective based on shared experience.

But at the same time, Nekrasov makes clear in the narrative that Kerzhentsev's relationships with friends and comrades in the army—and his movements within the physical landscape in and around Stalingrad—are built on personal relationships and spatial memories from his pre-war life. The juxtaposition of the two chronotopes, wartime life in the trenches and peacetime in Kiev, strengthens both. Merridale has argued that "the party took the credit" for this Stalingrad spirit, but in Nekrasov's narrative his hero's actions and thoughts during wartime did not differ greatly from those of his pre-war self.[21]

One of the strongest relationships Kerzhentsev forms is with his eighteen-year-old orderly, Valega.[22] Described in diminutives (a remarkable little guy, small, and round-headed [*zamechatel'nyi parenek, malen'kii, kruglogolovyi*]), Valega is a loyal servant, child, and wife to Kerzhentsev.

---

[21] "The brotherhood and selflessness to which the [Stalingrad] battlefield gave birth were rapidly adopted as the offspring of its ideology, its wise guidance. 'Thousands of patriots are proving themselves to be models of fearlessness, courage, and selfless dedication to the motherland,' the soldiers' front-line paper crowed" (Catherine Merridale, *Ivan's War: Life and Death in the Red Army, 1939–1945* [New York: Metropolitan Books: 2006], 179). In contrast, *In the Trenches* portrays an entirely different source for the soldiers' bravery and comradeship.

[22] This relationship was highlighted in the 1956 film made from the novel, *Soldiers* (*Soldaty*).

He knows how to cut hair, shave, repair boots, start a fire even in pouring rain. Every week I change my undergarments, and he darns socks almost like a woman. When we're stationed near a river—fish every day, in the forest—strawberries, blackberries, mushrooms. And everything silently, quickly, without any suggestions from me. In all nine months of our life together I have never had to get angry with him. (*V okopakh Stalingrada*, 26)

Kerzhentsev comments that he does not know much about Valega, merely that he is from Altai—a region in South-Central Siberia—and was orphaned as a child. Sentenced for a minor criminal offense, Valega was released early and volunteered for the war.[23] The boy's actions throughout the narrative demonstrate his loyalty and concern for Kerzhentsev; with his ubiquitous flask of milk and flask of vodka, Valega several times sneaks through enemy lines to supply these, or water, to Kerzhentsev and his fellow soldiers. As Alexander Prokhorov has noted, between Valega's sock darning and his jealousy when Kerzhentsev interacts with another orderly, Valega serves as the "necessary wife" for the narrator, feeding him, clothing him, and watching his back. At the same time, Kerzhentsev is a father figure to the fatherless Valega.[24] These pseudo–family relations again link peacetime and wartime through the common psychological and human needs of the characters.

Because he hails originally from Altai, Valega serves another purpose here as well—geographic and social diversity. Where else might a boy from the Kievan intelligentsia meet a peasant from the Far East but at war? One of the remarkable but incidental outcomes of the Soviet war experience was to bring a wide cross section of the Soviet empire together in common pur-

---

[23] Nekrasov notes that this is the only character in *In the Trenches* whose name he did not change; Valega was his orderly during the war and he continued to maintain a relationship with him and even wrote about him (in *Tri vstrechi*). See "Kommentarii vtoroi," in Viktor Nekrasov, *Na voine i posle*, 519–520. When Nekrasov and the actor Iura Solov'ev went to Altai to show the film "Soldiers," Valega was asked to speak. "Here is what he said, word for word: 'Well, how did we fight? Bit by bit. We placed mines, Bruno spirals, dug trenches. That's how we fought. Thank you'" (Nekrasov, *Na voine i posle*, 519).

[24] In another place, Kerzhenstev compares Valega to his mother, who used to hand him French rolls with butter as he headed out the door to school. As Kerzhentsev gets ready for the nighttime attack on Mamaev Kurgan, Valega begs, "Perhaps a bite to eat for the road? I have canned goods. Canned meat. You didn't even have a proper dinner. I'll open some," but Kerzhentsev refuses, so Valega shoves a piece of bread and lard, wrapped in newspaper, into his pocket (*V okopakh Stalingrada, 180*).

pose.[25] In one sentence in the middle of the story, Nekrasov introduces us to "Shapiro, Pengaunis, Samoilenko, and Sedykh," signaling a Jew, a Lithuanian, a Ukrainian, and a Belorussian. On the front lines and in the rear, Russian and Soviet people from the village and the city, from the university and fresh from the Gulag met in the army during wartime. This truth in wartime became a convention of Soviet military fiction. In *The Star*, for example, the reconnaisance group is made up of people from various parts of the Soviet Union, demonstrating that in wartime the "friendship of the Soviet peoples" helped them beat the racist and "racially pure" Nazi forces.

Almost the first thing Kerzhentsev notices when he reaches Stalingrad is the loudspeaker, over which Chekhov's story "Vanka" is being read. The plaintive (and hopeless) notes of Vanka's letter "to grandfather in the village" remind Kerzhentsev of the culture of pre-war civilization, as do the signs of normal life around Stalingrad:

> Blue skies. And dust... And slender acacias, and little wooden houses with carved roosters, and "Do Not Enter—Fierce Dogs." And nearby large stone buildings with female figures supporting something on the facades. The office of "Lower Volga Kooppromsbyt," "Patching of Galoshes," "Primus Repair," "The Molotov Regional Procurator's Office." (*V okopakh Stalingrada*, 56)

The inclusion of Chekhov in the story is a nice touch, a reminder of both high and popular culture. The story read over the radio of the indentured peasant boy—alone and lonely, out of place and out of his element, with no hope of rescue—reminds civilians and soldiers alike of the despair of pre-revolutionary life. In literary terms, though, Chekhov more than any other writer underscores what Nekrasov is trying to accomplish with *In the Trenches*. After all, no Russian writer better conveyed life bounded by inactivity and uncertainty, and Chekhov's detail-saturated, realistic prose, like Nekrasov's, lacks the "altitude" of the bigger picture.

When Kerzhentsev and his friend Igor arrive in Stalingrad, fresh from the disastrous retreat and now lacking a regiment, they find civilian life and discover that their attitude toward it has changed. Trying to chat with Igor's former commander's sister, Lyusya, Kerzhentsev realizes that the vestiges of culture no longer interest him:

---

[25] As Zubkova has written, "The war created its own special mode of association for people whose paths during peacetime rarely crossed" (*Russia after the War*, 17).

For some reason I don't feel right, and I don't want to talk about Blok or Esenin. All of this did once interest and concern me, and now it has retreated far, far into the distance. . . . Architecture, painting, literature . . . I have not read a single book since the war started. And I don't want to, I don't feel like it. All of that is for later, later. . . . (*V okopakh Stalingrada*, 65)

Though while in the trenches Kerzhentsev has dreamed of moments such as he now experiences with Lyusya—drinking tea, sitting on a couch, and listening to her play Liszt on the piano—these activities now make him uncomfortable. "After all, I'm no deserter, no coward, no hypocrite, but I feel somehow as if I were. . . ." (*V okopakh Stalingrada*, 60).

The military way of life has usurped civilian life, and Kerzhentsev feels a sense of betrayal in enjoying the beautiful while recalling the horrors of war—those behind him and those to come. Duty comes first, and though the city is in the midst of a period of inactivity, the feeling makes Kerzhentsev uneasy. During a trip to the city library, Kerzhentsev describes the comfortable woven chairs, the portraits of Turgenev, Tyutchev, "someone else with a mustache and a tiepin, some kind of Peruvian novellas from *International Literature*." These comforts of civilized life, the life of an intellectual, lure Kerzhentsev, and at home in his little room Valega has reheated a delicious borscht soup. But the narrative insists that this former reality, those peaceful days, are gone.

The city is filled with the sounds and smells of the first serious German air raid. Kerzhentsev's little room dissolves into dust, with shards of dishes and clumps of asphalt mixing with and destroying the borscht of which Kerzhentsev hasn't yet taken a spoonful. Peaceful life is over; the siege of Stalingrad has begun.

Kerzhentsev and Igor Svidersky (and their orderlies, Valega and Sedykh) are assigned to defend a tractor factory. Here they essentially prepare to blow the factory up, and in the meantime they have plenty of down time for reading and conversation. "We begin to make ourselves at home in our bunker": Valega and Sedykh decorate their little corner with a portrait of Stalin, a postcard of the Odessa Opera Theater, and a reproduction of Repin's *Zaporozhians*. Sedykh, who turns out to be a rather interesting young man, finds three books: Kruber's geography textbook, a volume of Chekhov's letters, and an issue of the magazine *Niva* from 1912. Kerzhentsev notes that "Sedykh is so curious as to be amusing," asking the most unexpected and naive questions and listening to the answers "as children do a fairy tale" (*V okopakh Stalingrada*, 93), reminiscent, perhaps, of the naïve Vanka from Chekhov's story, the peasant boy thrown into unknown circumstances and longing for a clear narrative. Here, in the comfortable atmosphere of the bunker, a conversation about "heroes and medals" ensues. Upon learning what is necessary, Sedykh decides, "That's it. I'll get a medal." As if such decisions, ultimately, were his to make.

War Heroes in an Industrial Age

World War II was a war fought on an industrial scale. We saw earlier in the propaganda of hatred promulgated by war journalists and poets, including Simonov and Ehrenburg, that the Germans were being portrayed as inhuman, as barbaric. They were also portrayed as machines, part of the new industrialized warfare that featured fighter planes and tanks rather than cavalry and infantry.[26]

At one point in the middle of Nekrasov's novel, three characters have an exchange about the war, about why they fight it, and about who they are. Kerzhentsev's fellow officer Igor takes the opportunity to puff his chest about the unbreakable mettle of the Russian people:

> France basically fell apart in two weeks. They pushed, and it fell into ruins, dispersed like sand. But we are fighting for the second year already ... [In France they have] Petains and Lavals. And we don't have those sorts. That's the main thing. Do you understand that that is the main thing? That our people are of a different sort. And that's why we're fighting. Still fighting. Even here, on the Volga, having lost Ukraine and Belorussia, we're fighting. And what country, tell me, what country, what people could withstand this? (*V okopakh Stalingrada*, 95)

But another member of the group argues that the outcome of war no longer depends on the strength of "the people," on the national ideal of the Russian warrior. Georgy Akimovich argues that modern war has become bigger than any people:

> Everything needs to be considered soberly. You can't do anything with heroism alone. Heroism is heroism, but tanks are tanks. [*Geroistvo*

---

[26] For a great collection of images of these hated foes, as well as images chronicling Soviet-American friendship during the war, see Jill Bugajski, "Paper Ambassadors: Friend and Foe in the War of Images," in *Windows on the War*, 104–135.

geroistvom, a tanki tankami.] [. . .] We will fight to the last soldier. Russians always fight like that. But nonetheless we have little chance. Only a miracle can save us. Otherwise we will be crushed. Crushed by organization and tanks. (*V okopakh Stalingrada*, 96–98)

Georgy Akimovich does not see the German soldiers as individuals: they are machines designed and destined to mow down their Russian enemies. Heroics, he argues, can only take the Russians so far. They will need technology and organization—in other words, a miracle—to prevent a massacre.

Kerzhentsev has an answer for Georgy Akimovich, though he keeps it to himself (and tells only the reader). Overhearing a song about the Dnieper River and a conversation between two privates about the rich, fertile soil of their homeland, Kerzhentsev muses:

There are details which you remember all your life. And they aren't just the memorable ones. Little, almost insignificant, they eat their way into you, become a part of you somehow, begin to grow, to grow into something big and significant, they take upon themselves the entire meaning of events, become something like a symbol. [. . .] Tolstoy called this the hidden warmth of patriotism. That may be the best definition. Perhaps this is the very miracle which Georgy Akimovich is expecting, a miracle that is stronger than German organization and tanks with black crosses.[27]

Reaching back across Russian literature and history, Nekrasov does not simply tie his novel (and the experience it details) to Tolstoy's *War and Peace*. After all, for Kerzhentsev, as the reader already knows, the Tolstoy who wrote *Anna Karenina* has no meaning in the trenches of Stalingrad. But the other Tolstoy, the one who knew about war and patriotism, speaks to him now.[28] Kerzhentsev and his comrades are sustained not by the party, or by the thought of Stalin, but by that "hidden warmth of patriotism."

---

[27] *V okopakh Stalingrada*, 99. There were half a million troops massed for the defense of Stalingrad in the summer of 1942. Over three hundred thousand of them would die defending the city. Cited in Merridale, *Ivan's War*, 174.

[28] William Nickell quotes an apt saying from the magazine *Vlast' truda*: "To Tolstoy the writer: peace / But to Tolstoi the prophet: war!" For our purposes it is the novelist of peace who is alien, while the novelist of war speaks to Kerzhentsev. Quoted in "Tolstoy in 1928: In the Mirror of the Revolution," *Epic Revisionism* (Madison: University of Wisconsin Press: 2006), 17.

This exchange, in which Tolstoy gets the last word, underscores that *In the Trenches* does not even pretend to adhere to the doctrine of socialist realism. Stalin makes several appearances in the novel, and a portrait of Stalin was one of the symbols of comfort and home at the tractor factory. But as Nekrasov noted, in all there were "only three lines about Stalin."

Individual as Heroic

We have defined Soviet heroism as bravery plus consciousness. However, in the second part of *In the Trenches*, we meet a character who introduces the reader to a different version of heroism. Nikolai Karnaukhov has recently returned from a month-long hospital stay to take the place of the now-dead commander of the fourth battalion. "Tall, pigeon-toed, with thick brows that met in the middle, gray-eyed," Karnaukhov speaks slowly, in a deep voice, carefully choosing his words. An efficient leader, Karnaukhov keeps his dugout very clean and neat ("*ne po-frontovomu*") and, what's more, appears to write poetry (*V okopakh Stalingrada*, 150–151). Brave and modest, Karnaukhov has also decorated his wartime lodgings:

> On the wall hung a calendar with days crossed out, a list of radio signals, a portrait of Stalin cut out of the newspaper, and of someone else—young, curly-headed, with an open, kind face.
> "Who is that?"
> Karnaukhov, catching my eye, looked bashful.
> "Jack London."
> "Jack London?"
> Karnaukhov is standing in the light, I cannot see his face, but by his translucent ears I can see that he is blushing.
> "Why Jack London all of a sudden?"
> "It's just. . . . I respect him. . . . Well, and. . . . Would you like some milk?" (*V okopakh Stalingrada*, 155)

It turns out that while in the hospital, Karnaukhov was reading everything he could find, and he did not have time to finish London's novel *Martin Eden*, so he took it with him. The conversation continues:

> "Do you like Jack London?"
> "Yes, I've read him several times."
> "I like him too."

"Everyone likes him. It's impossible not to like him."
"Why?"
"He's real somehow. . . . Even Lenin liked him. Krupskaya read him aloud." (*V okopakh Stalingrada*, 156)

The novel *Martin Eden*—London's semiautobiographical story of a self-educated, hardworking sailor who learns proper manners and grammar from a beautiful, young, college-educated bourgeois woman and then passes her by in sophistication, knowledge, and style—was published in 1909. A compelling and exciting narrative, the novel features a hero almost akin to Chernyshevsky's Rakhmetov in his asceticism and determination, whose loyalty to family and the lower classes despite his growing awareness of their limitations and his anger at his own disadvantage is matched only by his intellectual curiosity and incredible physical stamina. Kerzhentsev asks to borrow the novel when Karnaukhov has finished.

Eden's regime, which involves hard, intellectual labor nineteen to twenty hours a day (he only allows himself four to five hours of sleep), matches the labor of the men at the front line. As Kerzhentsev comments of Karnaukhov, "I know that he, like I, wants more than anything to sleep. But he will still sit down and draw the design of his defenses, sticking out the tip of his tongue, or he'll run to check whether dinner has been brought to the sergeants" (*V okopakh Stalingrada*, 151). Duty comes first.

This short conversation about fiction—very general, after all, with appropriate political approval from the father of the party—is not the end of *Martin Eden* in the trenches. Later on in the narrative, one of their superior officers, a colonel and the division commander, also notices the book lying on a table. Paging through it, he glances at the end and "furrows his brow in dissatisfaction": "Idiot. Dear Lord, what an idiot." The colonel had read the book long ago and has forgotten it. "I only remember that the young man was stubborn. And I don't like the end. It's a bad ending."

Suddenly, and without explanation, the colonel is assigning *Martin Eden* as reading material, not only to Kerzhentsev, but to Borodin, another soldier. "Then I'll organize an exam. Like we have on service regulations. We have a lot to learn from this Martin. Doggedness, persistence" (*V okopakh Stalingrada*, 167).

The colonel's insistence on this required reading is highlighted by the command he gives Kerzhentsev. Although Kerzhentsev and his men have been fortifying the area with mines, the colonel insists they attack Mamaev Kurgan, the famous hill outside Stalingrad, which at the moment is held by the Germans. Kerzhentsev, with only two companies of eighteen men each, agrees that the Germans' position, from which they are spraying the Russians with machine-gun fire, needs to be attacked, but he initially balks at the idea of an offensive.[29] Confident of their success, the colonel reminds the battalion commander, "And that guy, the one who drowns himself at the end, Martin Eden. . . . don't give [the book] to anyone. . . . If you don't bring it to me, I'll come to you on the knoll to get it" (*V okopakh Stalingrada*, 168). The offensive is successful, and Kerzhentsev's men gain the hill.

The novel *Martin Eden* is not mentioned again until about a hundred pages later, when Karnaukhov dies in battle. His body is not found; "someone said they saw him, along with four other soldiers, burst into the German trenches. Apparently he perished in there"—a real Soviet hero. The last time Kerzhentsev sees Karnaukhov, he asks him something and notices that "he raised his head, and for the first time I did not see in his eyes that smile, that deep, quiet smile somewhere in the very depths of his eyes, which I used to like so" (*V okopakh Stalingrada*, 265, 267). Perhaps Karnaukhov knows that his foray behind German lines, heroic though it might be, will end in his death.

Only twenty-five years old, Karnaukhov doesn't even get a proper burial. But in the narrative, he does get a kind of epitaph, as his love poetry becomes a talisman for Kerzhentsev, who keeps the poem in his pocket along with Lyusya's photo and a letter from his mother. "Simple, clear, pure—just like him. [. . .] I hang London's portrait on the wall beneath the mirror. They even look a bit alike—London and Karnaukhov" (*V okopakh Stalingrada*, 266).

Karnaukhov shares with London's Martin Eden a desire for love and poetry, trumped by the knowledge that duty and hard work are more important and must take precedence. When Kerzhentsev first gets to know Karnaukhov, he notes, he liked him immediately. And throughout the novel Karnaukhov continues to demonstrate an admirable quiet bravery.

---

[29] This is an idea first suggested to Kerzhentsev by Karnaukhov: "Oh, how we'd give it to the Fritzes if we took that hill. But what can you do with eighteen men?" The narrator continues, "Karnaukhov is right. If that risc was in our hands, we would make the third battalion's life better, and paralyze the bridge, and have the weapon emplacements that now flank the first battalion. But how to do it?" (Nekrasov, *V okopakh Stalingrada*, 158).

In Karnaukhov's case, we have bravery plus duty. Unlike many of the other officers, Karnaukhov not only follows military protocol (bringing daily reports to Kerzhentsev with detailed information on enemy fortifications and arms) but also acts Chapaev-like, one day taking trenches back from the Germans (and "losing only one man"), the next stealing a machine gun and six boxes of bullets from the Germans.

> His soldiers said that he himself went after the machine gun, but when I asked him, he smiled and, not looking me in the eye, said that it was only stories, that he'd never allow himself to do such a thing, and that going after machine guns is not what the company commander is for. (*V okopakh Stalingrada*, 151)

So what is the lesson of Jack London for Kerzhentsev and for the novel? Martin Eden *is* a heroic figure, but he is no Socialist. Rather, he demonstrates that an individual can be heroic even if he does not subscribe to a particular political ideology, and even if he chooses suicide in the end.

London defended his novel to Upton Sinclair using those very words: "Martin Eden is an individualist, I am a Socialist. That is why I continue to live, and that is the reason why Martin Eden died." Suicide is not a Socialist value. Sinclair noted:

> It is easy to understand the befuddlement of critics; for [London] had shown such sympathy with the hard-driving individualist that it would hardly occur to anyone that the character was meant to be a warning and a reproach.[30]

Nekrasov uses *Martin Eden* to offer his readers an alternative notion of heroism for his readers. Though an approved author for Soviet readers, London created in *Martin Eden* a hero who emphasizes individualism over the collective and who remains focused on the "I" in choosing to end his own life.

By drawing a parallel between Eden and Karnaukhov, Nekrasov leaves the questions of heroism and duty, love and poetry, the individual and the collective, in a state of ambiguity. Eden and Karnaukhov have positive qualities, but both end up dead. The reader is left to figure out the relationship between the characters and the meaning of their deaths.

---

[30] Upton Sinclair, quoted by Robert Hass, "Introduction," to Jack London, *Martin Eden* (Toronto: Bantam Books, 1986), xxi.

Beyond the Trenches

After the initial success of *In the Trenches*, Nekrasov wrote several more stories about the war. In all of them he maintained what he saw as the essential tone of everyday life and avoided the heightened rhetoric of heroism. His novel, originally published as *Stalingrad*, was renamed *In the Trenches of Stalingrad*, in part to acknowledge that contained within were no "great truths" about the battle as a whole, presented in a historical and panoramic view, but rather the "truth of the trenches," the details of life and *byt*.

In this way Nekrasov continued to struggle against the standard narrative of war even in the post-war period. For example, one critic praised his demobilization story *In My Native Town* (*V rodnom gorode*) thus:

> [it is] the first [narrative] to envision the soldiers' homecoming from the front not as an idyll or as a displacement of the battle to the front of Socialist development but realistically as a problem involving the partner who has become a stranger, the mistrustful Party official, the trials of everyday life.[31]

In other words, Nekrasov produced the truth of the postwar world in the same way as he had for the war itself. In this Nekrasov was more successful than Fadeev in his *Cement*, where those very same problems—the partner who has become a stranger, mistrustful party officials, the trials of everyday life—are precisely portrayed as a "displacement of the battle to the front of Socialist development." We can compare the experiences of Nekrasov's hero to Gleb Chumalov's and see that Nekrasov focused on real experiences and challenges, while Gladkov was enslaved to the rhetoric of *podvig*.

However, when *In My Native Town* was to be translated into the genre of film, Nekrasov fought with the director, who argued against that postwar truth:

> You must understand that a scenario in which the main character slugs the dean of the college in the face, is then excluded from the party and is not even reinstated by the end of the film, that this kind of scenario doesn't work. If you had shown an officer who returned from the front wounded, who was surrounded by attention and care by everyone: his

---

[31] See Kasack, *Dictionary of Russian Literature*, 266–267.

friends, the regional Party Committee, and the Commission for Fatherland War Veterans' Assistance, now that would be a different matter. . . .[32]

A different matter indeed. The scenario Nekrasov did not write would have conformed to the canonical rules of socialist realist fiction about war heroes, while the one he did write explored more pressing problems: the problems of mapping military experience and hierarchies onto the frustrations of civilian life.

In the end Nekrasov took his name off the film, and none of the motifs of his story remained. For Nekrasov, the portrayal of the postwar life of soldiers had to explore the conflict between military and civilian life and the psychological repercussions of that conflict, topics and approaches that the director didn't dare to use. Complaining about another film on the topic of adjusting to peacetime, Marlen Khutsiev's *The Two Fyodors* (1958), one critic wrote, "What kind of hero is that? Depressed, taciturn, unsociable. Do we need a man like that?" Nekrasov believed that such a hero, and such a portrayal, *were* needed. That's the kind of person Nekrasov himself could believe in.

The struggle over Nekrasov's work was essentially one of tone and detail. While Stalin inexplicably liked and praised *In the Trenches of Stalingrad*, the author's style was too ordinary, too "real" for socialist realism. Nekrasov was not a teacher; he had no desire to deliver ideologically correct content, especially about the war or about politics. His continual struggles with stereotypes and labels, with the categories of socialist realism and the heroism of war, reflect his more subtle approach to literature and life.[33] The true Soviet hero has been described as "intelligent, talented, kind, honest, brave, truthful, active, sincere, strong-willed, decisive, self-respecting, unselfish, persistent, trusting, proud, powerful. . . ." (Shtut 149). In a word, perfect. Nekrasov was more interested in psychological portrayals of the complexity of man, of the individual, than in producing a character who would inspire the collective with generalized "positive" characteristics.

The decline of Nekrasov's career tracked the way the Cold War settled into Soviet life in the decades of the 1950s and '60s. He never mentioned the Cold War as such, but it played a vital role in shaping his reputation. In 1947 Nekrasov was able to display his complicated set of heroes, a set of heroes that

---

[32] Nekrasov, "Slova 'velikie' i prostye," *Iskusstvo kino* 5 (1959): 58–59.
[33] "More than anything in life, I don't want to teach anyone." See Nekrasov, *Zapiski zevaki*, 194.

represents a retreat from the rigid oversimplification of the classic socialist realist novel and from the forced patriotic rhetoric of the typical Soviet war story, but which in decades to come would again prove too complex.

The retreat from socialist realist norms, like the military retreat with which the novel opens, was only temporary. Those "great and beautiful truths" that Panferov called for were not wanted for long, or perhaps the call itself was merely empty rhetoric. Instead, Stalin rapidly changed the course of Soviet war literature and war memory by banning the celebration of Victory Day and suppressing the memory of the war.

Ten years after *In the Trenches* had been published, the liberty that Nekrasov took with socialist realist prescriptions of heroism was corrected in the film version of the novel. For moviegoers, the heroic emphasis had shifted to Valega, a modernized, more efficient, and more effective version of Chekhov's peasant boy Vanka, a peasant-hero to parallel Vasily Tyorkin. The newly central, simple peasant Valega did not suffer from the ambiguity Kerzhentsev and Karnaukhov noticed in their experience of war. The film was a first step in moving the novel from prizewinning bestseller to suppressed contraband, the beginning of the novel's literary retreat.[34]

In effect, Nekrasov was asked increasingly which side of the barricades he was on. Khrushchev accused Nekrasov of writing like a "tourist with a walking stick," but Nekrasov was more than just a tourist. He may have been an observer, a flâneur, or, as he called himself, a *zevaka*, but he had also been a participant in the war, and his writing stemmed from those real experiences and the complex psychological reactions they had caused.

Throughout the 1960s, Nekrasov continued to insist, as he had from the very beginning, that he had defended his nation, his people, in the trenches, and he did so in the hopes that children would have the chance to grow up to be poets, musicians, or simply human beings. By the 1970s, that answer would no longer suffice. Under Brezhnev, human beings were not in high demand; the state continued to require heroes and feats, and there was no room for individuals with complex psychological makeups and personal desires.

In a March 5, 1974, letter published in several foreign newspapers, in a calm and rational tone Nekrasov asked, "Who needs this?" "This" was hav-

---

[34] In fact, the film was renamed *Soldiers* in 1957, although the posters had already been printed up advertising *In the Trenches of Stalingrad*. "In the end we were ordered to change the name; it was not permitted to use the word Stalingrad." See "Volgograd–Stalingrad," in Nekrasov, *Na voine i posle*, 554.

ing his apartment ransacked, his manuscripts confiscated, and his friends harassed in a continual search for "anti-Soviet materials." What, precisely, Nekrasov wondered, was the definition of anti-Soviet? If the poetry of Marina Tsvetaeva and translations of Pushkin into Hebrew (among the items confiscated) were anti-Soviet, then what about Molotov's October 1939 speech declaring it absurd to fight an idea like Hitlerism? And Beria's speeches? And the millions of people who died under Stalin? Were their deaths pro- or anti-Soviet actions?

In the end, Nekrasov had to retreat himself—this time across the border. By the end of 1974, he moved to France, where he continued to observe and write about life in Russia and across the world until his death in 1987. Why did it have to be that way, he asked himself: "People have left, they are leaving, they will leave. . . . Why are smart, talented, serious people leaving, people for whom the decision was not easy, people who love their homeland and oh! will miss it terribly?"

> Who needs this? The country? The government? The people? Aren't we needlessly discarding people of whom we should be proud? The artist Chagall, the composer Stravinsky, the aeronautical engineer Sikorsky, the writer Nabokov have all become the property of foreign cultures. With whom will we be left? KGB investigators won't create books, paintings or symphonies for us. . . .[35]

They won't contribute to Russian (or Soviet) culture. Nekrasov continued to insist on the use of "simple words" over "great" ones, and continued to assert the possibility that the ordinary and the great were not mutually exclusive, and in this he continued to fight the rhetoric of *podvig*, of socialist realist heroism:

> There is another kind of language—passionate, but not bombastic, truthful and utilitarian, the language in which ordinary people speak, ordinary people who sometimes achieve great deeds.[36]

That stubborn confidence in the capacity of language to tell the truth may have been most threatening of all to the Soviet state. Nekrasov came to

---

[35] "Komu eto nuzhno," reprinted in Viktor Nekrasov, *Kak ia stal sheval'e: Rasskazy. Portrety. Ocherki. Povesti.* (Ekaterinburg: U-Faktoriia, 2005), 5–12.
[36] Nekrasov, "Slova 'velikie' i prostye," 58, 61.

that faith through his experience of war, where he committed himself to describing only what he found under his nose, as honestly and compassionately as he knew how.

There is a resonance here, of course, with Ernest Hemingway. Hemingway too went off to war, and what he found most appalling about it was the way it perverted language. It does not exaggerate too much to say that his war experience forced Hemingway to invent a new literary language—a language that would exert an enormous influence on writing in English for the rest of the century, and on Russian writing as well.

* * *

After all, when he wasn't being banned, Hemingway was very popular in Russia.[37] By 1960, for example, there were over one million volumes of Hemingway in Russian circulating around the USSR despite the hiatus in publication of his works between 1939 and 1955. His popularity was greatest just before the war. Indeed, after Hemingway's suicide in 1961, Soviet writer Ilya Ehrenburg called Hemingway the most popular foreign author in the Soviet Union in the 1930s.[38]

We don't know, and perhaps we can never know, the full extent of the influence of Hemingway's writing on Nekrasov, although Nekrasov is on record for his opinions about Jack London. What we do know is that while the Nazi army advanced on Stalingrad, many Russian writers were thinking of Hemingway. Ilya Ehrenburg read the last pages of *A Farewell to Arms* aloud at a meeting of the All-Russian Theater Society, and the novel was slated to be published in 1941.[39] Anna Akhmatova included an epigraph from the novel in the 1942 redaction of her poem "Poem without a Hero." And in 1959—when Hemingway became possible again—Nekrasov published another Stalingrad story, "Dedicated to Hemingway."[40] So in order to think about what

---

[37] See Raisa Orlova, *Kheminguei v Rossii: Roman dlinoiu v polstoletiia* (Ann Arbor: Ardis, 1985).
[38] He said this to an American audience. See Ilya Ehrenburg, "In Memory of Hemingway," *Saturday Review* 4 (July 1961).
[39] It was rumored that Stalin nixed that publication (Orlova, *Kheminguei*, 30).
[40] In this story, the protagonist has the last Hemingway volume (*The Fifth Column and 37 Other Stories*, 1939) in the trenches at Stalingrad and won't allow it out of his hands; by the end of the story the familiar book is spattered with blood. See Orlova, *Kheminguei*, 36–37.

Nekrasov wanted to accomplish, it is worth quoting that famous passage in Hemingway's *Farewell to Arms* where a lieutenant talks about the relationship between war and language:

> I was always embarrassed by the words sacred, glorious, and sacrifice and the expression "in vain". . . . I had seen nothing sacred, and the things that were glorious had no glory and the sacrifices were like the stockyards of Chicago if nothing was done with the meat except bury it. There were many words that you could not stand to hear and finally only the names of places had dignity. Certain numbers were the same way and certain dates and these with the names of the places were all you could say and have them mean anything. Abstract words such as glory, honor, courage, or hallowed were obscene beside the concrete names of villages, the numbers of the roads, the names of rivers, the numbers of the regiments and the dates.[41]

Nekrasov too was embarrassed by words like "glory." He tried to introduce a language that would express honestly and with dignity what he had seen in war. It worked, briefly, but it would not be until the 1990s that Russian writers could again describe World War II in a language that was not obscene.

---

[41] Ernest Hemingway, *A Farewell to Arms* (New York: Scribner Classics, 1997), 169.

Part III
Cold War Repercussions

Chapter Five

From World War to Cold War: Tvardovsky, Solzhenitsyn, Voinovich, and Heroism in the Post-Stalin Period

> Life consists of more than just feats.
>
> Жизнь же состоит не из одних подвигов.
>
> -Vladimir Voinovich[1]

> The science of laughing at ourselves
> is an unloved child among sciences:
> it's not in fashion now, not honored,
> as if only ordeals will follow . . .
> But meanwhile, to protect your honor,
> you can't find a better medicine.
>
> Наука посмеяться над собой
> среди других наук—дитя дурное:
> она не в моде нынче, не в чести,
> как будто бы сулит одни мыстарства . . .
> А между тем, чтоб честь свою спасти,
> не отыскать надежнее лекарства.
>
> -Bulat Okudzhava[2]

In February 1946, less than a year after the Red Army had marched triumphantly into a defeated Germany, Stalin warned the populace that no relief was in sight: "As long as capitalism exists there will be wars, and the Soviet Union must be prepared."[3] This was a prophecy, a prophecy that Stalin himself would help to fulfill.

Perhaps Stalin had learned of George Orwell's October 1945 newspaper essay entitled "You and the Atomic Bomb," in which he coined the phrase "cold war."[4] Cold war was what Stalin described in his speech as he prepared Russians for an ongoing military and political struggle with the

---

[1] Vladimir Voinovich, Interview with Konstantin Mil'chin, *Russkii reporter*, 14 April 2010, №14 (142), http://www.rusrep.ru/2010/14/interview_voynovich/.
[2] "Vospitannym krovavoiu sud'boi," *Zal ozhidaniia: stikhi* (Nizhnii Novgorod: Izdatel'stvo Dekom, 1996), 24.
[3] February 9, 1946. Quoted in Brown, *Russian Literature since the Revolution*, 226.
[4] October 19, 1945, *Tribune*, London, Great Britain.

West. War, as Randolph Bourne had observed in 1918, allows the state to emerge and exercise its control over the populace. The Cold War, which replaced the Second World War within a matter of months, created a permanent condition of wartime readiness: the arms race, the space race, the race to influence events in the developing and postcolonial world—these races shaped life on both sides of the iron curtain, and they ensured that the Soviet Union remained in a state of war through much of the twentieth century.

The Second World War ended with the atomic explosions over Hiroshima and Nagasaki. Four years later, the Soviet Union detonated its own nuclear weapon. Both events were cause for celebration and dread at the same time. To an extent that Bourne could never have imagined, the Cold War became the health of the Soviet state.[5]

The Cold War, therefore, became the unavoidable circumstance for all those who would write in its shadow, a noise in the background, which sometimes grew louder and sometimes faded but never went quiet. But the Cold War was not limited to East-West conflicts.

Immediately after the Second World War, as the Cold War was settling in, the concept of heroics began to change. War had promoted enterprising individuals and created camaraderie among soldiers. In the aftermath of war, soldiers struggled to hang on to either. The kind of solidarity that soldiers might feel after the war was vividly rendered in Boris Slutsky's unpublished poem "Night Conversations," in which veterans find a bit of comfort as they compare experiences in the darkness of a railway carriage, only to part when the train pulls into their station. The poem's narrator emphasizes the "rank and file" nature of the soldiers: "My humble comrade, / An ordinary enlisted man" ("Tovarishch moi negordyi, / Obychnyi, riadovoi"). War had brought these men together in common cause, but now they went their separate ways.

Postwar support for demobilized soldiers was uneven. Some returned home to shattered families, some had to contend with their own physical

---

[5] On March 5, 2011, the fifty-eighth anniversary of Stalin's death, the Russian army newspaper *Krasnaia zvezda* carried an article claiming March 5, 1946, as the beginning of the Cold War. The article ends with the phrase, "In reality the cold war continues to this day, it's just that it has become less visible." See Natalia Yarmolik, "The Cold War Turns 65," http://www.redstar.ru/2011/03/05_03/3_02.html. Perhaps the Cold War is still the health of the Russian army.

and psychological injuries, others were taken directly from the front lines into the prison camp system. Still others, like Slutsky's characters, found fellowship in anonymous encounters and then went on with their lives. As another of his poet-personas declares, "When we returned from the war, / I realized that we were not needed."[6]

Both individualism and that sense of group solidarity posed potential threats to the Soviet system as World War II moved almost without interruption into the Cold War. Stalin needed to replace whatever "plastic juncture" the war might have created with a renewed control over the population. War, and the individual initiative that accompanies it, had in the past caused demands for internal reform in Russia. As historian Nina Tumarkin argues:

> [In the past] wars had given those who had fought in them, especially junior officers, a sense of entitlement, of self-respect, of independence that inevitably led to demands for change. In Stalin's eyes, the wartime reliance on individual initiative was utterly incompatible with his continued or, rather, renewed totalitarian control of the country. The resurgence of the Stalinist *apparat* was his main domestic goal in the spring of 1945. (*The Living and the Dead*, 92)

The reconstruction of this *apparat* meant a glorification of the abstract at the expense of concrete soldier-heroes.[7] Catherine Merridale has written about the construction of an "ideal soldier" who "took the place of all the diverse, the opinionated and self-confident fighters who came back from the front." As Hannah Arendt commented, in a "perfect totalitarian government . . . all men have become One Man." After the war, the ideal hero was praised, but the actual veterans, who were individual human beings, could not find their place in society.[8]

---

6 Slutsky, *"Bez popravok"* . . . , 226.

7 Postwar, Tumarkin claims, "Self-sacrificial wartime heroes were rapidly demoted. This was no time to rest on one's laurels, much less to expect rewards. The only postwar hero was Hero Number One, and he was not inclined to make room for any competition. Military heroism per se faded from the novel, which moved its focus from feats of valor to the practical business of economic and social reconstruction" (*The Living and the Dead*, 100).

8 Merridale, *Ivan's War*, 385. Merridale considers Tyorkin to be part of the "Soviet Union's hero myth" and calls Tvardovsky's treatment of war "euphemistic" (*Ivan's War*, 6–7). I disagree. Hannah Arendt, "Ideology and Terror: A Novel Form of

5. From World War to Cold War: Tvardovsky, Solzhenitsyn, Voinovich, and Heroism in the Post-Stalin Period

This chapter examines three writers and the postwar heroes they created within the context of the Cold War. We will look at what we might call the "posthumous" life of Tvardovsky's Vasily Tyorkin in the post-Stalinist era, as well as at a parody of the soldier's life story, Vladimir Voinovich's satirical and pointed *Life and Adventures of the Soldier Ivan Chonkin*, which couldn't be published in Russia until several decades after it was written. Between the two we find Solzhenitsyn's treatments of war and postwar life in his stories of the war and the Gulag. His Ivan Denisovich, a humble peasant-soldier akin to the one in Slutsky's poem, went straight from war to prison camp.

All three authors benefited from the patronage and personal endorsement of then–general secretary Nikita Sergeevich Khrushchev. Indeed, they wrote these works during Khrushchev's "thaw," and here an irony of semantics. The "thaw" initiated by Khrushchev, which permitted a certain level of cultural openness and allowed for a certain criticism of Stalinist excesses, occurred exactly when the Cold War became hardened and institutionalized. After all, between 1956 and 1964, Khrushchev presided over the suppression of the Hungarian Uprising, the launching of *Sputnik*, and the Cuban Missile Crisis (which most historians agree was the moment at which the world came closest to a nuclear exchange), and he pounded his shoe on the lectern of the United Nations, promising to "bury" the West. So without arguing the point too strenuously, we might suggest that the "thaw" amounted to replacing the terror of Stalinism with the terror of the Cold War and the threat of nuclear annihilation. The brief cultural thaw coexisted with a colder atmosphere in world politics than ever before. Russian writers must surely have seen that irony.

Soldiers in the post-Stalin era were no longer heroic. In the narratives of these three writers, soldier characters have survived the war to rejoin postwar society, whether they were "needed" or not, and they have lost their chance to be heroes. After all, a vital part of being a Soviet hero is death: from the moment Vasily Chapaev entered his watery grave, the death scene served to punctuate the hero's life in the mainstream Soviet narrative. In Soviet war novels, especially novels of World War II, it is virtually a rule that main heroes do not live to see the end of the book. In the 1970s this would again be the case: all five heroines in Boris Vasiliev's 1972 *The Dawns Here Are Quiet* per-

---

Government," in *The American Intellectual Tradition*, ed. David A. Hollinger and Charles Capper (New York: Oxford University Press, 2011), 340.

ish, though in the two-reel film version of the book the viewer keeps hoping that at least one will survive.

This narrative phenomenon can be connected with a larger discourse about masculinity and nationalism,[9] but it is also the case that once the early exemplary heroes had perished, other heroes were destined to follow suit. Chapaev's death set the agenda, and future war heroes tended to die as well. In contrast, during the Krushchev era we see soldiers who survive, including the nonheroic Chonkin.[10]

Each in their own way, Tvardovsky, Solzhenitsyn, and Voinovich rewrote the myth of the Soviet soldier in response to postwar life, when victory brought Cold War rather than peace.

Tyorkin Lives

There was nothing funny about the Second World War and its effect on the landscape and people of the Soviet Union, and yet Tvardovsky had created an amusing figure in his peasant-soldier character, and readers turned to *Vasily Tyorkin* for a laugh and a joke. Tyorkin was beloved in part because his adventures, his eternal cheerfulness, and the humor of his character made war into an everyday business, a daily task to be confronted with a positive attitude. Not didactic or ideological, Tyorkin's narrator presented the events of war as trying, difficult, but ultimately worth the effort. Tyorkin and his fellow soldiers believed they were fighting "for life on this earth"; readers too wanted to be convinced of that fact.

---

[9] Karen Petrone does just this in her article "Masculinity and Heroism in Imperial and Soviet Military-Patriotic Cultures," in *Russian Masculinities in History and Culture*, ed. Barbara Evans Clements, Rebecca Friedman, and Dan Healey (New York: Palgrave 2002), 172–193. She specifically argues that "Military-heroic masculinity is intimately connected with modern nationalism, for to be a soldier-hero is to be willing to fight and die for one's nation" ("Masculinity and Heroism," 173). Petrone's argument traces the continuity with the imperial period, specifically the literature and cultural paradigms of the Russo-Japanese War, but also emphasizes that narrative patterns continued well into the Soviet period *regardless of the fact* that the "traditional model of individual heroism ... contradicted Soviet commitments to the value of the collective" ("Masculinity and Heroism," 175).

[10] Voinovich's character draws his traits more from the folk character Ivan the Fool than from his fellow soldiers. In his review of *Chonkin* the year it was published, Geoffrey Hosking immediately connected the character with "Ivan-durak" (as well as with Jaroslav Hašek's Švejk). See "The Good Soldier Chonkin," *Times Literary Supplement* no. 3854 (23 January 1976): 93.

By the end of Tvardovsky's book, the name Tyorkin had become an eponym.[11] Just as Chapaev caught the imagination of Soviet readers and film buffs in the 1920s and 1930s, so too Tyorkin came to represent the peasant-soldier in World War II: inventive, creative, full of energy, and willing to die, if necessary, for his country. This kind of heroism both echoed what soldiers saw in their own regiments and gave them something to strive for, an attitude to emulate, a hero to admire.

According to the rules of the genre, an amusing poem with a picaresque hero should have ended with Tyorkin's triumph, perhaps even his marriage and the prospect of a happy family life. But this was wartime, and foregrounding goals of national and patriotic unity rather than genre conventions, Tvardovsky did not impose a cheerful conclusion onto his narrative. Instead, he left his hero's fate ambiguous; he admitted that he had to give up the idea of a plot, with its structure and conclusion, but instead "the genre of [his] work became not quite a chronicle, not quite a newsreel, but a 'book,' a living, moving, free-form book, inseparable from the real business of the people's defense of the Motherland, of their feats in the war" ("Kak byl napisan," 265).

Tyorkin thrived in the campaigns of World War II. From the very outset, however, his author intended to leave Tyorkin—alive or dead—on the field of battle. He had no interest in writing about Tyorkin after the war. But after a decade of resisting readers' requests that he write a sequel, Tvardovsky did return to his hero in 1954. He used Tyorkin to delineate the new era of openness and cultural thaw, penning a new poem in a familiar meter, "Vasily Tyorkin in the Other World" ("Vasilii Tyorkin na tom svete"), that, as the author explained, took up from the chapter "Death and the Warrior," where Tyorkin, "left half-dead" on the battlefield, really might have ended up in the other world ("Kak byl napisan," 263 n. 3).

Initially rejected by censors, the new poem lay in Tvardovsky's desk drawer for the next nine years. In 1963, he found himself at a gathering of Soviet and Western writers at Nikita Khrushchev's Georgian dacha in Pitsunda, and Khrushchev requested that Tvardovsky read the anti-Stalinist

---

[11] P. S. Vykhodtsev notes that the name became a "personification of the victorious people" when it began to be used as a password: "If you say Vasily Tyorkin gave it to you, / They'll let you through." Vykhodtsev, "A.T. Tvardovskii i narodnaia khudozhestvennaia kul'tura (*Vasilii Tyorkin*)," in *Tvorchestvo A.T. Tvardovskogo: issledovaniia i materialy*, ed. Vykhodtsev and N. A. Groznovaia (Leningrad: Nauka, 1989), 26–27.

poem aloud.[12] This was a satire on the "administrative-command system," and like all satires, it had to address the questions "against whom (or what) and in the name of what."[13] Three days later, on August 18, 1963, the poem was published in *Izvestiia* as well as in the August issue of *Novyi Mir*.[14] Tvardovsky used Tyorkin and Khrushchev . . . and Khrushchev used Tyorkin and Tvardovsky. The enemy was Stalinism; the goal was cultural thaw and conversations about the past.

Tvardovsky would make the other world work for him.

Tyorkin in the Other World

When Tvardovsky returned to Tyorkin a second time, some readers were decidedly not amused. One critic wrote, "Tvardovsky did not have the right to turn to the hero of the *Book about a Warrior* again."[15] Readers found the new Tyorkin to be too passive, too much of an observer. D. Starikov noted the change in tone in *The Other World*:

> Submission to the inevitability of fate, spiritual depression, the feeling that one cannot come back to life—a motif almost completely missing before, in *Vasily Tyorkin*—prevails in Alexander Tvardovsky's new poem. Persistently, continually, and frankly utterly annoyingly, giving the entire narrative the flavor of no way out. (196)

No way out. Now that Tyorkin had come "back to life," readers found him depressing and annoying. Yet another reader put it this way:

> In my opinion A. Tvardovsky violated his own authorial rights, if one can say it that way. Tyorkin personified an endless energy, optimism, resourcefulness. [. . .] In the new work the hero is placed—deliberately— into the artificial position of a resident of "the other world." [. . .] People will say to me: "You missed the point. This is a satire, a grotesque!" But

---

[12] As Michael Scammell writes, the poem's "daring political content, as daring in its way as *Ivan Denisovich*, . . . had condemned the poem to circulate underground . . ." (*Solzhenitsyn*, 477) I rely on Scammell's account below.

[13] For a recent comparison of "Tyorkin in the Other World" with the nineteenth-century satire of Saltykov-Shchedrin, see V. V. Prozorov, "*Tyorkin na tom svete* A.T. Tvardovskogo i shchedrinskaia satiricheskaia traditsiia," 105–119, in *Do vostrebovaniia . . . Izbrannye stat'i o literature i zhurnalistike* (Saratov: Izdatel'stvo saratovskogo universiteta, 2010).

[14] Below we will cite from "Terkin na tom svete," 377–404 in A. Tvardovskii and M. Gefter, *XX vek: Gologrammy poeta i istorika* (Moscow: Novyi Khronograf, 2005).

[15] D. Starikov, "Terkin protiv Terkina," *Oktiabr'* 10 (1963): 196.

for a grotesque, for a satire like this, our familiar and beloved Tyorkin is not appropriate.[16]

Instead of presenting a patriotic *Book about a Warrior* to do patriotic work, Tvardovsky used the character as a weapon to criticize current political conditions. Cranky readers missed the point. If in wartime Tyorkin had served to buoy up the common soldier and give him faith in the simple, clever Russian lads who were working together to save their fatherland, during the Thaw Tvardovsky wanted Tyorkin to serve another purpose entirely: to debunk some of the myths his character had participated in creating—for the sake of patriotic wartime rhetoric—and to highlight the horrors of the post-Stalinist Cold War bureaucracy.

Tvardovsky used Tyorkin as a Dante, a guide to an imaginary underworld, hoping to highlight problems in postwar Soviet life. In this underworld, Tvardovsky's hero meets with a fully bureaucratized society. His conversation with the general who greets him as he arrives clarifies for him that life in "the other world" is utterly hierarchical and leaves no room for individual endeavors. In a friendly tone, the general makes no bones about what awaits Tyorkin:

> The General laughed:
> All right. Go register.
> There's a system, brother,
> An order you need to know.
>
> We welcome all comers,
> Give each the place he deserves.
> But who's a coward and who's a hero
> Is not always clear and known.
>
> There must be discipline, you know,
> Discipline and order for all:
> It's not that kind of war, brother,
> Where each can fend for himself . . .
> ("Tyorkin na tom svete," 379)

---

[16] N. A. Shlykunov. "Razve eto tot geroi?" *Literaturnaia gazeta*, 21 November 1963. Tvardovskii himself argued that the new poem was no "continuation" of the old, but a completely separate satirical work ("Kak byl napisan," 275, n. 4). The journal battle surrounding the publication was explored in V. and O. Tvardovskaia, "Istoriia odnoi fal'shivki: Epizod bor'by vokrug 'Terkina na tom svete,'" *Voprosy literatury* 1 (2007): 36–52.

The spatial geography of the underworld mirrors the militarized discipline of the Soviet state above, and Tyorkin makes his way through the halls of bureaucracy, finding them familiar—not that relative freedom of movement he had during the war, but rather the iron hierarchies of postwar Soviet life.

Tvardovsky piled up details using straightforward poetic lines, but the reader, along with Tyorkin, becomes more and more astonished at the ridiculousness of it all. Tyorkin passes the registration desk and finds himself at the "check-in desk," its own kind of bureaucratic hell, with its "shelves, safes, niches, drawers . . . hefty books, folders, and card files."

> And in the silence, like a dying breath
> The words sound:
> "Write down your auto-bio
> Briefly and in detail. . . ."
>
> ("Tyorkin na tom svete," 380–381)

Both briefly *and* in detail. . . . Hell, it turns out, is just like life on earth, and all of the bureaucratic details of Soviet life are present, described as a parody of militarized order—the medical examination, the bedding distribution, even the editor's desk at the "Coffin Gazette." The only thing missing from this Soviet institution is the "complaint book" (*kniga zhalob*); in this "other world," good Soviet citizens have no complaints, or at least are not permitted to express them.

Tyorkin himself is called into question—after all, he's not really dead and should not be exploring the underworld. This too, though, is put down to his habit of not following the rules, not conforming, not fitting in with the collective. What in wartime was valued—individual initiative—is now denigrated:

> However, he'll say, it's no wonder,
> That you chose a wandering path.
> Since you tore yourself asunder
> From the collective—
> There's the rub.
>
> ("Tyorkin na tom svete," 386)

Upon meeting a friend, Tyorkin discovers that it's not merely the bureaucratic hurdles and the collectivist mores of Soviet society that are mirrored in the other world. Everything is the same, including the need for connections, as Tyorkin discovers when he gets sleepy and is looking for somewhere to bunk down, and his friend offers to use his connections to hook Tyorkin up.

It might seem that at least international political games would not pass beyond the border of death, but if Soviet ideology is present, capitalist ideology must be as well. As Tyorkin's friend explains, the Cold War is also being fought in the "other world"—indeed, as with life on earth, there are two "other worlds," separated by a version of the iron curtain:

> You might not know, it's not visible.
> There's the other world
> Where you and I are,
> And of course the bourgeois Other world.
>
> Each of them has its own walls
> With a shared ceiling
> Two other worlds,
> Two systems,
>
> And a border with a lock.
> Here and there—each with its rules
> And, as it should be—
> Everything is different, life and mores too. . . .
>
> ("Tyorkin na tom svete," 388)

Tyorkin is astonished, exclaiming, "How could it possibly matter after death?" ("*Da ne vse li zdes' ravno?*"), but the answer is expressed in an ideologically correct formula:

> Here's the most important thing:
> Our other world in the world beyond
> Is the best and most progressive.
>
> ("Tyorkin na tom svete," 389)

The fantastic setting of *Tyorkin in the Other World* permits Tvardovsky to use political clichés in his satire. Highlighting phrases from speeches and daily life ("best and most progressive," "our world," and "the bourgeois world"), the conversation approaches the Cold War competition between East and West as a normal status quo—even in the parallel world "below."

Tvardovsky did not stop with international politics, however; he turns his gaze on the Soviet Union itself. The narrator does not name names, but he doesn't have to. The many departments and desks that Tyorkin discovers include also a "special department," the leader of which is:

> He who sent us
> Into this processing plant.
> In whose name you fell, soldier,
> On the battlefield. [. . .]
>
> The organizer of all fates,
> While still alive in the Kremlin
> Organized a mausoleum
> For himself along the way.
>
> ("Tyorkin na tom svete," 395)

The unsentimental rendering of hell as a "processing plant" equates it with any large-scale industrial activity in the Soviet Union. Tvardovsky lays the blame for the militarized bureaucracy that only got more entrenched after the close of the Second World War squarely with Stalin himself. His "other world" features an exemplary military (which does its best to weed out the cowards), a highly developed bureaucracy, and, more importantly, the utter penetration of Stalinist values into daily life, including personal relationships. In fact, once Tyorkin's friend realizes that he is not really dead, he recognizes that he'll have to report him to "those who need to know" ("*kuda nuzhno*").[17]

Stalinist values before the war had implied that class distinctions were at an end.[18] Tyorkin's friend's experience in the "other world" belies that idea.

---

[17] Tvardovskii, "Tyorkin na tom svete," 398. This reads almost as a preparody of Chonkin, whose entanglement with those "who need to know" is chronicled at the end of the first book of *Chonkin* and into the second book, where he has been arrested as a spy and deserter. See also E. G. Arzamastseva, "'Uzh ne parodiia li on?': K voprosu o sootnoshenii obrazov Vasiliia Tyorkina i Ivana Chonkina," in *Literatura tret'ei volny*, ed. V.P. Skobelev (Samara: Samarskii universitet, 1997), 123–132.

[18] In his book *Stalinist Values: The Cultural Norms of Soviet Modernity, 1917–1941*, Hoffmann explores the ways in which the government promoted that sense of one classless, united society in the 1930s. See especially chapter 5, 146–183.

5. From World War to Cold War: Tvardovsky, Solzhenitsyn, Voinovich, and Heroism in the Post-Stalin Period

When the resurrected Tyorkin wants to bring his friend back with him to the "real" world, the friend has no desire to risk it:

> Yes, but [back home] I might not end up
> In the *nomenklatura*.
> Today in the underworld I occupy
> An important post.
> And there, who am I today?
> Should I toss my experience and rank to the dogs? . . .
>
> ("Tyorkin na tom svete," 400)

In contrast, the "other world" has no pull for Vasily Tyorkin. Rank- and class-consciousness, bureaucracy, reporting friends to the authorities—much of what was unpleasant in post–World War II Soviet Russia, and nothing at all to tempt Tyorkin to stay.

For Life on this Earth

The contrast between the sequel and the original *Vasily Tyorkin* measures the distance travelled from 1939 to the early 1960s. If Tyorkin and his comrades were willing to face all kinds of difficult situations during the war and felt a true comradeship in those days, when the word "comrade" really meant something, the postwar situation had deflated that patriotism. Life in either world was not particularly worth fighting for.

It was notable that in *A Book about a Soldier*, the wartime book about Tyorkin, the iconic character of political commissar familiar from *Chapaev* was missing. No one was telling Tyorkin what to do, and no one was looking over his shoulder. Even more importantly, perhaps, none of his comrades were reporting him to "those who needed to know." No betrayal, no complaints, just enemy fire, mined battlefields, dangerous river crossings, and strafing aircraft. There is, at one level, a purity and simplicity to a soldier's life during war.[19] In the simplicity of combat, Vasily Tyorkin thrived.

Depicting life in Cold War Soviet society turned out to be more complicated.

---

[19] As Walzer points out, it is a "great relief to follow orders" because it saves one from confronting any of the stickier moral and ethical questions about war (Walzer, *Just and Unjust Wars*, 311).

In his notebooks from the 1960s, Tvardovsky noted the sensation of life's passage:

> A third of my life has passed, and an important third at that—not that half-unconscious third of childhood and youth, nor that third remaining before me, but the most content-filled middle part. And it passed under the sign of war, first raging and burning day after day of its four years, and then hovering over my memory, over my consciousness and continuing to hover to this day—no matter what you're doing, no matter what you're thinking about, no matter what you're planning. Like that continual thought of death which some people—myself included—cannot escape.[20]

As Samuil Marshak wrote, these memories of the war include more than just horror; there is, after all, something good in them:

> Anyone who has spent several years at the front and survived, both physically and morally, holds in his heart not only the memory of the dangers, the bitter losses and bad luck that war brings with it. He remembers something more as well: the intense feeling of a clearly acknowledged common goal, frontline friendships, comradely unity, that unity of feelings which he sorely misses later, in peacetime.
>
> And at the very least, at the front a man is moving as one with his unit and thus he is at one with his time as well.[21]

In the postwar period, as mourning, hardship, and the difficulties of reconstruction were replaced by the fear and pressures of the Cold War, Soviet readers and writers held on to memories of the suffering and horrors of war and the triumph of victory. For Tvardovsky, the war was ever-present. But the postwar period brought terror and the Cold War, rather than peace, and Tvardovsky tried to take some responsibility for that as well.[22]

---

[20] 24 June 1964, A. Tvardovskii, "Iz rabochikh tetradei 60-kh godov," quoted in A. Tvardovsky and M. Gefter, *XX vek: Gologrammy poeta i istorika* (Moscow: Novyi Khronograf, 2005), 372.

[21] Marshak here explores an important idea for understanding Soviet life in wartime and beyond: for those who were willing to metaphorically "march in formation" in peacetime too, the transition was easier. But dissidents of any kind suffered before, during, and after the war. See Samuil Marshak, *Radi zhizni na zemle: ob Aleksandre Tvardovskom* (Moscow: Sovetskii pisatel', 1961), 63. See also discussion below of Joseph Brodsky's antipathy toward standardization and marching in formation.

[22] "With his every line," Marshak wrote, "the poet announces that he too must take responsibility for the past." Marshak, *Radi zhizni na zemle*, 77.

5. From World War to Cold War: Tvardovsky, Solzhenitsyn, Voinovich, and Heroism in the Post-Stalin Period

Tvardovsky believed that he was a part of history, and as such his poetry had to be more than just "a historical portrayal, a research paper, or an article; he is called upon as a contemporary, an involved *witness*."[23] That duty to witness, to give testimony, meant that Tvardovsky had to continue to report what he saw after the war, the bad with the good. His readers may have been unhappy that he "resurrected" Tyorkin, tried to use the peasant-soldier hero to indict a postwar bureaucracy and sterility that undermined any sort of Soviet "victory" in the Second World War, but Tvardovsky raised themes of postwar life in an attempt to preserve relations among comrades, to preserve the dignity of Soviet life during the Cold War. Stalin's terror could not be ignored, and the hypocrisy and betrayal that had penetrated Soviet life had to be acknowledged as well.

War and the Gulag

By the late 1930s, two topics in Soviet history begin to overlap: Stalin's terror against his own citizens and the looming confrontation between the two reigning totalitarian systems, Soviet Socialism and Hitler's National Socialism. Out of terror and war came the militarized state, which was perpetuated further during the Cold War.

In literature, those topics became connected throughout the midcentury for several reasons. First of all, the experience of war in some cases was quite similar to the experience of labor camps: the individual lost all autonomy, was subjected to the rules and regulations of a hierarchical system, often in ill-fitting uniforms and in unsanitary, unheated living conditions, with inadequate food and medical care. War was like a labor camp, but "for the good of the cause," to use Vasily Grossman's title. Secondly, and perhaps more importantly, some of those who served in the war went directly from the front to the system of Soviet prison and labor camps, where they served sentences of ten years or more. For several decades after the war, literature about the Gulag could not be published. Discussion of prison camps was completely suppressed.

A final reason that literary works about the Gulag and the experience of war are intertwined in the Soviet context is Alexander Solzhenitsyn. It was the end of 1962 when *Novyi Mir* first published *One Day in the Life of Ivan Denisovich* (in November, #11), a story in which the word *zek*, Russian slang

---

[23] Marshak, *Radi zhizni na zemle*, 74 [emphasis here mine].

for "prisoner" or *zakliuchennyi*, made its debut on the printed page, and immediately afterwards Solzhenitsyn published the war story "Incident at Krechetovka Station" (January 1963, #1, first excerpted in *Pravda* in December 1962). These two stories are both war stories, and both tell tales of betrayal. In a way, they represent two versions of the same story: both portray some Soviet soldiers following instructions in the militarized system and other soldiers arrested as spies, with no possibility of defending themselves.

As has been described many times, Tvardovsky was immensely excited when he received the manuscript submission of *Shch-854* via editor Anna Berzer at *Novyi Mir*.[24] There is no question that Tvardovsky saw the connection between the Second World War and the Gulag system; as he said somewhat euphemistically to Solzhenitsyn at one editorial meeting, "You show everyone both at the front and on the Siberian construction projects," i.e., in Soviet work camps.

Tvardovsky—and ultimately Khrushchev—loved Solzhenitsyn's manuscript in great part because the narrative was told from the point of view of a peasant, a simple, hard-working member of an agricultural kolkhoz who had served as a rank-and-file soldier during the war. As Kornei Chukovsky described the hero Ivan Denisovich in an unofficial review entitled "A Literary Miracle," "Shukhov was a generalized portrait of the Russian common man: resilient, stubborn, hardy, jack-of-all-trades, cunning, and kindhearted—close kin of Vasily Tyorkin."[25] Rather than telling the story of labor camps from the point of view of a member of the intelligentsia, as Dostoevsky did in his *Notes from the House of the Dead*, Solzhenitsyn wanted the everyman view, and that view spoke plainly and clearly to both the peasant-editor Tvardovsky and the peasant–general secretary Khrushchev. Indeed, Khrushchev praised *One Day in the Life of Ivan Denisovich* to Tvardovsky as "a life-enhancing work that was fully in the spirit of the Twenty-Second Congress."

---

[24] Scholars continue to speculate as to why this novella was published, rather than the work of Vasily Grossman, for example. The answers include, among others, the fact that Grossman wrote about a different set of prison camps, the Nazi camps at which Soviet POWs and European citizens, including Jews, were forced to work and/or put to death. The topic was discussed at the ASEEES Forty-second Annual Convention in Los Angeles in 2010, at the roundtable "Tolstoy and Grossman: Writing and Reading War and Peace in the Nineteenth and Twentieth Centuries."

[25] Quoted in Scammell, *Solzhenitsyn*, 424.

Interestingly, Solzhenitsyn's early war story, published just after *One Day in the Life of Ivan Denisovich*, made less of a splash. "Incident at Krechetovka Station" (*"Sluchai na stantsii Krechetovka"*)[26] takes place in 1941. The central character, Lieutenant Zotov, yearns to be sent to the front and chafes at his desk job at a train station, where he puts together trains to take troops, supplies, and so on to the various parts of the war zone. By 1962 the setting represents a retreat into the past, indeed, into the chaotic first year of the war about which Stalin and everyone else had maintained total silence for a decade and a half.

Scholars have suggested that in Lt. Vasily Zotov, "Solzhenitsyn portrayed, and satirized, his own younger self: puritanical, loyal, naive, idealistic, and fatally narrow in his blind devotion to the Soviet cause."[27] Ivan Denisovich too is a patriot; he dreams of returning to his kolkhoz and can't imagine its present, he willingly completes the work required during his sentence, and he regrets the lost years but is resigned to his fate. Not perhaps as cheerful as Tyorkin, Shukhov is nonetheless a hard worker, inventive and crafty, if only in hiding his tools and husbanding his strength so that he can work better again the next day. He is certainly more sympathetic to the general Soviet reader, especially one like Khrushchev or Tvardovsky, than intellectual characters such as the Moscow Art Theater actor Tveritinov in "Krechetovka" or the filmmaker Tsezar Markovich portrayed in *One Day*.

"Incident at Krechetovka Station" focuses on Zotov's single-mindedness, as he—like Travkin in *The Star*—refuses the companionship of women, no matter how tempted he might be. Instead, Zotov is almost fatally seduced by another man, the misplaced passenger Tveritinov. Tveritinov is personally pleasant, easy to talk with, and the frustrated Zotov enjoys his company. But at this important juncture of the war, Zotov needs to figure out why Tveritinov is travelling alone, and at first he wants to believe the story Tveritinov spins about losing his regiment. He does not understand Tveritinov's hints at the year 1937; readers might think that the traveller is actually escaping

---

[26] Solzhenitsyn's original title was "Incident at Kochetovka Station," the actual geographic location of the incident on which he based the story. However, because the editor of the right-wing journal *Oktiabr'* at the time was named Kochetov, Tvardovsky felt that the original title would cause unnecessary conclusions to be drawn about competition between himself and Kochetov, between *Novyi Mir* and *Oktiabr'*. Solzhenitsyn later restored his original title.

[27] Scammell, *Solzhenitsyn*, 438.

from a prison camp, but Zotov seems unaware that his guest might be a victim of Stalin's purges.[28] Instead he decides that he is probably an imperialist spy. Tveritinov asks what Stalingrad used to be called, but it was renamed from Tsaritysn in Stalin's honor in 1925. Zotov reacts: "A Soviet person who doesn't know Stalingrad? That is utterly impossible! Utterly! Utterly!" (*Rasskazy*, 209). He decides that he has to report Tveritinov to "those who need to know."

The story deliberately leaves the reader, like Zotov, in uncertainty. In the wake of his decisive action, Zotov cannot find out whether Tveritinov was really a spy or whether he has sent the hapless soldier into the Gulag system; in horror, when he realizes that he's been reported, Tveritinov shouts to Zotov, "What are you doing? What are you doing? This *cannot be corrected!!*" (*Rasskazy*, 215). The reader too cannot decide: was Tveritinov a prevaricating White officer, sent to interrogate Zotov about train routes, front lines, and other military secrets? Or did Zotov doom a fellow Soviet citizen to captivity, torture, and death in a system where nothing can be "corrected," a system from which Tveritinov might have recently escaped?

Was there room in the Soviet system for the human warmth, the "instinctive liking" for Tveritinov which Zotov felt? (*Rasskazy*, 201). After all, Tveritinov could have been telling the truth; he could really have been an *okruzhenets*, a soldier who had briefly been encircled by the enemy but who had escaped back to his own. Trying to justify his snap decision, Zotov thinks to himself that "instructions required one to take especial care with the encircled, especially when they were alone" (*Rasskazy*, 200).

One of the harshest Soviet policies during World War II was the one regarding prisoners of war and other soldiers caught behind enemy lines. The fact that Kazakevich's characters in *The Star* perished during their reconnaissance duty kept them from the fates of many Soviet soldiers, including Solzhenitsyn's peasant character Ivan Denisovich.

Solzhenitsyn begins *One Day in the Life of Ivan Denisovich* at reveille, and already in the first paragraph there is no doubt as to its location: the barracks and even the reveille itself signal a military setting, but the guard, *nadziratel'*, who is beating out the command and the two fingers' worth of frost on the windowpanes put us squarely in a Siberian prison camp.

---

[28] Ivan Denisovich and his fellow prisoners talk openly about 1937 and 1938 and comment that a "special camp" allows for such conversation, since all the prisoners are politicals. See Alexander Solzhenitsyn, *Rasskazy* (Moscow: ACT, 2003), 59.

5. From World War to Cold War: Tvardovsky, Solzhenitsyn, Voinovich, and Heroism in the Post-Stalin Period

The relationship between the militarized Gulag and the Red Army makes his imprisonment not that different for Ivan Shukhov, who is first and foremost a peasant-soldier. The narrator makes it clear that he was mobilized in the first days of the war: "Ivan Denisovich had left home on June 23, 1941." And he knew how to follow orders. Arrested before war's end, by the time of the novella's action, 1951, Shukhov remains in the power of his Soviet superiors.[29]

In the novel, each prisoner gets a backstory—how he ended up in the Gulag—and Ivan Denisovich's story ties his fate back to the war:

> According to his dossier, Ivan Denisovich Shukhov had been sentenced for high treason. He had testified to it himself. Yes, he'd surrendered to the Germans with the intention of betraying his country and he'd returned from captivity to carry out a mission for German intelligence. What sort of mission neither Shukhov nor the interrogator could say. So it had been left at that—a mission.
>
> Shukhov had figured it all out. If he didn't sign he'd be shot. If he signed he'd still get a chance to live. So he signed.

But what did Shukhov's confession really mean?

> What really happened was this. In February 1942 their whole army was surrounded on the northwest front. No food was parachuted to them. There were no planes. [. . .] Their ammunition was gone. So the Germans rounded them up in the forest, a few at a time. Shukhov was in one of these groups, and remained in German captivity for a day or two. Then five of them managed to escape. They stole through the forest and marshes again, and, by a miracle, reached their own lines. A machine gunner shot two of them on the spot, a third died of his wounds, but two got through. Had they been wiser they'd have said they'd been wandering in the forest, and then nothing would have happened. But they told the truth: they said they were escaped POWs. [. . .] If all five of them had got through, their statements could have been found to tally and they might have been believed. But with two it was hopeless. (*Rasskazy*, 47; *One Day*, 55)

---

[29] The Russian text of the novella can be found in Alexander Solzhenitsyn, *Rasskazy* (Moscow: AST, 2003), 7–116; English-language quotations come from *One Day in the Life of Ivan Denisovich* (New York: Signet Classic, 1998).

163

This prisoner, who was in the army from the second day of the war, was able to continue his life in a militarized setting. "During his long years in prisons and camps he'd lost the habit of planning for the next day, for a year ahead, for supporting his family. The authorities did his thinking for him about everything—it was somehow easier that way" (*Rasskazy*, 32; *One Day*, 35). Labelled a "spy," Ivan Denisovich remained a loyal soldier, obeying orders as much as possible, looking for shortcuts and ways to get what he needs (more food, warm clothing, tools for completing his work to his satisfaction). His position in the work squad resembled life in the regiment, which in turn resembles the ideal Soviet workplace, with each contributing according to his abilities. "Like a big family," Ivan Denisovich mused, "the work squad was a family" (*Rasskazy*, 58; *One Day*, 69).

Viktor Nekrasov, in a review that might have described Solzhenitsyn's work, remarked that official Soviet literature was, above all, "the most earnest literature in the world":

> Earnest, because it concerns itself only with earnest matters—life-affirmation, optimism, enthusiasm, love of toil, and, most importantly, the formation of a new man. There is no room for jocularity here. Irony, anecdote, allusion and innuendo are not its weapons. Its weapon is of quite another steel, unbending, impenetrable and always shining; and the name of this weapon is socialist realism.[30]

Although Solzhenitsyn's topics eventually got him expelled from the Soviet Union—in particular because he chose to publish them, especially *The Gulag Archipelago*, abroad—his style fit right in with the prevailing Soviet formulae.[31] These narratives consider soldiers in wartime and their postwar fates, and they suggest that loyalty to the state can have ambiguous consequences. The individual might find satisfaction in the daily tasks

---

[30] Victor Nekrasov, "Being Earnest Isn't Always Important," *Survey* 23.3 (104) (1977–1978): 42. The review was actually devoted to Venedikt Erofeev's *Moskva-Petushki* and Vladimir Voinovich's *Ivankiada* (1978).

[31] Writers as varied as Voinovich and Vladimir Sorokin have expressed their annoyance at and/or concern with Solzhenitsyn's messianic stance after he went into exile. See Voinovich's parodic *Moskva 2042* (Ann Arbor: Ardis, 1987) as well as his more serious *Portret na fone mifa* (Moscow: Eksmo, 2002). In Sorokin's novel *Tridtsataia liubov' Mariny* (Moscow: P. Elinin, 1995), the heroine—who is characterized by her random sexual encounters and dissident-worship—has a portrait of Solzhenitsyn in her apartment.

of war or even of Socialist construction projects in a Siberian camp. But as in *Cement*, the novel about postwar reconstruction after the Civil War, the individual had to be sacrificed to the collective. These soldiers did their duty for the state, but there was no *podvig* in their attempts to negotiate the Stalinist system.

The Hero as Parody: Chonkin

As Nekrasov argued, there was no room in Soviet literature for irony, jocularity, or parody. But that does not mean that no one wrote in that vein. Ironically, or perhaps tellingly for the Thaw period, Nikita Khrushchev himself was instrumental in securing the initial fame of parodic writer Vladimir Voinovich. As memoirists describe it, the general secretary "couldn't resist" singing along with what was to become the "unofficial hymn to Soviet cosmonauts" as he presided from the heights of Lenin's mausoleum over the welcome parade for Yury Gagarin on Red Square in 1960.[32]

That song featured words by Voinovich, who would go on to publish a number of his early stories in Tvardovsky's journal *Novyi Mir*. In his lyrics for "Fourteen Minutes to Take Off" ("*Chetyrnadtsat' minut do starta*") Voinovich celebrated the great Cold War triumph of the Soviet Union: the space program. The lyrics have a colloquial tone and include disarming details. Rather than the rhetoric of *podvig*, the song uses *byt*: the cosmonauts talk about having a smoke before getting into their rocket, and though it *seems* like a countdown, it really isn't. After all, they have fourteen minutes until takeoff—not ten seconds.

The song's themes are innocuous, but they reinforce Soviet Cold War doctrine. The cosmonauts are portrayed as friends, comrades who are performing a task together. They trust their navigator, who will ensure that they succeed, making space travel a simple feat. In fact they cherish the earth, their home planet, but they will win the space race, thus also becoming the earth's eventual masters. This easy task parallels the success of World War II, and the cosmonauts recall Tyorkin, who always had a good meal and a smoke before going out to smash the enemy. In later redactions, to negate the light humor Voinovich inserted into his lyrics, the cosmonauts were to "sing" before departing rather than have a smoke.

---

[32] Cornwell, "Voinovich," 880–882.

Voinovich's early stories, straightforward, realistic narratives of life in the "virgin lands" and provincial villages, received accolades from important writers and critics such as Ehrenburg, Grossman, Marshak, Simonov, and Tendriakov. V. Kardin called Voinovich one of "the most talented young prose writers" of his time, and Tendriakov responded to Voinovich's first story, "We Live Here" (published in *Novyi Mir* in 1961), by exclaiming, "A fresh voice has appeared!"[33]

Herein lay the conflict of the Thaw period: while the new journal *Yunost* (*Youth*) was founded in 1955 and Soviet literature yearned for "new voices," those voices faced severe restrictions on what they could say. In the end, they also had to remain loyal to the Soviet state. Voinovich began publishing in Russia, but it soon became clear that his kind of voice, a satirical voice, was not welcome in his native land. To the best of his ability, Voinovich continued to participate in the literary life of his country, joining the Writers' Union in 1962 and assisting in the adaptation of his narratives for the stage, but at the same time, over the next decade his literary activity took another direction: writing petitions and protests to defend and support dissident writers and intellectuals like Andrei Sinyavsky, Yuly Daniel, Solzhenitsyn, and Andrei Sakharov. Eventually exiled and stripped of his citizenship in 1980, Voinovich and his family had to leave the Soviet Union to avoid internal exile or worse, and he remained in Germany until being invited back by Gorbachev some ten years later.

His best and most beloved work, *The Life and Adventures of the Soldier Ivan Chonkin*, was published as *tamizdat* in France in 1969.[34] The novel comprises a parody of three genres: the folktale about Ivan the Fool, the saint's life, and the biographical novel about a heroic Soviet soldier.[35] In-

---

[33] L. B. Brusilovskaia, I. V. Konda, "Voinovich," in *Russkie pisateli 20 veka: biograficheskii slovar'*, ed. P. A. Nikolaev (Moscow: Izd. Randevu-AM, 2000), 159; Tendriakov's review was published in *Literaturnaia gazeta* 25 (February 1961).

[34] First published in *Grani* in 1969, possibly without the author's permission. An abridged version of the novel was published in *Iunost'*, 1988 (12) and 1989 (1–2).

[35] Originally planned as an "anecdote in five parts," *Chonkin* was the result of fifteen years of work for Voinovich throughout the 1960s and 1970s. Voinovich, *Zhizn' i neobychainye prikliucheniia soldata Ivana Chonkina* (Paris: YMCA-Press, 1975) was followed by a second volume in 1979, *Pretendent na prestol: novye prikliucheniia soldata Ivana Chonkina* (Paris: YMCA-Press 1981). As one Russian bookselling Web site had it, in advertising the final volume of Chonkin's adventures: "Chonkin lived, Chonkin lives, Chonkin will live." Voinovich, *Zhizn' i neobychainye prikliucheniia soldata Ivana Chonkina. Kniga III: Peremeshchennoe litso* (Moscow: Eksmo, 2007).

deed, *Chonkin* follows a decidedly non-heroic soldier, and in creating the character, Voinovich drew on the absurdist approach to chronicling war found in Jaroslav Hašek's 1923 *The Good Soldier Švejk*, part of what one critic has called "the tradition of anti-militarist satire."[36] Even the author is inclined to exclaim, "What kind of an absurd figure is this?!!"—as Chonkin fulfills his duty to his fatherland in the days and weeks before the German attack on the Soviet Union by guarding a downed airplane in a Soviet village. The narrator puts these words into the readers' mouths, continuing in outrage, "Where is the example for [our] maturing youth?" In his own pseudo-defense, the narrator announces, "The hero of a book is like a child; you take what you get, you can't just throw him out the window. Maybe others have better children, smarter children, but your own is always more dear because it's yours."[37]

This parody of a soldier gives us an inside-out view of life in the Soviet military, with a hero the narrator himself calls defective. Unlike other World War II heroes, Chonkin does not die a heroic death, or indeed any death. He never even really serves, but sits out much of the war in the countryside. As Natalia Ivanova and Peter Vail commented in a Radio Free Europe broadcast in 2006, the very idea of parodic war literature may be commonplace in other national literatures (from Švejk to Joseph Heller's *Catch-22*, among many other examples), but in the Russian tradition Voinovich and his Chonkin stand alone.[38]

Voinovich had hoped to publish *Chonkin* in the Soviet Union, and editor of *Novyi Mir* Alexander Tvardovsky immediately recognized Chonkin's kinship with his own Tyorkin. As Voinovich recalled:

> When I showed several chapters of *Chonkin* to Tvardovsky, he didn't like it, said that it wasn't funny or witty. Then he added that there were many such surnames: Travkin, Brovkin. . . . He was silent for a minute, and then added: "Tyorkin. . . ." I thought then that he might be right [. . .]: Travkins, Brovkins, Tyorkins, Chonkins. I went home and

---

[36] Peter Petro, "Hasek, Voinovich, and the Tradition of Anti-Militarist Satire," *Canadian Slavonic Papers* XXII.1 (March 1980): 116–121.

[37] Vladimir Voinovich, *Zhizn' i neobychainye prikliucheniia soldata Ivana Chonkina* (Moscow: Knizhnaia palata, 1990), 21. I will be citing from this edition of the novel.

[38] Petr Vail', "Geroi vremeni," 16 January 2006. http://archive.svoboda.org/programs/cicles/hero/21.asp.

tried to change the surname. I wasted a lot of time, but nothing came of it. Chonkin remains Chonkin.[39]

Chonkin's function is reflective: he is the contemporary version of the satiric mirror that Gogol's mayor holds up to the audience in his 1842 comedy *The Inspector-General*.[40] Voinovich recognized this difference:

> He is neither Švejk nor Tyorkin. Švejk and Tyorkin are active heroes, Chonkin is passive. He stands where he was told to stand and he stands at his post until relieved. But he stands to the end, as a true soldier should.[41]

One critic explained that Private Chonkin's main problem (for the fictional Soviet reality in which he lived, and for his author, living in actual Soviet space) is that he has no prejudices, makes no assumptions, and simply encounters phenomena in life with an open mind and heart.

> The thing is that every object, every phenomenon of everyday life is entangled with a multiplicity of connections and conditions, interwoven with invisible threads along with the conventional "rules of the game." But Chonkin is a natural man. He does not even suspect that these rules—required for all of us—exist. For him every object, every phenomenon exists, so to speak, in its primordial, pure state. And it only means what it means.[42]

In the novel, Voinovich uses various satirical devices to "expose the meaninglessness and mock the false grandeur" of the rhetoric of *podvig*.[43] He also employs estrangement, the technique Russian formalist theorists called

---

[39] Voinovich, quoted in Vail', "Geroi vremeni."
[40] On Gogol and Voinovich, see Victor Peppard, "Gogolian Substrata in *Zhizn' i neobychainye prikliucheniia soldata Ivana Chonkina*," *Russian Language Journal* 38.131 (1984): 131–138.
[41] Voinovich, "O sovremennosti i istorii," *Rossiia/Russia* 2 (1975): 233, quoted in Laura Beraha, "The Fixed Fool: Raising and Resisting Picaresque Mobility in Vladimir Voinovich's Chonkin Novels," *SEEJ* 40.3 (1996): 476.
[42] Benedikt Sarnov, "Estestvennyi chelovek v neestestvennykh obstoiatel'stvakh. O geroe etoi knigi i ee avtore," 523–539 in Vladimir Voinovich, *Zhizn' i neobychainye prikliucheniia soldata Ivana Chonkina* (Moscow: Knizhnaia palata, 1990), 532.
[43] See Khan, "Folklore and Fairytale Elements in Vladimir Voinovich's Novel *The Life and Extraordinary Adventures of Private Ivan Chonkin*," *SEEJ* 40.3 (1996): 494–518.

ostranenie, in highlighting Chonkin's natural or naive way of perceiving the world around him.[44] These literary devices aid Voinovich in deflating the very notion of the Soviet soldier. Everything from external situations—the uniform, language, and stance of a Soviet soldier—to internal inclinations undergoes transformation, as the false, inflated hero becomes a regular guy. Chonkin approaches his military service as he would normal life, and Voinovich chronicles his desires to sleep, have sex, and be comfortable in his surroundings—in other words, to live his life as best he can under the circumstances.

Orphaned early in life, Chonkin lost his foster parents as well. He is only semi-educated and tries to approach his military and political training humbly. These characteristics follow genre conventions for two Russian genres, the hagiographic story and the fairy tale. Halimur Khan argues that in a fairy tale, there are two possible kinds of heroes, victim-heroes and seeker-heroes. "Victim-heroes like Chonkin," he maintains, "begin their journey, or better even, their wanderings, without any particular goal in mind. Adventures thus *await* the victim-hero. He is the passive recipient of action."[45]

Chonkin is chosen to guard the downed aircraft (truly a valuable piece of state property) precisely because of his passive nature. He can be trusted not to *act* in any way, not to try and repair the plane, or sell it for parts, or in any way interfere with it. He is passivity personified, and his superiors depend on that, even when they have already forgotten about him entirely. Voinovich had intended to have Chonkin "stand at guard" until removed, indeed, until the end of the war, somehow "victorious over everyone" despite his total passivity.[46] Not bravery plus consciousness; in fact not brave and not conscious, just fulfilling his duty to the state without asking any questions.

Chonkin: A Real Man?

While Chonkin is a comedic figure on his own terms, the parody here refers more specifically to another famous story that centers around a plane. The hero of Boris Polevoi's Stalin-prizewinning 1947 novel *The Story of a*

---

44 Sarnov points out that Voinovich (in a story about the Great Leader of the Peoples) describes Stalin's house as standing "behind the high red brick fence that is known the world around. To call the steeped in legend 'walls of the ancient Kremlin' simply *a fence*—Lord almighty, this wouldn't occur to everyone," 535.
45 Khan, "Folklore," 512.
46 Voinovich quoted in Vail', "Geroi vremeni."

Real Man (*Povest' o nastoiashchem cheloveke*) takes off on an unauthorized mission and crashes his plane in enemy territory. This novel, based on the biography of Alexei Maresiev, became emblematic of the Soviet heroic feat in wartime.[47] The popular 1948 film *The Story of a Real Man* (directed by Alexander Stolper) cemented the image of the legless aviator in the Soviet imagination.[48]

The narrative weight of Polevoi's story falls on the hero's long and arduous crawl back to Soviet lines. Seriously wounded, legs and arms broken, without food or water, the hero-seeker drags his body for days on end in quest of his comrade soldiers. Readers of the narrative might ask, however, about the plane: this airman has destroyed not only his body but also a major piece of needed technology in a foolish, unnecessary run based on unreliable information.

Perhaps, however, the heroic struggle to survive was not what made Meresiev a real man; the second half of the narrative features a political commissar, also seriously wounded, who gives Meresiev the strength and motivation to stand up on his artificial legs and get back into a plane to fight the enemy. The transformation into a "real man" comes when Meresiev returns to the skies to continue to shoot down German planes.

Ivan Chonkin had no political commissar. His daftness at political meetings kept any well-meaning commissar from being able to influence his behavior. Voinovich deliberately undercuts any "positive" Soviet meaning that might be implied in his story. While Chonkin does not benefit from the advice and mentoring of a commissar figure, as Meresiev and Chapaev did, Voinovich does pair him with what Laura Beraha identifies as part of another traditional twosome: "the fool and the false pedant, part of the dialogical interanimating effect of foolish non-comprehension, the calling into question of power-based, established and thus moribund truths."[49] Chonkin's neighbor Gladyshev, in a parody of Soviet genetics, is attempting to create a hybrid tomato-potato plant so that in the most perfect of future societies, both the roots and the branches will bear fruit. Gladyshev's other experiments (which

---

[47] Polevoi named his character Aleksei Meres'ev.
[48] The film was seen by 34.4 million viewers and, like the novel, received a Stalin Prize (Youngblood, "Russian War Films," 92). The real pilot claimed never to have read the book or seen the movie; he lived the life of a "legend," dying only in 2001. For what must have been virtually his last interview, see Igor' Izgarshev, "Aleksei Mares'ev: Ia chelovek, a ne legenda!" *Argumenty i fakty* no. 19 (1072) (8 May 2001).
[49] Beraha, "The Fixed Fool," 485.

include creating vodka from fecal matter) point to the essentially sophomoric nature of this character and his role in the novel; if Chonkin is looking for knowledge and enlightenment, he won't find it next door.⁵⁰

But writing about a hero (in the style of a saint's life) and fecal matter also pushes the genre possibilities in ways that are important to Voinovich. As the author explained in an autobiographical note:

> One should keep in mind that I am a satirist. A satirist differs from writers working in other genres in that he concentrates his attention on the shady sides of life and on negative tendencies. More than others he emphasizes existing problems and even goes overboard. Without this there cannot be any satire.⁵¹

This kind of "overemphasis" was not welcomed in the late 1960s any more than it would have been in the early 1950s. When in 1952 Stalin pronounced, "We need our Gogols and Shchedrins," authors of the day knew that this call for critique and criticism, satire and savagery, was not authentic.

In the post-Stalin period, there was a little more wiggle room for satire, but not much. After Khrushchev was removed by political coup, the endorsement by the general secretary could no longer help Voinovich or Tvardovsky. Voinovich himself was "removed" from literary life, and even from "Fourteen Minutes to Take Off," which began to be performed without words—that is to say, without Voinovich's text. The author was expunged from his own popular patriotic song, and eventually from the Soviet Union, following the dissident Solzhenitsyn into exile. It may be that satire—like *samizdat* and *tamizdat*—was a medicine too bitter for the Soviet system to tolerate.

* * *

Cultural thaw in the early 1960s led to the publication of new authors like Voinovich, to new explorations with old characters—like Tvardovsky's expedition into the "other world" with his Tyorkin—and to new themes, such as

---

[50] Petro points to the "excremental" connection between Hasek's novel and Voinovich's, referencing Norman O. Brown, "The Excremental Vision," in *Life against Death: The Psychoanalytical Meaning of History* (Middleton, Conn.: Wesleyan University Press, 1959), 186–201. See Petro, "Hasek, Voinovich," 119.

[51] Qtd. in Sarnov, "Estestvennyi chelovek," 535.

Solzhenitsyn's exposés of wartime tattlers and post-war victims, including his peasant-soldier, sent to the Gulag. Khrushchev's cultural thaw ended when he was ousted and replaced by Leonid Brezhnev in 1964, but Cold War politics and internal persecution continued throughout the seventies and most of the eighties.

One tactic of the Brezhnev administration to try and create a social cohesion was to refocus the nation's attention on World War II. All publication of war memoirs was transferred to the Military Publishing House and subjected to strict censorial control. It was at this time—1965, the twentieth anniversary of the end of the war—that Victory Day became a national holiday and the cult of World War II began to grow.[52]

Literary critic and war veteran Lazar Lazarev recalled:

> Those of us who had fought in the war thought, at first, that at last the war was getting the attention it merited. But in fact that attention was purely an official attempt to turn the war into a show made up of concocted legends.[53]

In this new world, the old heroes had to be made extra-heroic in order to pass muster. War, and the memory and celebration of war, kept the Russian eye focused away from contemporary life, from the daily grind of the Brezhnev era. As Peter Vail argues:

> Russian life in peacetime was fairly impoverished and never very fun. That's why during wartime, when these conditions seemed less important, a certain unity, a kind of trench brotherhood, a clarity of ideas, emerged: here's the enemy, here's the friend, and all contradictions disappeared. And for that reason war was endowed with a particular purity and beauty. War was presented as a cleansing flame, and to speak about it with a grin was unseemly.[54]

---

[52] Tumarkin discusses the Grekov Military Art Studio and the 3-D panorama paintings of the Central Armed Forces Museum; the halls she describes were transferred intact to the new Museum of the Great Patriotic War, which opened in 1995. See *Pamiat' o podvige*, Moscow 1985, which Tumarkin cites, and compare it to the guidebook of the new Moscow museum.
[53] Quoted in Tumarkin, *The Living and the Dead*, 132–134.
[54] Vail', "Geroi vremeni."

No humor, only elevated words. Not life, but *podvig*. Even when war was not raging, a cult of war could keep that "pure," "cleansed" feeling of unity alive. If Khrushchev's thaw occurred during the hardening of the Cold War, then Brezhnev's cultural chill happened even as he explored detente and arms control with the United States. By 1974, ten years after Brezhnev took control of the Soviet Union, Nekrasov was in Paris, Solzhenitsyn was in Switzerland on his way to Vermont, and Alexander Tvardovsky was dead.[55] Six years later, Voinovich left for West Germany.

---

[55] When he was offered his Writers' Union membership back a decade later, Voinovich only laughed. See Vladimir Voinovich and Michael Henry Heim, "An Exile's Dilemma," *The Wilson Quarterly*, 14.4 (Autumn 1990): 114–120.

Chapter Six

Antiheroes in a Post-heroic Age: Sergei Dovlatov, Vladimir Makanin, and Cold War Malaise

I despise the word "we"
I hear in it the herd's lowing
The terrible silence of prison
And the thunder of the military parade.

Я ненавижу слово мы.
Я слышу в нем мычанье стада,
Безмолвье жуткое тюрьмы
И гром военного парада.

-Vladimir Korenatsky

In the dark twentieth century
With its clear sign of "Stalin"
If a man had a conscience,
He became a drunk.

В темном двадцатом веке
С четкой вывеской "Сталин"
Совесть была в человеке,
Если пьяницей стал он.

-Boris Slutsky

At the First Congress of Soviet Writers in 1934, Andrei Zhdanov had declared that "the whole life of our party, the whole life of our working class and its struggle combines the most stern and sober practical work with a supreme spirit of heroic deeds and magnificent future prospects." A directive had been handed down: documenting those "heroic deeds," those *podvigi*, and incarnating the heroes who performed them was the task of the official Soviet writer. As became clear in 1946, when Zhdanov presided over the purging of Anna Akhmatova and Mikhail Zoshchenko, there was no place in the Soviet Union for a nonofficial writer. This is what we have been examining in the preceding chapters: creating heroes was official policy.

What, then, happened to writers who refused to document heroic deeds? In many cases they "wrote for the long drawer," as the Russian saying goes; in some cases they published abroad, as did Voinovich, and in others they ceased to write at all. But living in the Soviet Union, they had to confront the discourse of *podvig*, the discourse of the heroic deed, on a daily basis—in the newspapers, in socialist realist fiction, at the movie theater, in their textbooks and their children's textbooks.

The generation of writers who came of age after World War II had to think about that heroic discourse, and about how their own fiction responded to it. These *shestidesiatniki*, "men (and women) of the sixties," had grown up on heroic narratives, whether of Civil War bravery demonstrated by Chapaev and other heroes, of "building socialism"—and the class warfare that entailed—one factory and kolkhoz novel at a time, or of partisans and frontline soldiers who defeated the evil Nazis and saved Europe from fascism. As children they also may have watched their neighbors and family members disappear into the Gulag. The terrors of their childhood—from Stalinism to the Second World War—had receded, but for many the taste of hypocrisy remained in their mouths.

Just a few years separated them from the myth of the happy Stalinist childhood; children born in the early to mid-1930s, in the view of one observer, frequently "managed to become dreamers."[1] For example, author Galina Shcherbakova, born 1931, remembered her postwar mind-set in 1952, just before Stalin's death, thus:

> Like everyone else, I lived under the impression of the Victory. It caused a kind of memory block. I forgot—even though I knew perfectly well—that my grandfathers were murdered during collectivization and my uncles were killed in the bloody year of 1937. I became a patriot to the very bones, and everything in me squealed with joy at my wonderful homeland.[2]

After the death of Stalin, for Shcherbakova and many like her this patriotism and belief in capital-V Victory—the transcendent meaning of Soviet victory in the Second World War—gradually began to disappear.

Many of those born in 1937 and later never reached that level of patriotism. Peter Vail and Alexander Genis argue that in the early 1960s, the "old heroes" of fiction (Pavel Korchagin, Alexander Matrosov, Alexei Stakhanov)—

---

[1] See Lev Anninskii, "Struktura labarinta: Vladimir Makanin i literatura 'seredinnogo' cheloveka," *Znamia* 12 (1986): 220.
[2] G. Shcherbakova, *Iashkiny deti* (Moscow: Eksmo, 2008), 241.

dreamers, who believed in the Soviet future and lived within the discourse of *podvig* in an effort to make it come true—were due to be replaced with "new heroes."[3] But those who might have created the new heroes were not themselves believers; they were "quiet skeptics," "implacable anatomists."[4] What kind of heroes would writers like those create? And was a protagonist necessarily a hero when the war was merely a "cold" one?

In this chapter we examine two authors, Sergei Dovlatov (1940–1990) and Vladimir Makanin (born 1937), themselves both "men of the '60s," to reveal the characteristics of what I call "antiheroism." These writers lived and wrote on the margins, had a phobia of the rhetoric of *podvig*, and adopted a tone of irony and even detached amusement. In this way they developed more fully the literary voice articulated by a previous generation, by Tvardovsky and especially Nekrasov.[5]

Dovlatov and Makanin were among a generation of writers who created characters perfect for their age, an age when only the truly deluded could believe any more in the grand Soviet experiment and when the Cold War too had become a stiff and stagnating fact of Soviet life.[6] This post-heroic age was presided over, fittingly enough, by Leonid Brezhnev, who had been a commissar, not a frontline soldier or a commander, during World War II. Men and women of the '60s around the world experienced a decade of cultural and political upheaval; those in the Soviet Union were not part of that social revolution. In 1964, the year Brezhnev assumed power, the first Beatles album was released in the United States. Needless to say, it was not released in the Soviet Union. Four years later, the Soviets brought the Prague Spring to a hasty conclusion.

---

[3] The critics discussed this in terms of "physicists" (i.e., scientists) and "lyricists" (i.e., humanists), terms that came from Boris Slutskii's 1959 poem of that name. See P. Vail', A. Genis, "Strana slov," *Novyi mir* 4 (1991): 239.

[4] Anninskii describes Makanin this way ("Struktura labarinta," 226).

[5] Mark Lipovetskii describes these two authors, among others, as having an "implicit existentialist orientation." See "Makanin's Existential Myth in the Nineties: 'Escape Hatch,' 'The Prisoner from the Caucasus,' and *Underground*," in Byron Lindsey and Tatiana Spektor, *Routes of Passage: Essays on the Fiction of Vladimir Makanin* (Bloomington, IN: Slavica, 2007), 97.

[6] For an extended exploration of this idea, see Alexei Yurchak, *Everything Was Forever, Until It Was No More: The Last Soviet Generation* (Princeton: Princeton University Press, 2006). Dovlatov and Makanin were a part of the "second-to-last" Soviet generation, but it may very well have seemed to them that the Brezhnev regime would last forever.

6. Antiheroes in a Post-heroic Age: Sergei Dovlatov, Vladimir Makanin, and Cold War Malaise

Sergei Dovlatov—who was perhaps the antithesis of an official Soviet writer—chronicled dropouts and misfits, frequently drawing on autobiographical events to document the other side of the heroic Soviet coin. Dovlatov was a stylist *par excellence*, and he wrote and rewrote his anecdotes and observations about Russian life in numerous stories, tales, and essays. Never published as an author of fiction in the Soviet Union, Dovlatov emigrated to the United States in 1979, and only there did he begin to publish. His popularity in Russia since the early 1990s has created an almost cultlike following of readers and of Dovlatov-style writers,[7] but through much of his life, Dovlatov was *persona non grata* in his homeland.

Vladimir Makanin's debut novel, *A Straight Line* (*Priamaia liniia*, 1965), was about a mathematician striving for good and justice. It was received positively by critics, who immediately ranked him with the "young writers" such as Vasily Aksyonov and Anatoly Gladilin. The issue of the literary journal *Moskva* in which *A Straight Line* was published also contained Bulgakov's long-awaited *Master and Margarita* and has been estimated to have been read by up to two million people. Reprinted a number of times, Makanin's novel remained popular and contributed to the wave of heroic literature of the Cold War, which featured scientists, engineers, and cosmonauts.[8]

After this splashy debut, Makanin describes his career in the seventies and eighties as akin to the experience of being buried in a pauper's grave: unable to publish in the literary journals, where his work would have been noticed, he published good books with provincial publishers. As he likes to say, no one read them, and they were promptly forgotten.[9] This status of marginalized writer parallels the characters in his work, who are outsiders and dropouts from society in one way or another. After the collapse of the Soviet Union, Makanin's career revived. He won the Russian Booker Prize for his 1993 novella *Baize-Covered Table with Decanter* (*Stol, pokrytyi suknom i s grafinom poseredine*), and his 1998 novel *Underground, or a Hero of Our Time* (*Andegraund, ili geroi nashego vremeni*) was an attempt to write the "big Rus-

---

[7] Author Mikhail Veller, who like Dovlatov lived in Tallinn, Estonia, has built a reputation on being an "anti-Dovlatov."
[8] See S. Iu. Motygin, *Priamaia liniia? . . . Evoliutsiia prozy V. S. Makanina* (Astrakhan': Izd. Astrakhanskogo gos. ped. universiteta, 2001), esp. 4–39.
[9] See Vladimir Makanin, "About Myself and my Contexts," in Lindsey and Spektor 19–20. Most of his books have since been republished, and in the 1990s he was the recipient of numerous literary prizes.

sian novel" for the post-Soviet era.¹⁰ In both of these texts, Makanin explored the ways in which Soviet life warped the consciousness of his generation.

By the late 1960s and 1970s, participation in the military and in countless other militarized collective enterprises had become increasingly empty of any meaning for many Soviet citizens. Those aspects of Soviet life where attendance was obligatory—from school to army service to meetings to October Revolution parades and May Day demonstrations—were part and parcel of a collective spirit that now felt hypocritical. As poet Vladimir Korenatsky wrote in the poem we cite as the first epigraph to this chapter, thoughts of the "collective" for this generation triggered scenes of prison, military parades, and psychiatric incarceration. The word "we," so central to post-revolutionary and World War II discourse, now made the poet sick. He did not want to be part of the "herd."

Dovlatov and Makanin raised antiheroism to the level of an individual ethical choice. In their work they focused on the individual who reacts against the rhetoric of war, collectivism, and patriotism and tries to make his own small mark in reduced, ironic, subtle ways. Lev Anninsky has argued that for Makanin, the ethical vacuum of Soviet life did not appear to be a tragedy. "We're used to it! This is no catastrophe—this is life. The norm. No apocalypse."¹¹ *Byt*. The norm. These are words in which some authors were able to find solace during the war but which in the postwar period became a betrayal of hopes and dreams. It seems to me, however, that Anninsky underestimated the bitter irony inherent in Makanin's approach to Soviet culture.

---

10 One of Makanin's other best-known stories is "The Caucasian Prisoner" (1994), in part because it seemed prescient, since it happened to be published just months before the onset of the first war in Chechnya. In that story, Makanin explored the "ambivalence of the idea of 'imprisonment.'" See Alla Latynina, "Ne igra, a prognoz khudozhnika," *Literaturnaia gazeta* 7 (June 1995): 4. For criticism on *Underground* see, for example, Ivanova, "Sluchai Makanina," *Znamia* 4 (1997): 215–220; Konstantin Kustanovich, "A Hero of a Bygone Time, or Russian Literature as an Ecological System in Vladimir Makanin's *Underground* and Other Works," in Lindsey and Spektor, 115–128; Vladimir Bondarenko, "Vremia nadezhda," *Zvezda* 8 (1986): 184–194; Irina Rodnianskaia, "Neznakomye znakomtsy," *Novyi Mir* 8 (1986): 230–244; Anninskii, "Struktura labarinta," *Znamia* 12 (1986): 218–226; Aleksandr Agaev, "Istina i svoboda: Vladimir Makanin. Vzgliad iz 1990 goda," *Literaturnoe obozrenie* 9 (1990): 25–33; Mariia Levina-Parker, "Smert' geroia," *Voprosy literatury* 5 (1995): 63–78; Latynina, "Ne igra, a prognoz khudozhnika."
11 Anninskii, "Struktura labarinta," 225.

6. Antiheroes in a Post-heroic Age: Sergei Dovlatov, Vladimir Makanin, and Cold War Malaise

For many, Makanin among them, the period of stagnation was tragic. The very fact that the underground emerged, that antiheroes tried to find their way in a society that failed to value them, created an irresolvable tension—between the "we" and the "I," the collective and the individual, the facts of life and the "truth" that they sensed was being betrayed. Makanin and Dovlatov, and others like them, sought the resolution in fiction, but rather than a solution, what they discovered for the most part was a means of distancing themselves from the norm.[12]

We can explore the *shestidesiatniki* in the seventies through Dovlatov's fiction, but with Makanin we will juxtapose two periods, his very early career and his post-Soviet fiction. In several early stories, we find a poignant depiction of postwar life, while in the post-perestroika novel *Underground, or a Hero of Our Time* he chronicled his own generation.[13] Makanin calls *Underground* a "memoir . . . a requiem for the Russian Underground," which he describes as "a whole generation of ruined, talented people. Some became alcoholics, some committed suicide. Some became completely degraded. Most of them could not do any real work."[14] The tragedy alluded to in Boris Slutsky's poem, quoted as the second epigraph to this chapter, was a real tragedy: conscience and sobriety were counterindicated in the age of Stalin, and even more so in the age of Brezhnev.

The ironic, matter-of-fact tone we find in these antiheroic authors was borrowed from Nekrasov and Tvardovsky, but their content was influenced enormously by Solzhenitsyn's *One Day in the Life of Ivan Denisovich*. For both Dovlatov and Makanin, the camps (and their reprisal in the second half of the twentieth century in the practice of psychiatric repression) represent the state's clear betrayal of its own citizens. Discussion of the Gulag in print opened the door for those considerations of the relationship between the individual and society which find full expression in their works.

The main characters of Dovlatov and Makanin's fiction push against Solzhenitsyn and Ivan Denisovich—a rank-and-file soldier turned *Lagermensch*—in order to present an antihero whose ironic worldview negates both socialist realism and the work ethic of the straightforward Solzhenitsyn.

---

[12] See Kustanovich, who insists that "the dialectical struggle between preserving the ego and merging with the swarm usually has no resolution in Makanin's works." Kustanovich, "A Hero of a Bygone Time," 120.

[13] Makanin's novella "He and She" ("Он и Она," 1987) chronicles the unhappy lives of the *shestidesiatniki*, men and women of the 1960s.

[14] Makanin, "About Myself . . .," 23.

Part of what was going on here was a keenly perceived generation gap. In talking about his favorite authors, Dovlatov had the following to say:

> Aksyonov and Gladilin were the idols of our youth. Their heroes were our peers. I myself was a bit like Viktor Podgursky. . . . Aksyonov and Gladilin were our personal writers. That is an inimitable sensation. . . . Then there were other idols. Sinyavsky. . . . Finally, Solzhenitsyn. . . . But they were already grownups. Sinyavsky was unreachable. Solzhenitsyn—even more so.[15]

Solzhenitsyn, after all, was some two decades older. Born in 1918, he lived through times that gave him the material he needed with which to create a hero, a peasant-hero who survived both war and Gulag. In fact, his own life was cast as one of the heroic artist, a survivor of war, Gulag, and even cancer. Makanin and Dovlatov, small children during the war, were never soldiers. And neither one could find anything heroic in Soviet life.

Sergei Dovlatov: Life in the Zone

War shaped Dovlatov in a very direct way. He was born in 1940 in the peripheral city of Ufa because his family had been evacuated there from Leningrad, then under Nazi siege, and after the war the family returned to a city marked by physical and psychological devastation.

As a writer, he does not easily fit into categories: a published journalist but a censored author, a "dissident" and emigre whose works published in America focused almost entirely on Soviet life and Soviet problems. In his fiction, Dovlatov documented heroic deeds, but he found them underground. In so doing, he incarnated unofficial Soviet antiheroes, confronting the problem of the socialist realist positive hero head-on.

Dovlatov matured both as a young man and an artist during the cultural thaw of the early 1960s. That space briefly allowed writers to ask questions about how an individual should act within the collective, about the individual's interactions with the state, about how the "I" negotiated with the "we." But it also gave birth to new ideas of how individuals could live honestly and

---

[15] Dovlatov, *Maloizvestnyi Dovlatov* (St. Petersburg: Zhurnal "Zvezda," 1995), 244. Later in emigration, Dovlatov was to reflect that Solzhenitsyn had "begun with earthshaking novels" ("Blesk i nishcheta russkoi literatury," in Igor' Sukhikh, *Sergei Dovlatov: Vremia, mesto, sud'ba* [St. Petersburg: Kul't-inform-press, 1996], 298), implying that his later work did not have as great an impact on Dovlatov and his contemporaries.

ethically within a society devoted to heroics and the hero. Dovlatov explored and developed these ideas especially in his first two fictional works, *The Compromise* (*Kompromiss*) and *The Zone* (*Zona*).[16]

Khrushchev's thaw really did seem to promise a new beginning. As Dovlatov described it, writing in New York in 1982:

> On the pages of the journals the names of talented young writers shone: Aksyonov, Gladilin, Voinovich, Okudzhava, Efimov, Akhmadulina, Shukshin, Iskander, Balter, and many others. This was a time of great illusions, enormous hopes. It seemed to many that the literary process could be renewed, that bridges could be built from classical Russian literature to the healthy artistic tendencies of the beginning of the sixties.

Dovlatov was a teenager at this time, and a young man when the Thaw ended. That hopefulness and subsequent disappointment constituted a formative experience for the writer. Looking back on the period from his forties, he continued:

> But alas, these illusions were not to come to fruition. The official process of the democratization of society quickly ran into a dead end, and what came to replace it was stunning in its even greater poverty, infertility, and boredom.
>
> If under Stalin talented writers were first published, then covered in filth in print, and finally shot or destroyed in the camps (Babel, Pilnyak, Mandel'shtam), now no one was shot, almost no one was put in prison, but no one was published. The best writers, making like conspirators, wrote, as they say, "for the drawer," and those less honest, trustworthy, and truthful served the government, receiving in turn access to very tempting material goods.[17]

That process gave birth to Dovlatov's idea of the "compromise"—the tacit agreement of the Soviet citizen to live and work in his homeland, an agreement that gradually ate away at the individual and his soul, turning him into a lackey of the state. The health of the state was not conducive to the mental health of the individual writer.

---

[16] All quotes from *Zona* and *Kompromiss* in volume 1 of Sergei Dovlatov, *Sobranie prozy v trekh tomakh* (St. Petersburg: Limbus-Press, 1993), 25–172 and 173–324.

[17] "Blesk i nishcheta," 300–301.

Like Solzhenitsyn and his contemporaries Varlam Shalamov and Evgeniia Ginzburg, Dovlatov contributed to the literature of the Gulag, the literature describing life in what Russians call the Zone—a widespread Soviet nickname for what Solzhenitsyn termed the "Gulag Archipelago," the system of prison camps that dotted the landscape of the Soviet Union. But the other three writers were in direct conflict with the state when they were imprisoned, and directly benefitted from official permission when they published works about their experience. Their understanding of the Gulag was political and personal. In contrast, Dovlatov belonged to a completely different generation, and as Ilya Serman—another victim of Stalin's camps—has pointed out, Dovlatov's prison camp was also completely different.[18] Not imprisoned themselves, Dovlatov's generation understood the idea of *Lagermensch* metaphorically.

Even so, the Gulag loomed in the Soviet imagination in the 1960s and beyond. In an essay entitled "The Gulag as Civilization," Andrei Bitov has argued that "with time, between the zones freedom evaporated like water; the straits became parched, and it all became one zone. [. . .] whatever reality you take, you can describe it as a prison camp. [. . .] the prison camp is the very model of our world."[19] The Zone was a real place, but it also became a metaphor for life in the Soviet Union. The narrator of Dovlatov's novel *The Zone* would have agreed with Bitov. He claimed, "There is a suspicious similarity between guards and prisoners. Or even more broadly, between 'prison camp' and 'freedom.'"[20]

Dovlatov's biography forms a mirror image of the fictional Ivan Denisovich's life in the Gulag. Ivan was a World War II soldier turned prisoner, arrested for imagined crimes against the state, while Dovlatov fulfilled his military service to the Soviet state as a prison guard in the camps. But during his service, Dovlatov did not feel part of a grand project launched by the collective against enemies of the state; rather, as a guard he felt as powerless as the prisoners he guarded.[21]

Basing his stories in *The Zone* on his own experience, Dovlatov deliberately blurred the boundaries between this world and the Soviet world

---

[18] "Teatr Sergeia Dovlatova," *Grani* 136 (1985): 138–162.
[19] Andrei Bitov, "Gulag kak tsivilizatsiia," *Zvezda* 5 (1997): 6.
[20] Dovlatov, *Zona*, 26.
[21] See Mark Lipovetskii, "'Uchites', tvari, kak zhit'' (paranoiia, zona i literaturnyi kontekst)," *Znamia* 5 (1997): 199–212. Lipovetsky argues that for Shalamov and Solzhenitsyn, the zone is primarily a time-space of violence, while for Dovlatov it is an example of the absurd as a universal principle ("Uchites'," 209).

surrounding it, revelling in the metonymic shift that suggested the Soviet Union was also a Zone, a prison camp on a larger scale. As late as 1997, Bitov continued to assert that he personally had not yet left the Zone—in other words, his worldview and psychological makeup remained that of a prisoner long after the walls came down. Many Soviet and post-Soviet citizens have experienced something similar.

Dovlatov's hero in his autobiographical narratives does not fulfill the category of positive hero according to the doctrine of socialist realism. But this understated, picaresque hero—the antihero—is still Soviet. His definition of "*svoi*" ties his Soviet hero back to the nineteenth century: "[Alexander] Herzen was 'our kind,' a down-to-earth and precise person, . . . intelligent and honorable."[22] These were the qualities that characterized the antihero of Dovlatov's generation: a dissident, "outsider" antihero, who deflates the very Soviet discourse within which he lives, helping us to measure the meaning of heroic for a post-heroic age.

What Is a Hero If There Is No Truth:
Dovlatov's *The Zone* and *The Compromise*

In his "Soviet" works, specifically *The Zone* (1982) and *The Compromise* (1978, published 1981), Dovlatov highlighted the hypocrisy of life in the Soviet Union. Each of these narratives has a structure complicated by the presence of one or more autobiographical heroes.[23] In *The Zone*, for example, on the level of plot Dovlatov exploited the complexities of life in a totalitarian society, and he also did so on the level of the construction of the text. In his narrative, the reader sees that not just content but form was affected by Soviet conditions.

Dovlatov complained that his manuscript seemed fragmentary because it was fragmentary—having had to be smuggled out of the Soviet Union by

---

[22] As a young man conducting an epistolary courtship, Dovlatov made a list of books he thought the future actress Tamara Urzhumova should read—which would also show her what kind of books *he* liked. He started with Russians: "If you haven't read it, you should definitely take up Herzen, *My Past and Thoughts*. You will be surprised to what extent Herzen was 'our kind' ['*svoi*'], a down-to-earth and precise person, to what extent he was intelligent and honorable. No need to read his fiction. It is very disappointing." Dovlatov, Letter to Tamara Urzhumova, 1 July 1963, published in *Zvezda* 8 (2000): 140–142.

[23] Karen Ryan succinctly characterizes *The Zone* as featuring a "relatively complex narrative strategy" (*Contemporary Russian Satire*, [Cambridge: Cambridge University Press, 1995], 180).

well-meaning Frenchwomen in small microfilmed excerpts. Dovlatov left it up to the reader to imagine the connotations here. Further, he undercut these "Soviet" complaints by adding others unrelated to Soviet conditions. In the capitalist "free" country where he finally published the manuscript, neither publishers nor the public really cared about his collection of camp stories, and his ability to assemble the manuscript was further hampered by technical details, such as the need to rent a photo enlarger.

The Zone itself incorporated all these complaints and more, becoming a doubled chronicle of writing and self-discovery in Soviet Russia and publishing and reflection in the United States. As such, *The Zone* owes much to the genres of epistolary novels, story cycles, and autobiographical fiction.[24] Allegedly first written in the mid-1960s, the final published book became a completely different work thanks to the letters added to the text on publication in 1982.[25] This technique, of co-creating a narrative space between two very different times (1960s and 1980s), two very different places (a Soviet prison camp and New York City), and two necessarily different narrative voices (a prison guard and an emigre to America), may very well be unique to Dovlatov and to this work in particular.

Since his subject matter, Soviet prison camps, had by the time of publication been vividly and indelibly illustrated by both Solzhenitsyn and Shalamov, Dovlatov was in a sense forced to compete with his predecessors, as he himself acknowledged in the text. Through innovations in narrative voice as well as through generic play, Dovlatov told his story of life in, and escape from, the Zone of the Soviet Union.

In contrast, *The Compromise* retells Dovlatov's experiences as a journalist in Estonia in 1972–1975. Again, part "document," part fictionalized memoir,

---

[24] This technique is reminiscent of what Galya Diment described in her book *The Autobiographical Novel of Co-Consciousness: Goncharov, Woolf, Joyce* (Gainesville: University of Florida Press, 1994).

[25] In fact, one of the reasons Dovlatov went to Estonia in 1972 was to try and publish *The Zone. Notes of a Camp Guard*, which was accepted by a publisher in Tallinn, as the conditions of censorship there were less strict than in the "centers" of Leningrad and Moscow. However, although *The Zone* reached the stage of page proofs, in the end it was banned. This story becomes a part of the text of *The Compromise*, thus linking the two works and strengthening the autobiographical background of the Estonian novella. For more on this, see Jekaterina Young, "Dovlatov's *Compromise*: Journalism, Fiction and Documentary," *Slavonica* 2 (2000): 44–67 as well as her book, *Sergei Dovlatov and his Narrative Masks* (Evanston: Northwestern University Press, 2009), chapter 4.

the novel presents a series of so-called "compromises" that defined life for Dovlatov in the Soviet Union. His autobiographical character works for the newspaper *Soviet Estonia*—a "party newspaper." The overt conflict of the work is between what the journalist publishes in the paper and the "back-story," the events and people who are transformed by Soviet journalistic convention into the somewhat mundane narratives that pass muster for print.

Divided into an introduction and twelve chapters, the novel ostensibly investigates the relationship between Soviet print media and "reality." Each chapter includes a news item (complete with dateline and headline) and a second narrative, often rich with dialogue.

In the pages of *The Compromise*, Dovlatov delineated his own moral categories of right and wrong, truth and falsehood, exploring totalitarian myth-making from the inside, from within Soviet journalism. As Andrei Ar'ev has written, "Sergei Dovlatov valued truthful invention over the truth of fact."[26] A journalist observing not the mud and blood of war but the workings of the Socialist state on the kolkhoz and in the city, Dovlatov refused to believe in facts as such. Instead, he saw that everything was relative.

Accused by his fictional editor of "political nearsightedness" and "moral infantilism" in the first compromise, i.e., the first chapter of the novel, Dovlatov dismissed the charges as unimportant. After all, he claimed, he was not writing for the newspaper in order to exercise his creative mind, or indeed to further the goals of the Communist Party, but rather to earn a living. "They paid me two rubles for the notice. I'd hoped it would be three . . ." In this work, a send-up of journalism, Dovlatov pretended that writing for a newspaper can be a simple cash exchange. But in fact, he had a conscience, and as Slutsky so poignantly put it, the only alternative for a man with a conscience in Soviet society was to become a drunk.

Dovlatov described his editor as an "oily, marzipanish man, a kind of reserved rascal," and this scared and angry Soviet bureaucrat presented a clear antagonist for the journalist.[27] Editors generally fall into this category— "them" and not "us," "*chuzhoi*" and not "*svoi*." One editor, trying to teach

---

[26] Andrei Ar'ev, introduction, "Sergei Dovlatov: Deviat' pisem Tamare Urzhumovoi," *Zvezda* 8 (2000): 137.

[27] Dovlatov, *Sobranie prozy*, 1: 177. Turonok is not the total hack he purports to be; it is important to Dovlatov that despite everything, the journalist's talent is recognized. Turonok sends Dovlatov on assignment because, much as he hates to admit it, and much as he recognizes Dovlatov's ideological unreliability, he also knows that Dovlatov can write and the other journalists working for him are decidedly mediocre.

Dovlatov the rules of Socialist journalism, explained, "All your characters are scoundrels. If your hero has to be a scoundrel, then you should bring him to a moral crisis through the logic of the story. Or to retribution. But in your work scoundrels are something natural, like rain or snow. . . ." (*Sobranie prozy*, 1: 182).

These scoundrels were precisely the antiheroes whom Dovlatov championed. In a kind of artistic manifesto, Dovlatov explained his attitude toward the concept of the heroic: "In this story there are no angels and no villains. . . . No sinners and no saints. And there are none in life, either. [. . .] I'm not certain that in life repentance invariably follows crime, or that feats are rewarded by bliss. We are what we feel. Our traits, merits and sins are brought into the world by close contact with life. . . ."[28]

"No sinners and no saints." "We are what we feel." "I'm not certain that . . . feats are rewarded by bliss." These phrases represented Dovlatov's stance as a *bytopisatel'*, an existential writer of the everyday, who resisted the rhetoric of *podvig* with all of his being. Writing in the era of stagnation, with Cold War repercussions all around, facilitated this stance.

As he struggled to define his characters—in *The Compromise*, represented by fictional versions of himself and his friends—he wrote against any remnants of the socialist realist positive hero, searching out other categories of good and evil, to finally define a new kind of hero in a post-heroic world, an antihero who also has a right to live and to love. Not only did Dovlatov question the moral categories offered by official Soviet literary doctrine and Communist upbringing, he even doubted—and perhaps mourned, in a way—the clear moral imperatives of nineteenth-century fiction. For Dostoevsky, it was unquestionable that crime had to have punishment, and indeed "repentance"—without moral regeneration Dostoevsky's Raskolnikov could not have experienced the rebirth that comes to him in his Siberian exile. That is one trajectory of heroism.

For Dovlatov, though, everything was more ambiguous. He and his friends were drawn together by "a slight distaste for the official side of

---

Dovlatov is the "lyricist" Turonok needs for certain assignments where "the human element" (*chelovechinka*) is required.

[28] Dovlatov, *Sobranie prozy*, 1: 182. This section trails off with the characteristic: "'Nature, you are my goddess!' And so on . . . Well, anyway . . ." Dovlatov's dislike of purple prose keeps his ironic tools sharp. Literary and moral musings are too rhetorically overheated for him.

newspaper work [and] a certain healthy cynicism, which helped us avoid fine-sounding words. . . ." (*Sobranie prozy*, 1: 182). Perhaps ironically, it was a lack of discipline on the "ideological front" that had gotten the Dovlatov character fired from his previous job, in Leningrad. And in a work devoted to the continual compromises of life under the Soviet regime, it was hypocrisy that pushed Dovlatov over the edge. In journalism, he explained:

> Everyone could do one thing. Violate the principles of Socialist morality in one area. That is to say, one person was allowed to drink. Another— to play the hooligan. A third—to tell political jokes. A fourth—to be Jewish. A fifth—to not belong to the Party. A sixth—to lead an amoral life. And so on. But each person, I repeat, was allowed one thing. It was not possible to be both Jewish and a drunk. A hooligan and a non-party member. . . . I myself was fatally universal. That is to say, I allowed myself everything in small doses. I drank, behaved scandalously, showed ideological nearsightedness. In addition, I was not a Party member, and I was even somewhat Jewish. Finally, my personal life was becoming more and more complicated.[29]

In refusing to follow the unwritten rules of Socialist life and morality—and indeed lampooning them as ridiculously arbitrary—Dovlatov pushed against the official line. When at a party meeting at his Leningrad newspaper it was suggested he "go to the people" and write about "real life," Dovlatov burst out, "[If I gave you] real life you would shoot me without a trial!" It was this refusal to sign on to official hypocrisy in Leningrad that led to Dovlatov's move to Estonia.

Dovlatov's greatest antihero in *The Compromise* is the unconquerable Ernest Leopoldovich Bush, an anarchist who despite his best efforts to join in state activities always undermines himself in the end, ruining his chances for jobs, apartments, and promotions. When Dovlatov's alter ego in "The Ninth Compromise" asks, "Who is Bush?" his friend Shablinsky replies, "Bush is something fantastic. You'll see. I think you'll like him."[30] That shine and that breadth (*blesk, razmakh*) are the qualities that best characterize the individualist, who in the final account is glad to have dropped out of society—and

---

[29] Dovlatov, *Sobranie prozy*, 1: 269. Dovlatov's mother was Armenian and his father was Jewish. His personal life was indeed complicated: married three times, he had four children with three different women.

[30] Sergei Dovlatov, *Vstretilis', pogovorili* (St. Petersburg: Azbuka, 2003), 205.

who in Dovlatov's fictional world usually gets the girl, the vodka, and the reader's admiration as he does so.

But the autobiographical Dovlatov character in these stories cannot come to terms with life as an outsider. At one point in the narrative, Dovlatov and his friend Mikhail Zhbankov—a photojournalist and confirmed alcoholic fifteen years Dovlatov's senior, and thus fifteen years further along in his cynicism, and his alcoholism—are sent to the Estonian countryside to prepare a story on a true Socialist heroine, a Stakhanovite milkmaid, which is funny, almost absurd, just on its face, although of course a common theme in the Soviet press.

Met at the train station by the Regional Party Committee secretary, Dovlatov and Zhbankov are taken to a government dacha, where they are coddled, wined, and dined by two women, the thirty-year-old representative of the regional Komsomol and her younger colleague, supposedly an aspiring young journalist. Mostly—as is often true in what might be called the "alcoholic chronotope" of Dovlatov's fiction—they are wined.

Over the course of his assignment, Dovlatov is unable to enjoy the charms of the young Evi Sakson.[31] Instead the journalist is tormented by that eternal Russian question, inherited from Chernyshevsky via Lenin: "What is to be done?" Zhbankov tells Dovlatov, "Don't think. Drink vodka." Evi concurs, in her Estonian-accented, amusingly halting Russian, but she has other ideas for how Dovlatov should spend his time not thinking: "You should think less. Enjoy the good that exists. [. . .] That's enough drinking. Let's go. I'll make you like me. [. . .] Don't think. Sometimes it's better to be stupid." "Too late," Dovlatov answers, "I'll have to drink" (*Sobranie prozy*, 1: 256–257). Unable to avoid contemplation of his wasted life, focused on the bitter truth that "there's only one life, there won't be another," Dovlatov drinks himself into oblivion.

Regional Party Committee Secretary Liivak, whose first allegiance is to party discipline, offers a stark contrast with the anti-authoritarian Dovlatov. When Liivak commends Dovlatov for his work in the provinces, he delivers an utterly standard and banal speech: "Comrades, I am satisfied. You worked well, enjoyed some cultured leisure time. I was pleased to meet you. I hope

---

[31] Evi is female company specifically provided for him by the party secretary. Konstantin Kustanovich has explored this ritual—of providing sexual partners for visitors—in his essay "Erotic Glasnost: Sexuality in Recent Russian Literature," *World Literature Today* 67.1 (Winter 1993): 136–144. See 138.

that our friendship will become a tradition. After all, party workers and journalists are in a way, I would say, colleagues. I wish you success on the difficult ideological frontlines. Perhaps you have a question?" (*Sobranie prozy*, 1: 259). The hypocrisy is stunning, but the military context is equally striking: Liivak assumes that these journalists are working hand in hand with Communist party hacks in the struggle for Cold War domination over the West.

Dovlatov and Zhbankov have been anything but good workers or cultured tourists; they have spent their entire business trip drinking heavily. The short letter that Dovlatov produced in five minutes on the morning after was barely literate: "Dear and Much Respected Leonid Ilich! I would like to share with you a happy event. In the last year I managed to reach unheard of work results." Double entendres also permeated the text of the telegram: "And one more happy event occurred in my life. The communists of our farm have united to choose me as their member!"[32] Dovlatov's ghostwritten telegram to Brezhnev, penned with a shaking hand, was published in the newspaper along with Brezhnev's reply to the prizewinning Estonian milkmaid—received *before* the telegram was written. The ritualistic nature and ultimate insignificance of the entire assignment both justifies and causes the drunkenness of the journalist. Conscience and sobriety are two incompatible concepts.

In answer to Liivak's query, "Perhaps you have a question?" Zhbankov articulates the only question the two Tallinn journalists can imagine, their existential answer to the thought that their work had brought them into such close contact with party hacks and political idealogues: "Where's the bar?" ("*Gde bufet?*") The uncomplicated Evi Sakson, bidding Dovlatov good-bye at the station, reminds him, "Don't drink so much . . . or else you can't make sex" (*Sobranie prozy*, 1: 259, 260).

All of these characters demonstrate the boundaries of Dovlatov's own moral strictures. Willing to take a business trip to help prop up the ideological underpinnings of the Brezhnev regime, the journalist can only stomach his assignment by drinking heavily. Aware that he is too clever to hoodwink himself about the meaning of his own work, Dovlatov chooses to drown his sorrows (and perhaps his intellect) at the party-provided provincial dacha. The open corruption of the party system, with sexual and alcoholic favors

---

[32] Dovlatov, *Sobranie prozy*, 1: 258–259. As he comments, "Here the style was clearly shaky, but I hadn't the strength to correct it" (1: 259).

guaranteed, forms the backdrop for the hero's despair; his linguistic and professional accomplishments are utterly pointless, for Brezhnev's telegram would arrive with or without Dovlatov's service as a ghostwriter. But unlike Ernst Leopoldovich Bush, he cannot drop out but remains on the margins of the system: drunk and without the girl.

The autobiographical hero in *The Compromise* is obviously no hero, in any traditional sense, at all. He is nothing like the hardworking peasant-prisoner protagonist of Solzhenitsyn's *One Day in the Life of Ivan Denisovich* from two decades earlier. But the reader recognizes the difficulties the journalist faces. His faults—drinking, amorality, being "somewhat Jewish"—stem from his intellect, his hatred of hypocrisy, his search for the truth and for individual integrity in a society that denies him even that much. As he articulates the problem to a friend, "Under our conditions, it's more worthy to lose than to win."

There could not be a starker indictment of the rhetoric of *podvig*. In the post-heroic age of Brezhnev, Dovlatov's antihero exhibits many admirable characteristics, among them his particular brand of honesty and foolish bravery. These traits in turn complicate his life and keep him from being able to bridge the gap between the official Socialist "what is to be done" and his own cynical experience. In a common-enough response for the dissident hero of the 1970s and '80s, instead of the reaction, "I should drink less," Dovlatov's hero determines, "I should drink more." Not "pit' nado men'she," but "pit' nado bol'she."[33]

Dovlatov's antihero in the 1970s is the man behind the media, working within the dishonest discourse of Soviet journalism to support the by-now stagnant Soviet regime. Though the newspaper snippets of *The Compromise* suggest that the journalist writes what he must to receive his pay, continuing to help manipulate popular opinion, he exists in such a disillusioned time that neither he nor his readers subscribe to the nonsense he publishes in *Soviet Estonia*. Yet in his self-deprecating, ironic way, Dovlatov creates a hero the reader *can* believe in, even if we don't believe in his enterprise of propping up the Soviet regime. Dovlatov's hero did not accomplish great feats, but neither did Brezhnev. Dovlatov's alcoholic, amoral journalist represents an antihero

---

[33] Compare to the hero of the popular 1975 Soviet film *The Irony of Fate* (*Ironiia sud'by* [dir. Eldar Ryazanov]). This statement also begs comparison with Venedikt Erofeev and his famous alcoholic narrative. On *Moskva-Petushki* see especially Ryan, *Contemporary Russian Satire*, 58–100.

living in hypocritical times, and he finds his dignity not in labor or in *podvig*, as a socialist realist hero should, but in irony and at the bottom of a bottle.

In his work, Dovlatov asserted that "there are no angels and no villains. . . . No sinners and no saints. I long ago ceased to categorize *people* as positive or negative." And, he concluded, "or literary characters either." Not agreeing to the rules of the game—whether the propaganda game, the socialist realism game, or the party game—represented a certain line in the sand for Dovlatov, but he, and his antiheroes, played anyway, understanding that losing is itself a protest and in that sense a kind of winning.

The Compromise began with Dovlatov, unemployed, looking through his portfolio of newspaper clippings: "Yellowed pages. Ten years of lies and pretense. But still, here are people, conversations, feelings, reality. . . . Not in the pages themselves, but beyond, on the horizon. . . . The path from *pravda* to *istina* is a difficult one" (*Sobranie prozy*, 1: 176).

Pravda is of course truth, but so is *istina*. Dovlatov here was playing with untranslatable words; *istina* is generally speaking *more* "true" than *pravda*, but in the Soviet period, when *pravda* was contaminated, claimed as its own by the Communist Party through their party organ, the newspaper of that name, *istina* could be even more difficult to find.

We have been looking at this question of truth and fact throughout the Soviet period. Truth is what gives meaning to fact; details fill it out to portray the experiences of war and peace. But postwar Soviet society was so permeated by hypocrisy, by "compromise," that Dovlatov and his generation struggled to address the question under new circumstances.

This fungible concept of truth undergirds *The Compromise*. When is it permissible to lie? When should one tell the whole truth? What do those truths mean in a society permeated by lies? And finally, what is a hero if there is no truth?

Individual vs. Collective—I vs. We: Makanin's Protest

Vladimir Makanin describes the 1960s as a time when the whole idea of the individual (*Lichnost'*) had passed. His first novel, *A Straight Line*, was in his words about "an unsuccessful Individual who could not survive in the twentieth century when everything was being worked out by collectives."[34] This theme—the theme of the individual trying to live in a collective cul-

---

[34] "A Conversation with Vladimir Makanin," in Lindsey and Spektor, *Routes of Passage*, 175.

ture—became central to Makanin's work. Mary Ann Szporluk identifies this as Makanin's protest against socialist realism and Soviet society. She writes:

> The politically correct writer was expected to give the reader moral guidance and correct social and political interpretations. According to the Bolshevik adaptation of Marxist theory, the Soviet Union would evolve into a perfect social system in which the individual would be subordinated to the collective. Makanin responded to this all-too-real cultural pressure by making the repression of the individual in the collective culture one of his major themes. He examines the effects of collective thinking on the individual as well as the responsibilities of individuals to society.[35]

Makanin's personal history gave him private lessons in the tensions of individual versus collective and the ironies that often resulted from that friction. After World War II, his father—as if in a parody of Gladkov's plot from *Cement*—was attempting to make repairs at the plant where he worked and was instead arrested for sabotage. Makanin's uncle came to the rescue: he "donned his patriotic medals, took his civil war gun, and went to the Orsk prosecutor's office to demand his brother's release."[36] The power of the war hero in this case worked, and Makanin's father was let go, but his son learned an important lesson: that socialist realism as featured in *Cement* was a fiction. The lone worker cannot put the factory back on line, and by isolating himself he becomes extremely vulnerable to the repressions of the state. Makanin's success as a chess *wunderkind* singled him out as an individual who could dominate in an intellectual game; his father's arrest in 1948 taught him the dangers of being singled out.

This dislike of the collective characterizes Makanin's entire literary career. In his assessment of Makanin some years ago, Deming Brown pointed out that Makanin had been identified with a number of literary trends—the "forty-year-olds," "city prose," and the "Moscow school"—and had been considered both an heir to the "confessional prose" of the 1960s and a kinsman of "village prose."[37] In fact he belongs to no school. Makanin's work varies from stories of life in the Urals to allegorical tales of dystopia. In all his fiction, the

---

[35] "Afterword," in Vladimir Makanin, *Escape Hatch and the Long Road Ahead. Two Novellas* (Ardis: Dana Point, 1996), 186.
[36] Recounted in Lindsey, "Translator's Preface," from Makanin's memories, x.
[37] *The Last Years of Soviet Russian Literature: Prose Fiction 1975-1991* (Cambridge: Cambridge University Press, 1993), 102.

protagonist finds himself alienated from collective enterprises, suffering from attempting to fit in, or otherwise lost in the society that surrounds him.

The dislocations of postwar reconstruction featured prominently in his early novellas *Fatherlessness* and *The Soldier and the Soldier's Wife*, both from 1971.[38] The first is an urban narrative that centers around a group of children who grew up in an orphanage since "their fathers remained in the trenches," i.e., perished during the war, leaving them both homeless and fatherless. *Fatherlessness* is a wonderful group portrait of lost boys, not heroes as in Libedinsky's optimistic novel *Birth of a Hero*, but young men searching for meaning and purpose in life.

The second novella features two individuals in a village: a woman whose fiancé did not return from the war—a "Russian soldier's wife, a Russian Penelope, who sat and waited"—and a married soldier who longs for the "speed, the intensity of military life" and who cannot find his way in peacetime (Makanin 154, 205). In an ironic twist, demobilized soldier Ivan Semenych starts an affair with Katya and insists that she procure wild ducks from the market to provide legitimacy for his cover story that he spent the night hunting.

When Katya is desperate because she cannot obtain the duck, a helpful driver assumes it is for her sick child: "He could just see it: somewhere a child is dying, the country doctor is useless, and a special bouillon, made from wild duck, was essential [to save the child from death]" (Makanin 175–176). Thus the childless woman uses a stranger's humane assumption to cover for her irresponsible lover.[39] In the end, the protagonists of this story find themselves alone and hopeless, utterly lacking a connection to the social and cultural life around them and as a result lacking any ethical grounding.

This lost feeling is common among Makanin's characters and is accompanied by an absence of personal and collective responsibility. One critic describes this as a trait of the "barracks" lifestyle in the Soviet Union: "I didn't think it up, so I can't change it; if they're giving, take, if they're beating you, run; that's how things are, you just have to fit in."[40] Militarized life was unsustainable, especially in the absence of war.

---

[38] Makanin, *Bezotsovshchina. Soldat i soldatka. Povesti* (Moscow: Sovetskii pisatel', 1971).
[39] This wild duck motif appears in a tragic form in Viktor Astafiev's late story "A Bird of Passage," where in the postwar period a real child is dying of starvation, but even the duck bouillon cannot save him.
[40] Anninskii, "Struktura labarinta," 220.

Rather than maintaining a patriotic spirit, Soviet citizens began to avoid responsibility. This "adaptation" to life and to the unchanging situation of the Brezhnev stagnation (what Yurchak has called, "Everything was forever until it was no more") represents perfectly the refusal of a whole generation of Russians to believe in the hopelessly corrupt system that surrounded them and clarifies a kind of "keep your head down" attitude that ran counter to the official rhetoric of *podvig* and in the end contributed to the system's failure. Brezhnev followed on Stalin's 1946 insistence that the Soviet Union would always be at war with the capitalist West, but already at the beginning of his era people had ceased to believe that this war could be won, or even that it was being fought at all effectively.

War, and Gulag, Updated:
Soviet Punitive Psychiatry in *Underground, or a Hero of Our Time*

For Makanin, the psychiatric asylum represents the logical extension of what a permanently militarized nation would do to its citizens. If life in the army imposed order, discipline, and regimentation on the population, that life also held out the possibility of heroic validation. If life in the Gulag removed troublesome individuals from the body of the nation, the camps still provided hope for camaraderie and individual resistance. Diagnosing individuals as mentally ill removed them physically not only from the rest of Soviet society but, in a sense, from the human race as well. This was Soviet policy.

The use of psychiatry as part of the apparatus of an oppressive state was formalized in 1959, when Nikita Khrushchev defined any kind of dissent or social deviation as a mental illness. Quoted in *Pravda* as saying that "a crime is a deviation from the generally recognized standards of behavior, frequently caused by mental disorder,"[41] Khrushchev gave *carte blanche* to psychiatric panels working under the aegis of the KGB to diagnose, hospitalize and isolate, and frequently to engage in medical torture.

Under Brezhnev the use of mental institutions took a particularly cynical turn. Among other things, during these years the psychiatric hospital was

---

[41] *Pravda*, May 24, 1959, cited in Cornelia Mee, *Internment of Soviet Dissenters in Mental Hospitals* (Cambridge, Eng., 1971), 1. There is some evidence that the diagnosis "creeping schizophrenia" was invented in response to Khrushchev's idea that only a madman could be critical of the Socialist system. See George Windholz, "Soviet Psychiatrists under Stalinist Duress: The Design for a 'New Soviet Psychiatry' and its Demise," *History of Psychiatry*, vol. X (1999): 329–347, 344.

used as a part of a public relations campaign. While prisons and camps might make for bad press in the West, a therapeutic institution like an asylum might bring good press. As Zhores Medvedev, a victim of forced committal in 1970, reasoned:

> Someone had the simple idea that the increasing number of trials and political prisoners made a very poor public impression, while an increase in the number of patients under treatment in hospitals would be a very good indication of social progress. From this moment, psychiatric hospitals began to expand.[42]

Schizophrenia, or split personality, was far and away the most common diagnosis made by Soviet psychiatrists, particularly in the Brezhnev era, and therefore the medical rationale usually given out for the incarceration of patients during the most intense period of punitive psychiatric practice.[43] As Teresa Smith has argued, the Soviet case was unusual, particularly because of the large number of individuals involved in various dissident movements and subsequently subjected to psychiatric evaluation and incarceration. Soviet psychiatry came to serve the interests of the repressive state thanks to a set of circumstances which Smith explores, most importantly the "unusually ambiguous definition of mental disease."[44] The Soviet definition of schizophrenia was so expansive that it came to include an "asymptomatic form," in which doctors argued that "outwardly well-adjusted behavior, formally coherent utterances, and retainment of former knowledge and manners [are] characteristic of a pathological development of the personality."[45] Thus so-called "normal behavior" could actually be used to indicate the presence

---

[42] Roy and Zhores Medvedev, *A Question of Madness* (London: Macmillan, 1971), 200. Incidentally, the PR campaign did not work, and the World Psychiatric Association censured the Soviet psychiatric organization for the use of repressive psychiatric practices. Indeed, the Soviet professional society of psychiatrists was in 1989 only provisionally readmitted to the World Psychiatric Association. See Teresa Smith with Thomas Oleszczuk, *No Asylum: State Psychiatric Repression in the Former USSR* (New York: New York University Press, 1996), 28.
[43] For a detailed description of the history of Soviet theories of schizophrenia, see Martin A. Miller, "The Theory and Practice of Psychiatry in the Soviet Union," in *Psychiatry* 48 (February 1985): 16.
[44] Smith and Oleszczuk, *No Asylum*, 4–5.
[45] See Mee, *Internment*, 6–10 on the famous case of Major-General Petr Grigorenko. See also Smith and Oleszczuk, *No Asylum*, 7.

of insanity. Psychiatric diagnosis by George Orwell. Not really good public relations at all.

It bears repeating that the madhouse—or the threat of it—was a real fact of Soviet life, a central part of the brutal treatment of individuals during the 1960s and '70s and even '80s. While it is fascinating to explore literary uses of the madhouse, we should always keep in mind that these were real institutions, doing real and barbaric things to real and broken people. The two so-called special psychiatric hospitals in Leningrad and Kazan each had a capacity for as many as one thousand patients, and we may never know just how many patients were "treated" throughout the system during the worst years of psychiatric repression. As Smith cautions, in Soviet Russia it was "no secret to anyone that you can have schizophrenia without schizophrenia."[46] Given the practices of Soviet psychiatry, depictions of the madhouse and Soviet psychiatrists such as we find in Makanin seem more like reportage than caricature.

The psychiatric hospital has acted as a potent metaphor for a number of cultures—after all, Ken Kesey's 1962 *One Flew over the Cuckoo's Nest* investigated similar ideas and conditions as we see in the Russian wards. The parallel of institution and restrictive regime is not uniquely Soviet. But when Tom Stoppard set his 1978 play *Every Good Boy Deserves Favor* in an asylum, he chose to set that asylum in Brezhnev's Russia, not in America or Britain.[47] Issues of psychiatric repression were widely publicized by concerned humanists in the West in the 1970s, and they plagued Russians trying to figure out how to live and make choices in a collectivist, coercive state.

---

[46] Smith and Oleszczuk, 1, quoting V. M. Morozov from Andre Koppers, *A Biographical Dictionary on the Political Abuse of Psychiatry in the USSR* (Amsterdam: International Association on the Political Use of Psychiatry, 1990), 36. Smith also suggests that post-Soviet society will continue to turn to psychiatrists for aid with problems of state, unless new standards of professional conduct are developed to counter habitual connections between medicine and politics (Smith and Oleszczuk, 199).

[47] The details of Stoppard's play, down to the address of the special psychiatric hospital in Leningrad in which his hero is interred, seem to be culled directly from human rights reports of the 1970s, including the samizdat newsletter *Chronicle of Current Events*. In fact the play is based on Vladimir Bukovsky's memoirs, *To Build a Castle: My Life as a Dissenter*, trans. Michael Scammell (New York: Viking, 1978). See Stoppard, *Every Good Boy Deserves Favor and Professional Foul* (New York: Grove Press, 1978). A Russian review of Stoppard's *Arcadia* fifteen years ago noted that none of Stoppard's "dissident" plays, including *Every Good Boy*, had been translated into Russian. The reason given was that "political theater is out of fashion." See *Otrazhenie nastoiashchego, Novyi mir* 9: 657 (1996): 216.

It is no accident that Makanin revived those concerns in contemporary post-Soviet fiction.[48] While the history of the Russian asylum and the history of Russian madness are surely tied to a larger history of these questions in the West, *Underground, or a Hero of Our Time* serves to remind us of the particularly Russian way in which the issues resonate. Under conditions of punitive psychiatry, issues of power and language overlap with problems of psychiatric "care." For Makanin, truth is historically conditioned, and the power wielded by authorities—whether military hierarchies, police, or medical doctors—called out to be analyzed. The medical repression of the "I" in the service of the "we" deserved its own fictional treatment.

In the novel *Underground, or a Hero of Our Time*, the author foregrounds the deeply conscious, indeed self-conscious, nature of his connection to the Russian past and to Russian literary history, and in so doing he also highlights the question of the hero in history. Both Dostoevsky and Lermontov are present: Makanin has written a new version of *Notes from Underground*, with a new hero for a new time. The novel's epigraph comes from Lermontov's novel *A Hero of Our Time* (1840): "The hero . . . is a portrait, but not of one man: it is a portrait compiled from the sins of our entire generation in its fullest development." As Lermontov did for the late Romantic era, Makanin was trying to identify what kind of hero (or heroes) lived in *fin de siècle* post-Soviet Russia and to parse the meaning of "heroic" for the era.

Beyond the title, the novel makes thickly layered references to other works within the Russian literary canon. Makanin recalls, overtly or allusively, Saltykov-Shchedrin, Chekhov, Olesha, Pasternak, and Venedikt Erofeev, along with Dostoevsky, Lermontov, and many others. In fact, his hero Petrovich resembles no one more than Venichka Erofeev, both in life and in Erofeev's novel *Moscow to Petushki* (first publication 1973): often drunk, but just as often uttering philosophical truths, Petrovich loves to ride the Moscow Metro just as the fictional Venichka rode the suburban electric trains.[49] With these referential devices, the author is writing his novel into the history of

---

[48] In the United States, Stoppard's play, with Andre Previn's original score, was revived in November 2002 by the Wilma Theater and the Philadelphia Orchestra. The Czech directors of the Wilma, Blanka and Jiri Zizka, are old friends and fans of Stoppard's and frequently stage his work.

[49] Scholars have also suggested a similarity to the sculptor Mikhail Shemiakin. See Aida Khachaturian, *Roman V.S. Makanina Andegraund, ili geroi nashego vremeni: Homo Urbanis v pole 'Usredneniia'* (Tallinn: PhD diss., Tallinn University, 2006), 124, note 71.

Russian literature, with its "accursed questions" and its social agenda of helping the individual find his way within the collective.

The novel also builds on the rich Russian tradition of literary madness. In his study of Rabelais, Mikhail Bakhtin brought the analysis of literary madness back to the ancient ideas of Menippean satire, which when filtered through the lens of Romanticism rendered insanity as both a place of individual refuge and the source of individual revelation. Bakhtin went on to note the deep connection between freedom of speech and expression and the freedom of the spirit made possible through madness. Since neither was tolerated within Russian or Soviet culture, the possibilities offered by madness were particularly charged. The mad individual in the Russian tradition has always been an independent thinker. Perhaps his madness was precisely in his lack of respect for authority and his search for asylum, and inspiration, beyond the reach of civil society.[50]

This Menippean madman, flirting with freedom and death, can be found throughout Russian literature and history. Nineteenth-century philosopher Peter Chaadaev, mentioned in virtually every book on Russian psychiatry, ranks as the first prominent victim of punitive psychiatry.[51] Literary heroes bristled on the pages of nineteenth-century Romantic literature, from Griboedov's Chatsky—misunderstood and frustrated by Moscow society—to the impoverished heroes of Gogol and Dostoevsky, to Lermontov's Pechorin, perhaps not mad, but certainly alienated and bitter. Beaten down by *byt*, these characters were not accepting of the norm but rather acted out their opposition to society's norms through pointed remarks, affronted behavior, drunken scenes, and even murder, exempting themselves from the standards of social behavior and claiming the freedom to act as they chose.

---

[50] Citing Lucian's "Dialogues"—"Independence, every inch of him: he cares for no one. 'Tis Menippus!"—Bakhtin writes, "Let us stress in this Lucianic image of the laughing Menippus the relation of laughter to the underworld and to death, to the freedom of spirit, and to the freedom of speech" (*Rabelais and his World*, trans. by Helene Iswolsky [Cambridge, MA: MIT Press, 1968], 70). In Makanin, the "underworld" receives new metaphoric realization, but the principle of the relationship between independence, death, and freedom remains the same.

[51] In fact, psychiatric diagnosis as a political instrument has a much longer history in Russia, dating back to eighteenth-century rationalist philosophy as absorbed by Russian rulers from Peter the Great to Catherine the Great. See Ilya Vinitsky, "A Cheerful Empress and her Gloomy Critics," *Madness and the Mad in Russian Culture*, ed. Brintlinger and Vinitsky (Toronto: University of Toronto Press, 2007), 25–45. For further discussion of the treatment and representation of the insane in Russia, see the entire volume.

6. Antiheroes in a Post-heroic Age: Sergei Dovlatov, Vladimir Makanin, and Cold War Malaise

But whatever freedoms madness might bring to individuals, there was nothing of refuge about the institutional context of Russian madness. Both Gogol and Chekhov portrayed the asylum as a place of torture and betrayal. The larger chronotope of the repressive state institution, whether hospital or prison, continues to appear throughout modern Russian literature, from Dostoevsky and his *Notes from the House of the Dead* to Chekhov's "Ward No. 6," Solzhenitsyn's *One Day* and *Cancer Ward*, even Liudmila Petrushevskaia's *The Time: Night*. Each of these narratives uses the prison or the medical and psychiatric ward to force confrontations, to strip characters of their external differences, to reveal and explore their essential humanity, their strengths and weaknesses. These texts, many of them part of the realist tradition, depicted the asylum as a social microcosm. Others, such as Bulgakov's *Master and Margarita*, returned to the topos of asylum as refuge, and the Master finds a modicum of peace in Dr. Stravinsky's psychiatric clinic, far from the insanity of 1930s Moscow life.

Makanin draws freely from these literary and cultural traditions of madness, not distinguishing particularly between the paradigms of refuge and torture when concocting his postmodern melange of references. Each of the heroes explores the Menippean promises of madness, without ever quite fully realizing them. In Makanin's work, the psychiatric hospital is a refuge. Even though conditions in his hospital are abysmal and the orderlies are sadistic, ultimately the stark environment, like a stripped-down version of outer society, forces the hero Petrovich to confront the most basic of human needs—the need for empathy.

Upon first ending up in the madhouse, Makanin's Petrovich reminds himself that "the loony bin [*psikhushka*] is a piece of the state" and thus very similar to a police station or a prison (*Andegraund*, 343). Thus Makanin's psychiatric space is reminiscent of Chekhov's in "Ward No. 6"—a space of ultimate oppression, where the few rights of the individual which exist in everyday society have been abrogated. But Makanin gives his hero an individual quest that ends in almost optimistic success; in that absence of rights, Petrovich takes back his own humanity through an act of empathy and thus benefits from the oppression around him.

By the 1990s, such optimism was possible. If Dovlatov's characters sought solace and forgetfulness in alcohol and irony, Makanin took the historical circumstances of Soviet punitive psychiatry and showed the contrast between their practice in the 1970s and what the madhouse chronotope might reveal two decades later. In the novel, the path to the hospital leads backward in time to a more heroic age of overt struggle with clearly defined totalitarian enemies, whose eclipse in the post-Soviet era the hero paradoxically mourns. Beyond Brezhnev, beyond socialist realism, beyond the ideological hierarchies of Soviet society, Makanin's heroes must search for their own enemies without and within. The historical complexities confronted by the characters set them adrift in contemporary life, and their search for a mooring leads them to lunacy. As Makanin clearly shows, there is nothing Romantic about madness.

Let me now pull the lens back, to ask briefly how Makanin's novel reflects the experiences of the Soviet "man of the '60s." In *Underground, or a Hero of Our Time*, Makanin used the psychiatric hospital as a funhouse mirror on civil society in order to question and explore Soviet ideas about and experiences of the hero—the writer, the artist, the poet, the creative individual—and to begin to place those experiences within a post-Soviet context. In the process he resurrected Russian and Soviet literary experiences and characters—whether from the nineteenth century or the Brezhnev era of underground culture. He also reexamined those cultural moments, their cultural representatives, and the Soviet experiment of seventy years' duration—when being in the "*andegraund*" really meant something. This novel recalls a time of true opposition in the Soviet Union, when, as Philip Roth once said, nothing was possible, and everything mattered.

No apologist for the Soviet regime, Makanin was not using this novel as a simple act of nostalgia for the bad old days when it was easy to identify heroes and villains. Instead, the novel struck at the heart of the Russian intelligentsia's post-Soviet dilemma. Makanin was not celebrating the restrictive regimes of Khrushchev, Brezhnev, etc., and the crippled psyches of the Soviet population of those years.

Nonetheless, he and his compatriots are without doubt products of that history and that system. Just as in the pre-1917 era, when the intelligentsia struggled with tsarist censorship and repression, the Soviet-era Russian intelligentsia grew dependent on their own struggle with the even more controlling and interventionist totalitarian government. After the collapse of that government, the intelligentsia too lost its mooring. Having hoped and fought for the end of socialism and the Socialist state, they became confused as to what exactly their victory meant. They had won the Cold War, but were they heroes?

6. Antiheroes in a Post-heroic Age: Sergei Dovlatov, Vladimir Makanin, and Cold War Malaise

By placing the madhouse at the center of this novel, Makanin confronted a central chronotope in nineteenth- and twentieth-century Russian history. In that confrontation, he recognized that while that history is horrible, it is the only history upon which he can draw. In the end, it may not be a history to celebrate, but it is *his* history. In that sense, writers at the end of the twentieth century resembled the writers of Russia after the Revolution: sifting through the debris of Russian history, they were searching for that which they could use to understand better their present moment. Could the individual find a path outside of the collective culture? What would become of the underground when the repressive agents were themselves repressed?

Makanin created his characters against the backdrop of the very strong tradition of the protagonist-centered Russian novel—from Gogol's Poprishchin to Lermontov's Pechorin, Turgenev's Bazarov, Rudin, etc., and Dostoevsky's Raskolnikov in the nineteenth century, and Chapaev (the socialist realist positive hero), Zhivago, Venichka, and so on in the twentieth. Whether in wartime or not, each of these heroes of the literary past confronted the problems of his own time, but by the end of the twentieth century with the collapse of the imperial mind-set of both tsarist Russia and its Soviet successor state, Makanin's protagonists were lost in their own societies. Makanin's Petrovich—a flawed dissident hero to be sure, but the only one capable of functioning in the post-Soviet world—found the answer to Russian and Soviet historical dilemmas in the actions of a true madman, his own brother Venya.

At the end of *Underground*, in a section entitled "One Day in the Life of Venedikt Petrovich" (an obvious reference to Solzhenitsyn's *One Day in the Life of Ivan Denisovich*), Petrovich brings Venya out of the asylum for a day of celebration. It seems that one or two of Venya's paintings have been published in a German art book, and to commemorate this event, Venya gets a twenty-four-hour furlough from the hospital. During this day, Petrovich tries to offer Venya everything the madman has been missing in his decades of asylum life: fame, friendship, women (what Petrovich calls "my contribution to his therapy"), material goods, homemade food, and tea. Venya, of course, decides that he does not want to go back to the madhouse, just as his psychological ability to function is nearing its end. Scared by Venya's increasingly erratic behavior, Petrovich gives him a tablet the doctor prescribed for just such an emergency, and as it begins to take effect, he says, "I began to lose my brother" (*Andegraund*, 540, 551).

But even in his drug-induced psychological absence, Venya maintains a certain level of self-awareness, and this is the lesson he teaches his brother Petrovich. As Petrovich tries to drag Venya to the metro station, Venya pronounces two words: "I myself." I'll do it myself, he says, thus negating Petrovich's idea of what the state had done to Venya; while it may be true that Soviet psychiatric practices destroyed Venya and left him a childlike psychological cripple, Venya still maintains a kind of independence. Arriving at the asylum, he says again to the orderlies, "Don't push me, I [will go] myself." Petrovich hears this "I myself" through the silence of his own post-Brezhnev-era existence and understands that these are the words that he has been waiting to hear, the answer to his own questions in life:

> And [Venya] even straightened up, proud for this one moment—a Russian genius, beaten down, humiliated, pushed around, in his own shit, and yet don't push, I'll get there, *I myself!*[52]

Venya may need the madhouse, the only place where he can live after the Soviet psychiatric abuse visited upon his psyche, but he remains an artist and an independent soul. And having recognized the value and worth of this independence, the other hero, Petrovich, may find a way to function outside the madhouse as well.[53]

Makanin used his writer, Petrovich, along with the genius brother Venya, to describe the underground, to indict the system that forced it into existence, and to explore the meaning of both in a post-Soviet context. The madhouse functions as the main chronotope, as the plot circles back to it and to the protagonist's double: the better, wittier, purer brother on the inside. But the madhouse also functions to cleanse Petrovich of murder. Like Dostoevsky's

---

[52] Makanin, *Andegraund*, 555, 556. Tim Sergay sees in this line a reference to the murdered priest Alexander Men, whose last words are purported to be "*ia sam*." Personal communication.

[53] G. S. Smith reads Petrovich as a "violent anti-social hero" and sees a "solipsistic sense of personal identity" as his central core (Smith, "On the Page," 457). He finds Venya's "*ia sam*" to be a mere "pathetic insistence on doing things for himself" (Smith, "On the Page," 457 n. 44). In contrast, I argue that Petrovich learns two lessons in the madhouse. Petrovich discovers that the isolation that comes with murder, with transgression, can be overcome through human empathy; he also sees Venya's independence, his "*ia sam*," as the word he has been waiting for, the clue to reentering a creative state that, perhaps, gives the reader this very novel.

Raskolnikov over a hundred years earlier, he has undergone an almost religious rebirth. After committing that most transgressive of acts, the taking of another's life, Petrovich finds a way to reenter the community of humankind. And his fellow post-Soviet citizens who welcome him back in turn recover some of their own humanity by discovering forgiveness. Makanin used the madhouse as a place where people could work out a sense of their larger humanness. It is almost cliched to repeat that Soviet society and the constant state of war stripped its citizens of much of their humanity. Makanin's novel underscored how complicated and problematic it became to restore that humanity in the post-Soviet era.

* * *

Joseph Brodsky commented that readers could sense in Dovlatov's tone a refusal to be victimized. That stance—of the individual who chooses his own fate, not willing to have his life scripted by the authorities or anyone else— was one that Brodsky knew well from personal experience, including his own experience in psychiatric institutions. Brodsky went on to say:

> Serezha belonged to a generation which took the idea of individualism and the principle of the autonomy of human existence more seriously than had ever been the case before anywhere. I can speak about this authoritatively since I have the honor—the great and sad honor—to belong to this generation myself.[54]

This is the generation about which Makanin wrote his memoir, and that stance of the autonomous individual was the same stance that Makanin's Venya, despite the serious damage that has been inflicted on him, managed to take at the end of the novel.[55]

Brodsky and Dovlatov were born at almost the same moment to Leningrad families—one just before the siege and one during evacuation—and both ended up ejected from their homeland. They, like Makanin and even

---

[54] Joseph Brodsky, "O Serezhe Dovlatove: 'Mir urodliv, i liudi grustny,'" in Dovlatov, *Sobranie prozy*, 3: 360.

[55] On Brodsky and the psychiatric hospital, see especially Lev Loseff, "On Hostile Ground: Madness and Madhouse in Joseph Brodsky's 'Gorbunov and Gorchakov,'" in *Madness and the Mad*, 90–104.

more so his hero Petrovich, were men of the sixties. In one of his autobiographical essays, Brodsky describes his set of friends, who even if they made it through their higher education were unable to perform the "lip service" required to work in the system:

> We ended up doing odd jobs, menial or editorial—or something mindless, like carving tombstone inscriptions, drafting blueprints, translating technical texts, accounting, bookbinding, developing X-rays.[56]

They represent that generation of dropouts sometimes known as the "boiler room" generation; unable to stand the militarized Soviet institutions, almost allergic to marching in formation, they dropped out of school and university and took menial jobs—or wrote about characters who did. In another essay, Brodsky explained why he hated even his school uniform:

> That uniform, too, was semi-military: tunic, belt with a buckle, matching trousers, a cap with a lacquered visor. The earlier one starts to think of himself as a soldier, the better it is for the system. That was fine with me, and yet I resented the color, which suggested the infantry or, worse still, the police.[57]

The classroom, the infantry, the police, the prison, and finally the asylum—at some level, for this generation of post-heroic Russian men, these Soviet institutions all merged together seamlessly. In the age of Brezhnev, when all aspects of life from childhood on were regimented and disciplined, and when the threat of physical and psychological violence always loomed, heroism in the old sense was impossible. Preserving one's own integrity, whether as a drunk in Dovlatov's fiction or in a madhouse in Makanin's, was the best one could aspire to.

---

[56] Joseph Brodsky, "Less than One," in *Less than One: Selected Essays* (New York: Farrar, Straus, Giroux, 1986), 29.
[57] Brodsky, "In a Room and a Half," in *Less than One*, 468.

Part IV
Chapaev and War: Russian Redux

Monument to Chapaev, Samara

Chapter Seven

Revisiting War: Viktor Astafiev and the Boys of '24

> War is the Soviet people's great feat, war is a test of the soundness of all human qualities. Thanks to war we saved our own country and the entire world from the brown plague. War represents one of the best pages of our entire history.
>
> *Война есть великий подвиг советского народа, война есть проверка на прочность всех человеческих качеств, благодаря войне мы спасли свою страну и весь мир от коричневой чумы. Война есть одна из лучших страниц всей нашей истории.*
>
> -Alexander Shpagin[1]

> I'll tell you, there's nothing cheerful about war . . .
>
> *Я вам скажу, ничего веселого в войне нету . . .*
>
> -Bulat Okudzhava (1969)

Call it a perfect cultural storm. The early 1990s witnessed a remarkable confluence of cultural forces that both enabled and forced Russians to confront the meaning and memory of their wartime history.

All over the world, the fiftieth anniversary of World War II was marked with somber speeches, with monuments and museum exhibits, and with recollections and memoirs. But in Russia the fiftieth anniversary of the war was commemorated with particular enthusiasm. In Moscow, Victory Park was reinvigorated, and that vast shrine to World War II now includes the Museum of the Great Patriotic Wars well as an the open-air museum of World War II–era armaments with a new obelisk and statue of St. George, plus three houses of worship: a new, gold-domed Orthodox church (1993–1995), a memorial mosque, and a memorial synagogue with a Holocaust museum inside.

---

[1] Aleksandr Shpagin, "Religiia voiny," *Iskusstvo kino* 5 (2005): 57. Here Shpagin is characterizing the myth of World War II, not asserting the truth of this view.

Something for everyone, and a way to recall the glory of the victory, as writer Galina Shcherbakova remembered it. But for veterans of World War II, this moment was marked by a certain urgency. Put bluntly, they were all nearing the end of their lives. As Bulat Okudzhava wrote in the year before his death:

> My generation is dying,
> We've gathered at the hallway doors.
> Perhaps there's no inspiration any more,
> Or perhaps no hope. None at all.[2]

Aging veterans were revisiting the locations and tropes of their youth, whether actual battlefields of the war with Nazi Germany or the parallel sites of Stalin's war on his own people.

Those who were not veterans, like Moscow mayor Yury Luzhkov, saw these late-twentieth-century sites as a chance to participate in the glory remaining from the only great Soviet victory, the victory over the Fascists. In either case, this was the moment when the events of World War II were passing from the realm of living memory into the realm of history.

These commemorations were taking place during a time of failure and defeat. Even as new memorials to World War II were rising, monuments to the Soviet past were toppling—from the Dzerzhinsky statue on Lubyanka Square to the Lenin and Stalin monuments that for some time rested in Moscow's Fallen Monument Park, to the many statues throughout the former Soviet republics that have been removed.[3] The collapse of the Soviet Union came about, in no small measure, because of the humiliating defeat suffered in the Afghan war, and it simultaneously signaled, if not the loss of the Cold War, then at least a diminishment of Russia on the world stage.

No wonder, then, that even while the reminders of the Soviet Union disappeared, projects like Victory Park and its *Poklonnaya gora* memorial complex, built for enormous crowds of tourists both foreign and domestic,

---

[2] Quoted in Dmitrii Bykov, *Bulat Okudzhava* (Moscow: Molodaia gvardiia, 2009), 24.
[3] The Fallen Monument park in Moscow began to form after 1991, but now the statues have been righted and the park has been renamed Muzeon Park of Arts and transformed into an open-air sculpture garden. Even that park may soon disappear, if Sir Norman Foster's Golden Orange mixed-use complex is built on the site of the park and the Central House of Artists as proposed. Similar open-air parks featuring Communist-era statues and monuments exist in Budapest (Memento Park) and Lithuania (Grutas Park).

kept the Second World War fresh in the minds of Russian citizens as the new century loomed.[4] As historian Michael Ignatieff remarked about Soviet days, "The Great Fatherland War can be made to seem the one moment of genuinely collective effort which was not tarnished by terror and fratricide."[5] That discourse about war prevailed through much of the twentieth century, and in the face of Soviet defeat, many yearned to regain that sense of collective pride.[6]

The issue of the collective versus the individual, "we" versus "I," that we have been examining across the literary history of the Soviet period was also a central part of the Soviet war myth. Thus for writers, the collapse of the Soviet Union created the space to reevaluate World War II free from the strictures of official censorship and the mythology created about the war even while it was still going on. It wasn't simply that new things about the war could be known, though the opening up of state archives flooded the Russian imagination with an overwhelming, sometimes bewildering, amount of information.

More than that, the space that opened up even while the fiftieth-anniversary bands played included an indictment of the history of the Soviet Union as a whole. The Revolution and the Civil War seemed now to have been waged for naught. Millions dead and imprisoned in purges, campaigns of terror, and famines had suffered and perished in vain. The Soviet Union had lost the Cold War to Western powers. What would be the legacy of World War II?

---

[4] For a detailed discussion of the development of the *Poklonnaia gora* complex in the 1980s and early 90s, see Nina Tumarkin, "Story of a War Memorial," in *World War 2 and the Soviet People*, ed. John and Carol Garrard (New York: Macmillan Press, 1993), 125–146. Tumarkin's book *The Living and the Dead* completes the story. When I visited the museum in 2008, I found many aspects of the experience truly amazing, but among the strongest impressions I had was of the bathroom—long gleaming white rows of ceramic-tiled stalls in the women's room, all of the Japanese-style "squat" variety that I usually only find at old Soviet railway stations and provincial restaurants. The bathroom was designed to accommodate a large volume of visitors quickly and efficiently.

[5] Michael Ignatieff, "Soviet War Memorials," *History Workshop* 17 (Spring 1984): 160.

[6] It isn't true, of course, that nothing and no one was forgotten. In retelling Shalamov's story of the lend-lease bulldozer that moved skeletons in Kolyma to make room for new victims, Viktor Nekrasov recalls a parallel incident on the hill of Mamaev Kurgan, which when he visited after the war was still covered with the bones and skulls of war dead. "Several years later bulldozers dug up these bones and skulls and moved them into one large mass grave" ("Stalingrad i Kolyma," in *Kak ia stal sheval'e*, 100). The only monument to the millions of dead in Kolyma in 1986, when Nekrasov was writing these words, was Shalamov's story, although ten years later another war veteran, the sculptor Ernst Neizvestny, would install his monolithic Mask of Sorrow—a monument to the victims of Stalinism—in Magadan.

The central questions Michael Walzer asked for us in the introduction to this book became even more pressing: What is a just war? And is anything that occurs within a just war moral? With the dissolution of the Soviet Union, Russians began to confront the questions of *jus ad bellum* and *jus in bellum*, of whether the war was just and whether there was justice in it, or whether the whole history of the Soviet World War II experience was simply a collection of myths and errors.

Boys of '24

World War II changed the face of Soviet culture and history. It also shaped the lives and careers of a remarkable generation of writers, writers who experienced war at a young age. This generation, what I call the "boys of '24," included war writers and poets—such as Bulat Okudzhava, Yury Bondarev, Vasil Bykov, and Boris Vasiliev—and literary critics like Lazar Lazarev.

Children of the Soviet experiment, many of these writers were orphaned in the 1930s as a result of collectivization and the Stalinist purges. For example, Bulat Okudzhava (1924–1997) was raised by relatives after his father was arrested in 1937 under suspicion of being a Trotskyite and executed, and his mother disappeared into the camps in 1939. Off to the front at age eighteen, the boys of '24 came to maturity in the trenches fighting the Germans.

These soldiers were witnesses to war and deprivation. They began their writing careers after World War II, in some cases studying in courses for writers, in others finding their way themselves, but all gripped by the sense that they wanted to document the experience of their generation and their nation. Indeed, with their uniquely Soviet biographies, this generation of writers became metonymic representatives of the entire Soviet twentieth century.

The literature they produced and the frequent interviews they gave for the Soviet press for the anniversaries of the beginning and end of the war changed as the landscape of Soviet culture changed. Subscribing, as was necessary, to the doctrine of socialist realism, some of them wrote on other topics or muted their responses to the war in their fiction, but as they reached their sixties and Mikhail Gorbachev launched his campaign of *glasnost*, they began to realize that they could now speak out and that they could write and talk about the war in a new way.

To take one example, Bulat Okudzhava published his first story about the war in 1961. He wrote poetry and songs and made a respectable career for himself performing concerts with "author's songs" (*avtorskie pesni*), accompanying himself with three chords on an acoustic guitar. These songs were sometimes ironic, but always gentle, such as the "Song of the Cheerful Soldier" (*"Pesenka vesëlogo soldata"*)—which focuses on the simplicity of life for the member of the armed forces who follows the call of his motherland and in turn is excused from taking personal responsibility for his actions—or "The Paper Soldier" (*"Bumazhnyi soldat"*), about the bravery of a toy soldier. Other songs did not mention the war at all.

But at the very beginning of *glasnost*, in 1986, Okudzhava demanded a new kind of honesty:

> I value people who know how to think independently, in any situation. I value people who don't build their happiness on someone else's unhappiness. I value people who respect the individual (*lichnost'*). Not the collective, but the individual. Because we have long ago learned to respect the collective; it's time to begin to respect the individual. I especially hate lies [...] especially now, when we are finally allowed to speak the truth.[7]

Almost ten years later, this singer of songs about cheerful soldiers found himself confessing that the victory over the Nazis was a Pyrrhic one. "The sad part," commented Okudzhava, "is that though we may have won a victory, we turned out to be vanquished."[8]

The Angriest Boy of '24: Viktor Astafiev

This generation entered the war with enthusiasm and naive ideas of fighting to save their country. They were responding to the shock of the Nazi attack, war propaganda, and an adolescent desire to be a part of something big and important. But on a personal level, many of these young soldiers were traumatized by the mud and blood they encountered day after day, week after week.

No one felt that trauma more deeply than Viktor Astafiev. And no member of his generation staked his literary ambition on describing those traumas more than he did when he published his epic novel *The Accursed and the Damned* in 1994. That novel changed the conversation about World War II in the post-Soviet period, even as the celebrations of the fiftieth anniversary were winding down.[9]

---

[7] 14 September 1986. "Ia nikomu nichego ne naviazyval..." 51.
[8] 4 April 1995. "Ia nikomu nichego ne naviazyval..." 16.
[9] Frank Ellis writes about Astafiev, Georgii Vladimov, and Vladimir But in his chapter "The Russian War Novel of the 1990s: A Final Reckoning?" in *The Damned and the Dead: The Eastern Front through the Eyes of Soviet and Russian Novelists*, 212–267.

Viktor Astafiev (1924–2001) lost his parents when his father was arrested for "sabotage," identified as an enemy of a state at war with its own people, and his mother perished in 1931 in a tragic boating accident on her way to visit his father. As a result, he spent his childhood years in an orphanage in the Yenisei region of Siberia. He entered the Red Army in 1942 as an eighteen-year-old who hadn't even finished the tenth grade, serving in a number of capacities, and was awarded a medal for bravery in 1943.

When he returned from the war, he worked at various jobs until finding a place at a newspaper and publishing his first book of stories in 1953. Accepted into the Writers' Union in 1958, he studied at the Moscow Higher Literary Courses in the early 1960s.

It was at this time that he began to think about how one should write about World War II. According to his own account, he felt the need to register a "protest against the 'lacquered' literature about war." He published throughout the Soviet period and was awarded state prizes for his fiction. Best known in the West for his prose works about village and provincial life in Siberia, including such masterpieces as "Liudochka" (1989), a chilling tale that ranks with the best fiction of the twentieth century, Astafiev was at heart a writer formed by war, and the experience of war was central to much of his work.

Several of his early works highlighted World War II, including the novella *The Shepherd and the Shepherdess* (*Pastukh i pastushka*, 1971) and the play *Forgive Me* (*Prosti menia*, 1980), about love and death in a military hospital. He returned to the theme of the war and wrote about it throughout the 1990s, publishing the novel *The Accursed and the Dead* and the novellas *The Cheerful Soldier* (*Veselyi soldat*, 1998) and *A Bird of Passage* (*Proletnyi gus'*, 2001).[10] In these war stories, heavy with autobiography, Astafiev commemorated the suffering and deaths of the many young soldiers sacrificed to the war effort, and the postwar trials of those who survived. Like his younger

---

10 For more on "Liudochka" see Julian D. Moss, "Violence in Viktor Astafiev's Fiction," and Nadya L. Peterson, "Death and the Maiden: Erasures of the Feminine in Soviet Literature of the Fin-de-siècle," in *Times of Trouble: Violence in Russian Literature and Culture*, ed. Marcus C. Levitt and Tatyana Novikov (Madison: University of Wisconsin Press, 2007), 236–245 and 246–255, esp. 247–250. In his article Moss looks at *The Accursed and the Dead* as well as "Queen Fish," *A Sad Detective Story*, and "Liudochka" and concludes that the role of violence in Astafiev's work is "to castigate some aspect of Russia: sometimes the Soviet system and its operatives, sometimes the state's destruction of Siberia, sometimes Russian Man's failure to live in harmony with Nature, sometimes contemporary Russia's sliding morals and casual violence" (Moss, "Violence," 244).

colleague Makanin, Astafiev took the Soviet regime to task for the way it destroyed and deformed its citizens. An eyewitness and participant in war, he took advantage of the new opportunities to write openly, as if answering Okudzhava's call to stop telling lies.

Astafiev explored these themes of war most thoroughly and bitterly in his magnum opus, *The Accursed and the Dead*. Given the autobiographical source of Astafiev's writing and the vast discourse of war fiction, rhetoric, and memory with which this novel interacts, we might imagine that with his testimony he aimed to obliterate previous historical narratives with a new narrative of victimhood.

This war fiction was Astafiev's final act. He wrote the novel to honor his fellow "boys of '24," the orphans and marginalized misfits from Siberia with whom he served in the war, and to claim his own status as a representative victim of twentieth-century Soviet history. In so doing, he both rejected the Soviet rhetoric of *podvig*, of feats of glory associated with World War II, and reinscribed his own version of *podvig* into history—as a writer of unwanted truths and unpopular memories.

The Accursed and the Dead: Truth from the Trenches

Written between 1990 and 1994, *The Accursed and the Dead* was first published in journal form in *Novyi Mir* in the last decade of Astafiev's life. This book—which he called his main work ("a novel about the war, *that* war, the trench [war], *my* war")—was for him a holy obligation and an act of civil defiance, and it was designed to bring Astafiev into a certain category of Russian writers. "Shalamov branded them with the camps," he mused. "I will brand them with the front. If I can manage to get it done."[11] This concern with aging and the increased urgency of getting the words on paper was shared by many writers of Astafiev's war generation.

The novel is a diptych and sprawls over many months of the war and over six hundred pages. The first book, "The Devil's Pit," is devoted to the recruit training period in Siberia, while the second book, entitled "The Bridgehead," focuses on a river crossing in European Russia, a trope that echoes the river crossing in *Chapaev*. The novel brings together dozens of characters, many of them orphans and children of exiles, and throws them into the cauldron of war.

---

[11] Gennadii Trifonov, "Rubtsy voiny (pamiati V. P. Astaf'eva)," *Kontinent* 214 (2002).

In fact, Astafiev had planned a third part to the novel but published it separately as the story "A Cheerful Soldier" when it became clear that he couldn't pull the novel together into one whole.[12] For the author, as for the reader, *The Accursed and the Dead* was a real challenge. Though filled with fascinating descriptions of geographic spaces, personal interactions, and army protocol, the novel lacks a specific narrative or plot trajectory. If, as we discussed in the introduction, the challenge for any war writer is to give meaning to what is otherwise chaotic violence interspersed with long periods of boredom, Astafiev resisted that impulse to make meaning out of this war with the very structure of the novel.[13]

His ambitions in writing the novel were captured by the title he gave it, which echoed the titles of other "big" Russian books like Vasily Grossman's 1959 (published 1980) *Life and Fate* or Tolstoy's nineteenth-century *War and Peace*, both epic novels about the struggles of the individual in wartime, featuring enormous casts of characters and vast expanses of the European landmass.[14] Thus for readers, Astafiev's title signalled that the book would grapple with the eternal questions about just and unjust wars, the role of the individual in a war-torn society, and the role of God, fate, and the government in the personal lives of human beings.[15]

In Russian the title is even more violent—*prokliaty* both reminds us of the nineteenth century's "accursed questions" and represents a label that cannot be reversed; the dead are not merely dead but have been killed, *ubity*, a word that points to the inherent search for criminal intent, for someone to

---

[12] Astafiev was also struggling with health crises and the difficulties of writing this epic novel; he himself felt "that I didn't quite get there with this novel." See personal letter to Il′ia Grigor′evich (surname unknown), 26 May 1994, *Net mne otveta: Epistoliarnyi dnevnik, 1951–2001* (Irkutsk: Izdatel′ Sapronov, 2009), 555.

[13] In her article "Tvorchestvo Viktora Astaf′eva," Czech scholar M. Zahradka writes that "the unity of the novel is destroyed by the excessive number of characters and episodes that lead to the fragmentary nature of the text and an excessively publicistic tone." See *Starodub: Astaf′evskii ezhegodnik: Materialy i issledovaniia*, vyp. 1 (Krasnoyarsk: 2009).

[14] The English-language reader might even think of Norman Mailer's 1948 *The Naked and the Dead* about his experiences in the Philippines during the war. Konstantin Simonov's *The Living and the Dead* (1959) follows the same title format.

[15] The tone of the novel veers from descriptive and evocative into that of a moralizing screed. Frank Ellis has argued that it is really two novels, a "conventional war novel" and a "discourse on Russia's suffering." See Ellis, "Sons of the Soviet Apocalypse: Viktor Astafiev's *The Damned and the Dead*," *The Modern Language Review* 97.4 (October 2002): 909–923; 912.

blame.[16] "Who is to blame?" (*Kto vinovat?*) is a question that the reader asks and strives to answer even before opening the covers of the book, and the heft of the volume promises that the answer will be complex and multilayered.

Igor Dedkov reminds us that Astafiev's literary goal was to write the "most truthful novel about the war."[17] Perestroika and the collapse of the Soviet regime were accompanied by the collapse of official history, and documents and fictional works revealing details about the Stalinist terror and the labor camp system dominated the periodical press and bookstore shelves. New documents and fiction about World War II followed almost immediately.

But by using the word "truth," Dedkov also reminds us that the truth about Soviet history, and who got to tell that truth, had shifted throughout the twentieth century. In the wake of World War II, as we explored in previous chapters, eyewitnesses had a certain authority that lent authenticity to their accounts. Astafiev too was an eyewitness and participant. However, in this novel he was not reporting from the trenches but revisiting them many years later, in a completely different social and political setting, when the Soviet Union had collapsed. The truth he was reaching for was about witnessing in the moral sense, not in the reportorial sense. His novel was about setting the record straight.

The 1980s and early 1990s saw a host of republished fictions and narrating witnesses, including the stories of Varlam Shalamov about the prison camps of Kolyma. When thinking about his own act of moral witness, Astafiev believed that it was as important and paradigm-changing as these memoirs about the Gulag had been. He also hoped that, given the kinds of new truths that had emerged during *glasnost* about Stalin and the camps, the Russian people were ready for a new look at the experiences of World War II. He was to be disappointed.

When the novel came out, many veterans found the graphic and uncompromising story of World War II to be an attempt to blacken their heroics. Wedded to the rhetoric of *podvig*, they did not want to revisit the trenches in a new way. Instead, they wanted to continue to read reminders that fit the

---

[16] Critics have translated the novel's title variously as *The Damned and the Dead* (Frank Ellis) and *The Cursed and the Slain* (Julian D. Moss).

[17] Igor' Dedkov, "Ob"iavlenie viny i naznachenie kazni," *Druzhba narodov* 10 (1993): 185–202; 187. For more criticism on the novel, see Vladimir Zubkov, "Ozhidanie? Proshchanie?: Segodnia i zavtra khudozhestvennoi prozy o Velikoi Otechestvennoi voine," *Ural* 5 (2010); V. F. Gladyshev, "My za tsenoi ne postoim? (Dve pravdy o voine)," *Ural* 5 (2004); V. M. Mikhailiuk, "Velikii truzhenik pera," *Ural* 5 (2004).

slogans to which they had become accustomed: "We are heroes, we won the war" or "Nothing is forgotten, no one is forgotten."[18]

But Astafiev's campaign of moral witness had a different agenda, and he claimed to have anticipated his mixed reception:

> I already knew what kind of reaction [my novel] would evoke in a reader who had been raised on an utterly different kind of literature. I knew also that many would say: "I haven't read the novel, but the novel is shit anyway, since my comrade and the Veterans Council of N Region both say it's bad."

Astafiev said in another context, after publishing "A Cheerful Soldier," that he had decided not to return to the war theme anymore

> because it is difficult and pointless. The young cannot understand, hardly anyone understands, and older folks don't want to be reminded. If you must write about the war, it should be about the one that was made up, where they look heroic, where it wasn't the Germans beating them, but them beating the Germans.[19]

As the Soviet Union collapsed and the project of revising history accelerated, the conflict of the standard narrative and the revisionist narrative grew more acute, especially with anniversary dates looming and veterans beginning to disappear from the scene. Astafiev admitted, "Now I see that my Belorussian friend Vasil Bykov's words were not so preposterous, when he wrote: 'You know, Viktor, sometimes I'm glad that I'll die soon.'"[20]

Monuments for and against History

The post-Soviet literary landscape was a place of postmodern experimentation and frivolous wordplay, as authors reveled in the opportunity to publish whatever they liked. Astafiev's work, which leans toward didactic naturalism, formed quite a contrast. In fact, one favorable reviewer noted about *The Accursed and the Dead*, "Against the background of the literary games

---

[18] Moss points out that "many hundreds [of veterans] wrote to [Astafiev] to thank him for having the courage to tell the truth" (Moss, "Violence," 237). See also the discussion of Astafiev's afterword to the novel, below, which quotes supportive veterans.
[19] See Nikolai Kavin, ed., "Besedy s Viktorom Astaf'ievym," *Znamia* 5 (2009): 132.
[20] See Ella Karaseva, "Beri, da pomni," review of *Starodub*, in *Oktiabr'* 5 (2010).

at the beginning of the 90s Astafiev's novel stands as a majestic and terrible monument."²¹

The timing of the novel's publication in the 1990s was not accidental. Nor was its irony. Astafiev wanted to offer his own monument to the fiftieth anniversary of World War II, one that would destroy the standard narrative of the war and accuse those who cling to it—especially after Stalinism and Socialist values have been eclipsed—of naïveté and dishonesty. This is what Okudzhava meant when he decried those who continued to lie "especially now, when we are finally allowed to speak the truth."

In looking at the task Astafiev set himself in his novel, we can use terms coined by scholar Yomi Braester in his analysis of twentieth-century texts from another totalitarian culture fraught with historical tragedy: China. Braester distinguishes between texts that "bear witness for history"—i.e., speak "in the name of 'history' to evoke a sense of events as tangible and purposeful"—and those that function as a witness "against history." He argues that in "claiming that writing is divorced from 'history' (understood as the sign of reality, progress, and national destiny), authors challenge their own capacity to bear witness. Bearing witness against history perforce becomes bearing witness against testimony itself."²² Writing *for* and *against* history is one way to parse discourses about the Second World War.

We can also borrow from Susan Rubin Suleiman's work to contextualize Astafiev's project of remembering World War II. Astafiev knew that the long, state-sponsored program of patriotism, war propaganda, and war memories would get in the way of his book's reception among many whom he would have liked to reach. The Soviet mechanisms of constructing war memories and memorials perforce included within them what Suleiman identifies as the role *forgetting* plays as "the active agent in the formation of memories." She goes on to say:

> Like the sea sculpting the land it surrounds, forgetting gives memories their shape and relief. [. . .] What forgetting accomplishes is the highlighting of some past impressions and experiences and the elimination—or at least the bracketing—of others.²³

---

21 Sergei Beliakov, "Prokliatie Viktora Astafieva," *Ural* 5 (2005).
22 Braester builds his book around this distinction between "for" and "against." See Yomi Braester, *Witness against History: Literature, Film and Public Discourse in Twentieth Century China* (Stanford, CA: Stanford University Press, 2003), ix-xii.
23 Susan Rubin Suleiman, *Crises of Memory and the Second World War* (Cambridge, MA: Harvard University Press, 2006), 215.

Many of Astafiev's readers, veterans themselves who were invested in the heroism of war—especially as their pensions decreased and their war wounds and other physical ailments increasingly pained them—were engaged in precisely this kind of forgetting, this "bracketing" of experience, a state-sponsored process that went on for decades under Brezhnev and continued beyond perestroika on a voluntary basis. In the years following Gorbachev's cancelling of all history exams in 1988, veterans became entrenched in their remembering and forgetting, clinging to certain official versions of history so as to maintain the physical and psychological benefits of having served the fatherland.

If during certain periods of Soviet history war memorials were designed and erected as a vindication of Stalin's terror,[24] Astafiev in the final years of his life worked to remind his fellow countrymen that the disastrous war was *caused* by Stalinism and that the Victory, such as it was, could not serve as a vindication of the injustices perpetrated by the government and its leader against the populace.

Swimming entirely against the currents of Russian memory, Astafiev was not interested in whether World War II was a just war. What he really cared about were individual actions during the war that he saw as fundamentally immoral. In his fiction, Astafiev created a memorial in words that indicted both the terror and the war and that saw little distinction between the two.

Alexander Shpagin has pointed out that the narrative created about the Great Patriotic War continued to ossify until by the end of the twentieth century it had been transformed into something closer to a religious dogma. As he describes the war myth in the epigraph to this chapter:

> War is the Soviet people's great feat, war is a test of the soundness of all human qualities, thanks to the war we saved our own country and the entire world from the brown plague. War represents one of the best pages of our entire history.[25]

---

[24] Ignatieff, "Soviet War Memorials," 160.

[25] Shpagin, "Religiia voiny," 5: 57. It is worth comparing Astafiev's direct attack on the discourse of *podvig*, through realism and naturalistic detail, with the lampooning of *podvig* in such parodic novels as Viktor Pelevin's 1992 *Omon Ra*, in which a young cosmonaut is subjected to preparatory courses such as "The Strong of Spirit," which features speakers "whose profession was feats" (Viktor Pelevin, *Omon Ra* [Moscow: Vagrius, 1999], 48). See chapter 8 below.

That paradigm was fully functional through the entire Soviet period, and new militaristic and patriotic government stances in the twenty-first century are striving to keep it alive.

Astafiev, however, wrote against that paradigm. Readers can't help but notice that his condemnation of the Soviet government, political establishment, and totalitarian military regime lacks the heroic individuals necessary for great feats. Astafiev wrote instead about ill-prepared, ill-fed, ill-trained boys thrown to slaughter without a thought for the individual human being.[26]

Thus his goal in the novel was to subvert the paradigm of heroism, of *podvig*, in the witnessing for history that had dominated the discourse about the war. However, Astafiev could not escape the idea that there was a heroic feat being accomplished, and he defined his own work as an author in those terms:

> To write about war, about any war—is an extremely difficult task, almost insurmountable, but to write about the past war, the Patriotic war, requires an unbelievable effort, because nowhere and never in the history of humanity has there been such a terrible and bloody war. And although there's a saying that people lie about war and hunting, there has been so much lying about this war, everything connected with it has been so confused, that in the end the "made up" war eclipsed the real one.[27]

Telling the truth becomes an act of heroism, and the author himself becomes a hero. The rhetoric of *podvig* was inescapable, even as Astafiev tried to chronicle its falseness, and his efforts to eradicate official history seemed to him to be his biggest feat yet. In a personal letter to Yury Nagibin, Astafiev wrote:

> I have written the war, terrible, murderous; perhaps there is not much artistry there, but there is plenty to rub people's noses in. I wrote a work the like of which has not yet been seen in our literature; there are such works in American literature, and they speak to each other—[Dalton]

---

[26] Ellis notes that Astafiev's descriptions of the training camp conditions seem as if they came from the pages of *The Kolyma Tales* or *The Gulag Archipelago*. See "Sons of the Soviet Apocalypse," 913–914, and *The Damned and the Dead*, 218.

[27] Astafiev, "Afterword," in *Izbrannoe: Prokliaty i ubity* (Moscow: Terra, 1999), 619–620. I will cite from this edition of the novel throughout the chapter.

Trumbo's [1939] *Johnny Got His Gun*, for example, which I read in *Siberian Fires* one time...."[28]

Heroic Soviet history, the official history, was chronicled in what Astafiev called the "lacquered" literature about war, and Astafiev wanted to unwrite it all, to create a new class of works of truth that might speak to each other as American novels do. This was an enormous task.

As Boris Vasiliev, a fellow war novelist and another "boy of '24," wrote, Soviet memories of the war were fabricated. "Deliberately, over a long period of time, any historical sense was destroyed in us; we have been trained to [believe in] constructed history, the stereotypes of shameless lies."[29] That constructed history, those lies, were a powerful part of Soviet memory and identity. Writing in connection with the fortieth anniversary of the war, Viktor Nekrasov was made uncomfortable by the Soviet declarations of "20 million dead" that were supposed to prove the heroic sacrifice of the Soviet people. He asked:

> Is it really worth focusing on this number? Doesn't it speak to a certain, to be gentle, error (if not a crime)? There are people, even here in the [Russian] emigration [in Paris], who assert that Stalin's prewar reprisals against the military elite were orchestrated not out of cowardice and suspicion, but deliberately, so as to renew the officers' corps with young commanders.[30]

Invented history. "Lacquered literature." Errors and crimes.

In the midst of the fiftieth-anniversary celebrations, Astafiev wrote to a friend to express the same thought we quoted above from Okudzhava, questioning whether the war had even been won:

> Let them beat their drums, those aged phantoms of war, who so eagerly take in the beautiful lies to which they have become accustomed, let

---

[28] 10 June 1994 (Astaf'ev, *Net mne otveta*, 558).
[29] Boris Vasil'ev, "Liubi Rossiiu v nepogodu," interview with Elena Iakovich, *Literaturnaia gazeta*, 30 May 1990 (No. 22, 6296). See also Anna Krylova, "Neither Erased nor Remembered: Soviet 'Women Combatants' and Cultural Strategies of Forgetting in Soviet Russia, 1940s-1980s," in *Histories of the Aftermath: The Legacies of the Second World War in Europe,* ed. Frank Biess and Robert G. Moeller (New York: Berghahn Books, 2010), esp. 90–91.
[30] "6 June 1944," in Viktor Nekrasov, *Na voine i posle,* 560.

them go into the next world with the conviction that they were not defeated in the war, that they won a Victory. But there's no need to convince anyone that it was we, not Germany, who suffered defeat, leaving ourselves beautiful words while our country and people were destroyed in the war.[31]

"Beautiful words." By the 1990s, other words were needed. In the afterword to the 1999 edition of his novel, Astafiev quoted reactions by veterans who were grateful for his "correction" of the narrative. Astafiev enlisted the words of veterans themselves, which use the voice of authenticity and the first person, to confirm his fictional panorama, to testify to the author's own *podvig*. One veteran wrote:

> Words cannot express the depth of my reaction, Viktor Petrovich. You have created something unique. This work shows immense bravery and will. And also heart. To pass again along those bloody paths, torturing your heart and memory—without exaggeration, this was a feat [*podvig*]. The quiet, everyday feat of a camp victim. There's no other word for it. I can only replace the epithet: not a camp victim, but a soldier.[32]

Using this letter, Astafiev added authenticity to his own narrative and to his parallel between war and Gulag. These "true soldiers of the trenches" ("*istinnye okopniki-soldaty*"), as he called them, wrote to share their "confessions, entrusted to paper, the confessions of people who are not used to pretending and whose memories are tired."[33] But in this afterword he also noted that there is no one all-encompassing truth. Truth depends on individual experience. Each soldier experienced the war differently; each brought home his own stories.

The official truth did not acknowledge such differences, and it is that hypocrisy that Astafiev could not forgive:

> Appearance. The appearance of truth, the appearance of activity. The appearance of knowledge, education, the appearance of concern for the

---

[31] See personal letter to Il'ia Grigor'evich (surname unknown), 26 May 1994, *Net mne otveta . . .* , 556.

[32] M. Popov, *Arkhangel'sk*. Quoted in "Kommentarii," in Viktor Astaf'ev, *Izbrannoe*, 619.

[33] Astaf'ev, "Afterword," *Izbrannoe*, 621.

people and the soldier. The appearance of a strong defense. The appearance of a powerful army. The appearance of unshakeable unity. The appearance of a united state that fell apart in three days. . . .

Appearance, delusion, lies . . . daily lies, haunting lies, and you already begin to doubt: maybe the lies are the truth, and the truth really is lies. . . . (*Izbrannoe*, 620)

This concern with the "real truth" dominated Astafiev's last years.

Heroes—or Orphans?

In *The Accursed and the Dead*, many of the soldiers are orphans, often the children of criminals and "enemies of the people," of "eternal pioneers," of exiled kulaks and the resettled (*spetspereselentsy*), of Old Believers and collective farmers. Most of the recruits are weak, unhealthy, and terrified. These ragtag eighteen-year-olds from the margins of society are unformed by life and fate, their characters not yet solidified and their bodies undernourished.

Early on, sustained by songs and speeches, the boys imbibe a mass enthusiasm that enables them to feel a unity as a group, to feel their potential as fighters allied against the enemy, Hitler and his fascist forces. War songs (such as "Rise up, rise up, enormous country! Rise up to face the fatal battle") bring the wandering recruits together, "and not even noticing, they fell into step, began to stamp their feet along the beaten-down path of sand mixed with snow to the beat of that dread song." (*Izbrannoe*, 8, 9) They believe the narrative proclaimed on the radio by the great leader himself:

> We have overcome our difficulties, and now our factories, kolkhozes and sovkhozes, our military factories and the enterprises connected with them are supplying the Red Army honestly and regularly . . . our country has never had such a strong and well-organized rear. . . . (*Izbrannoe*, 33)

But as they experience the "training camps"—with their inadequate food, shelter, and sanitary facilities, in places rife with disease and bugs, with only ill-fitting, used uniforms (b/u: *byvshie v upotreblenii*) and minimal footwear—what spirit they do have quickly evaporates.

Astafiev gives the background of numerous individual soldiers, some of whom the narrator labels "*dokhodiagi*," using the prison camp word for sick and starving boys who will not live long enough to fight for their homeland. This parallel—of Siberian training camps for recruits and the work camps that were spread across Siberia and the rest of the Soviet Union—is one that Astafiev made in speaking about the novel, but here in the text it has a special poignancy, since the emphasis is on very young characters, just eighteen years old, neither criminals nor the political enemies of the regime, but merely boys caught in the gears of history.

Arguably the low point of the "Devil's Pit" comes during the recruits' training. The soldiers utterly lack discipline and are impervious to efforts to train them, but Astafiev wants us to see that these boys just didn't understand the point of all this discipline and how arbitrary it can be. Two of them, the sweet and naive Snegirev twins, go AWOL for a few days to see their mother and return to camp with food gifts for all:

> "Eat, eat," they shout out happily, carefree, "Mama sent a lot, she wanted us to treat everyone. Whom can I feed, she said, all alone here by myself?"
> "Where were you?" asked the commander of the battalion.
> "Home of course. What's the big deal? We came back." (*Izbrannoe*, 159)

All the soldiers await forgiveness for the Snegirevs. They even imagine the words that will be pronounced: "but moved by humanistic ideas and considering the young age of the criminals and their exemplary behavior during peaceful times, our most humane party, headed and led by the father and teacher toward ultimate victory . . ." (*Izbrannoe*, 168).

Instead, the battalion commander hands down a death sentence. The boys react with utter shock: "What is this all about? We're all in this together" (*Izbrannoe*, 169). This distinction—*svoi/chuzhie*—doesn't help the Snegirev brothers, and their martyrdom hangs over the entire novel; even in the final battle scenes on the bridgehead hundreds of kilometers and pages later, their fellow recruits and officers will think of them, wondering whether they have in this unexpected and unfair martyrdom been spared a more horrible fate, the fate of survival (*Izbrannoe*, 504).

This execution is followed by a change in the daily lives of the rest of the battalion. Recognizing that the conditions which led the Snegirevs to seek

7. Revisiting War: Viktor Astafiev and the Boys of '24

their mother's help—the filth and near starvation to which the recruits have been subjected—have not made ideal soldiers of them, the officers send the recruits to the village. They are temporarily loaned out to a nearby sovkhoz to harvest winter wheat.

The local military administration is afraid that the army will not accept the "emaciated, sickly soldiers" of the Twenty-first Regiment. The narrator explains:

> The supreme leader announced at a meeting in the Kremlin: "We have never had such a reliable and strong rear," and he will not tolerate contradiction of his words, and so a solution to the situation was found (*Izbrannoe*, 177).

Astafiev never renders any blame for the conditions of the camp, for the misery of the young recruits; neither Colonel Azatyan nor Captain Shchus nor *starshina* Shpator are at fault. Instead, blame hovers somewhere far away, in the Kremlin, with the "father" of them all. In these passages set in the countryside, Astafiev demonstrates to his readers that the boys really are orphans, suffering from a lack of family feeling. The temporary homes they find at the sovkhoz show them to be human beings, capable of work if treated with love and understanding. Their fates at the front seem that much more tragic after this section of the novel, where the reader finally gets to know the soldiers a little better as individuals. In the end, virtually all of these soldiers die, not as heroes, but as orphans, orphaned by the state.

Much later in the text, the character Major Zarubin—who functions as a kind of father figure for the boys of '24 once they reach the front—is seriously wounded. His voice tired with bitter irony, the major sums up yet another failed day on the bridgehead:

> That's how we fight, that's how we'll be victorious ... here it is, the third year of the war, and we are still encountering the results of the brilliant war preparations. And there's nothing we can do, other than heroically overcome these difficulties.

A few pages later, Zarubin thinks to himself, "I may die tonight. But what about them, hungry and abandoned by everyone?" (*Izbrannoe*, 466, 473).

The Commissar-Hero Vanishes

Stalin barely enters into the narrative, except as a disembodied radio voice. As a representative of political power, Astafiev substituted the figure of the commissar. However, the shape of the novel, with opening chapters devoted to the Siberian training camp for recruits in the winter of 1942–1943 and most of its second book set on the bridgehead, the dangerous side of the river where no political officers ventured, means that commissar figures barely make an appearance in the novel.

All the more important, then, that the novel ends with Colonel Musyonok, the regiment's political commissar, as the half-dead remnants of the regiment return from the bridgehead to the left bank of the river. Universally hated (by everyone, from the commander of the regiment, Beskapustin, to his own driver, Brykin), Musyonok is portrayed by the narrator as utterly blind to the condition of the troops (who are "naked, starving," and "exhausted" [*Izbrannoe*, 601, 602]) and indifferent to the inappropriateness of his own diction when he addresses them.

> They hated Musyonok and feared him. He knew this perfectly well, and he crawled into every hole, was present at every meeting, including operational ones; even in small military councils he would advise how best to defeat the enemy. (*Izbrannoe*, 604)

His verbal attack on the returning officers and soldiers who, in his words, "had shamed the battle flag of the guards division with their behavior," clarified the situation for Captain Shchus, who decides, "I'll kill the bastard!"

Shchus organizes an "accident," sending Musyonok's driver away and making sure that the commissar's vehicle leaves the road and ends up in a minefield. Musyonok, killed in the explosion, enters history as a martyr, and the irony of this "promotion" is not lost in the telling. The division's artist sketches a scene, which he entitles "Funeral of the Commissar-Hero," and the narrator contrasts the pomp that accompanies the burial ceremony with the burial of soldiers who perished on the right bank, who were "thrown into big shallow pits" with all their belongings.

Musyonok's funeral is attended by military dignitaries in full uniform, with an orchestra playing a list of revolutionary songs and even chamber music chosen by Musyonok's lover.[34] Accompanied by a fancy coffin, speeches, honors, and a temporary wooden obelisk with words engraved in gold, Musyonok is buried on a hill with flowers, wreaths, and a rifle salute to mark his passing. Official history, with all its trappings, records the death of the commissar-hero. Astafiev's soldiers—and his readers—know that the honor is false.

The contrast between soldiers and the commissar continues as the narrator describes the deliberate flooding of the area a decade later. The "white soldiers' bones" remain on the bottom of a new man-made sea, while "the head of the political department of the guards rifle division's grave will be transferred":

> The decomposing coffin with its tarnished silver, again covered with the colors of the guards division, to the sound of an orchestra, ceremoniously, with speeches and a still more impressive salute will be interred in the earth in a new place. Every year pioneers and veterans of war will come to this heroic gravesite with flowers and wreaths, they will bow down to the monument, pronounce . . . speeches and drink a memorial glass, here on the green banks, with banquet tables groaning. (*Izbrannoe*, 616)

Critic Evgeny Ermolin insists that Astafiev is not didactic.[35] Regardless, in these concluding pages of his novel, his point is very clear. The narrator mourns the soldiers—who have perished in a tragically undersupported, perhaps even unnecessary, battle on the periphery of the front—and depicts their mass graves in graphic terms. While the dead bodies await burial, rats make nests in their filthy clothing, and those digging the shallow graves drive the rats away with shovels and stones. But the dignity of the "clean white bones" in the fast-forward scene of the future undercuts the bitter irony of the pilgrimages to the monument to the "commissar-hero." The lies are there, Astafiev tells his reader, but we know they are lies.

---

[34] The lover wears a black lacy handkerchief over her head "in violation of military uniform codes" (*Izbrannoe*, 612, 613).

[35] See Evgenii Ermolin, "Mestorozhdenie sovesti: Zametki o Viktore Astaf'eve," *Kontinent* 100 (1999).

The Crossing

Uneven though this novel might be in quality, it has some amazingly stirring passages. The second volume chronicles day after day as the Soviet army tries to cross the River Dnieper and loses thousands of soldiers. Born in Siberia and in the heart of Russia, very few of them know how to swim, and they perish in the cold water without functional rafts or boats of any kind.

This "crossing" evokes other scenes of forced river crossings, like the more successful *"Pereprava, pereprava"* chapter of Tvardovsky's *Vasilii Tyorkin*, and like Chapaev, who dies while trying to escape by swimming across a river. In this sense, it takes on mythological meanings. In a normal state of affairs, one side is "ours," Russian, and the other belongs to the enemy, "them." In wartime, with a push to enter the enemy's territory and conquer it, or to reclaim one's own territory, the crossing can have a symbolic meaning of progress, of heading toward success and the reintegration of two halves, two banks, into one whole, "ours."

But this river becomes a watery grave for most of the soldiers who try to cross. Those who do make it onto the bridgehead spend over a week struggling to attain Height #100 and then maintain their position. Without proper supply lines, with only one communication line, which is constantly endangered, the regiment holds on, eventually "winning" and returning to unite with their forces on the other side of the river. Throughout the battle scenes, relationships between individual soldiers become more real, with trust and mutual effort facilitating their working together, even though they continue to perish in great numbers.

As the novel nears its end, Astafiev devotes several sections to the German side, as if to remind his reader that Hitler was as much to blame as Stalin, and that the Germans were only following orders. But the point was not to compare dictators, or even political systems. Rather Astafiev's novel is concerned with the individual soldiers themselves.

As he tells it, to be a German boy in the war was a better fate. The Germans have better supply lines, and their regular dinner hour sticks in the craw of the Russian soldiers, who eventually begin to steal off and intercept meal packets, willing to risk all for a piece of bread. Astafiev refused to condemn the ordinary German soldier, but the weight of the reader's pity stays with the Russians.

This turn to the German point of view was an audacious choice that mirrored, perhaps, Leo Tolstoy's legacy of glancing into the enemy camp in his masterpiece *War and Peace*. Astafiev imagines war as the greatest baseness, as a betrayal of humanity, and he portrays it as a duel between two military machines, two ideologies—Stalinism and Fascism—in which individual rank-and-file participants are equally vulnerable, equally likely to be victims. Those millions of people, his characters among them, in Astafiev's view are deprived of agency, of personal responsibility, and of the chance for a future.[36] Astafiev insists that for the soldiers who fought on either side, the larger causes did not matter. For them, the notion of a just war was irrelevant.

And this was Astafiev's goal, in the end. In a letter to one veteran who attacked the novel, Astafiev pulled no punches in declaring his purpose in writing: "I am writing a book about the war in order to show people, especially Russians, that war is a monstrous crime against man and morality." Veterans who want to uphold the lies about war, the fiction created by the Soviet government in its celebrations of victory, cannot accept Astafiev's work. Astafiev summed up what he saw as the problem with memories about war by saying:

> Only according to the Soviet moral code can one send 120 million of one's fellow citizens to their graves in order that front line morality and all-inclusive Soviet happiness triumph. Only here can a general be considered great and pure of heart after murdering 47 million of his countrymen and currying favor with his leader and the Party in peacetime by driving an entire army of Russian boys into the territory of atomic bomb testing like laboratory rabbits, which your beloved Zhukov did. He has other black deeds and crimes to his name about which you would rather not know, would rather forget, and most importantly you wish that everyone should forget everything, but instead remember the past war as if it were one heroic deed after another, where Russians only beat their enemies to the sounds of patriotic cries, following the lead of a fearless commissar.[37]

---

[36] Beliakov, "Prokliatie Viktora Astaf'eva," *Ural* 5 (2005). One critic asserts that his heroes—"good young guys who landed at the front"—are cursed by God, according to the author. "For being born with the Soviet religion of hate in their hearts . . . they fell into the hands of the devil and burned up in that fire." But are they "good guys"? It seems to me that Astafiev for the most part deprives them even of that opportunity. Another critic argues that the characters are cursed not by God, nor by the author, but by fate itself—the mere fact of experiencing war (a "kingdom of hatred") curses them. See Dedkov, Zubkov, and Lev Anninskii, "Za chto prokliaty?" *Literaturnaia gazeta*, 3 March 1993.

[37] Astafiev's numbers here are highly exaggerated, and we can see the degree of his agitation in this letter.

Those patriotic cries, those uniting songs, and those fearless commissars are for the most part missing from *The Accursed and the Dead*. In his correspondence, Astafiev contrasts writers who created "the war you needed, the heroic war" with honest writers like himself who "perceive the war as disgusting, despicable, killing the human in man."[38]

We can look at Astafiev's war writings as the confession, the *ispoved'*, of the soldier-writer, the *frontovik*. Andrei Nemzer notes, "Astafiev is not recollecting; he is living the pain, which cannot be dismissed as 'yesterday's,' 'past,'"[39] regardless of the fifty-year distance in time. As Suleiman pointed out, paraphrasing French ethnographer Marc Augé, "It is forgetting that makes movement toward the future and beginning anew possible."[40] Perhaps at the end of the twentieth century, the Russians were not yet ready for that kind of forgetting. In the Russian case, decades of state-sponsored "bracketing" had to be overcome before any post-traumatic healing might begin.

For Astafiev and some veterans of World War II, the sacrifices made by unwitting Russian boys were not being valued in the reassessing process of historical reflection. There could be neither amnesty nor amnesia. Astafiev blames Stalin and the Stalinist system for the pain and suffering visited upon the Russian countryside and the Russian populace, including the lost boys of '24 (and '23 and '25, and so on), sacrificed by the thousands.[41] But in his eyes there is no future at all for this country. Writing in 1997, he indicted Russia in category after category:

> A country with a population almost incapable of labor, masses physically and psychologically ill; a country where mortality rates continue to surpass birth rates at an ever increasing speed; a country where millions of people are imprisoned and millions more are headed there; a country where the military is only pretending to make reductions and

---

[38] Letter to Comrade Kulikovskii, summer 1995, Astaf'ev, *Net mne otveta . . .* , 585–588.
[39] Nemzer, "Prigovor i molitva," *Novyi Mir* 10–12 (1992), reprinted in *Literaturnoe segodnia: O russkoi proze. 90-e* (Moscow: Novoe literaturnoe obozrenie, 1998), 35–38 37.
[40] Suleiman, *Crises of Memory*, 225.
[41] In his personal letters, Astafiev also places blame for the ruin of the Russians on Jews, including Lenin, whom he indicts not only for his ruinous Communist theories and his own historical acts but also for his supposed Jewish grandmother. Astafiev can sometimes demonstrate in letters and fiction a virulent anti-Semitism, which came to light especially in his published correspondence with historian Natan Eidel'man in the mid-1980s. See Vladimir Shlapentokh, *Soviet Intellectuals and Political Power: The Post-Stalin Era* (I. B.Tauris, 1990), 269–270.

reforms; a country where thievery and drunkenness are the norm; a country where the ethical, talented, and intelligent people are either dying or emigrating; a country that has lost its spiritual center; a country that is beaten down by banality, by out of control prodigal behavior, poisoned long ago by words of vanity and lies, lack of professionalism, laziness.[42]

The war is one concrete cause of what Astafiev sees as the horrors of the present. "The betrayal," he writes in the novel, "begins in the highest, most important offices of leaders, presidents—they betray millions of people, sending them to their deaths."[43] For Astafiev, the purpose of fiction about the Second World War was to prevent future wars, to bear witness to the inhumanity of war and the military, and to bring mankind to its senses. Shortly after the novel came out, the new Russia launched a war in Chechnya.

If, as Suleiman argues, shaping memory is a collective process, in time forgetting can allow for a higher truth, a truth for the nation. But Astafiev in the 1990s was invested in remembering, in indicting, in painting a panorama of the past that included every unfairness, every injustice. This is not just the "truth of the trenches," it is the truth of the victims, who cannot allow anything to be forgotten, nor can they admit to errors or weaknesses, or in any way take responsibility for their own exploitation and victimization.

How could Astafiev take revenge for the loss of childhood, of family, of any semblance of normal life, suffered by the boys of 1924? The anger and hatred, the cry half a century after war's end, the naturalism and exactitude of the evidence he brought to bear indicted the Communist regime and the country that permitted their ascent to power. Dedkov called the novel "material evidence of the enormity of the state's transgression and inveterate communist criminality."[44] In an era when state archives were opening and historical documents had become available, Astafiev's novel still functioned as "material evidence." This is the kind of witnessing he wanted to achieve.

---

[42] See Vladimir Zubkov, "Razryv: Viktor Astaf'ev posle 'derevenskoi' prozy," *Ural* 5 (2005).

[43] *Prokliaty i ubity, Novyi Mir* 12 (1994): 111. Quoted from A. Iu. Bol'shakova, *"Astaf'ev,"* in *Russkie pisateli 20 veka. Biograficheskii slovar'*, ed. V. P. Skobelev (Moscow: Randevu-AM, 2000), 47–49.

[44] Dedkov, "Ob"iavlenie viny," 187.

We can also read the novel as a "cry of the tortured soul," as Vasil Bykov called it, of an orphan and a victim who could not continue to permit his wounds and those of his generation to be overlooked.[45]

* * *

This novel, long and complex, with its many characters and several important iconic settings—the training camp, the village and sovkhoz, the bridgehead—is like Panova's an ensemble novel, although the vast number of characters makes it an epic on the order of *War and Peace*. But despite the fact that the novel is based on the war experiences of the author, it does not feel particularly autobiographical.

Nonetheless, one of Astafiev's boys, Lyoshka Shestakov, represents the voice of the author, and when the reader looks back on the novel after finishing it, Shestakov seems to speak Astafiev's truth more than some other characters. The narrator explains that Lyoshka, upon arrival at training camp, "quickly came to feel what must always come in the barracks and in prison—a listless consent to everything that was happening, a submission to fate" (*Izbrannoe*, 9). It is this helplessness, this lack of agency among all the boys of 1924, rather than any narrative structure, that drives Astafiev's novel.

While the author described the young soldiers as lacking basic necessary moral and ethical codes, he never condemned them for this. The novel is infused by pity and sorrow, by anger at the waste of these young lives, an entire generation of young men (and even women) sacrificed for no real reason even before the war began. Astafiev mourned each of those lives in his six-hundred-plus-page novel, precisely for their efforts in a game that was fixed against them. As Freud believed, trauma is never perceived in real time. The trauma and the tragic fate of Astafiev's generation, the boys of '24, haunted him throughout his life and in the end made him a witness against history, against that history that had made of him a victim, not a victor. That victim was a human witness to the crimes of the Soviet state, perpetrated against its own citizens.

In the end, Astafiev was a survivor of '24, but his experiences and those of his generation left them fragile and haunted. They carried their wounds,

---

[45] Bykov, quoted in Zubkov, "Razryv."

physical and psychological, with them until the end of their lives. To honor the memory of those killed in the war, Astafiev felt compelled to reinterpret the meaning of the war and the war hero. For this former soldier, what that meant was to say out loud that at a basic human level, those deaths were meaningless. By the 1990s, the naïve claims of bravery in the face of war collapsed, victim to their own statistical irrelevance. Chapaev had perished, and he would not be resurrected.

Chapter Eight

Revisiting Chapaev: Viktor Pelevin and Vasily Aksyonov

> Boys! Recall the famous story of the legendary character celebrated by Boris Polevoi!
>
> Ребята! Вспомните знаменитую историю легендарного персонажа, воспетого Борисом Полевым!
>
> -Viktor Pelevin[1]

But Chapaev was revisited, over and over. In this final chapter we come full circle. Despite Astafiev's indictment of traditional Soviet war literature, in the post-Soviet period the figure of Chapaev continued to resonate. As we have seen, he and his comrades, literary depictions of war heroes and Cold War antiheroes, were constants across the Soviet twentieth century.

Long after people ceased reading Furmanov's 1923 novel, Vasily Chapaev lived on. In 1941 he was mobilized to help with the war effort and featured in the short film *Chapaev Is with Us!*[2] The Vasiliev brothers' film too remains beloved, although in post-Stalinist times more for its humor than for its historical portrayal of the Civil War era.[3] Even in twenty-first-century Russia, Soviet-era Chapaev anecdotes still make up a significant percentage of all jokes told. History and humor. The appropriation of Chapaev by the Soviet and post-Soviet populace speaks to the centrality of the myth of the peasant-warrior and to the necessity of treating Soviet sacred myths with a grain, or a *gorst* (handful), of salt.

---

[1] Viktor Pelevin, *Omon Ra. Zhizn' nasekomykh. Zatvornik i Shestipalyi. Prints Gosplana* (Moscow: Vagrius, 1999), 7–122; 28–29.

[2] http://www.youtube.com/watch?v=UChik40rcrw&feature=related. Also interesting is the "Hollywood-style" trailer created by recent fans to accompany the original film: http://www.youtube.com/watch?v=t-ORc8hQjR0&feature=fvsr.

[3] See Graham, *Resonant Dissonance*; Lilya Kaganovsky, *How the Soviet Man was Unmade: Cultural Fantasy and Male Subjectivity under Stalin* (Pittsburgh: University of Pittsburgh 2008); and John Haynes, *New Soviet Man: Gender and Masculinity in Stalinist Soviet Cinema* (Manchester: Manchester University Press, 2003) for discussions of Chapaev and *Chapaev*. Upon its release in 1934, the film was lauded by *Pravda*, whose editorial read, "The whole country is watching Chapaev!" Graham credits the surge of Chapaev jokes to the thirtieth anniversary of the film in 1964, after which it began to be shown frequently on television (*Resonant Dissonance*, 6).

8. Revisiting Chapaev: Viktor Pelevin and Vasily Aksyonov

In this chapter we look at two writers who in the post-Soviet era came back to the figure of Chapaev in order to explore the definition of the military hero in a post-heroic, post-Soviet nation. Both Viktor Pelevin and Vasily Aksyonov returned to Chapaev and used him as a touchstone to help evaluate the legacy of the Soviet century and the Socialist realist hero, Pelevin in his novel *Chapaev and Pustota* and Aksyonov in his short story "The Ship of the World: *Vasily Chapaev*."[4]

Socialist realist heroes were ripe for parody, and Pelevin has a field day with them in his 1991 *Omon Ra*. We'll open our analysis below with this novella. But if Astafiev demonstrated that even World War II could not produce heroes in the same way any more, Chapaev and the legacy of the Civil War were a virtual playground for writers. By the 1990s, the figure of the literary war hero as he was created in the 1920s was utterly inconceivable. Pelevin and Aksyonov could not even get angry about this loss as Astafiev did. For them, he was fodder for postmodern play.

Exposing the Soviet Military Complex: Viktor Pelevin and *Omon Ra*

When Viktor Pelevin won the Booker Prize in 1993,[5] the panel of judges recognized that he was among the most exciting figures in the contemporary post-Soviet literary world. Born in 1962, Pelevin grew up in the dark twilight of the Soviet Union, the son of a military instructor and a school teacher of English, and his fiction offered dystopian visions of the modern world. His early work tended to incorporate the experiences of youth culture: Western film and television, computer games, drug experimentation, advertising lingo. Though he differs in several ways from his older contemporary Vladimir Makanin—Pelevin dark, cynical, and amusing; Makanin more serious and brooding—he wound up locating one of his novels in the same place as Makanin's *Underground*: the madhouse.

Pelevin published the novella *Omon Ra* in 1991. The first-person narrative features a character who initially seems like a Soviet success story. The

---

[4] Vasily Aksyonov, "Korabl' mira: *Vasilii Chapaev*," in *Negativ polozhitel'nogo geroia* (Moscow: Vagrius, 1996), 159–177. First published in *Znamia* no. 1 (1995).

[5] Pelevin was honored with the Small Booker for his debut collection of stories, *The Blue Lantern*. He has won numerous prizes since and was named the Best Writer of 1996 by the journals *OM* and *Ogonek*. See O. Bogdanova, S. Kibal'nik and L. Safronova, *Literaturnye strategii V. Pelevina* (St. Petersburg: Petropolis, 2008), 114. Viktor Erofeev has supposedly stated that "in the post-*Metropole* generation [that is to say, his own and Vasily Aksyonov's generation—AKB], there is no generation, only Pelevin by himself" (Bogdanova et al, *Literaturnye strategii*, 6).

young man is a virtual orphan, escaping his personal family (where his father is a drunk and his deceased mother a distant memory) to join the big Soviet family. Just like the boys of '24, he enlists in the Soviet military, in this case an elite military academy where he hopes to be trained to be a part of the vaunted Soviet space program. He plans to fly to the moon. As we saw in Voinovich's song about the space race, if the Cold War can be said to have produced any real heroes, surely they were the cosmonauts who beat the United States into outer space.

The narrative is utterly conventional: told by Omon himself, who describes his childhood, schooling, and first job, occasionally falling into reminiscences as he interacts with the social structures and individuals whom he meets in his daily life.

That life—like the Soviet Union itself—turns out to be patently absurd, and this text is driven by a different heroic model. Not the Civil War peasant leader Chapaev, with his spontaneous energy and his love of horses and the elemental, but the Soviet war hero Alexei Maresiev. We discussed Polevoi's 1946 classic postwar socialist realist novella *The Story of a Real Man* by Boris Polevoi and its cinematic counterpart, Alexander Stolper's 1948 film of the same name, briefly in chapter 5.[6] To reiterate, Maresiev was a famous World War II pilot who crashed his plane behind enemy lines and crawled back through the woods, broken legs and all, to eventually fly again as a double amputee. This, Polevoi had asserted, was a real man.

The institute where Omon has enrolled is dedicated to making "real men" out of its cadets. In other words, in a surreal and sadistic realization of Maresiev's path to heroic martyrdom, the boys all undergo an operation to simulate his fate. In this send-up of the macho military code, according to which boys become men through training and experience, the cadets are given a mechanized and surgical shortcut to heroism. However, our hero Omon, along with his friend Misha, is tapped for an even more elite program. Their instructor says, "There's time for you to become real men later," and puts off their double amputations.[7]

---

[6] In an interview for Victory Day in 2001, the real Mares'ev claimed, "I'm a person, not a legend!" See Izgarshev, "Alexei Mares'ev: 'Ia chelovek, a ne legenda.'"

[7] Pelevin, *Omon Ra*, 32. In the English translation this reads, "You have been registered immediately for the first-year course at the KGB secret space-training school—so you'll just have to wait a bit before you become Real Men. Meanwhile, get ready to go to Moscow." *Omon Ra*, trans. Andrew Bromfield (New York: New Directions, 1998), 36.

Pelevin is not interested in providing a new path to martyrdom or even heroism in his fiction. Rather, he ridicules the symbols and discourses of Soviet life, pointing out that the Emperor is not wearing any clothes, that the Wizard is simply a man behind the curtain. In this novella he does so in an utterly flat, realistic narrative, with only the occasional philosophical aside or metaphorical image. For Pelevin, there is nothing sacred, except perhaps the individual consciousness. It is the only space left, perhaps, for heroic action.

In *Omon Ra* he lampoons the food, the summer camps, the poetry, even the military training of his homeland (focusing more on the jokes instructors tell than on any actual space aeronautics). Omon was named by his father for the Soviet special forces in the hopes that his future would be bright. But the reader questions that future when it emerges that even as a small child on the playground little Omon felt in his "soul a loathing for the state."[8]

As it turns out, Omon is no Soviet hero. In *Omon Ra*, Pelevin has conflated two episodes of Soviet history and the heroes that they produced—the heroes of World War II and the cosmonauts of the Cold War—and turned them into a macabre parody. Pelevin has collapsed history, thus denying Soviet history any motion or change.

Only in one small paragraph of the narrative does it seem like this parodic Soviet world of cosmonauts may all be a dream. The reader (and eventually the protagonist) becomes aware that Omon's "flight" is a fake, and his travel across the face of the moon turns out to be underground in an abandoned tunnel of the Moscow Metro system, something Pelevin, who studied to be a transportation engineer, would have known plenty about. Omon travels on a converted bicycle. When asked what he's thinking about during the journey, Omon responds reluctantly:

> Well, I often remember my childhood [. . . .] How I used to go riding on my bike. It was a lot like this. And to this day I don't understand it—there I was, riding along on my bike, with the handlebars down low, and it was really bright up ahead, and the wind was so fresh. . . . [. . .] I thought I was riding towards the canal. . . . So how can it be that I. . . .[9]

Perhaps in some "realistic" version of the narrative, this whole novella is a dream, and Omon himself has crashed his bicycle into the canal as a ten-year-

---

[8] *Omon Ra*, 11; 8 in the English translation.
[9] *Omon Ra*, English translation, 129; 102 in original.

old and is spending the rest of his life in a semi-coma. But it is the components of the dream—the mockery of adults toward the "cadets," the yearning of the young men to accomplish something in their otherwise empty lives, their equal parts anticipation and dread at the thought of the feats they may be asked to achieve—that create the poignancy of this text, produced when "everything [...] was no more."

During late socialism, as Yurchak has argued, much of the force of Soviet authoritative language "came through rhythm, sound, and phraseology that looked and sounded impressive."[10] Pelevin's *Omon Ra* demonstrates the emptiness of that rhetoric.[11] Some critics have seen the entire story as deliberately surreal, and it is surely the irony-free presentation of the amputation ritual more than anything else that indicts both Soviet myths of heroism and Soviet official history itself.[12]

Chapaev Rides Again—with a Madman for a Sidekick

Four years after *Omon Ra*, Pelevin published *Chapaev and Pustota* and reached back even further in Soviet history to the ur-text of Soviet heroism. In fact, the title of *Chapaev and Pustota* connects the novel to other texts of Russian literary history, not only fitting the model of "this and that" (as in *Fathers and Sons*, *Crime and Punishment*, *War and Peace*) but, in its use of proper names, also repeating the model of *Taras Bulba*, *Oblomov*, *Anna Karenina*, among others.[13] However, instead of the cheerful swashbuckling peasant we see, particularly in the Vasilievs' 1934 film *Chapaev*, in Pelevin's incarnation Chapaev is a tuxedo-wearing philosophical guru, much smarter and deeper than anyone around him. By the 1990s, the naif has become the sophisticate. In the novel, Furmanov and the entire Soviet political system are dismissed as if they had no historical relevance nor power.

---

[10] Yurchak, *Everything Was Forever*, 78. Pelevin was a member of what he himself calls *Generation P*, that last Soviet generation about whom Yurchak writes.

[11] Mark Lipovetsky writes about the "hyper-reality of Soviet simulacra [as] produced by Soviet ideology" and argues that in this first book both Pelevin and his protagonists were on a "quest for reality within the world of simulacra." Lipovetsky, "Russian Literary Postmodernism in the 1990s," *Slavonic and East European Review* 79.1 (January 2001): 47.

[12] Lilya Kaganovsky believes that in this text Omon is given a "way out." See "How the Soviet Man Was (Un)made," *Slavic Review* 63.3 (Autumn 2004): 596.

[13] We might add *The Accursed and the Dead* to this list of titles. For further analysis of the Buddhist logic inherent in the title, see Aleksandr Zakurenko, "Iskomaia pustota," *Literaturnoe obozrenie* 3: 269 (1998): 93–94.

Like Makanin, whom we discussed in chapter 6, Pelevin chose to set his novel at a Moscow hospital for the insane in the 1990s. The narration switches back and forth between this "real" time and the delusional time of Pelevin's main hero, who believes that he is actually living in 1919–1920 as a somewhat unwilling participant in the Russian Civil War. In *Chapaev and Pustota*, the reader is unsure for roughly the first third of the novel where, and more importantly *when*, "reality" actually is—revolutionary and Civil War Russia in 1919 or the post-Soviet insane asylum. Thus the historical context and time itself are from the outset doubled in the novel, which is built around the hero, Peter Pustota. In his own mind Pustota is a modernist poet turned Civil War commissar, although in 1990s "reality" he is a delusional young man in his mid-twenties undergoing psychiatric treatment.

The rest of the cast of characters is a rather humorous lot as well, drawn from the types of contemporary life and the pages of military history: the psychiatrist, Dr. Timur Timurovich Kanashnikov, whose name rhymes with the Kalashnikov rifle; the four patients who are the subjects for his dissertation research (Peter, "Simply Maria"—who takes his name from the eponymous Mexican television serial, Serdiuk, and Volodin); a new version of the Civil War commander Chapaev; and Baron Yungern, whose name is both a play on Karl Jung and a fictionalization of the historical Baron Roman von Ungern-Sternberg, a World War I hero who fought for the White Army during the Civil War.[14] This postmodern narrative is consciously non-linear, folding back upon itself across time and space, though the main settings are the psychiatric hospital and the various landscapes of Civil War Russia, from Moscow streets, nightclubs, and apartment houses to the provincial manor home and estate commandeered by Chapaev's detachment.

The hero's name, Peter Pustota, has a rich and ambiguous significance, which gets lost in translation: *pustota* means "emptiness."[15] Though the hero does to some extent act as an empty vessel into which others (his psychiatrist, fellow members of his group therapy, Chapaev, etc.) pour content, this explanation oversimplifies his character, which might benefit rather from

---

[14] Baron Ungern, like Pelevin's fictional creation, was famed for his interest in Buddhism. Ungern fought against the Reds in Siberia and then in Mongolia during the Civil War.

[15] In my discussion, I will call the hero "Pustota." Andrew Bromfield solves the punning problem in English by making him "Pyotr Voyd" in his translation of the novel.

being viewed through the lens of "secular kenosis."[16] Peter also embodies the solipsistic existence of the paradigmatic modernist poet, whom Pelevin lampoons in this pseudo-historical novel. Finally, the hero's surname of "emptiness" announces the philosophical underpinnings of the novel, as Pelevin and his narrator propose a self-absorbed variant of Buddhism in answer to late-twentieth-century Russian social problems.

Buddhism and religion take the place of politics, science, and medicine in Pelevin's hierarchy of values. It is no accident that the good doctor Kanashnikov in Pelevin's *Chapaev and Pustota* is writing his dissertation on the split personality. Here we have an historical allusion—his name also recalls the Kanatchikova dacha, one of the most famous insane asylums in Russia—within another important historical allusion, neither of which Pelevin really takes seriously. We discussed in chapter 6 how the definition of schizophrenia has been deeply significant in the history of Soviet psychiatric practice.[17] Fittingly, Pustota's doctor—who is experimenting with therapies and treatments—slaps this diagnosis on the main character and his fellow patients and gives them the status of guinea pigs in a post-Soviet medical laboratory where the rights of the individual are no more respected than they were during the age of Brezhnev.

Again like Makanin, Pelevin draws freely from literary and cultural traditions of madness, not distinguishing particularly between the paradigms of refuge and torture when concocting his postmodern melange of references. Pustota explores the Menippean promises of madness without ever quite fully realizing them. For the patients, Pelevin's psychiatric ward is both a refuge from the insanity of newly capitalist Moscow and a door to other, transcendent worlds, and for Pustota this refuge and escape offers more excitement and intellectual stimulation than anything in Moscow on the "outside."

Peter Pustota understands that the madhouse is like any other repressive system: right away he notices the willingness of the other patients to participate in their various therapies and concludes that "the atmosphere of a madhouse obviously must instill submissiveness" (*Chapaev i Pustota,* 105). Pustota and his ward mates find themselves traveling in time and space as their dream therapy takes them into imaginary landscapes. The fact that these imaginary landscapes are primarily violent and militaristic—from Pustota's Civil War battles to mafia *razborki* to futuristic Hollywood film narratives featuring Arnold

---

[16] See Wieda, "Secular Kenosis."
[17] For a detailed description of the history of Soviet theories of schizophrenia, see Miller, "Theory and Practice of Psychiatry in the Soviet Union," 16.

Schwarzenegger—ties the repressive atmosphere of the mental hospital to a post-Soviet society still struggling with the after-effects of a century of war.[18]

Emptiness, Pelevin-Style[19]

By collapsing 1919 into the 1990s, Pelevin links the beginnings of both of these new eras with a profound sense of emptiness. He explores the persona of his "empty" hero both through interactions with the characters from the Soviet "Chapaev text"—including Anka the machine gunner, but casting Peter as a smarter version of Chapaev's traditionally dense adjutant, Petya—and through psychotherapy. In the madhouse, Dr. Kanashnikov's group therapy sessions give the patients the opportunity to interact with each other's delusions and fantasies. The sessions—which have links to real Soviet psychiatric practice—involve collective hypnotic dreaming.[20] As the doctor explains the therapy to his patient Pustota:

> When the session comes to an end, a reaction sets in as the participants withdraw from the state that they have been experiencing as reality . . .

---

[18] On the connections between *Chapaev and Pustota* and *Master and Margarita*, see Bogdanova et al, *Literaturnye strategii*, especially 45–64.

[19] For Russian criticism on Pelevin and this novel, see Pavel Basinskii, "Iz zhizni otechestvennykh kaktusov," *Literaturnaia gazeta* 22: 5604 (29 May 1996): 4; Dmitrii Bykov, "Pobeg v Mongoliiu," *Literaturnaia gazeta* 22: 5604 (29 May 1996): 4; Andrei Nemzer, "Kak ia upustil kar'eru" (May 1996), reprinted in *Literaturnoe segodnia*, 313–315; Irina Rodnianskaia, "I k nei bezumnaia liubov'," in *Novyi mir* 9 (1996): 857; 212–216; Karen Stepanian, "Realizm kak spasenie ot snov," *Znamia* 11 (1996): 194–200; Zakurenko, "Iskomaia pustota." See also the admiring profile by Jason Cowley, "Gogol à Go-Go," *New York Times Magazine* (23 January 2000): 20–23; Alexander Genis, "Borders and Metamorphoses: Viktor Pelevin in the Context of Post-Soviet Literature," in Mikhail Epstein, Alexander Genis and Slobodanka Vladiv-Glover, *Russian Postmodernism: New Perspectives on Post-Soviet Culture* (New York: Berghahn Books, 1999), 212–224; and Marina Kanevskaia, "Istoriia i mif v postmodernistskom russkom romane," *Izvestiia AN*, seriia Literatury i iazyka, 59.2 (2000): 37–37. Gerald McCausland looks at *Chapaev and Emptiness* in the context of Pelevin's other work in his "Viktor Pelevin and the End of Sots-Art," in *Endquote: Sots-Art Literature and Soviet Grand Style*, ed. by Marina Balina, Nancy Condee, and Evgeny Dobrenko (Evanston: Northwestern University Press, 2000), 225–237.

[20] According to Miller, the favorite modes of psychotherapy in the Soviet Union were "hypnosis, 'culture-therapy' (using art, music, etc.), and work therapy" (Miller, "Theory and Practice of Psychiatry," 17). In *Chapaev and Pustota* we see examples of both hypnosis and "culture therapy." Miller goes on to state that in Soviet psychiatry "there is an assumption . . . that psychotherapy is a process in which the patient overcomes his disorder through a realization of the facets of the disorder," a description that matches closely the theories of Kanashnikov.

your ideas and your mood might infect the others taking part in the session for a certain time, but as soon as the session comes to an end, they return to their own manic obsessions, leaving you isolated. And at that moment—provided the pathological psychic material has been driven up to the surface by the process of catharsis—the patient can become aware of the arbitrary subjectivity of his own morbid notions and can cease to identify with them. (*Chapaev i Pustota*, 38)

In the novel, Dr. Kanashnikov's group therapy and the madhouse itself—with all its odd characters—play and experiment with the idea of individual identity.

As we have discussed, questions of the self and the collective were key to Soviet discourse and have become even more charged in post-Soviet times both within and outside fiction. As Russia struggled—and still does—to understand what form of government and civil society will be its next incarnation, self and society have become central to the novel as well. In a post-collective society, what is the meaning and role of the individual? What is a split personality, and what is a whole personality? If in fact there is anything wrong, how can healing take place? Who, in the end, is the hero, and in what social context is he created? The therapies that go on in the madhouse are a metaphor for the struggle to determine exactly what the nature of individuality will be in this new post-Soviet society.[21]

Kanashnikov's psychotherapy raises these questions for the four patients in his post-Soviet madhouse, as well as for those on the outside, since the patients represent four types of post-Soviet citizen—the philosophical loner who imagines he's a poet (Peter), the young (and "Westernized") homosexual who has fallen under the influence of Mexican soap opera and American film culture (Maria), the unemployed alcoholic who has raised drinking to an almost metaphysical level (Serdiuk), and the mafia boss who experiments with psychedelic drugs (Volodin).[22]

---

[21] In Pelevin, as might be expected, the madhouse is only a metaphor, unlike in Makanin where the narrative's irony does not preclude a portrayal of real suffering.

[22] Several Russian critics have identified these patients as representatives of contemporary Russian types. For example, Rodnianskaia calls the patients "four modes of the 'Russian soul': the man of the people, the bum/dreamer [*mechtatel'nyi bosiak*], the 'New Russian' and, of course, the Russian intellectual with his 'split false personality' and his call to free ourselves from 'so-called inner life'" (Rodnianskaia, "I k nei," 214). Nemzer argues that the illnesses of Petr's three fellow patients are "built on the stereotypes of contemporary mass culture" ("Kak ia upustil kar'eru," 314).

Pelevin's novel has a higher aim than mere imaginative representation of reality. Peter Pustota experiences his 1919 self as his true self, and the scenes in the lunatic asylum as "nightmares." But even within what he sees as his true self, he is engaged with the idea of the individual, the "I," and how he interacts with community and society. As a modernist poet, he titled one of his books of poetry *The Kingdom of I*, and he explains, "I used to do a lot of traveling, and then at some moment I suddenly realized that no matter where I might go, in reality I can do no more than move within a single space, and that space is myself" (*Chapaev i Pustota*, 282). So for the protagonist, the entire world has collapsed into himself; he is his very own kingdom.

In a political sense, after the 1917 Revolution the kingdom actually did disappear, leaving individuals to seek new direction for their lives. And in a literary sense, Peter Pustota would not have been the only modernist poet to find all meaning within himself. For post-Soviet times, the situation is remarkably similar: the Union has dissolved, and the poet seeks meaning in the fragments of history that constitute his own essence. Post-Soviet solipcism is isolating, to say the least.

Both Peter and Pelevin would say the novel takes place "nowhere" (*nigde*): within the head of the individual and therefore outside of time and space. Indeed, Pelevin himself has punned that "this is the first novel in world literature whose action takes place in absolute emptiness."[23] Kanashnikov's psychiatric notes state that Pustota "does not find placement in a psychiatric hospital oppressive, since he is confident that his 'self-development' will proceed by 'the right path' no matter where he lives" (*Chapaev i Pustota*, 104). In his travels with Baron Yungern, who is a kind of metaphysical guide,[24] Peter comes to understand that "I myself . . . constitute the only possibility of being, the exclusive means by which all these psychiatric clinics and civil wars came into the world" (*Chapaev i Pustota*, 220).

The pseudo-Buddhist Yungern explains to Peter that he should strive to reach that "nowhere," which is a place of "eternal freedom and happiness":

---

[23] See Sally Laird, "Viktor Pelevin," *Voices of Russian Literature* (Oxford: Oxford University Press, 1999), 181. Rodnianskaia has argued that the novel takes place both in post-revolutionary and post-Soviet times, and that "these two epochs 'rhyme'" (Rodnianskaia, "I k nei," 214), while Stepanian contends that "the entire narrative follows the stylistics of a dream" (Stepanian, "Realizm kak spasenie ot snov," 195).

[24] Yungern officially "heads up one of the branches of the afterlife"; Zakurenko characterizes him as a "contemporary colleague of Woland's" (Zakurenko, "Iskomaia pustota," 94).

"Why should you . . . not find yourself in this 'nowhere' while you are still alive? . . . No doubt you are fond of metaphors—you could compare this to discharging yourself from the mental home." Chapaev, resurrected as a tuxedo-wearing guru who in the Civil War scenes is both Peter's military commander and his philosophical mentor, also advises his disciple to discharge himself from the hospital (*Chapaev i Pustota*, 223, 270).

Pelevin rejects the madhouse as a place of medical practice, lampooning psychiatric techniques such as drug therapies, hypnosis, and group sessions. In the world(s) of *Chapaev and Pustota*, madness takes on a complete subjectivity, with all objective scientific discourse evaporating.

One thing that does go on in the clinic is joke telling. Near the end of the novel, the patients in the mental hospital participate in this popular culture ritual, retelling Chapaev jokes—and the patient Peter Pustota "corrects" them, explaining the "real event" behind each anecdote. Like Dovlatov, with the back stories of his Soviet journalistic feuilletons, and other writers we've looked at, Pelevin is exploring issues of fact and myth. But here the facts are part of a patient's delusion, and the myths are the beloved popular culture jokes that poked fun at the heroic figure of Chapaev in the first place. The patient stands in for Soviet citizens as a whole, who somehow needed to believe in those facts about Soviet wars and Soviet heroes.

Unexpectedly, in an almost surreal scene, the doctor gives in to the hero's desire to check himself out of the asylum and facilitates the exit of the post-revolutionary poet into contemporary Moscow. The novel ends with our hero Peter leaving the hospital, which has been his home for over three hundred pages, underscoring yet another joke—that nothing gets cured in the clinic.

No Way Out

Thus *Chapaev and Pustota* ends where it began, almost as if the intervening Soviet years between 1919 and 1991 had no significance. After Peter has let himself out of the institution, he returns to downtown Moscow. The narrative repeats word for word the opening paragraphs of the novel:

> Tverskoy Boulevard appeared exactly as it had been when I last saw it—once again it was February, with snowdrifts everywhere and that peculiar gloom which somehow manages to infiltrate the very daylight. The same old women were perched motionless on the benches,

watching over brightly dressed children engaged in protracted warfare among the snowdrifts; above them, beyond the black latticework of the wires, the sky hung down close to the earth as though it were trying to touch it. Some things, however, were different . . . (*Chapaev i Pustota*, 323–324)

In the very first scene of the novel—which takes place in early 1919—the narrator noticed that the statue of Pushkin on Tverskoy Boulevard looked different than it had two years previously when he had last seen it. Pushkin now seemed a little sad because he was wearing a red banner proclaiming, "Long live the first anniversary of the Revolution." At the end of the novel Peter comments that "the bronze Pushkin had disappeared, but the gaping void that had appeared where he used to stand somehow seemed like the best of all possible monuments."

In actual historical Moscow, of course, the Soviets moved the Pushkin statue across the street, so that when Peter looks at the space where he expects the statue to stand, he finds only an empty square. Pustota continues to survey his surroundings: "Where the Strastnoy Monastery had been, there was now an empty space [*pustota*], with a sparse scattering of consumptive trees and tasteless street lamps" (*Chapaev i Pustota*, 324). In the meantime, too, between Peter's two realities, Tverskoy Boulevard had been called Gorky Street from 1935 to 1990. Tverskoy also came full circle.

Pelevin uses the historical circumstance of Pushkin's peregrination to create a metaphor of post-Revolutionary and post-Soviet Russia: in Pustota's imagination, in 1919 Pushkin was Bolshevized and forced to wear a revolutionary banner, and Pustota himself left the spent field of decadent poetry for the battlefields of the Civil War. In "real" 1990s Moscow, the statue of Pushkin has been replaced by emptiness, or void, and the abiding Russian hero, Pushkin, makes way for the banal and delusional Peter. With the monastery gone as well, Peter finds himself without direction, and wryly quotes Dostoevsky's Marmeladov: "And have you any idea what it is like, my dear sir, when you have nowhere left to go?"

Pelevin's hero encapsulates the fate of the individual under the Soviets: in post-revolutionary Russia, the hero was forced into the collective, but in the postmodern world, without any meaningful collective, the hero is absent, an emptiness in and of himself. This novel with its circular narrative brings to mind Alexander Blok's 1912 poem:

> Night, a street, a lamp, a chemist's shop,
> A meaningless and dim light.
> Even if you live for another quarter of a century,
> Everything will be like this. There is no way out.[25]

In his own "no way out," which reads as a pseudo-Buddhist turn, Peter chooses to retreat within that emptiness, into a solipsistic state, which Pelevin names with a geographic pun: "Inner Mongolia."[26]

For Pelevin the madhouse serves as a stage upon which to explore the notion of how to define one's individuality, but in his work he also explores the time-tested tropes of Soviet fiction, including the trope of Vasily Ivanovich Chapaev, war hero and socialist realist icon. The business of war, particularly the Civil War and World War II, is a serious one, but in a culture like Russia's, where the official became bureaucratized and anything state-sponsored was ripe for underground parody, these wars too presented material for satire.

As a historical and cultural figure, Chapaev bridges the gap between the serious realist presentation of the experience of the hero in wartime and the *anekdot*-alized parody of that high-flown portrait. These two strands of Soviet literature, both with a version of war hero at their center, include such opposite texts as Solzhenitsyn's *One Day in the Life of Ivan Denisovich* and Dovlatov's *The Zone* and *The Compromise*. Though opposite sides of the coin, they encourage their readers to question "history," to approach both the past and the present with a critical eye—a necessary corrective after decades of belief in the "appearance" of truth.

The Feast of the Soul: *"Pir dukha"*

Reconsidering and reshaping the Chapaev myth and other Soviet myths has been part of a larger trend of post-Soviet life. Confronting the heritage of war and its symbols, authors have used characters like Chapaev and Stalin, what a recent Russian critic called "branded historical figures" ("*brendovye*

---

[25] Blok's "no way out" explored the rash of suicides in his time, and in that sense Pelevin is more optimistic. See D. S. Likhachev, "Iz kommentariia k stikhotvoreniiu A. Bloka 'Noch', ulitsa, fonar', apteka,'" *Russkaia literatura* 1 (1978), 186–188.

[26] This is what made the novel controversial in Russia: if the pseudo-Buddhist message of this and some of Pelevin's other works really is "check out of reality, find your own Inner Mongolia," just as Gus Van Sant's characters dreamed of doing in the 1991 American film *My Own Private Idaho*, then certainly Pelevin is an antiprophet for the new Russia, a writer promoting the further disengagement of already disaffected youth.

istoricheskie figury"),²⁷ to engage the past while also selling books. The term "branding," along with "business," "marketing," and many other new vocabulary words, came to Russia from the commercialized and capitalist West, and these terms participate in a discourse that takes history and turns it into a commodity. In the literary world, contemporary writers in Russia are taking a page from Umberto Eco (and hoping for the monetary success that comes from Hollywood films like his *The Name of the Rose*): they want to maintain a highbrow profile while also selling enough books to become famous.²⁸

This is the context in which Vasily Aksyonov (1932–2009) published his short post-Socialist, postmodern tale "The Ship of the World: *Vasily Chapaev*" (1995).²⁹ In this entertaining story, Aksyonov explodes some of the same Soviet and post-Soviet myths and stereotypes that Pelevin tackles (including Chapaev, socialism, the Komsomol, mafia *razborki*, and new age religion). Also like Pelevin, and like *Chapaev*, his narrative features two important tropes of Soviet Russian literature: a river as central to the topos of the story and a hero who in the end saves the day.

Aksyonov uses his story to draw implicit parallels between the beliefs and practices of Communist ideology, business, and religious cults. He also valorizes his inventive and essentially honorable—if perhaps also drunken, lassitudinous, and lustful—young hero, the guide and translator Lev. We see here a late-twentieth-century version of Dovlatov's antihero. Not surprising, since Aksyonov was one of the writers Dovlatov read as a young man.

The title of the story could also translate as "The Ship of Peace," which might fit better the Hare Krishna passengers on board, but given that the text is very much about attempts to bridge cultural differences, "Ship of the World" works as well. Certainly Aksyonov was exploiting the dual meaning of "*mir*," and he may also have been referring to the "Ship of Fools" concept, related both to madness and to philosophers, especially in the context of exile from one's homeland (cf. the 1922 "ship of philosophers," intellectuals expelled from Soviet Russia much as Aksyonov and many of his generation were half a century later).

Aksyonov's text illustrates some important points about post-1991 relations between Russians and foreigners and about contemporary uses of history and heritage in post-Soviet Russia. Thus not only does Aksyonov write

---

27 Vladimir Elistratov, "Filosofiia mifokitcha," *Znamia* 5 (2006).
28 This is a paraphrase of Elistratov's argument.
29 V. Aksyonov, "Korabl' mira: *Vasilii Chapaev*."

about the confrontation of culture and commodity, as we'll explore below; as a Russian American fiction writer, his work also *exemplifies* that clash.[30]

Aksyonov engages the West in this narrative by using a collection of Australians in search of a spiritual experience, thus creating the effect of estrangement: these non-Russian characters perceive Russia and Chapaev using utterly "other" parameters. They hear Russian words and names that "sound like" their own foreign vocabulary. Their only other route to Russian culture is via their assigned translator, who tries to present them with the historical Chapaev and his place in Russian history and culture and to shape that information into a satisfactory customer service experience as offered by his firm, the touring agency Wandering Soul.

In the story, Aksyonov overlays contemporary clichés on top of deep Soviet symbols of war and heroism, from revolutionary figures to their socialist realist permutations, to the trauma of World War II that resonates with the trauma of Soviet communism and totalitarian rule. The plot concerns the arrival in Russia of a Hare Krishna sect led by a former dental prosthetist from Australia. Derek Door, who took the name Swami Shrila Prabhavishnu, brings a group of followers from the so-called Ashram of the Four-Armed One to Russia. Their goal is "to irrigate the earth with the eternally refreshing chants of Hare-Rama" ("Korabl' mira," 160, 161).

The narrative presents the Australians' quest as an utterly plausible effort, made possible by the fall of the Soviet Union and the resulting freedom for alternative religious groups. Indeed, it *is* utterly plausible: the twin lure of Mother Russia with her attendant "Russian soul" (part of an old pilgrimage tradition that we can trace at least as far back as Tolstoyans crossing the ocean to catch a glimpse of the master) and the sudden economic and political accessibility of Russia, after decades of restricted travel, has brought hordes of tourists, curiosity seekers, culture mavens, history buffs, and evangelical missionaries of all stripes to the Russian Federation since 1991.

These particular travelers have chosen the Volga River, symbol of Mother Russia and the longest river in Europe, for their cruise, and they plan to

---

[30] Russian commentators have over the years emphasized Aksyonov's status as a "feel-good" writer. In the words of Evgenii Popov, before his emigration Aksyonov "radiated fun, swagger, victory by his very life and image." But even after his emigration, in the words of another critic, Aksyonov "remained a truly Soviet writer." See Popov, "Dve liubvi: Aksyonov i Dovlatov," *Vsemirnoe slovo* 9 (1995): 12–13: 12 and Evgenii Ponomarev, "Sotsrealizm karnaval'nyi," *Zvezda* 4 (2001): 213–219: 216.

cleanse the waters of the "miasma of collapsed Communism" and facilitate the "renaissance of the shores" ("Korabl' mira," 161)—an inverted baptism of the vital waterway and its adjacent lands. Like the fiction of the 1970s, Aksyonov's story uses irony to chronicle the relationship between the central protagonist and his surroundings. Inverting the war-hero relationship, the action of the story takes place in the wake of Soviet "defeat," and the hero has been reduced to giving tours of that defeat to some of the westerners who have "won" the Cold War.

Aboard a rusty steamer called *Vasily Chapaev*, Prabhavishnu and his shaven-headed, saffron-robed followers set off on the Volga in the direction of Samara.[31] Their guide and translator, Lev Obnag, at first holds himself aloof from the cult members but, as part of his duties, translates their speeches to the surprised sailors of other passing crafts, ending each with a heartfelt "Hare-Rama!" As the steamer floats along the river, the naïve, happy "bhagavats" dance and chant. The contrast with post-Soviet life is stark; as the narrator puts it in one instance, "The gloomy industry of exhausted socialism watched from the banks as the crowd entered into ecstasy" ("Korabl' mira," 163). The river, a symbol of travel and communication, brings the foreign tourists/cult members into a somewhat distant contact with the ordinary post-Soviet life on its banks.

The central figure in the narrative is the Russian translator Lev, who is described as a Muscovite, a graduate of the Maurice Thorez[32] Institute of Foreign Languages, "as worldly-wise and tattered" as the steamer itself. His appetites know no measure; indeed, the reader is told, "He had grown a belly of a size rather surprising in a man of 28 years."

> It could be stuffed into his jeans only with difficulty and could not be sucked in beneath his ribs when girls were approaching. His patchy beard and ringlets of hair—which resisted a comb—left little of his face on view; you could just glimpse his nose, the pillows of his cheeks, or his eyes, shining with a lazy cynicism, sometimes the left eye, sometimes the right, depending on which way his hand was pointing at the given moment. ("Korabl' mira," 163)

---

[31] For the Swami, the name Samara is evocative of the words "Samvara," or "highest good" as well as "Samantabhadra," which signifies the entirely good power that moves the universe, and reminds him of the "Samaritans," those "bearers of peace and love" (Aksyonov, "Korabl' mira," 161).

[32] Maurice Thorez (1900–1964), the leader of the French Communist Party, had ties both to Stalin and the Comintern.

His physique is anything but heroic and instead borders on the grotesque. Lev is a highly unlikely hero, but one whose role as cultural interpreter places him as mediator between the tourists and his fellow Russians.

The foreign passengers are shocked at the unclean Lev, whose habits of eating meat and drinking alcoholic beverages violate both the body and the mind, and they assume that proximity to them will make the sinner want to imitate their ways. Lev in turn finds the diet of the cult—mostly nuts and other foods that can be harvested without "pain" to the tree—horrific. "These schizos have created for themselves a voluntary gulag, if you don't take into account the ritual fucking," thinks Lev ("Korabl' mira," 164). The foreigners' reaction to Lev highlights their own righteousness and symbolizes a widespread attitude of the West toward Russia: "Once Russians see the light, they will emulate us and believe in our gods and our markets!"

The irony here is lost on the deliberately self-abnegating Australians: Russians were forced to endure hardships and deprivations that the Australians simply could not imagine. They suffered through the complications of the Civil War, starved and froze through the deprivations of the Second World War period, and lived in and through a real Gulag. Finally free of those historical circumstances, their country has become a playground for foreigners. And here the Australians have come to Russia to play at hardship.

But as a post-Soviet citizen, Lev evaluates the Krishnaites' code of behavior using his own cultural parameters; in the post-Socialist explosion of possibilities that enables him to make his living with Wandering Soul, self-limitations do not seem to him desirable. As Konstantin Kustanovich has argued, Soviet culture was maimed precisely by the curtailment of freedom, and not only in prison camps: "Deprived not only of political freedom, but also of the freedom to choose a job or a place of habitation (because of the infamous *propiska* laws), the freedom to possess property, and the freedom to conduct business, the Soviet people had only two freedoms left: drinking and sex."[33]

Lev, when the opportunity arises, indulges in both—as frequently as possible. Aksyonov, for his part, indulges in another favorite Russian pastime: punning. Lev's speaking name gives him the chance when Lev decides he'd like to take part in the "morning ritual of universal union," the "ritual fuck-

---

[33] K. Kustanovich, "Erotic Glasnost," 138. Joseph Brodsky put it somewhat differently, arguing that in the Soviet period, the free enterprise was limited to "adultery, moviegoing, Art" ("Less than One," 22).

ing": the "bhagavats undressed Obnag to the skin,"³⁴ a sentence that offers wonderful internal rhymes and repetitions. From this point in the narrative on, Lev maintains a more pure lifestyle while with his charges, although he continues to drink beer and vodka and indulge in meat products while alone in his cabin. Is he becoming more naked, more pure, in falling under the influence of his Western charges, or is he merely fulfilling his role as a mediator and translator of language, history, and culture?

It is Lev's purpose to prevent mistranslation of Russian and Soviet culture. Generally, the swami and Lev speak past one another, each with his own agenda. For example, the swami asks, "After whom is our boat named, Lev? I sense an echo of the eighteenth main purana."

"Not surprising," Lev answers immediately. "Vasily Chapaev is an historical hero and at the same time the source of good moods." Lev has given a perfect definition of the meaning of Chapaev; these two aspects have defined his role in Soviet culture since the 1920s.

The joking image is perhaps more contoured and significant than the ideological symbol itself. The tourist boat on which Lev works represents the fame of Chapaev and the simultaneous neglect of that fame. The fact that the socialist realist heritage industry could appropriate the naming rights of this branded historical figure and put that name on a rusting hulk—or put that name on a tourist steamer, which is subsequently permitted to fall into decay and become a rusting hulk—adds yet another dimension to the tradition of Chapaev jokes. Predictably, the story will end happily—Aksyonov's stories usually do—and in the end the simultaneity of Soviet ideology, "live" post-Soviet culture, and the exploitation of heritage will all come together.³⁵

Knowing the peace-loving nature of his charges, Lev deliberately avoids mentioning the violence inherent in Chapaev's service to his nation. As the steamer continues to sail, Aksyonov's post-Soviet readers, recalling our favorite Chapaev jokes, might still have in mind the tragedy of the Civil War—or indeed the travesty of what socialist realism and government intervention meant for Russian literature in the Soviet era—but the Krishnaites, the outsiders, have none of that context.

Lev does not try to present the complexity of Chapaev's image to the swami and his naïve followers, nor perhaps does he initially understand it

---

34 "Bkhagavaty razdeli Obnaga donaga." "Korabl' mira," 165.
35 Ponomarev writes about Aksyonov in almost offended tones, claiming that his heroes are always happy and always win the day ("Sotsrealizm karnaval'nyi," 215).

himself. In response to Lev's description, "the Bhagavats beamed with joy. To sail on a ship bearing the name of a hero who is also the source of good moods—what a blessing, what good luck!" ("Korabl' mira," 163). Nor does Lev explain the complexities with which the very term "hero" is invested in the Soviet and now post-Soviet context.

The ship sails on to Samara, which turns out to be a historically important tourist destination on a number of levels: it features the Soviet Chapaev industry as well as several significant World War II sites, *and* it is the home of the oldest Russian beer factory, Zhigulyovskoe (which, alas, Lev does not manage to visit, given the teetotaling nature of this particular group of tourists).[36]

In Samara, things get serious. The tourist fantasy is transformed into a confrontation with history. The "epicenter" of the story,[37] according to the otherwise fairly unobtrusive narrator, is the central square of the ancient city of Samara.[38] On that square—arranged around a sculptural group representing Chapaev and his fellow soldiers—stand four buildings:

> The theater building, a Russian cake-like building of stone, from the end of the nineteenth century . . . the Museum of Weaponry, in a formerly luxurious private home in the modernist style . . . the tall, constructivist dildo of the Volga-Ural Military Region Headquarters . . . and the large square building in the Soviet-Communist Party style poised atop the thirty-seven meter tunnel to the cave of the beast, Joseph Stalin. ("Korabl' mira," 167)

Samara, then known as Kuibyshev, was the location to which the Soviet government was to evacuate if necessary during the Second World War; and Stalin's bunker—twice the size and depth of Hitler's famous bunker, though

---

[36] The narrative mentions the hundred-year-old beer factory in one breath with "underground weapons factories" (Aksyonov, "Korabl' mira," 166).

[37] The first meaning of "epicenter" is geological, a point, directly above the true center of disturbance, from which the shock waves of an earthquake apparently radiate. The designation of the Samara square in this way invests the monument to Chapaev and the buildings surrounding it with the power to mark a cataclysm. The "cave of the beast" below may very well indict Stalin as the cause of the Soviet cataclysm.

[38] One post-Soviet description of Samara calls it an "industrial, provincial city, that is to say calm and kind [. . .] Samara is known for its modernist architecture and its very decent dramatic theater. And also for the constant efforts of certain of its citizens to throw off the calm and complacency of everyday life." Galina Ermoshina, "Molodoi chelovek iz intelligentnoi sem'i," Review of *Performance* (2000). Ermoshina also quotes Boris Svoiskii as stating, "I think that real Samaravites must seem strange to people of strong nerves and principles. Frivolous. They hold nothing sacred."

never actually used by Stalin—was only discovered and turned into a museum in the 1990s.[39]

This square, with its buildings ranging from the 1880s through the mid-twentieth century, memorializes the military twentieth century. Chapaev Square represents the crossroads of Soviet life: the theater and the sculptural group are surrounded by the military and the Communist Party, and all turn toward the institutional repository of power, history, and heritage—the Museum of Weaponry.

And beneath it all, the "cave of the beast," the fantastic and secret bunker that was to secure the life of the "father of the peoples" in case of military disaster. The "constructivist dildo," sexualized by Aksyonov's narrative, is mirrored by the bunker's shaft below ground, and this vertical axis contrasts with the horizontal axis of the riverbank. For Aksyonov, the historical landscape presented by this ensemble of buildings encircling the Chapaev monument, along with the square's underground secret, offers a perfect toponymic setting for exploring history and heritage.[40] Aksyonov didn't have to invent a place to parody; Samara exists in all its multilayered history. He only tinkers with the cityscape by populating it with his characters.

As Lev launches into his tour-guide spiel about the history of Samara during the Second World War, his linguistic faculties begin to falter for the first time. The swami reacts strongly to the sound of "Kuibyshev," and Lev assumes he is reacting to the Russian three-letter word with which its first syllable rhymes (*khui*, or cock), but there is some other meaning that throws the bhagavats into a frenzy of dancing. "I feel that a storm is approaching, the Swami muttered. I don't like this! Kuibyshev has a bad sound to it! Pray, so that it does not hear us! Go away! Go away!"

This ridiculous scene distills the way Russians in the post-Soviet period struggled to come to terms with the Soviet past in general and with World War II in particular. At this epicenter of the story, what was taken as sacred

---

[39] The Wikipedia entry on Samara includes the following, with no citation: "The life of Samara's citizens has always been intrinsically linked to the Volga river, which has not only served as the main commercial thoroughfare of Russia throughout several centuries, but also has great visual appeal. Samara's river-front is one of the favorite recreation places for local citizens and tourists. After the Soviet novelist Vasily Aksyonov visited Samara, he remarked: 'I am not sure where in the West one can find such a long and beautiful embankment. Possibly only around Lake Geneva.'"

[40] A review of Aksyonov's novel *Moskva-kva-kva* congratulates him on creating his own genre, "lyrico-ironic retromyth/kitsch," based on his use of Moscow streetscapes and toponyms in that work. See Elistratov, "Filosofiia mifokitcha."

almost instantly becomes foreboding, and the swami begins to chant for it all to "go away."

Lev distracts the bhagavats with explanations and directs them to the center of the square. The sculptural group is described thus, beginning with Lev's tour-guide diction and continuing with the narrator's voice:

> Splendid metallurgy, cast in bronze. The sculpture consisted of seven human figures and one horse. On horseback sat a man with a saber, behind him a sailor dragged a machine gun, a combat woman clutched a rifle, a Cossack bared his blade, a proletarian prepared a hand grenade, a country peasant also raised something or other in threat . . . Also there was a man unmarked by social rank who had an enemy bullet in him and was preparing to fall. All the faces of this sculpture were filled with uncontrollable hatred. ("Korabl' mira," 168)

Instead of greeting the monument to Vasily Chapaev with cheerful animation, the group reacts with horror, and "a mute scene ensued, or even a kind of alternative sculptural group, where the Manizer bronze was counterbalanced by the devotees' folds of orange cloth and heads shaven to the shininess of a billiard-ball" ("Korabl' mira," 169). The two frozen-action scenes mirror each other, as the Krishnaites come into contact with the Soviet myth of the Civil War. Chapaev, the swami shouts, is no ship of the world—or of peace, for that matter—but rather an incarnation of the demon.

The official Sovietized square is sterile, empty, but the post-Soviet people's reaction to that space recalls Bakhtin's argument about the regenerative folk laughter of the public square. The almost Gogolian mirroring of sterile (but long-standing) monument and foreign "other," the bhagavats who recoil in horror, is in turn mirrored by a post-Komsomol group that calls itself Interknowledge (*Interznanie*, although the locals' nickname for the group is *Isterzanie*, torment; "Korabl' mira," 171).

The Australians' plan to "cleanse the miasma . . ." is in turn mirrored by the post-Komsomol group's plan to stage an "action" or show entitled "Feast for the Soul," in Russian "*Pir dukha*," a homonymic expression that allows Lev and the Komsomol leader to share a laugh over bathroom humor—a form of Russian male bonding that supersedes any ideological, political, or commercial differences the two may have. In a parody of the post-Soviet estrada stage, "*Pir dukha*" features a "star of the Russian battlefields" singing at an open-air theater, surrounded by young people (heads shaven) who dance and clap.

In tight, colored bicycle shorts, laced-up combat boots, and a camouflage bustier above her muscled abdomen, Anka-the-Machinegunner held the huge "penis of a microphone" near her red—like the rose of revolution—lips and sang:

> Hey, once, and again!
> He saved me from a bullet!
> And who is right and who is not
> Is known only to the Commissariat!
>
> ("Korabl' mira," 173)

It is in this show that Lev finds inspiration to "save" his tourists. Concerned about his passengers, his ship, his employer, and the reputation of the firm paying his salary, Lev wants to avert what he senses is a potential "David Koresh–style" ending to their mission. All the swami's wordplay suddenly reveals itself to him: the impending "final dousing" involves a rope to avoid "pointless floating"—in other words, the "Great Dousing" is a mass-suicide plan, a battle plan against the "triumvirate of devils in the form of Chapaev" ("Korabl' mira," 175).

The Samara residents have taken the seriousness out of Soviet history by celebrating it in their ridiculous pop "Feast for the Soul," and Lev too backs the outsiders away from the horror of Soviet history by evoking the humor of Chapaev. In his final speech to the bhagavats, the new post-Soviet hero saves the day.

In order to do so, he calls to some of his own gods for inspiration and protection, and Aksyonov reveals the true meaning of "obnag": to convince the cult to abandon their suicide plan, Lev has to become utterly craven, "polnost'iu obnaglev," and he calls to "St. George (the patron saint of Moscow) . . . Fyodor Dostoevsky, Vasily Rozanov, and the young heroes of the revolution Leonid Kannegiesser and Fanny Kaplan." Wishing he had a glass of Absolut, Lev begins his speech:

> Your great and holy leader Shrila Prabhavishnu Swami with his eagle eye, inherited from a host of blessed incarnates, has seen directly into the essence of the Russian human landscape. This land was possessed by demons, and Vasily Ivanovich Chapaev was indeed the incarnation of Vritri, Madhu and Mur, who so unexpectedly revealed themselves in the bronze on the main square of Samara, formerly the city of Kuiby-shev. However, the question is whether our steamer, this rusty barge,

was a trap prepared for us by these powerful demons. It's not merely that the touring agency "Wandering Soul" offers its clients a bona fide guarantee of 100 % cooperation; this goes much deeper.

The fact is that Chapaev himself—who was unquestionably a Fury of the Civil War, and was reflected later in demonic works in paper, cellulose, and bronze—over the years, that is to say about forty years after his own personal Final Dousing in the waters of the Ural, suddenly began to show signs of freedom from his demonic source, coming to life in an unending series of amusing anecdotes, with the help of which our barely alive people tried to free ourselves from the devils of communism. I will tell you a few of these little stories and you can judge for yourselves.[41]

Revisiting the river toponym and the traditional river crossing from countless Soviet war stories, Aksyonov also links Chapaev's watery death to the cult followers' planned "final dousing." Lev's speech is a summation of the militarized twentieth century and the meaning of Chapaev for that century.

As a finale to his tale, Aksyonov presents a third mirrored sculptural group that arrives post-Soviet style: mounted on the bed of a KAMAZ truck, the "Feast for the Soul" celebration rolls down the street, including Anka-the-Machinegunner and Chapaev himself with a gladiolus in his hand instead of a saber. This bit of street theater is a way to demilitarize the military, and the gladiolus strikes the final blow. These are neither neo-Nazis nor flower children, but simply participants in a tasteless send-up of all that Soviet society claimed to hold sacred.[42]

On this basic level, Aksyonov's story is utterly straightforward: "outsiders" such as the Krishnaites can understand neither the heritage of the Russian Civil War nor the tragedy visited upon the Russian people by Soviet leaders, the Soviet economic system, and world history in the form of continual warfare throughout the twentieth century; and their attempts to "purify" the waters of Russia are laughable and over the top. Insiders too parody the cult of war and the heritage industry, but their sexualized ritual of public display in the end mocks the tragedy of the Russian twentieth century.[43]

---

[41] Aksyonov, "Korabl' mira," 176.
[42] Could this be a parody of present-day Samara-ites themselves, whose reputation is that they hold nothing sacred? See above.
[43] Compare to the sexualized street "actions" of Iurii Mamin's 1990 film *Bakenbardy* (*Sideburns*). Aksyonov's *Interznanie* would fit right in with the "clubs" in that film; both texts parody provincial life, with its extreme and excessive reactions.

The "Feast of the Soul" marks a ritual consumption of the self, a destructive sexual act that mocks the past and offers nothing for the future—except the laughter of Russian self-awareness and the bitter sense of irony that has enabled Russians to keep on. Lev tells Chapaev jokes to his clients, including one about cleanliness and hygiene:

> Vasily Ivanovich and Petya go to a bathhouse. "Vasily Ivanovich," Petya exclaims, "you're so much dirtier than I am!"
> "Well, of course," replies Chapaev, "I'm older than you."[44]

However, even in the midst of a ridiculous story about an exaggerated cult visiting Russia, Lev's Chapaev jokes represent something more serious: the "essence of Russia's process of struggling with the demon."[45] Lev Obnag is no warrior and no ideal hero, but his is the attitude of a survivor: he finds his happiness in the ever-present Russian *kolbasa*, in beer and vodka and sex—and in the popular reinvention of the heritage industry that brought us the Chapaev anecdote.[46]

* * *

The "heritage industry" is scholar David Lowenthal's term. Lowenthal argues that "history tells all who will listen what has happened and how things came to be as they are. Heritage passes on exclusive myths of origin and continuance, endowing a select group with prestige and common purpose. . . . History is for all, heritage for ourselves alone."[47] In the post-Soviet condition, history became compromised, and prestige and common purpose all but disappeared, leaving only the heritage industry with its empty symbols intact.

Lowenthal stresses that "to serve as a collective symbol heritage must be widely accepted by insiders, but inaccessible to outsiders. Its data are social,

---

[44] Interestingly, in a novel in which he wants to "reclaim" the "real" Vasily Chapaev, Eduard Volodarsky permits himself this same joke. See *Strasti po Chapaiu* (St. Petersburg: Amfora, 2007), 220.
[45] "Sut' demonoborcheskogo protsessa Rossii." "Korabl' mira," 177.
[46] Graham argues that Chapaev jokes "liberate Chapaev from both the civil war chronotope in which he was 'crystallized' by Furmanov and the Vasil'evs and from the abstract epic of Soviet history." He continues, "The *anekdot*-al Vasilii Ivanovich is a positive cultural figure, a hero." See *Resonant Dissonance*, 112.
[47] David Lowenthal, *Possessed by the Past: The Heritage Crusade and the Spoils of History* (New York: Free Press, 1996), 128.

not scientific."[48] Pelevin's novels *Omon Ra* and *Chapaev and Pustota* and Aksyonov's "The Ship of the World: *Vasily Chapaev*" explore these social data and the gap between insider and outsider access to Soviet heritage. In socialist realist texts (fiction, film, and sculpture), Chapaev represented a fulfillment of the spontaneity/consciousness dialectic, a "modern-day *bogatyr*," in John Haynes's words, forging a new Socialist life.

But if the indictment of Stalin's cult of personality, as Haynes has argued, "undermin[ed] the quasi-religious faith in leadership that constituted ... much of Chapaev's heroic status,"[49] then in postmodern post-Soviet texts, Chapaev is both hero and joke. Both a representation of the death and destruction that overwhelmingly filled the pages of history in the Soviet era and an example of the ability on the part of the Soviet/Russian people to rise above that tragedy. Both the marker of the epicenter of Russia's twentieth-century topos of war and the negation of Stalin and his secret underground bunker through the tool of laughter. For writers at the end of the twentieth century, what's the difference?

The Chapaev monument in Samara was constructed by the German Russian sculptor Matvei Genrikhovich Manizer. This is the same sculptor who memorialized the partisans, sailors, and soldiers of the Revolution in statues that still grace the Moscow Metro. He also produced Stalin's death mask.[50]

His monument stands on Chapaev Square in today's Samara, marking the "epicenter" of Russia's twentieth-century problems. It stands on top of the secret underground bunker built for Stalin's use during World War II and thus unites the two wars that undergird Russia's self-identity in the twentieth century.

Stalin may have left the building, but Chapaev lives on.

---

[48] David Lowenthal, "Identity, Heritage and History," in John R. Gillis, ed., *Commemorations: The Politics of National Identity* (Princeton: Princeton University Press, 1994), 49.
[49] Haynes, *New Soviet Man*, 160, 164.
[50] Manizer also helped train Ernst Neizvestny, the World War II veteran and sculptor who was exiled in the 1970s. His enormous Mask of Sorrow, installed at Magadan in 1996, commemorates the victims of Stalin's Kolyma camps.

Afterword

> It fell to us to save the Motherland,
> and you will need to guard the Fatherland.
>
> Нам Родину спасать досталось,
> а вам—Отечество беречь.
>
> -Mikhail Dudin[1]
>
> It's just too bad that the motherland has faded,
> no matter what they sing about her still.
>
> Жалко лишь, что родина померкла,
> что бы там ни пели про нее.
>
> -Bulat Okudzhava

The "short" twentieth century began in 1917 and ended in 1991, according to historian Eric Hobsbawm. Across that seventy-five-year century, one of the primary experiences for Soviet citizens was of war—the physical, social, and economic consequences of it; continual preparations for future wars; and finally, the struggle over how to remember it all. If we were to do a crude arithmetic, we could calculate that across those seventy-five years, Russians spent more than two decades in direct conflicts with other nations, and if we add to that number the period of the Cold War—which intermittently became "hot" in the third world in places like Angola, the Horn of Africa, and Cuba—we can see that for the Soviet twentieth century, Mikhail Epstein was not exaggerating when he described every generation as having been shaped by war and a militarized society: "For every generation its own war and its own victims. . . ."

The end of Hobsbawm's short twentieth century provides a bookend to poet Anna Akhmatova's prescient statement that the "real twentieth century" began with the Russian Revolution. And if that century began with the events of World War I and the Revolution, then it ended because of the events of the Cold War and the hot war in Afghanistan.

In the end, the United States and the Soviet Union did not exchange intercontinental ballistic missiles. But it is quite clear that the arms race and the military empire the Soviet Union built and had to maintain after the Second World War contributed significantly to bankrupting the country's economy.

---

[1] Dudin was a poet and a defender of Leningrad during the siege.

Afterword

The Soviet system collapsed so quickly and so completely in large part because its military spending had hollowed the economy out from the inside.

Even while the Soviet Union attempted to keep pace in the 1980s with Ronald Reagan's enormous arms buildup, it was fighting a genuine war on the periphery of its empire in Afghanistan. Between 1979 and 1989, over six hundred thousand Soviet men served in that war; more than fourteen thousand returned home in coffins. We will never know with any real certainty how many Afghans were killed, but the best estimates range between one and two million. In addition to leaving the country physically devastated, the Soviet war displaced two million Afghans internally, and five to ten million more became refugees. Indeed, through the 1980s, half of all the refugees in the world were Afghans. And as we are now all painfully aware, the unanticipated consequences of that war were the rise of the Taliban, Al Qaeda, and America's own involvement in the quagmire that remains of Afghanistan.

The 1990s might have been a moment for Russians to reckon with that war. By and large, that didn't happen. As we have seen, the collapse of the Soviet Union in the wake of the Afghan war opened up a cultural space for the "men of the '60s" and even the "boys of '24." They crowded out the survivors of Afghanistan. In the west the war was routinely compared to America's fiasco in Vietnam, and like many of those who returned from that long war, the veterans of Afghanistan came home traumatized, drug addled, and largely ignored. But unlike Vietnam vets, they fought for a country that when they got back home soon ceased to exist. A lost generation of young Russian men. Certainly the war produced no nationalist pride nor any heroic moments. The legacy of the war remains to be assessed.

Though the Soviet Union was dissolved soon after those boys came home, the nation that replaced it in many ways continued much like the old. War and political struggles have occupied the leaders hip and populace alike, and journalists and writers continue to be assassinated and attacked with virtual impunity. The "rule of law" Gorbachev announced as his goal in the mid-1980s has not come to fruition.

In the wake of 1990s attempts to come to terms with the atrocities that accompanied the Soviet Victory in World War II, Russia under Vladimir Putin has worked to make sure that the memory of World War II remains the heroic, just war that the Soviets constructed.

In honor of the sixty-fifth anniversary of the Victory in World War II, on May 9, 2010, military parades took place in eighteen cities of the Russian Federation as well as in Sevastopol, Ukraine: Moscow, St. Petersburg, Rostov-on-Don, Ekaterinburg, Chita, Khabarovsk, Vladivostok, Kaliningrad, Murmansk, Voronezh, Smolensk, Tula, Vladikavkaz, Nizhny Novgorod, Novorossiysk, Volgograd, Astrakhan, Novosibirsk all saw tanks and soldiers commemorating the Victory.[2] On this date one year earlier, the new law "Against the Rehabilitation of Nazism" made it illegal to criticize the actions of the Soviet army and government during World War II or to deny that the Soviet Union had won the war. Some foreign commentators noted, "As Russians celebrate their victory over the Nazis, they may also be celebrating the defeat of freedom of speech."[3]

On Victory Day in 2011, President Dmitry Medvedev emphasized in one of his speeches to veterans and workers at a military museum that "in order to be true patriots, people must be active. Those who lie about on the couch are unlikely to become real patriots." He continued, "We can only feel like a united nation if we have a history, if we remember that history."[4] In light of the law against criticizing Soviet actions during World War II, it is clear that the history Russians should remember is only the one they were fed during Soviet times. No new historical discoveries, views, or opinions welcome.

War seems to be central to the health of Putin's state.

Typical of this new political climate is the way in which one of the mid-century stories we looked at has returned to the cinema. Alexander Lebedev's 2002 remake of Kazakevich's *The Star* stripped it of its detail and humanity in favor of spectacular pyrotechnics and adrenaline-pumping action. In the novella, beyond the doomed reconnaissance mission, there are two real points: on the one hand, true loyalty is not valued, but loyalty without obedience causes Travkin's death; on the other hand, Travkin's holy image as a hero "cures" the radio operator Katya of her promiscuous ways.

In the 2002 film version, the characters are very poorly differentiated.[5] Oddly enough, the principle of "friendship of the peoples" seems to have been used to bring together the little reconnaissance band—the Russian Travkin,

---

[2] Viktor Khudoleev, "Chekania shag po vsei strane," *Krasnaia zvezda*, 3 March 2010, http://www.redstar.ru/2010/03/18_03/1_01.html.

[3] John Wendle, "Russia moves to ban criticism of WW II win," *Time World*, 8 May 2009, http://www.time.com/time/world/article/0,8599,1896927,00.html.

[4] Marina Eliseeva, "Pod znamenem pobedy," *Krasnaia zvezda*, 11 May 2011. http://www.redstar.ru/2011/05/11_05/1_01.html.

[5] Youngblood describes the characters in the film as "carefully individualized," but that is certainly not what I observed.

Afterword

the Ukrainian Annikanov, the Siberian/shaman with the Asian features, and the thin German-speaking Sparrow—but through most of the film physical characteristics are not noticeable: covered in mud and wearing their camouflage, the soldiers all look alike.

Katya does not undergo any transformation but remains virtuous during the entire film. The soldier she imagined herself with in the novella, Barashkin, preys on her instead in the film, and when she realizes that he's making moves on her, she immediately stands up and walks away. The actions that highlighted loyalty and disobedience in the novella (Annikanov's disobedience in returning from the hospital to Travkin's unit and Mamochkin's taking the SS officer against orders) were marked positive and negative in the book, whereas in the film both are accompanied by the only true grins we see, as if the soldiers involved were proud of themselves: "Aren't we hooligans, acting as we please . . ."

The voice-over giving us information on how the Germans are reacting to the actions of our little reconnaissance unit is simply lazy cinema. Three times we get an update, since the actual film is not showing us what's happening. The characteristics Kazakevich gave his individual soldiers are occasionally alluded to, but they serve no plot or characterization function in the film. They seem like obligations the filmmaker felt toward the original novella, but they do no work for the film.

Instead, what the film tells us (differently than the novella) is that all the soldiers are young (as with the "boys of '24"). They are willing to go on their mission, but they don't have much military discipline. In the end there are isolated acts of pointless bravery, and the "green ghosts" perish in a conflagration. War, twenty-first-century style. No heroes, no real message, just entertainment. Just the thing for citizens who want to lie about on their couches, staying out of political trouble.

* * *

War requires narrative in order to give it meaning. Without it, men wouldn't go off to fight. Narratives require heroes, and war produces them at a great rate. As we've seen in this book, the way in which war creates heroes and the nature of that heroism was a central concern for Russian writers in the twentieth century. The official rhetoric of *podvig* competed with detailed descriptions of *byt* or the necessary rhetoric of *est'*, what Frank Ellis calls

Afterword

"heroic pragmatism": the need to get the job done, the desire to do one's duty before the fatherland.

The narratives we have explored from the first half of the Soviet century were more likely to fall into the patriotic mode. Living in the shadow of the doctrine of socialist realism, these writers followed an easy formula where heroism equalled bravery plus consciousness. There was little room for satire or irony in the midst of Civil and World War, and even less in light of Stalin's Terror. By the second half of the century, that version of heroism began to ring hollow, and a second set of protagonists began to emerge, some antiheroes, some committed to the integrity of the individual, and others pushing against the status quo. They fulfilled their duties but did so in an alcoholic haze or with bitter and ironic complaints, or they went "underground" and chose their own set of values, which contradicted official Soviet paradigms.

It remains to be seen what a twenty-first-century Russian literary hero looks like. In 2008, Galina Shcherbakova published a collection of short stories entitled *Yashka's Children* in which she tried to argue that Soviet and post-Soviet people descended from Chekhov's peasant-turned-lackey Yasha from *The Cherry Orchard*. In postmodern style, she reuses Chekhov's titles to write new stories of her own time.[6] But titles notwithstanding, Shcherbakova's stories chronicle another facet of Russian life: the fear of war.

One of Shcherbakova's heroines regularly performs sexual acts with the recruiting officer in charge of her twin nephews' *uchastok* in advance of their eighteenth birthday—and tears her hair out in despair when the twins are picked up on the street, drafted into the armed services, and killed during their first week of service.

The grandfather of today's Vanka—who has left home voluntarily to avoid the cruel attacks of the man who killed his baby sister, drove his father away and his mother to her death, and even shot the family pet—learned his cruelty the honest way, as a military guard in charge of sending Baltic "traitors" to labor camps after the Second World War.

A boat captain in uniform follows a lady with a dog back to her apartment—and robs her blind before disappearing, not off to sea as he claimed,

---

[6] For an analysis of Shcherbakova, see my essay "'A Cigar in the Fresh Air': Chekhov's Yashka Lives!" in *Chekhov for the 21st Century*, ed. Carol Apollonio and Angela Brintlinger, forthcoming at Slavica, 2012.

but in search of another naive victim. His status as a military hero was suspect from the beginning, given the strong scent of alcohol he emitted.

These are three examples of the ways in which Shcherbakova digested and represented the twentieth-century history of war, from forced recruitment and the famed *dedovshchina* (army hazing), which traumatizes so many Russian young men, to the ethnic profiling that filled the Gulag, to the abuse of power by men in uniform. Her book teems with even more examples. Are her characters Yashka's children or Chapaev's comrades? Regardless, it's lucky that she published the book when she did. Some of what she wrote might have gotten her prosecuted in 2011.

References

Abramov, Anatolii. *Lirika i epos Velikoi otechestvennoi voiny: problematika, stil', poetika*. Moscow: Sovetskii pisatel', 1972.
Agaev, Aleksandr. "Istina i svoboda: Vladimir Makanin. Vzgliad iz 1990 goda." *Literaturnoe obozrenie* 9 (1990): 25–33.
Akimov, V. M. *Ot Bloka do Solzhenitsyna: Sud'by russkoi literatury XX veka (posle 1917 goda)*. St. Petersburg: St. Petersburg State Academy of Culture, 1994.
Aksyonov, Vasily. "Korabl' mira: *Vasilii Chapaev*." *Negativ polozhitel'nogo geroia*, 159–177. Moscow: Vagrius, 1996.
Aleksievich, Svetlana. *U voiny ne zhenskoe litso*. Moscow: Vremia, 2007; Pal'mira, 2004.
Aliger, Margarita. "Tropinka vo rzhi." *Vospominaniia ob Aleksandre Tvardovskom: sbornik*. Moscow: Sovetskii pisatel', 1982. Second Edition.
"Andegraund vchera i segodnia." *Znamia* 6 (1998): 172–199.
Anninskii, Lev. "Struktura labarinta: Vladimir Makanin i literatura 'seredinnogo' cheloveka." *Znamia* 12 (1986): 218–226.
———. "Za chto prokliaty?" *Literaturnaia gazeta*, 3 March, 1993.
Appleby, Joyce, Lynn Hunt, and Margaret Jacobs. *Telling the Truth about History*. New York: Norton, 1994.
Arendt, Hannah. "Ideology and Terror: A Novel Form of Government" (1953). Reprinted in *The American Intellectual Tradition, vol. 2: 1865 to the Present,* edited by David A. Hollinger and Charles Capper, 338–348. New York: Oxford University Press, 2011.
Ar'ev, Andrei. Introduction, "Sergei Dovlatov: Deviat' pisem Tamare Urzhumovoi." *Zvezda* 8 (2000): 137–138.
———. "Nasha malen'kaia zhizn'." In Sergei Dovlatov, *Sobranie prozy v trekh tomakh*, 1: 5–24. St. Petersburg: Limbus-press, 1993.
Arkhangel'skii, Aleksandr. "Gde skhodilis' kontsy s kontsami: nad stranitsami romana Vladimira Makanina *Andegraund, ili Geroi nashego vremeni*." *Druzhba narodov* 7 (1998): 180–185.
Arzamastseva, E. G. "'Uzh ne parodiia li on?': K voprosu o sootnoshenii obrazov Vasiliia Terkina i Ivana Chonkina." *Literatura tret'ei volny*, edited by V. P. Skobelev, 123–132. Samara: Samarskii universitet, 1997.
Astaf'ev, Viktor. *Izbrannoe: Prokliaty i ubity*. Moscow: Terra, 1999.
———. *Net mne otveta: Epistoliarnyi dnevnik, 1951–2001*. Irkutsk: Izdatel' Sapronov, 2009.
———. "Proletnyi gus'." *Novyi Mir* 1 (2001).
———. "Veselyi soldat." *Novyi Mir* 5–6 (1998).
Bakhtin, Mikhail. *Rabelais and His World*. Translated by Helene Iswolsky. Cambridge, Mass.: MIT Press, 1968.
Baklanov, Grigorii. "Vozvrashchenie." *V okopakh Stalingrada*, 3–6. Moscow: Khudozhestvennaia literatura, 1990.

Ball, Alan. *And Now My Soul Is Hardened: Abandoned Children in Soviet Russia, 1918–1930.* Berkeley: University of California Press, 1996.

Barker, Adele. "V. F. Panova." *Dictionary of Russian Women Writers*, edited by Marina Ledkovsky, Charlotte Rosenthal, and Mary Zirin, 483–485. Westport, CT: Greenwood Press, 1994.

Barratt, Andrew and Edith W. Clowes. "Gor'ky, Glasnost' and Perestroika: The Death of a Cultural Superhero?" *Soviet Studies* 43.6 (1991): 1123–1142.

Barratt, Andrew and Barry P. Scherr, trans. and eds. *Maksim Gorky: Selected Letters.* Oxford: Clarendon Press, 1997.

Basinskii, Pavel. *Gorky.* Moscow: ZhZL, 2005.

———. "Iz zhizni otechestvennykh kaktusov." *Literaturnaia gazeta* 22: 5604 (29 May 1996): 4.

Beevor, Antony and Lara Vinogradova, eds. and trans. *A Writer at War: Vasily Grossman with the Red Army, 1941–1945.* New York: Pantheon, 2005.

Beliakov, Sergei. "Prokliatie Viktora Astaf'eva." *Ural* 5 (2005).

Beraha, Laura. "The Fixed Fool: Raising and Resisting Picaresque Mobility in Vladimir Voinovich's Chonkin Novels." *SEEJ* 40.3 (1996): 475–493.

Bibikhin, V. "Ex libris *Nezavisimoi gazety*," *Nezavisimaia gazeta* (13 May 1998).

Bird, Robert. "The Functions of Poetry: TASS Windows and the Soviet Media System in Wartime." *Windows on the War: Soviet TASS Posters at Home and Abroad, 1941–1945*, edited by Peter Kort Zegers and Douglas Druick, 92–103. New Haven and London: The Art Institute of Chicago and Yale University Press, 2011.

Bitov, Andrei. "Gulag kak tsivilizatsiia." *Zvezda* (5) 1997: 3–30.

Blake, Casey Nelson. *Beloved Community: The Cultural Criticism of Randolph Bourne, Van Wyck Brooks, Waldo Frank and Lewis Mumford.* Chapel Hill, NC: UNC Press, 1990.

Bocharov, Anatolii. *Vasilii Grossman: Zhizn', tvorchestvo, sud'ba.* Moscow: Sovetskii pisatel', 1990.

Bogdanova, O., S. Kibal'nik, and L. Safronova. *Literaturnye strategii V. Pelevina.* St. Petersburg: Petropolis, 2007.

Boiko, Aleksandr. "Geroi strany, kotoroi net." *Sovetskaia Rossiia* (16 February 1995).

Bol'shakova, A. Iu. "Astaf'ev, Viktor Petrovich." *Russkie pisateli 20 veka: biograficheskii slovar'*, edited by P. A. Nikolaev. Moscow: Randevu-AM, 2000.

Bondarenko, Vladimir. "Vremia nadezhdy." *Zvezda* 8 (1986).

Borenstein, Eliot. *Men without Women: Masculinity and Revolution in Russian Fiction, 1917–1929.* Durham, NC: Duke University Press, 2000.

Bourne, Randolph. "War Is the Health of the State" (1918). *Bourne Mss.* Columbia University Libraries, www.bigeye.com/warstate.htm.

Braester, Yomi. *Witness against History: Literature, Film and Public Discourse in Twentieth-Century China.* Stanford, CA: Stanford University Press, 2003.

Brik, Osip. "Pochemu ponravilsia Tsement." *Na literaturnom postu*, 2 (1926): 30–32. Republished as O. M. Brik. "Pochemu ponravilsia 'Tsement'?" *Epigony khudozhestva, Literatura fakta: pervyi sbornik materialov rabotnikov Lefa*, edited by N. F. Chuzhak, 84–88. Moscow: Federatsiia, 1929.

Brintlinger, Angela. *Writing a Usable Past: Russian Literary Culture, 1917–1937*. Evanston, IL: Northwestern University Press, 2000.

———. "'A Cigar in the Fresh Air': Chekhov's Yashka Lives!" *Chekhov for the Twenty-first Century*, edited by Carol Apollonio and Angela Brintlinger. Bloomington, IN: Slavica, 2012.

Brintlinger, Angela and Ilya Vinitsky, eds. *Madness and the Mad in Russian Culture*. Toronto: University of Toronto Press, 2007.

Briskman, T. Ia., ed. *Viktor Petrovich Astaf'ev: zhizn' i tvorchestvo*. Moscow: Pashkov dom, 1999.

Brodsky, Joseph. *Less than One: Selected Essays*. New York: Farrar, Straus, Giroux, 1986.

———. "Literature and War: A Symposium. The Soviet Union." *Times Literary Supplement* 17 May, 1985: 543–544.

———. "O Serezhe Dovlatove: 'Mir urodliv, i liudi grustny.'" In Dovlatov, *Sobranie prozy* (3: 355–362).

Brooks, Jeffrey. *Thank You, Comrade Stalin! Soviet Public Culture from Revolution to Cold War*. Princeton: Princeton University Press: 2000.

Brown, Deming. *The Last Years of Soviet Russian Literature: Prose Fiction 1975–1991*. Cambridge: Cambridge University Press, 1993.

Brown, Edward J. *Russian Literature since the Revolution*. London: Collier-Macmillan, 1969.

Bugajski, Jill. "Paper Ambassadors: Friend and Foe in the War of Images." *Windows on the War: Soviet TASS Posters at Home and Abroad, 1941–1945*, edited by Peter Kort Zegers and Douglas Druick, 104–135. New Haven and London: The Art Institute of Chicago and Yale University Press, 2011.

Burtin, Iu. "Nestareiushchaia pravda." *"Zhivaia pamiat' pokolenii." Velikaia Otechestvennaia voina v sovetskoi literature. Sbornik statei*, 136–153. Moscow: Khudozhestvennaia literatura, 1965.

Busch, Robert. "Gladkov's Cement: the Making of a Classic." *SEEJ* 22.3 (1978): 348–361.

Bykov, Dmitrii. *Bulat Okudzhava*. Moscow: Molodaia gvardiia, 2009.

———. *Byl li Gor'kii*. Moscow: AST, Astrel', 2008.

———. "Pobeg v Mongoliiu." *Literaturnaia gazeta* 22: 5604 (29 May 1996): 4.

Carlyle, Thomas. *On Heroes, Hero-Worship, and the Heroic in History*. New York: D. Appleton and Company, 1841.

Chances, Ellen. *Conformity's Children: An Approach to the Superfluous Man in Russian Literature*. Columbus, OH: Slavica, 1978.

Clark, Katerina. "Socialist Realism and the Sacralizing of Space." *The Landscape of Stalinism: The Art and Ideology of Soviet Space*, edited by Evgeny Dobrenko and Eric Naiman, 3–18. Seattle: University of Washington Press, 2003.

———. *The Soviet Novel: History as Ritual*, 3rd ed. Bloomington, IN: Indiana University Press, 2000.

Cornwell, Neil, ed. *Reference Guide to Russian Literature*. London, Chicago: Fitzroy Dearborn, 1998.

Cowley, Jason. "Gogol à Go-Go." *New York Times Magazine* (23 January 2000): 20–23.
Dedkov, Igor'. "Ob"iavlenie viny i naznachenie kazni." *Druzhba narodov* 10 (1993): 185–202.
Diment, Galya. *The Autobiographical Novel of Co-Consciousness: Goncharov, Woolf, Joyce*. Gainesville: University of Florida Press, 1994.
Dobrenko, Evgeny. *The Making of the State Reader: Social and Aesthetic Contexts of the Reception of Soviet Literature*. Translated by Jesse M. Savage. Stanford: Stanford University Press, 1997.
Dovlatov, Sergei. "Blesk i nishcheta russkoi literatury (Lektsiia, prochitannaia 19 marta v universitete Severnoi Karoliny)," in *Igor' Sukhikh, Sergei Dovlatov: Vremia, mesto, sud'ba* [St. Petersburg: Kul't-inform-press, 1996], 290–304.
———. *Kompromiss. Sobranie prozy v trekh tomakh*, vol. 1, 173–324.
———. *Maloizvestnyi Dovlatov*. St. Petersburg: Zhurnal "Zvezda," 1995.
———. "Sergei Dovlatov: Deviat' pisem Tamare Urzhumovoi." *Zvezda* 8 (2000): 137–147.
———. *Vstretilis', pogovorili*. St. Petersburg: Azbuka, 2003.
———. *Zona (Zapiski nadziratelia). Sobranie prozy v trekh tomakh*, vol. 1, 25–172.
Efimov, Nina. "The Confession of an Underground Hero." *Routes of Passage: Essays on the Fiction of Vladimir Makanin*, edited by Byron Lindsey and Tatiana Spektor, 141–156. Bloomington, IN: Slavica, 2007.
Eidinova, N. "Negasnushchii svet Zvezdy (O povesti Em. Kazakevicha)." *Slova, prishedshie iz boia*, edited by A. G. Kogan. Moscow: Kniga, 1980.
Eliseeva, Marina. "Pod znamenem pobedy." *Krasnaya zvezda*, 11 May, 2011. http://www.redstar.ru/2011/05/11_05/1_01.html.
Elistratov, Vladimir. "Filosofiia mifokitcha." *Znamia* 5 (2006).
Ellis, Frank. "Army and Party in Conflict: Soldiers and Commissars in the Prose of Vasily Grossman." In John and Carol Garrard (1993), 180–201.
———. "The Problem of Remarquism in Soviet Russian War Prose." *Scottish Slavonic Review* 11 (1988): 91–108.
———. "Sons of the Soviet Apocalypse: Viktor Astafiev's *The Damned and the Dead*." *The Modern Language Review* 97.4 (October 2002): 909–923.
———. *The Damned and the Dead: The Eastern Front through the Eyes of Soviet and Russian Novelists*. Lawrence: University of Kansas Press, 2011.
———. *Vasiliy Grossman: The Genesis and Evolution of a Russian Heretic*. Oxford: Berg Publishers, 1994.
Emerson, Caryl. *Cambridge Introduction to Russian Literature*. Cambridge: Cambridge University Press, 2008.
Epstein, Mikhail. "Posle karnavala, ili vechnyi Venichka." *Ostav'te moiu dushu v pokoe*, by Venedikt Erofeev, 3–30. Moscow: Izdatel'stvo XGS, 1995.
Ermolin, Evgenii. "Mestorozhdenie sovesti: Zametki o Viktore Astaf'eve." *Kontinent* 100 (1999).
Ermoshina, Galina. "Molodoi chelovek iz intelligentnoi sem'i." Review of *Performance* (2000).

Etkind, Efim G. "Intonatsiia." In "Iz knigi druzei—Viktoru Nekrasovu. Vospominaniia o pisatele," in *Vremia i my* 98, ed. Efim Etkind (New York, Jerusalem, Paris: Vremia i my, 1987), 213–215.

Fitzpatrick, Sheila. "Everyday Stalinism: Ordinary Life in Extraordinary Times." Excerpted in *Stalinism: The Essential Readings*, edited by David L. Hoffmann, 161–178. Malden, MA: Blackwell, 2003.

Faust, Drew Gilpin. "Race, Gender, and Confederate Nationalism: William D. Washington's Burial of Latane." Southern Review 25 (1989): 297–307.

———. 2011 Jefferson Lecture in the Humanities. "Telling War Stories: Reflections of a Civil War Historian." www.neh.gov/news/humanities/2011-05/TellingWarStoriesWeb.pdf.

Frankel, Edith Rogovin. "The Tvardovsky Controversy." *Soviet Studies*, Vol. 34.4 (October 1982): 601–615.

Friedberg, Maurice. "New Editions of Soviet Belles-Lettres: A Study in Politics and Palimpsests." *American Slavic and East European Review*, 13.1 (February 1954): 77–88.

———. Untitled review of *The Life and Extraordinary Adventures of Private Ivan Chonkin*. Slavic Review 39.4 (1980): 717–719.

Furmanov, Dmitrii. *Chapaev*. Moscow: Gosizdatel'stvo khudozhestvennoi literatury, 1961.

———. *Nezabyvaemye dni*, in series Biblioteka molodogo rabochego. Leningrad: Lenizdat, 1983.

Garrard, John and Carol. *The Bones of Berdichev: The Life and Fate of Vasily Grossman*. New York: Free Press, 1996.

———, eds. *World War 2 and the Soviet People*. New York: St. Martin's Press, 1993.

Gasiorowska, Xenia. *Women in Soviet Fiction, 1917–1964*. Madison: University of Wisconsin Press, 1968.

Genis, Alexander. "Borders and Metamorphoses: Viktor Pelevin in the Context of Post-Soviet Literature." *Russian Postmodernism: New Perspectives on Post-Soviet Culture*, edited by Mikhail Epstein, Alexander Genis and Slobodanka Vladiv-Glover, 212–224. New York: Berghahn Books, 1999.

Gessen, Keith. "Under Siege: A beloved Soviet writer's path to dissent." *The New Yorker* 6 March, 2006: 82–87.

Gibian, George. "World War 2 in Russian National Consciousness: Pristavkin (1981–1987) and Kondratyev (1990)." In John and Carol Garrard (1993), 147–159.

Gladkov, Fedor. *Cement*. Translated by A. S. Arthur and C. Ashleigh. New York: Frederick Ungar, 1980.

———. "Moia rabota nad 'Tsementom' (V poriadke samokritiki)." *Sobranie sochinenii v 8-i tomakh*, vol. 2, Moscow: Gosizdatkhudlit, 1958.

———. *Tsement*. In *Krasnaia nov'* (1925) nos. 1–6.

Gladkovskaia, L. A. "Emmanuil Kazakevich." *Emmanuil Kazakevich, Sobranie sochinenii*, vol. 1 of 3. 5–24. Moscow: Khudozhestvennaia literatura, 1985.

Gladyshev, V. F. "My za tsenoi ne postoim? (Dve pravdy o voine)." *Ural* 5 (2004).

Gorky, A. M. *Sobranie sochinenii v tridtsati tomakh.* Moscow: Izdatel'stvo khudozhestvennoi literatury, 1949–1955.
———. *Childhood.* Translated by Graham Hettlinger. Chicago: Ivan Dee, 2010.
———. *Mat'.* Leningrad: Khudozhestvennaia literatura, 1986.
———. *Mother.* Secaucus, NJ: Citadel, 1972.
Graham, Seth. *Resonant Dissonance: The Russian Joke in Cultural Context.* Evanston, IL: Northwestern University Press, 2009.
Grishunin, A. L. "Vasilii Tyorkin A. Tvardovskogo." *Vasilii Terkin: Kniga pro boitsa,* by Aleksandr Tvardovskii, 406–488. Moscow: Nauka, 1976.
Gutkin, Irina. *The Cultural Origins of the Socialist Realist Aesthetic.* Evanston, IL: Northwestern University Press, 1999.
Hass, Robert. "Introduction." *Martin Eden,* by Jack London, v–xxii. Toronto: Bantam Books, 1986.
Haynes, John. *New Soviet Man: Gender and Masculinity in Stalinist Soviet Cinema.* Manchester: Manchester University Press, 2003.
Heberle, Mark. *A Trauma Artist: Tim O'Brien and the Fiction of Vietnam.* Iowa City: University of Iowa Press, 2001.
Hellebust, Rolf. *Flesh to Metal: Soviet Literature and the Alchemy of Revolution.* Ithaca: Cornell University Press, 2003.
Hemingway, Ernest. *A Farewell to Arms.* New York: Scribner Classics, 1997.
Hodgson, Katharine. *Written with the Bayonet: Soviet Russian Poetry of World War Two.* Liverpool: Liverpool University Press, 1996.
Hoffmann, David L., ed. *Stalinism: The Essential Readings.* Malden, MA: Blackwell, 2003.
———. *Stalinist Values: The Cultural Norms of Soviet Modernity, 1917–1941.* Ithaca: Cornell University Press, 2003.
Holmgren, Beth. "Writing the female body politic (1945–1985)." *A History of Women's Writing in Russia,* edited by Adele Marie Barker and Jehanne M. Gheith, 225–242. Cambridge: Cambridge University Press, 2002.
Homer. *The Odyssey,* translated by Robert Fagles. New York: Penguin Books, 1996.
Hook, Sidney. *The Hero in History: A Study in Limitation and Possibility,* 1943. Boston: Beacon Press, 1955.
Hosking, Geoffrey. *Beyond Socialist Realism: Soviet Fiction since Ivan Denisovich.* London, New York: Granada, 1980.
———. "The Good Soldier Chonkin." *Times Literary Supplement* no. 3854 (23 January 1976): 93.
Iakovich, Elena. n.t. *Literaturnaia gazeta,* 30 May 1990 (No. 22, 6296).
Ignatieff, Michael. "Soviet War Memorials." *History Workshop* 17 (Spring 1984): 157–163.
Isbakh, Aleksandr. *Furmanov.* In series Zhizn' zamechatel'nykh liudei. Moscow: Molodaia gvardiia, 1968.
Ivanova, Natal'ia. "Sluchai Makanina." *Znamia* 4 (1997).
Ivantsov, Vladimir. "A Conversation with Vladimir Makanin." In Lindsey and Spektor, 171–191.

Izgarshev, Igor'. "Aleksei Mares'ev: Ia chelovek, a ne legenda!" *Argumenty i fakty* no. 19 (1072), 8 May 2001.

Kaganovsky, Lilya. *How the Soviet Man Was Unmade: Cultural Fantasy and Male Subjectivity Under Stalin*. Pittsburgh: University of Pittsburgh Press, 2008.

———. "How the Soviet Man Was (Un)made." *Slavic Review* 63.3 (Autumn 2004): 577–596.

Kanevskaia, Marina. "Istoriia i mif v postmodernistskom russkom romane." *Izvestiia AN*, seriia Literatury i iazyka, 59.2 (2000): 37–47.

Karaseva, Ella. "Beri, da pomni." Review of *Starodub*, in *Oktiabr'* 5 (2010).

Kasack, Wolfgang. *Dictionary of Russian Literature since 1917*, translated by Maria Carlson and Jane T. Hedges. New York: Columbia University Press, 1988.

Kataev, V. B. *Igra v oskolki: Sud'by russkoi klassiki v epokhu postmodernizma*. Moscow: Izdatel'stvo moskovskogo universiteta, 2002.

Kavin, Nikolai, ed. "Besedy s Viktorom Astaf'evym." *Znamia* (5): 2009.

Kazakevich, Emmanuil. *Zvezda: povest'*, in *Velikaia otechestvennaia*, edited by V. Kozhevnikov, K. Simonov, and A. Surkov, 7–80. Moscow: Khudozhestvennaia literatura, 1966.

Kelly, Catriona. *A History of Russian Women's Writing, 1880–1992*. Oxford: Clarendon Press, 1994.

Kemp-Welch, A. *Stalin and the Literary Intelligentsia, 1928–1939*. Basingstoke: Macmillan, 1991.

Khachaturian, Aida. *Roman V. S. Makanina Andegraund, ili geroi nashego vremeni: Homo Urbanis v pole 'Usredneniia.'* Tallinn: PhD diss., Tallinn University, 2006.

Khan, Halimur. "Folklore and Fairytale Elements in Vladimir Voinovich's Novel *The Life and Extraordinary Adventures of Private Ivan Chonkin*." *SEEJ* 40.3 (1996): 494–518.

Khodasevich, V. F. "Gor'kii." *Koleblemyi trenozhnik*. 353–374. Moscow: Sovetskii pisatel', 1991.

Khudoleev, Viktor. "Chekania shag po vsei strane." *Krasnaia zvezda*, 3 March 2010, http://www.redstar.ru/2010/03/18_03/1_01.html.

Kolesnikov, Mikhail. *Bez strakha i upreka*. Moscow: Voennoe izdatel'stvo, 1971.

Kopelev, Lev. "Pervoe znakomstvo." In "Iz knigi druzei," 224.

Koppers, Andre. *A Biographical Dictionary on the Political Abuse of Psychiatry in the USSR*. Amsterdam: International Association on the Political Use of Psychiatry, 1990.

Kornblatt, Judith. *The Cossack Hero in Russian Literature: A Study in Cultural Mythology*. Madison: University of Wisconsin Press, 1992.

Krasnoshchekova, Elena. "Two Paradoxical Fellows: Dostoevsky and Makanin's Underground Men." In Lindsey and Spektor, 129–140.

Kreutzer, Ruth. "Vera Panova." *Russian Women Writers*, edited by Christine Tomei, 1019. New York: Garland, 1999.

Krylova, Anna. "Dancing on the Graves of the Dead: Building a World War II Memorial in Post-Soviet Russia." *Memory and the Impact of Political Transformation in Public Space,* edited by Daniel J. Walkowitz and Lisa Maya Knauer, 83–102. Durham, NC: Duke University Press, 2004.

———. "'Healers of Wounded Souls': The Crisis of Private Life in Soviet Literature, 1944–1946." *Journal of Modern History* 73.1 (2001): 307–331.

———. "In their own words? Soviet women writers and the search for self." *A History of Women's Writing in Russia,* edited by Adele Marie Barker and Jehanne M. Gheith, 243–263. Cambridge: Cambridge University Press, 2002.

———. *Neither Erased Nor Remembered: Soviet "Women Combatants" and Cultural Strategies of Forgetting in Soviet Russia, 1940s–1980s.* New York: Bergahn Books, 2010.

Kudriashova, A. "Kakoi ty, chelovek?" *Voprosy literatury* 7 (1965): 199–204.

Kupriianovskii, Pavel V. *Gor'kii. Furmanov. Serafimovich. A. Tolstoi.* Ivanovo: Ivanovo knizhnoe izdatel'stvo: 1960.

Kustanovich, Konstantin. "Erotic Glasnost: Sexuality in Recent Russian Literature." *World Literature Today* 67.1 (Winter 1993): 136–144.

Kustanovich, Konstantine. "A Hero of a Bygone Time, or Russian Literature as an Ecological System in Vladimir Makanin's Underground and Other Works." In Lindsey and Spektor, 115–128.

Laird, Sally. "Viktor Pelevin." *Voices of Russian Literature: Interviews with Ten Contemporary Writers,* 178–192. Oxford: Oxford University Press, 1999.

Lakshin, Vladimir. "Solzhenitsyn, Tvardovskii i *Novyi Mir.*" *The Twentieth Century: A Socio-political Digest and Literary Magazine,* vol. 2. London: TCD Publications, Ltd., 1977. English translation by Michael Glenny Cambridge, Mass.: MIT Press, 1980.

Latynina, Alla. "Autsaidery: Spor vokrug 'lishnikh liudei' sovremennosti." *Oktiabr'* 7 (1987): 178–184.

———. "Ne igra, a prognoz khudozhnika." *Literaturnaia gazeta* 7 June, 1995, 4.

Lazarev, Lazar. "Vo imia pravdy i dobra: o poezii Borisa Slutskogo." In B. A. Slutsky, *Bez popravok...,* 5–72. Moscow: Vremia, 2006.

Levina-Parker, Maria. "Smert' geroia." *Voprosy literatury* 5 (1995): 63–78.

Levine, Lawrence W. *The Unpredictable Past: Explorations in American Cultural History.* New York: Oxford University Press, 1993.

Levitt, Marcus C. and Tatyana Novikov, eds. *Times of Trouble: Violence in Russian Literature and Culture.* Madison: University of Wisconsin Press, 2007.

Libedinskii, Iurii. "Bol'shevik, voin, pisatel'." In A. Isbakh and D. Zonov, *Furmanov v vospominaniiakh sovremennikov,* 172–192. Moscow: Sovetskii pisatel', 1959.

———. *Rozhdenie geroia.* Leningrad: Gosudarstvennoe izdatel'stvo khudozhestvennoi literatury, 1931.

Likhachev, D. S. "Iz kommentariia k stikhotvoreniiu A. Bloka 'Noch', ulitsa, fonar', apteka,'" *Russkaia literatura* 1 (1978), 186–188.

Lindsey, Byron. "Translator's Preface." *The Loss. A Novella and Two Stories,* ix–xvi. Evanston: Northwestern University Press, 1998.

——— and Tatiana Spektor. *Routes of Passage: Essays on the Fiction of Vladimir Makanin.* Bloomington, IN: Slavica, 2007.

Lipovetsky, Mark. *The Charms of Cynical Reason: Tricksters in Soviet and Post-Soviet Culture*. Boston: Academic Studies Press, 2010.

———. "Makanin's Existential Myth in the Nineties" ("Escape Hatch," "The Prisoner from the Caucasus," and "Underground") in Lindsey and Spektor, 97–108.

———. "Russian Literary Postmodernism in the 1990s." *Slavonic and East European Review* 79.1 (January 2001): 31–50.

———. *Russian Postmodernist Fiction: Dialogue with Chaos*, edited by Eliot Borenstein. Armonk, NY: M.E. Sharpe, 1999.

———. "'Uchites', tvari, kak zhit'' (paranoiia, zona i literaturnyi kontekst)." *Znamia* 5 (1997): 199–212.

———. "War as the Family Value: Failing Fathers and Monstrous Sons in *My Stepbrother Frankenstein*." *Cinepaternity: Fathers and Sons in Soviet and Post-Soviet Film*, edited by Helena Goscilo and Yana Hashamova, 114–137. Bloomington, IN: Indiana University Press, 2010.

London, Jack. *Martin Eden*. Toronto: Bantam Books, 1986.

Loseff, Lev. "On Hostile Ground: Madness and Madhouse in Joseph Brodsky's 'Gorbunov and Gorchakov.'" In Brintlinger and Vinitsky, 90–104.

Lowenthal, David. "Identity, Heritage and History." *Commemorations: The Politics of National Identity*, edited by John R. Gillis. Princeton: Princeton University Press, 1994.

———. *Possessed by the Past: The Heritage Crusade and the Spoils of History*. New York: Free Press, 1996.

Luzianina, L. N. "Dukhovnyi smysl kontsepta 'zvezda' v odnoimennoi povesti E. Kazakevicha." *Dukhovnost' kak antropologicheskaia universaliia v sovremennom literaturovedenii*, 96–99 (Kirov, 2009).

Macdonald, Dwight. Preface, *Alexander Herzen's My Past and Thoughts*, abridged edition. New York: Knopf 1973.

McCausland, Gerald. "Viktor Pelevin and the End of Sots-Art." *Endquote: Sots-Art Literature and Soviet Grand Style*, edited by Marina Balina, Nancy Condee, and Evgeny Dobrenko, 225–237. Evanston: Northwestern University Press, 2000.

Makanin, Vladimir. "About Myself and My Contexts." In Lindsey and Spektor, 19–24.

———. "Andegraund, ili geroi nashego vremeni." *Znamia* 1–4, 1998.

———. *Andegraund, ili geroi nashego vremeni*. Moscow: Vagrius, 1999.

———. *Bezotsovshchina. Soldat i soldatka. Povesti*. Moscow: Sovetskii pisatel', 1971.

Makarenko, A. "Chapaev D. Furmanova." *Literaturnyi kritik* 1934, no. 10–11.

Marsh, Rosalind J. *Soviet Fiction since Stalin: Science, Politics, Literature*. Totowa, NJ: Barnes and Noble Books, 1986.

Marshak, Samuil. *Radi zhizni na zemle: ob Aleksandre Tvardovskom*. Moscow: Sovetskii pisatel', 1961.

Mikhailiuk, V. M. "Velikii truzhenik pera." *Ural* 5 (2004).

Miller, Martin A. "The Theory and Practice of Psychiatry in the Soviet Union." *Psychiatry* 48 (February 1985): 13–24.

Mathewson, Jr., Rufus W. *The Positive Hero in Russian Literature*. New York: Columbia University Press, 1958.

Medvedev, Roy and Zhores. *A Question of Madness*. London: Macmillan, 1971.
Mee, Cornelia. *Internment of Soviet Dissenters in Mental Hospitals*. Cambridge, Eng.:Working Group on the Internment of Dissenters in Mental Hospitals, 1971.
Merridale, Catherine. *Ivan's War: Life and Death in the Red Army, 1939–1945*. New York: Metropolitan Books, 2006.
"Mesto literatora v Otechestvennoi voine." *Literaturnaia gazeta* 20 August, 1941, 1.
Mikhailov, O. N. "Put' Bunina-khudozhnika." *Literaturnoe nasledstvo* vol. 84, part 1, *Ivan Bunin*. Moscow: Nauka, 1973.
Miller, Frank. *Folklore for Stalin: Russian Folklore and Pseudofolklore of the Stalin Era*. Armonk, NY: M.E. Sharpe, 1990.
Moss, Julian D. "Violence in Viktor Astafiev's Fiction." In Levitt and Novikov, 236–245.
Motygin, S. Iu. *Priamaia liniia? . . . Evoliutsiia prozy V.S. Makanina*. Astrakhan: Izdatel'stvo Astrakhanskogo gosudarstvennogo pedagogicheskogo universiteta, 2001.
Nekrasov, Victor. "Being Earnest Isn't Always Important." *Survey* 23.3 (104): 1977–1978, 42–51.
———. *Kak ia stal sheval'e: rasskazy. Portrety. Ocherki. Povesti*. Ekaterinburg: U-Faktoriia, 2005.
———. *Saperlipopet. Esli b da kaby, da vo rtu rosli gryby*. London: Overseas Publications, 1983.
———. "Slova 'velikie' i prostye." *Iskusstvo kino* 5 (1959): 55–61.
———. *Stalingrad*. Frankfurt-am-Main: Posev, 1981.
———. *V okopakh Stalingrada*. St. Petersburg: Azbuka-klassika, 2005.
———. *Zapiski zevaki*. Moscow: Zakharov, 2003.
Nemzer, Andrei. "Kak ia upustil kar'eru." (May 1996) Reprinted in *Literaturnoe segodnia. O russkoi proze. 90-e*, 313–315. Moscow: Novoe literaturnoe obozrenie, 1998.
———. "Kogda? Gde? Kto? O romane Vladimira Makanina: opyt kratkogo putevoditelia." *Novyi mir* 10 (1998): 183–195.
———. "Prigovor i molitva," *Novyi Mir* 10–12 (1992), reprinted in *Literaturnoe segodnia: O russkoi proze. 90-e* (Moscow: Novoe literaturnoe obozrenie, 1998), 35–38.
———. n.t. *Segodnia*, 2 March, 1993.
Nickell, William. "Tolstoy in 1928: In the Mirror of the Revolution." *Epic Revisionism*, edited by Kevin M. F. Platt and David Brandenberger, 17–38. Madison: University of Wisconsin Press: 2006.
Nikolaev, P. A, ed. *Russkie pisateli 20 veka. Biograficheskii slovar'*. Moscow: Randevu-AM, 2000.
Nivat, Georges. "Monsieur Nekrasov!" In "Iz knigi druzei," 217–219.
Norris, Stephen. N. *A War of Images: Russian Popular Prints, Wartime Culture, and National Identity, 1812–1945*. DeKalb, IL: Northern Illinois University Press, 2006.
Novikov, Tatyana. Review of Vladimir Voinovich's *Portret na fone mifa*. *World Literature Today* 77.2 (2003): 134.

O'Brien, Tim. *The Things They Carried*. New York: Broadway Books, 1998.
Okudzhava, Bulat. *"Ia nikomu nichego ne naviazyval . . ."* Edited by Aleksandr Petrakov. Moscow: Biblioteka zhurnala "Vagant-Moskva," 1997.
———. *Zal ozhidaniia: stikhi*. Nizhnii Novgorod: Izdatel'stvo Dekom, 1996.
Orlova, Raisa. *Kheminguei v Rossii: Roman dlinoiu v polstoletiia*. Ann Arbor: Ardis, 1985.
Panova, Vera. *Moe i tol'ko moe: o moei zhizni, knigakh, i chitateliakh*. St. Petersburg: Izdatel'stvo zhurnala Zvezda, 2005.
———. "Otkuda vzialias' kniga Sputniki." *Sputniki*. Leningrad: Sovetskii pisatel', 1967.
———. *Sputniki*. Leningrad: Sovetskii pisatel', 1967.
Pelevin, Viktor. *Chapaev i Pustota*. Moscow: Vagrius, 1999.
———. *Omon Ra. Zhizn' nasekomykh. Zatvornik i Shestipalyi. Prints Gosplana*. Moscow: Vagrius, 1999.
———. *Omon Ra*. Translated by Andrew Bromfield. New York: New Directions, 1998.
Peppard, Victor. "Gogolian Substrata in *Zhizn' i neobychainye prikliucheniia soldata Ivana Chonkina*." *Russian Language Journal* 38.131 (1984): 131–138.
Peteli, Viktor. *Zhizn' Maksima Gor'kogo*. Moscow: Tsentrpoligraf, 2007.
Peterson, Nadya L. "Death and the Maiden: Erasures of the Feminine in Soviet Literature of the Fin-de-siècle." In Levitt and Novikov, 246–255.
Petro, Peter. "Hasek, Voinovich, and the Tradition of Anti-Militarist Satire." *Canadian Slavonic Papers* XXII.1 (March, 1980): 116–121.
Petrone, Karen. "Family, Masculinity, and Heroism in Russian War Posters of the First World War." *Borderlines*, edited by Billie Melman, 95–120. New York: Routledge, 1998.
———. "Masculinity and Heroism in Imperial and Soviet Military-Patriotic Cultures." *Russian Masculinities in History and Culture*, edited by Barbara Evans Clements, Rebecca Friedman, and Dan Healey, 172–193. New York: Palgrave 2002.
Petrov, N. and O. Edel'man, "Novoe o sovetskikh geroiakh." *Novyi mir* 6 (1997): 140–151.
Piskunova, Svetlana. "Observations on the Poetics of Vladimir Makanin." In Lindsey and Spektor, 109–114.
Polianskii, Valer'ian. "Tsement i ego kritiki." *Na literaturnom postu* 5–6 (1926): 50–53.
Ponomarev, Evgenii. "Sotsrealizm karnaval'nyi." *Zvezda* 4 (2001): 213–219.
Popov, Evgenii. "Dve liubvi: Aksyonov i Dovlatov." *Vsemirnoe slovo* 9 (1995): 12–13.
Potresov, Vladimir. "Vozvrashchenie Nekrasova." In Nekrasov (2003), 5–26.
Prozorov, V. V. "*Tyorkin na tom svete* A.T. Tvardovskogo i shchedrinskaia satiricheskaia traditsiia," 105–119. *Do vostrebovaniia . . . Izbrannye stat'i o literature i zhurnalistike*. Saratov: Izdatel'stvo saratovskogo universiteta, 2010.
Rancour-Laferriere, Daniel. "From Incompetence to Satire: Voinovich's Image of Stalin as Castrated Leader of the Soviet Union in 1941." *Slavic Review* 50.1 (1991): 36–47.

Reed, Walter. *Meditations on the Hero: A Study of the Romantic Hero in Nineteenth-Century Fiction*. New Haven and London: Yale University Press, 1974.
Rodnianskaia, Irina. "I k nci bezumnaia liubov'." *Novyi mir*, 9: 857 (1996): 212–216.
———. "Neznakomye znakomtsy." *Novyi Mir* 8 (1986).
Rollberg, Peter. *Invisible Transcendence: Vladimir Makanin's Outsiders*. Washington, DC: Occasional Papers at the Kennan Institute for Advance Russian Studies, August 1993.
Romanova, Regina. *Aleksandr Tvardovskii: Trudy i dni*. Moscow: Volodei Publishers, 2006.
Rosenthal, Bernice Glatzer. *New Myth, New World: From Nietzsche to Stalinism*. University Park, PA: Penn State University Press, 2002.
Ryan-(Hayes), Karen. *Contemporary Russian Satire: A Genre Study*. Cambridge: Cambridge University Press, 1995.
Sarnov, Benedikt. "Estestvennyi chelovek v neestestvennykh obstoiatel'stvakh. O geroe etoi knigi i ee avtore." In Voinovich (1990), 523–539.
Scammell, Michael. *Solzhenitsyn: A Biography*. New York, London: Norton, 1984.
Scherr, Barry. "Gorky and God-Building." *William James in Russian Culture*, edited by Joan Delancey Grossman and Ruth Rischin, 189–210. Lanham, MD: Lexington Books, 2003.
———. *Maxim Gorky*. Boston: Twayne, 1988.
Serman, Ilya. "Teatr Sergeia Dovlatova." *Grani* 136 (1985): 138–162.
Shapir, M. "Dante i Tyorkin 'na tom svete': O sud'bakh russkogo burleska v XX veke." *Voprosy literatury* 3 (May-June 2002): 58–72.
Shlapentokh, Vladimir. *Soviet Intellectuals and Political Power: The Post-Stalin Era*. Princeton: Princeton University Press, 1990.
Shlykunov, N. A. "Razve eto tot geroi?" *Literaturnaia gazeta* (21 November 1963).
Shpagin, Aleksandr. "Religiia voiny." *Iskusstvo kino* 5 (2005): 57–68; 6 (2005): 73–89.
Shtut, Sarra. *Kakov ty, Chelovek?: geroicheskaia v sovetskoi literature*. Moscow: Sovetskii pisatel', 1964.
Slutsky, B. A. *"Bez popravok..."* Moscow: Vremia, 2006.
———. *Stikhi raznykh let. Iz neizdannogo*. Moscow: Sovetskii pisatel', 1988.
Smirnov, Igor'. *Roman tain: Doktor Zhivago*. Moscow: Novoe literaturnoe obozrenie, 1996.
Smirnova, L. N. "Kak sozdavalsia *Tsement*." *Tekstologiia proizvedenii sovetskoi literatury: Voprosy tekstologii* 4 (1967): 140–227.
Smith, Alexandra. "Tvardovskii." In Cornwell, 852–53.
Smith, G. S. "On the Page and on the Snow: Vladimir Makanin's *Andergraund* [sic], *ili Geroi nashego vremeni*." *Slavonic and East European Review* 79.3 (July 2001): 434–458.
Smith, Teresa with Thomas Oleszczuk. *No Asylum: State Psychiatric Repression in the Former USSR*. New York: New York University Press, 1996.
Snyder, Timothy. *Bloodlands: Europe Between Hitler and Stalin*. New York: Basic Books, 2010.

Sofronitskii, Vladimir. "Dolg khudozhnika." *Literatura i iskusstvo* no. 46 (7 November, 1942): 1.
Solzhenitsyn, Aleksandr I. *The Oak and the Calf: Sketches of Literary Life in the Soviet Union*, translated by Harry Willetts. New York: Harper and Row, 1975.
Solzhenitsyn, Alexander. *One Day in the Life of Ivan Denisovich*. New York: Signet Classic, 1998.
———. *Rasskazy*. Moscow: Izdatel'stvo ACT, 2003.
Sotskova, M. N. *Dmitrii Furmanov*. Moscow: Prosveshchenie, 1969.
Starikov, D. "Terkin protiv Terkina." *Oktiabr'* 10 (1963): 193–207.
Stepanian, Karen. "Krizis slova na poroge svobody." *Znamia* 8 (1999): 204–214.
———. "Realizm kak spasenie ot snov." *Znamia* 11 (1996): 194–200.
Stoppard, Tom. *Every Good Boy Deserves Favor and Professional Foul*. New York: Grove Press, 1978.
Struve, Gleb. *Russian Literature under Lenin and Stalin*. Norman, OK: University of Oklahoma Press, 1971.
Sukhikh, Igor'. *Knigi XX veka: russkii kanon*. Moscow: Nezavisimaia gazeta, 2001.
———. *Sergei Dovlatov: Vremia, mesto, sud'ba*. St. Petersburg: Kul't-inform-press, 1996.
Suleiman, Susan Rubin. *Crises of Memory and the Second World War*. Cambridge, MA: Harvard University Press, 2006.
Svirski, Grigori. *A History of Post-War Soviet Writing: The Literature of Moral Opposition*, translated by Robert Dessaix and Michael Ulman. Ann Arbor: Ardis, 1981.
Szporluk, Mary Ann. "Afterword: On Reading Makanin." *Escape Hatch and the Long Road Ahead: Two Novellas*, by Vladimir Makanin, 183–193. Ardis: Dana Point, 1996.
Tal, Kali. "Speaking the Language of Pain: Vietnam War Literature in the Context of a Literature of Trauma." *Fourteen Landing Zones: Approaches to Vietnam War Literature*, edited by Philip K. Jason, 215–250. Iowa City: University of Iowa Press, 1991.
Tolczyk, Dariusz. "Who is Ivan Denisovich? Ethical Challenge and Narrative Ambiguity in Solzhenitsyn's Text." *One Day in the Life of Ivan Denisovich: A Critical Companion*, edited by Alexis Klimoff. Evanston, IL: Northwestern University Press 1997.
Toper, P. M. *Radi zhizni na zemle: Literatura i voina. Traditsii. Resheniia. Geroi*. Third edition. Moscow: Sovetskii pisatel', 1985.
Trifonov, Gennadii. "Rubtsy voiny (pamiati V.P. Astaf'eva)." *Kontinent* 214 (2002).
Tumarkin, Nina. *The Living and the Dead: The Rise and Fall of the Cult of World War II in Russia*. New York: Basic Books, 1994.
———. "Story of a War Memorial." In John and Carol Garrard (1993), 125–146.
Tvardovskaia V. and O., "Istoriia odnoi fal'shivki: Epizod bor'by vokrug 'Terkina na tom svete." *Voprosy literatury* 1 (2007): 36–52.
Tvardovskii, Aleksandr. "Kak byl napisan 'Vasilii Terkin." Reprinted in *Vasilii Terkin: Kniga pro boitsa*, 229–283.

———. "S Karel'skogo peresheika (Iz frontovoi tetradi)." Reprinted in *Vasilii Terkin: Kniga pro boitsa*, 284–286.
———. "Terkin na tom svete." In *XX vek: Gologrammy poeta i istorika*, by Aleksandr Tvardovskii and Mikhail Gefter, 377–404. Moscow: Novyi Khronograf, 2005.
———. *Vasilii Terkin: Kniga pro boitsa*. Moscow: Nauka, 1976.
Vail', Petr. "Geroi vremeni." 16 January 2006. *Radio Free Europe*. http://archive.svoboda.org/programs/cicles/hero/21.asp.
——— and A. Genis, "Strana slov." *Novyi mir* 4 (1991): 239.
Vaksberg, Arkady. *Gibel' burevestnika: Maksim Gor'kii, poslednie dvadtsat' let*. Moscow: Terra-Sport, 1999.
Van Baak, Joost. *The House in Russian Literature: A Mythopoetic Exploration*. Amsterdam, New York: Rodopi, 2009.
Vanshenkin, Konstantin. "A.T. Tvardovskii. 'Ia ubit podo Rzhevom'. Opyt novogo prochteniia." *Neva* 6 (1996), 178–181.
Vasil'ev, Boris. "Liubi Rossiiu v nepogodu." Interview with Elena Iakovich, *Literaturnaia gazeta*, 30 May 1990 (No. 22, 6296).
Vavra, Edward. "Afterword." In *Cement*, by Fedor Gladkov (1980), 313–352.
Vinogradov, I. "Chelovek i voina." *V okopakh Stalingrada and Poslednie zalpy*, by Viktor Nekrasov and Iurii Bondarev, 470–495. Moscow: Izvestiia, 1968.
Voinovich, Vladimir. Interview with Konstantin Mil'chin. *Russkii reporter*, 14 April 2010, №14 (142), http://www.rusrep.ru/2010/14/interview_voynovich/.
———. "O moem neputevom bludnom syne." *Iunost'* 1 (1990): 76–78.
———. "O sovremennosti i istorii." *Rossiia/Russia* 2 (1975): 228–235.
———. *Portret na fone mifa*. Moscow: Eksmo, 2002.
———. *Pretendent na prestol: novye prikliucheniia soldata Ivana Chonkina*. Paris: YMCA-Press, 1981.
———. *Zhizn' i neobychainye prikliucheniia soldata Ivana Chonkina*. Moscow: Knizhnaia palata, 1990.
———. *Zhizn' i neobychainye prikliucheniia soldata Ivana Chonkina. Kniga III: Peremeshchennoe litso*. Moscow: Eksmo, 2007.
——— and Michael Henry Heim. "An Exile's Dilemma." *The Wilson Quarterly*, 14.4 (Autumn 1990): 114–120.
Volodarsky, Eduard. *Strasti po Chapaiu*. St. Petersburg: Amfora, 2007.
Vroon, Ronald. "Dmitrii Furmanov's Chapaev and the Aesthetics of the Russian Avant-Garde." In *Laboratory of Dreams: The Russian Avant-Garde and Cultural Experiment*, edited by John E. Bowlt and Olga Matich, 219–236. Stanford: Stanford University Press, 1996.
Vykhodtsev, P. S. "A.T. Tvardovskii i narodnaia khudozhestvennaia kul'tura (Vasilii Terkin)." *Tvorchestvo A.T. Tvardovskogo: issledovaniia i materialy*, edited by Vykhodtsev and N. A. Groznovaia, 5–42. Leningrad: Nauka, 1989.
Walzer, Michael. *Just and Unjust Wars: A Moral Argument with Historical Illustrations*, fourth edition. New York: Basic Books, 2006.
Wendle, John. "Russia moves to ban criticism of WW II win." *Time World*, 8 May, 2009, http://www.time.com/time/world/article/0,8599,1896927,00.html.

References

Wieda, Nina. "Secular Kenosis in Boris Vasil'ev's *And Dawns Are Quiet Here*," ASEEES 2010, Los Angeles, CA.

Windholz, George. "Soviet Psychiatrists under Stalinist Duress: The Design for a 'New Soviet Psychiatry' and its Demise." *History of Psychiatry*, vol. X (1999): 329–347.

Yarmolik, Natalia. "'Kholodnoi voine' – 65 let." *Krasnaia zvezda*, 5 March, 2011. http://www.redstar.ru/2011/03/05_03/3_02.html.

Young, Jekaterina. "Dovlatov's Compromise: Journalism, Fiction and Documentary." *Slavonica* 2000 (2): 44–67.

———. *Sergei Dovlatov and his Narrative Masks*. Evanston, IL: Northwestern University Press, 2009.

Youngblood, Denise J. "*Ivan's Childhood* and *Come and See*: Post-Stalinist Cinema and the Myth of World War II." *World War II, Film and History*, edited by John Whiteclay Chambers II and David Culbert, 85–96. New York and Oxford: Oxford University Press, 1996.

———. *Russian War Films: On the Cinema Front, 1914–2005*. Lawrence: University Press of Kansas, 2007.

Yurchak, Alexei. *Everything Was Forever, Until It Was No More: The Last Soviet Generation*. Princeton: Princeton University Press, 2006.

Zagradka, M. "Tvorchestvo Viktora Astaf'eva." *Starodub: Astaf'evskii ezhegodnik: Materialy i issledovaniia*, vyp. 1 (Krasnoiarsk: 2009).

Zakurenko, Aleksandr. "Iskomaia pustota." *Literaturnoe obozrenie* 3: 269 (1998): 93–96.

Zhuk, Sergei I. *Rock and Roll in the Rocket City: The West, Identity, and Ideology in Soviet Dniepropetrovsk, 1960–1985*. Baltimore: Johns Hopkins University Press, 2010.

Zubkov, Vladimir. "Ozhidanie? Proshchanie? Segodnia i zavtra khudozhestvennoi prozy o Velikoi Otechestvennoi voine." *Ural* 5 (2010).

———. "Razryv: Viktor Astaf'ev posle 'derevenskoi' prozy." *Ural* 5 (2005).

Zubkova, Elena. *Russia After the War: Hopes, Illusions and Disappointments, 1945–1957*, translated and edited by Hugh Ragsdale. Armonk, NY: M.E. Sharpe, 1988.

Index

"accursed questions," 30, 198, 213, 214
   "What is to be done?" 46, 188, 190
   "Who is to blame?" 214
   "Who lives happily in Russia?" 72 n. 10
Akhmadulina, Bella, 181
Akhmatova, Anna, 143, 174, 257
   and "Poem without a Hero," 143
Aksyonov, Vasily, 9, 27, 30, 31, 119 n. 7, 177, 180, 181, 233, 244-255, 256
   "The Ship of the World: *Vasily Chapaev*", 233, 233 n. 5, 244-255, 256
   Moskva-kva-kva, 251 n. 40
Aleksievich, Svetlana, 102 n. 23
Aliger, Margarita, 95 n. 10, 96
Anninsky, Lev, 175 n. 1, 176 n. 4, 178, 227 n. 36
"antiheroism," 109, 176, 178
Arendt, Hannah, 148
Ar'ev, Andrei, 185
arms race, 8, 147, 257
"art for art's sake," 44
Astafiev, Viktor, 9, 29, 118, 210-231, 232, 233
   The Accursed and the Damned, 29, 210, 211, 211 n. 10, 212-215, 215-216, 218-219
   Afterword to *The Accursed and the Damned*, 219-220, 221-228, 229-230
   biography, 211-212
   A Bird of Passage, 193, n. 39
   A Cheerful Soldier, 211, 213, 215
   other works: *A Bird of Passage*, "Forgive me," "Liudochka," "Queen Fish," *A Sad Detective Story*, "Shepherd and the Shepherdess," 211 an. 211 n. 10
"author's songs" (*avtorskie pesni*), 209-210

Bakhtin, Mikhail, 198 an. 198 n. 50, 252
Ball, Alan. 63 n. 53
Balter, Boris, 181
Barker, Adele, 94 n. 8
Basinskii, Pavel, 36 n. 6, 239 n. 19
Beevor, Antony and Lara Vinogradova, 26 n. 22, 92 n. 3
Beliakov, Sergei, 216 n. 21, 227 n. 36
Beraha, Laura, 168 n. 41, 170
Bestuzhev-Marlinsky, Alexander, 54 n. 36
Bird, Robert, 69 n. 5, 75 n. 20, 125 n. 19
Bitov, Andrei, 182
   "Gulag as Civilization," 182, 182 n. 19
"boiler room generation," 204
Bondarev, Yury, 209
Borenstein, Eliot, 16 n. 8, 40 n. 16
Bourne, Randolph, 10, 18, 31, 37, 45-46, 67, 147
   "War is the Health of the State," 10, 31, 45-46, 67, 147
"boys of '24," 29, 85 n. 24, 209, 212, 223, 228, 230, 234, 258, 260
Braester, Yomi, 216 an. 216 n. 22
Brezhnev, Leonid, 141, 172-173, 176, 176 n. 6, 179, 189-190, 194-196, 200, 202, 204, 217, 238
Brik, Osip, 35 n. 4, 61, 67
   and heroism and *byt*, 61, 67
Brodsky, Joseph, 28, 109, 109 n. 30, 119 n. 7, 158 n. 21, 203-204, 203 n. 55, 204, 248 n. 33
Brown, Deming, 192
Brown, Edward, 103 n. 24, 146 n. 3
Brown, Norman O., 171 n. 50
Bugajski, Jill, 133 n. 26
Bukovsky, Vladimir, 196 n. 47
Bulgakov, Mikhail, and *Master and Margarita*, 177, 199, 239 n. 18
Bunin, Ivan. 84

Busch, Robert, 35 n. 3, 54 n. 36
But, Vladimir, 210 n. 9
Bykov, Dmitry, 36 n. 6, 207 n. 2, 239 n. 19
Bykov, Vasil, 209, 215, 230
byt, 21, 22, 26, 61, 67-68, 81, 82 n. 28, 84, 88, 92, 108, 110, 112, 125, 126, 139, 165, 178, 186, 198, 260

Carlyle, Thomas, 12-14, 36, 42
  On Heroes, Hero-Worship, and the Heroic in History, 12-14
Chaadaev, Peter, 198
Chances, Ellen. 15
Chapaev jokes and anecdotes, 42 n. 18, 83, 232 an. 232 n. 3, 242, 249, 254, 255, 255 n. 46
Chapaev model, 25
Chapaev "text," 30, 42, 239
Chekhov, Anton. 42, 56, 58, 79 n. 25, 131, 132, 133, 141, 197, 199, 261
  The Cherry Orchard, 261
  "The Darling," 42
  "Letters," 132
  "Vanka," 131, 133, 141
  "Ward No. 6," 199
Chernyshevsky, Nikolai, 43, 44, 46, 136, 188
  Rakhmetov and *What is to Be Done?*, 46, 136
Chistiakov, Vasilii, 72 n. 11
Chkalov, Valery, 30
Clark, Katerina, 24 n. 19, 41 n. 17, 53
Cold War, 30, 63, 140, 146-150, 147 n. 5, 153, 155 and ff., 165, 172-173, 176-177, 186, 189, 200, 207-208, 232, 234-235, 247, 257
Cowley, Jason. 239 n. 19

Daniel, Yuly, 166
Dedkov, Igor, 214, 227 n. 36, 229
Diment, Galya, 184 n. 24
Dobrenko, Evgeny, 35 n. 4, 47, 60 n. 49

Dobrolyubov, Nikolai, 43
Dostoevsky, Fyodor, 15, 43, 46, 50, 97, 160, 186, 197, 198, 201, 202-203, 243, 253
  Notes from the House of the Dead, 160, 198
  Notes from Underground, 197
  Marmeladov and *Crime and Punishment*, 243
  Raskolnikov and *Crime and Punishment*, 43, 46, 50, 186, 201, 202-203
Dovlatov, Sergei, 9, 28, 30, 38 n. 12, 94 n. 8, 119 n. 7, 176 n. 6, 176-191, 199, 203, 204, 242, 244, 245, 246 n. 30
  as *bytopisatel'*, 186
  biography, 176-177, 180
  The Compromise, 181, 183, 184-191
  The Zone, 180, 181, 183-184
Dudin, Mikhail, 257 an. 257 n. 1
Durova, Nadezhda and *The Cavalry Maiden*. 14, 42

Efimov, Igor, 181
Ehrenburg, Ilya, 26, 69, 91, 133, 143, 166
  and Hemingway, 143
  "Kill!" 69
Elistratov, Vladimir, 245 nn. 27 an. 28, 251 n. 40
Ellis, Frank, 26 n. 22, 101 n. 19, 119 n. 5, 125 n. 20, 210 n. 9, 213 n. 15, 214 n. 16, 218 n. 26, 260-261
Emerson, Caryl, 72 n. 12
Epstein, Mikhail, 7, 9-10, 12, 239, 257, 201
Ermolin, Evgen. 225
Erofeev, Venedikt, 9 n. 1, 197
  Moskva-Petushki, 164 n. 30, 190 n. 33, 197
  Venichka, 9 n. 1, 197, 201
Erofeev, Viktor, 233

est', 67-68, 82, 84, 108, 112, 125, 260
   rhetoric of, 67, 82, 84, 108, 125, 260
Etkind, Efim, 122

Faust, Drew Gilpin. 18 an. 18 nn. 10 an. 11, 75, 85
Fitzpatrick, Sheila, 78 n. 24
Friedberg, Maurice, 35 n. 3
Furmanov, Dmitry, 9, 25, 34, 35, 42-52, 62, 74, 77, 83, 92, 94, 95, 232, 236, 255 n. 46
   biography, 43-44
   Chapaev (novel), 42-52
      as ur-text of Soviet heroism, 236

Gagarin, Yury, 29-30, 29 n. 27, 30 n. 28, 165
Gasiorowska, Xenia, 94 n. 8
Genis, Alexander, 175, 176 n. 3, 239 n. 19
Gessen, Keith, 26 n. 22
Gladilin, Anatoly, 119 n. 7, 177, 180, 181
Gladkov, Fyodor, 9, 15, 25, 34, 35, 38, 52-62, 66, 139, 192
   biography, 54
   Cemen. 52-62
   zhivuchest', 54
Gladyshev, V.F., 214 n. 17
glasnost, 36 n. 9, 96, 188 n. 31, 209, 210, 214, 248 n. 33
Gogol, Nikolai, 14, 46, 117, 168, 168 n. 40, 171, 198, 199, 201, 239 n. 19, 252
   Poprishchin. 201
Golding, William, and *Lord of the Flies*, 63
Gorbachev, Mikhail, 28-29, 29 n. 25, 166, 209, 217, 258
Gorky, Maxim, 16, 25, 30, 34, 35, 35-42, 43, 51, 52, 54, 56, 60-61, 79, 92
   and Dmitrii Furmanov, 51, 92
   and Fyodor Gladkov, 52, 54, 56, 60-61

   and *Lives of Remarkable People*, 37, 38 n. 12
   biography, 35-38
   Mother, 16, 25, 34, 35, 35-42, 43
      Nilovna as Mother of Socialist Realism, 42
   "Song of the Stormy Petrel," 36 an. 36 nn. 7, 8, 9
   speech at the First Congress of Soviet Writers, 79
Graham, Seth, 42 n. 18, 232 n. 3, 255 n. 46
Grekov Military Art Studio, 172 n. 52
Griboedov, Alexander, 98
   and Chatsky, 198
   Woe from Wit, 72 n. 11
Grigorenko, Major-General Peter, 195 n. 45
Grishunin, A.L., 73 n. 13, 82 n. 28, 83 n. 30
Grossman, Vasily, 26, 26 n. 22, 91, 92 n. 3, 114, 119 n. 5, 122 n. 14, 128, 159, 160 n. 24, 166, 213
   Life and Fate, 213
Gulag, 32, 131, 149, 159-165, 172, 175, 179, 180, 182, 182 n. 19, 194, 214, 218 n. 26, 220, 248, 262
Gutkin, Irina, 17

Hartzok, Justus, 16 n. 8, 25 n. 20, 38 n. 12, 42 n. 18
Hašek, Jaroslav, 79 n. 24, 150 n. 10, 167, 171 n. 50
   The Good Soldier Švejk, 79 n. 24, 150 n. 10, 167, 171 n. 50
Haynes, John. 232 n. 3, 236, 256 n. 49
Heller, Joseph, and *Catch-22*, 167
Hemingway, Ernest, 91, 143-144
heroism, 15, 20, 24, 27, 30-31, 32, 24, 43, 49, 52, 61, 68-69, 72, 103, 113-114, 118, 122, 125, 133, 138-142, 186, 204, 217, 260
   amputation as a shortcut to, 234
   and sacrifice, 100, 114, 148 n. 7

and truthtelling, 218
as a way of disciplining violence, 51
bravery plus consciousness, 21, 43, 135, 169, 261
bravery plus duty, 138
models and definitions of, 16-18, 34, 35, 43, 45, 51, 91, 135, 218,
myths of, 236
"heroic pragmatism" (Frank Ellis), 125 n. 20, 261
symbols of war and, 246
Hettlinger, Graham, 36 n. 6
Hodgson, Katharine, 70 n. 7, 74, 81 n. 27
Hoffmann, David L., 59 n. 46, 156 n. 18
Holmgren, Beth, 104-105
Hosking, Geoffrey, 11 n. 3, 27 n. 23, 150 n. 10

Ignatieff, Michael, 208
Irony of Fate (film), 190 n. 33
Iskander, Fazil, 181
Ivanova, Natalia, 167, 178 n. 10

Kaganovsky, Lilya, 232 n. 3, 236 n. 12
Kanatchikova dacha, 238
Kanevskaia, Marina, 239 n. 19
Karamzin, Nikolai, 13
Kataev, Vladimir, 66 n. 1
Kazakevich, Emmanuil, 9, 26, 91-102, 111, 112, 117, 122, 122 n. 14, 162, 259, 260
  biography 93-94
  The Star 95-102
Kazan. 196
  special psychiatric hospital in. 196
Kelly, Catriona, 103
Kemp-Welch, A., 35 n. 5, 54 n. 35
Kesey, Ken. 196
Khan, Halimur, 168 n. 43, 169
Khodasevich, Vladislav, 37 an. 37 n. 10
Khrushchev, Nikita, 141, 149, 151-152, 160, 161, 165, 171, 172, 173, 181, 194, 200

and psychiatric repression. 194
  an. 194 n. 41
and the Thaw, 149, 172, 173, 181
Kochetov, Vsevolod, 151 n. 26
Kopelev, Lev, 122, 124
Korenatsky, Vladimir, 174, 178
Kornblatt, Judith, 13, 46, 49 n. 28
Kreutzer, Ruth, 103 n. 24
Krylova, Anna, 91 n. 2, 102 n. 23, 105 n. 26, 219 n. 29
Kryuchkov, Kozma, 46, 47
Kukolnik, Nestor, 46
Kustanovich, Konstantin. 178 n. 10, 179 n. 12, 188 n. 31, 248

Lagermensch, 182
Lakshin, Vladimir, 71 n. 9, 72 n. 11, 75 n. 19
Latynina, Alla, 178 n. 10
Lazarev, Lazar, 73 n. 16, 119 n. 5, 120 n. 9, 171, 209
Lebedev, Alexander and *The Star*, 97, 116, 116 n. 42, 259-260
Lebedev-Kumach, Vasily, 80, 81 n. 27
Leningrad, 104, 119 n. 7, 180, 187, 203
  as center, 184 n. 25
  blockade of, 109, 180, 203, 257
  special psychiatric hospital in. 196, 196 n. 47
Lermontov, Mikhail, 14, 36, 83 n. 30, 197, 198, 201
  A Hero of Our Time, 14, 83 n. 30, 197
  "A Lonely White Sail Gleams" (*Beleet parus odinokii*), 36
Pechorin. 14, 198, 201
Libedinsky, Yury, 25, 44, 50, 51 n. 31
  Birth of a Hero, 25, 62-64, 193
"literature of fact," 45, 51
London, Jack, 27, 135, 137, 138, 143
  and *Martin Eden*. 27, 135-136, 138
Loseff, Lev, 203
Lowenthal, David, 255-256
Luzhkov, Yury, 207

281

Index

McCausland, Gerald, 239 n. 19
Magadan. 30, 208 n. 6
Mailer, Norman, *The Naked and the Dead*, 213 n. 14
Makanin, Vladimir, 9, 28, 175-179, 180, 212, 233, 237, 238, 240 n. 21
   Baize-Covered Table with Decanter, 177
   biography, 191-193
   "The Caucasian Prisoner," 176 n. 5, 178 n. 10
   Fatherlessness, 193
   "He and She," 179 n. 13
   The Soldier and the Soldier's Wife, 193
   A Straight Line, 177, 177 n. 8, 191
   Underground, or a Hero of Our Time, 176 n. 5, 177, 178 n. 10, 179, 194-204, 233
Makarenko, Anton. 47-48
Manizer, Matvei, 252, 256, 256 n. 50
Maresiev, Aleksei 170, 234
Marshak, Samuil, 75 n. 20, 158-159, 158 nn. 21, 22, 159 n. 23, 166
Mathewson, Rufus, 11 n. 3, 15
Maurice Thorez Institute of Foreign Languages, 247
Medvedev, Dmitry, 259
Medvedev, Zhores, 195
   and Roy Medvedev, 195 n. 42
Mee, Cornelia, 194 n. 41, 195 n. 45
mentor/disciple pattern. 24, 40, 48,
Meresiev, Alexei (character of Polevoi novel), 170
Merridale, Catherine, 129, 134 n. 27, 148 an. 148 n. 8
Miller, Frank, 42 n. 18
Miller, Martin. 195 n. 43, 238 n. 17, 239 n. 20
Mordovtsev, Daniil, 46
Moscow, 93, 119 n. 7, 199, 206, 207, 237, 238, 242-243, 251 n. 40, 259
   as center, 63, 90, 101, 115, 127, 184, 234 n. 7
   bookstores, 23

Fallen Monument Park (Muzeon Park of Arts) 207 and n. 3
Gorky Street/Tverskoy Boulevard, 243
Institute of History, Philosophy and Literature, 72 n. 11
Izvestiia, 44
literary journal *Moskva*, 177
Moscow Art Theater, 161
Moscow Higher Literary Courses, 211
Moscow metro, 197, 235, 256
"Moscow School" of literature, 192
Moscow society, 198
Moscow State University, 44
Museum of Medical Defence, 108
St. George, 253
Victory Park and "*Poklonnaia gora*" complex, 172 n. 52, 206, 207, 208 n. 4
Moss, Julian. 211 n. 10, 214 n. 16, 215 n. 18

Nagibin, Yury, 218
Neizvestny, Ernst (and Mask of Sorrow), 208 n. 6, 256 n. 50
Nekrasov, Nikolai, 72 n. 10, 79
Nekrasov, Viktor, 9, 23, 26-27, 71 n. 9, 82 n. 28, 91, 117-144, 164, 165, 173, 176, 179, 208 n. 6, 219
   biography, 119-121
   In the Trenches of Stalingrad, 26-27, 117-144
Nemzer, Andrei, 228, 239 n. 19, 240 n. 22
Nickell, William, 134 n. 28
Norris, Stephen. 46
Novyi Mir (*New World*), 71, 71 n. 9, 75 n. 19, 96, 113, 152, 159, 160, 161 n. 26, 165, 166, 167, 212

O'Brian, Tim, 18, 91, 112-113
Okudzhava, Bulat, 91, 146, 181, 206, 207, 209-210, 212, 216, 219, 257

biography 209
Olesha, Yury, 197
Orlova, Raisa, 143 nn. 37, 39, 40
Orwell, George, 146, 196
  "You and the Atomic Bomb," 146
ostranenie, 169
Ostrovsky, Nikolai, 66 n. 1

Panfilov heroes (*Panfilovtsy*), 113-116
Panova, Vera, 9, 23, 26, 71, 91, 92, 93, 95, 102-104, 105-112, 116, 117, 122, 126, 230
  biography 94, 103 n. 24, 104
  memoirs, 94 n. 8, 103 n. 24, 104 n. 25, 109
  porozhny reis / gruzhyony reis, 108, 126
  The Train Companions, 92, 93, 95, 103-112, 117, 122 n. 14
Pasternak, Boris, 71, 197
  Doctor Zhivago, 201
Pelevin, Viktor, 9, 30, 232, 233-244, 244 nn. 25, 26, 245, 256
  biography, 233, 233 n. 5, 235
  Chapaev and Pustota, 30, 233, 236-244, 245, 256
  Generation P, 236 n. 10
  Omon Ra, 30, 217 n. 25, 232, 233-236, 256
Peppard, Victor, 168 n. 40
Peteli, Viktor, 36 n. 6
Peterson, Nadya, 211 n. 10
Petro, Peter, 167 n. 36, 171 n. 50
Petrone, Karen. 46 n. 25, 150 n. 9
Petrushevskaia, Liudmila, *The Time: Night*, 199
Pisarev, Dmitry, 43
Podgursky, Viktor, 180
podvig, 21, 22, 32, 34, 45, 48, 52, 66, 67, 68, 70, 80 and ff, 90, 94, 97, 98, 101, 102 n. 23, 109 and ff. , 114, 165, 168, 172 n. 52, 173, 174, 175, 176, 186, 190, 191, 194, 212, 214, 217 n. 25, 218, 220, 260

culture of *podvig*, 114
rhetoric [discourse] of, 21, 22, 32, 52, 67, 80 and ff, 84, 85 n. 34, 94, 97, 109, 125, 139, 142, 165, 168, 175, 176, 186, 190, 194, 212, 214, 217 n. 25, 218, 260
Polevoi, Boris, 26, 34, 52 n. 33, 169, 232
  The Story of a Real Man [novel], 52 n. 33, 169-170, 234
  The Story of a Real Man [film by Alexander Stolper], 170, 234
Ponomarev, Evgenii, 246 n. 30, 249 n. 35
Popov, Evgenii, 246 n. 30
Prozorov, V.V., 152 n. 13
psychiatric practice, Soviet, 8, 178, 179, 194, 195 an. 195 n. 42, 196, 197, 198 n. 51, 202, 237-238, 239, 241-242
psychiatric asylums, clinics and hospitals, 194, 196, 199, 200, 203, 203 n. 55, 237-238, 241-242
Pushkin, Alexander, 13, 46, 96, 142, 243
  Eugene Onegin. 83 n. 30
  statue of in Moscow, 243
Putin, Vladimir, 29, 29 n. 25, 116 n. 42, 258, 259

Remarquism, 119 an. 119 n. 5
Rodnianskaia, Irina, 178 n. 10, 239 n. 19, 240 n. 22, 241 n. 23
Rolland, Romain. 37 an. 37 n. 11
Romanova, Regina, 71 n. 8, 72 n. 11
Rozanov, Vasily, 253
Ryan-(Hayes), Karen. 183 n. 23, 190 n. 33

Sakharov, Andrei, 166
Saltykov-Shchedrin, Mikhail, 152 n. 13, 171, 197
Samara, 205, 247, 247 n. 31, 250-255, 250 nn. 37 an. 38, 251 n. 39
  Chapaev monument in. 205, 251, 256
Sarnov, Benedikt, 168 n. 42, 169 n. 44
Scammell, 152 n. 12, 196 n. 47

Index

Scherr, Barry, 38 nn. 12 an. 13, 39
Sedakova, Olga, 7
Sergay, Tim, 202 n. 52
Serman, Ilya, 182
Shalamov, Varlam, 182 an. 182 n. 21, 184, 208 n. 6, 212, 214
   Kolyma Tales, 208 n. 6, 214, 218 n. 26
Shcherbakova, Galina, 175, 207, 261, 262
shestidesiatniki ("men [and women] of the sixties"), 175, 179, 179 n. 13, 204
Shpagin, Alexander, 206, 217-18, 217 n. 25
Shtut, Sarra, 140
Shuksin, Vasily, 181
Shvarts, Evgenii, 72 n. 12
Simonov, Konstantin. 20 n. 15, 26, 69-70, 78, 91, 133, 166
   "Kill him," 69
   The Living and the Dead, 213 n. 14
Sinclair, Upton. 138
Sinyavsky, Andrei, 71, 166, 180
Slutsky, Boris, 66, 67-68, 73, 91, 147, 148, 149, 174, 179, 185
   "Est'!" [Yessir!], 66, 67-68
   "Night Conversations," 147, 149
   "Physicists and Lyricists," 176 n. 3
Smith, Alexandra, 79 n. 24
Smith, G.S., 202 n. 53
Smith, Teresa and Thomas Oleszczuk, 195-196
Smolensk, 70, 72, 259
   Smolensk Pedagogical Institute, 70, 72 n. 11
socialist realism, 15-17, 28, 42, 54, 79, 92, 99, 101, 117, 135, 141, 164, 179, 191, 209, 249, 256, 261
   and Makanin. 192, 200
   and novel, 13, 23, 24, 34, 52 n. 33, 53, 66, 83, 141, 175, 234
   and "positive hero," 11, 15-16, 24, 28, 32, 48, 73, 79 n. 24, 102, 141, 142, 180, 201
   and Dovlatov, 183, 186, 191
   parodies of, 233
   and war, 72, 91, 116, 140
   and war hero, 246
   codification of, 35
   definition of, 99
   and Nekrasov, 119 an. 119 n. 7
   socialist realist heritage industry, 249
   socialist realist "kitsch," 103
   trope of Chapaev and, 244
Solzhenitsyn, Alexander, 9, 27, 71, 73, 149, 150, 159-165, 166, 171, 173, 179, 180, 182, 184, 190, 199, 201
   Cancer Ward, 199
   Gulag Archipelago, 164, 174, 182, 182 n. 21, 218 n. 26
   "Incident at Krechtovka," 160, 161-162
   One Day in the Life of Ivan Denisovich, 27, 149, 152 n. 12, 159-160, 162-164, 179, 190, 199, 201, 244
   The Oak and the Calf, 71 n. 9, 73
   and Dovlatov, 180 an. 180 n. 15, 182, 184
   and Khrushchev, 160
   and Tvardovsky, 71 n.9, 73, 160
Sorokin, Vladimir, 164 n. 31
space race, 8, 30, 147, 165, 234
Stalin, Joseph, 22, 23, 27, 35 n. 5, 38 n. 12, 42 n. 18, 54 n. 35, 59 n. 46, 72 n. 10, 73, 75 n. 19, 78, 84 n. 34, 93, 96, 102, 114, 115, 119, 119 n. 5, 120, 121, 132, 134, 135, 140, 141, 142, 143 n. 39, 146, 147 n. 5, 148, 156, 159, 161, 162, 169 n. 44, 171, 174, 175, 179, 181, 194, 207, 214, 221, 224, 226, 228, 244, 247 n. 32, 250, 250 n. 37, 256
   as Hero Number One, 148 n. 7
   myth of the happy Stalinist childhood, 175
   "Not One Step Backward" speech, 114

Stalin Prize, 26, 93, 95 n. 9, 96, 103, 104, 120, 169, 170 n. 48
Stalin's bunker, 250-251, 256
Stalin's cult of personality, 75 n. 19, 256
Stalin's death mask, 256
Stalinism [and Stalinist system], 27, 53 n. 34, 78 n. 24, 148, 149, 152, 156, 165, 175, 194 n. 41, 208 n. 6, 216, 217, 227, 228
Stalinist purges [and camps], 104, 149, 162, 182, 207, 209, 214, 217, 219
Stalingrad, 27, 30, 31, 90, 117-144, 162, 208 n. 6
Starikov, D., 152
Stepanian, Karen. 239 n. 19, 241 n. 23
Stolper, Alexander, 170, 234
Stoppard, Tom (*Every Good Boy Deserves Favor*), 196 an. 196 n. 47, 197 n. 48
Struve, Gleb, 72 n. 10
Sukhikh, Igor, 74 n. 17, 180 n. 15
Suleiman, Susan Rubin. 216, 228, 229
Szporluk, Mary Ann. 192

Tal, Kali, 20, 85
Tallinn. 177 n. 7, 184 n. 25, 189,
Tendriakov, Vladimir, 166
Terror, the, 7, 22, 103, 104, 149, 158, 159, 175, 208, 214, 217, 261
"Thaw," the, 104, 149, 151, 152, 171-173, 180, 181
Thorez, Maurice, 247 n. 32
Tolstoy, Leo, 14, 15, 42, 46, 91, 92 n. 4, 134, 134 n. 28, 135, 160 n. 24, 213, 226-227
  Anna Karenina, 42, 128, 236
  Sevastopol Sketches, 14, 92 n. 4
  War and Peace, 14, 74, 92 n. 4, 134, 213, 226-227, 230
Tolstoyans, 246
Toper, P.M., 91 n. 1
Trifonov, Gennadii, 212

Trifonov, Yury, 27, 28
Trumbo, Dalton, *Johnny Got His Gun*. 218-219
Tsvetaeva, Marina, 142
Tumarkin, Nina, 78 nn. 23 an. 24, 148 an. 148 n. 7, 172 n. 52, 208 n. 4
Turgenev, Ivan. 15, 43, 44, 54, 55, 58, 97, 97 n. 13, 132, 201
  Bazarov, 43, 201
  Rudin. 201
Tvardovsky, Alexander, 9, 23, 25, 26, 27, 66-90, 91, 92, 95-96, 99, 101,118-119, 122 n. 14, 125, 146, 148 n. 8, 149, 150-159, 171, 173, 176, 179, 226
  biography 70-72
  Vasily Tyorkin: A Book about a Soldier 75-90, 153, 226,
  Tyorkin's heroism, 151
  Tyorkin in the Other World 151, 152-159
  and *Novyi Mir* 71, 71 n. 9, 75 n. 19, 96, 160-61, 161 n. 26,165, 167

Vail, Peter, 167, 172, 175
Vaksberg, Arkady, 36 n. 9
Van Baak, Joost, 55 n. 39
Vasiliev, Boris, 23, 29 n. 26, 209, 219, 219 n. 29
Vasiliev, Sergei and Georgy, 46, 232, 236
  Chapaev (film), 25, 29 n. 27, 46, 232, 236
Vavra, Edward, 60 n. 47
Veller, Mikhail, 177 n. 7
Vladimov, Georgii, 210 n. 9
Voinovich, Vladimir, 9, 23, 27, 119 n. 7, 146, 149, 150, 173
  and Tvardovsky, 167-168
  biography, 165-166
  "Fourteen Minutes to Take Off," 27, 165, 171
  Ivankiada, 164 n. 30
  Life and Adventures of the Soldier Ivan Chonkin. 23, 27, 149, 166-171

Chonkin. 150 n. 10, 165
Moskva 2042, 164 n. 31
Portret na fone mifa, 164 n. 31
"We Live Here," 166
Volodarsky, Eduard, 255 n. 44
Voronsky, Alexander 35 n. 5
Vroon, Ronald, 50
Vykhodtsev, P.S., 90 n. 42, 151 n. 11

Walzer, Michael, 21-22, 157 n. 19, 209
Wieda, Nina, 116 n. 41, 238 n. 16
Wilma Theater, 197 n. 48
Windholz, George, 194 n. 41
word and deed [*slovo* and *delo*], 43, 44, 97

Young, Jekaterina, 184 n. 25
Youngblood, Denise, 24 n. 17, 102 n. 23, 170 n. 48, 259 n. 5
Yunost, 27, 166
Yurchak, Alexei, 176 n. 6, 194, 236

Zakurenko, Alexander, 236 n. 13, 239 n. 19, 241 n. 24
Zhdanov, Andrei, 174
Zizka, Blanka and Jiri, 197 n. 48
Zoshchenko, Mikhail, 174
Zubkov, Vladimir, 124, 214 n. 17, 227 n. 36, 229 n. 42
Zubkova, Elena, 118 n. 3, 125 n. 20, 131 n 25